AMSTERDAM

RODNEY BOLT

About the author

Rodney Bolt is seldom happier than when rattling along the canals of Amsterdam on his Miss Marple Dutch bicycle, or burrowing through papers in the Municipal Archive. Having lived in Greece, South Africa, Britain and Germany, he arrived in Amsterdam in 1991, and now nothing can convince him to leave. He has also written Cadogan Guides to Germany, Bavaria and Madeira, as well as other books and numerous articles on the Netherlands. In 1994 he won the German National Tourist Office's 'Travel Writer of the Year' award.

Cadogan Guides
Highlands House, 165 The Broadway, London SW19 1NE
info@cadoganguides.co.uk
www.cadoganguides.com

The Globe Pequot Press
246 Goose Lane, PO Box 480, Guilford, Connecticut
06437–0480

Copyright © Rodney Bolt 1997, 2000, 2002, 2004
Updated by Rodney Bolt 2004

Series book design: Andrew Barker
Series cover design: Sheridan Wall
Art direction: Sarah Rianhard-Gardner
Photography: OLIVIA, © Olivia Rutherford
Maps © Cadogan Guides, drawn by Oxford Cartographers
Map Co-ordinator: Angie Watts

Managing Editor: Christine Stroyan
Editor: Tim Locke
Contributors: James Alexander and Caroline Mudd
Proofreading: Daphne Trotter
Indexing: Isobel McLean
Grid-referencing: Tori Perrot
Production: Navigator Guides
Printed in Italy by Legoprint
A catalogue record for this book is available from the British Library
ISBN 1-86011-120-3

The author and the publishers have made every effort to ensure the accuracy of the information in this book at the time of going to press. However they cannot accept any responsibility for any loss, injury or inconvenience resulting from the use of information contained in this guide.

Please help us to keep this guide up to date. We have done our best to ensure that the information in this guide is correct at the time of going to press. But places and facilities are constantly changing, and standards and prices in hotels and restaurants fluctuate. We would be delighted to receive any comments concerning existing entries or omissions. Authors of the best letters will receive a copy of the Cadogan Guide of their choice.

Contents

Introduction

Amsterdam sits snug on the northern seaboard of mainland Europe, a knot of elegant waterways and neat 17th-century canal houses. It bears no comparisons the world over, and not just because of its famously liberal attitude to soft drugs and its showpiece Red Light District. For Amsterdam is a city pared down to its essentials and then drawn carefully to human scale. Beneath the tourist gloss is a fully grown-up place: set foot in Amsterdam and you are soothed by a sense of order, a composure that makes other world cities look like gawky teenagers. It's tidy for a start: the streets are litter-free and (with most locals rolling around on two wheels) there's a noticeable lack of car fumes, while the Golden Age pong of canal water has long since been dispelled by high-tech pumps that replenish the entire contents of the waterways each day. And, unlike the transient populations of London or New York, people come here and stay for years, seduced by the maturity of the place, the extraordinary concentration of museums and galleries, the beauty of the canals (there are more here than in Venice) and the unsurpassed standard of living.

Amsterdam keeps a delicate balance between apparent contradictions. Alternative cultures rub shoulders with sturdy traditionalists. Young party-seekers enjoy the clubs or stagger between coffeeshops; businessmen roll by on bicycles, ties flapping in the wind. Sleazy types lurk about in dim alley-ways, while just two steps away smartly dressed burghers file into church for a classical concert. And to the surprise of the newcomer, everyone gets along just fine.

The city's long history of tolerance, which culminated in its status as a hippy mecca during the 1960s, is the key to its present sensibilities, though its growing prosperity as a world finance centre has muffled some of the old radical elements. Squatters are moving on; graffiti (other than state-sponsored pieces by Fabrice) have been wiped from trams and brickwork; young professionals have colonized the dockland islands of the River IJ, transforming old warehouses into bold new developments; and business parks glitter on the outskirts of town. But, still, as a visitor you could hardly find a more welcoming place. Stray into a neighbourhood bar beyond the tourist limits and you might expect to be run through with icy stares – you're more likely to be greeted in perfect English, or left quietly to your own devices. After all, Amsterdam's seen it all before.

The Neighbourhoods

6 Begijnhof, p.99

4 Brown cafés and *hofjes* in Jordaan, p.162

The Centre: New Side

Grand Canals and Jordaan

The Centre: Old Side

8 Antique-shopping in the Spiegelkwartier, p.125

Museumplein and Vondelpark

1 Museumplein – the Rijksmuseum, Stedelijk Museum and Van Gogh Museum, p.130, p.136 and p.138

7 Vondelpark, p.143

9 Brouwersgracht, p.150

10 The view from the Westerkerk tower, p.122

Outside the Centre

5 Albert Cuypmarkt, p.146

Waterlooplein and the Plantagebuurt

2 Anne Frankhuis, p.123

3 Gable-spotting on the Grand Canals, p.118

In this guide, the city is divided into the six neighbourhoods outlined on the map above, each with its own sightseeing chapter. This map also shows our suggestions for the Top Ten activities and places to visit in Amsterdam. The following colour pages introduce the neighbourhoods in more detail, explaining the distinctive character and highlights of each.

The Centre: Old Side

The Old Side is known to Amsterdammers as De Walletjes ('the little walls') after the city walls that once ran through the area; it is better known to visitors for its Red Light District, which has cast its come-hither stare over this side of town for centuries. Brash bars and smoke-filled coffeeshops hold their ground next to sex shops and brothels, while shifty-looking men cruise the streets, and curious tourists and stag-weekenders find it all very funny. In the middle of everything, the Oude Kerk provides refuge of a more respectable kind, hosting concerts and exhibitions. Close by are the fanciful medieval turrets of De Waag; the remarkable Amstelkring Museum, a 17th-century clandestine church; and countless relics from the age of trade.

From top: Red Light District, Old Side hotel, Zeedijk at night.

The Centre: Old Side

Clockwise from top left: Begijnhof, Bloemenmarkt, Damrak, the Dam.

The Centre: New Side

The main drag of Damrak and Rokin follows the old path of the River Amstel to form the backbone of the New Side – a mixed bag of historic landmarks, atmospheric cafés and mainstream shops. The sedate court-yard of the Begijnhof provides an improbable refuge behind café-strewn Spui, while Kalverstraat, the city's main shopping artery, runs up against the floating flower market. As darkness falls, queues form outside some of the city's top club nights on boisterous Rembrandtplein – all bright lights and blaring music – while to the north all things converge on the grey expanse of the Dam, built in early medieval times to stop the River Amstel in its tracks.

All photos: Waterlooplein scenes.

Waterlooplein and the Plantagebuurt

The Nazi occupation reduced the Jewish Quarter that had grown around Waterlooplein to dereliction. The community that contributed much to Amsterdam life is now all but invisible, commemorated by a few sombre monuments. But Waterlooplein itself is once again at the heart of city life, home to the City Hall and national opera house. The Portuguese-Israelite Synagogue stands across the road from the Joods Historisch Museum, while the Waterlooplein fleamarket attracts bargain-hunters in their hundreds. Out to the east stretches the Plantagebuurt, an old Jewish suburb which now holds the Hortus Botanicus and the Artis Zoo.

Waterlooplein and the Plantagebuurt
Waterlooplein and the Plantagebuurt chapter p.103
Hotels p.209 Restaurants p.227 Bars p.236

Grand Canals and Jordaan

Built for wealthy merchants during the Golden Age boom, the Grand Canals, lined with gable-crowned houses and crisscrossed with cobbled lanes, are the lingering image of any visit to Amsterdam. When the rich moved in, the poor had to move out, so the artisans and labourers settled the tight-packed streets of nearby Jordaan, now home to chichi Amsterdammers and pock-marked with *hofjes* (almshouse courtyards) and brown cafés.

Clockwise from top: Canal by night, brown café, Jordaan shop window, almshouse.

Pick your canal and follow its leisurely course round the city's belly; ferret about the antique shops of the Spiegelkwartier; or pay your respects to the Anne Frankhuis. And by night join the loud crowd on Leidseplein, the city's tourist vortex.

Clockwise from top: Anne Frankhuis, Egelantiersgracht gables, Leidseplein, Jordaan antique shop, Westerkerk.

Grand Canals and Jordaan

Museumplein and Vondelpark

Beyond the girdle of the Grand Canals, the city's favourite park, Vondelpark, stretches its leafy limbs alongside the diamond showrooms and designer boutiques of the haute couture shopping district, centred on P.C. Hooftstraat. Next door is

Clockwise from top: Stedelijk Museum, Rijksmuseum garden, Vondelpark, Rijksmuseum arches.

Clockwise from top: Rijksmuseum, Vondelpark, Van Gogh Museum window.

Museumplein, a grassy square bordered by the city's greatest cultural institutions. The monumental Rijksmuseum (mostly closed until 2008, although a wing will remain open) steals the show with the nation's finest collection of Golden Age art, while the Van Gogh and Stedelijk museums display more recent masterpieces. At the southern tip of the square stands the Concertgebouw, often acknowledged as the world's greatest concert hall.

Museumplein and Vondelpark

Museumplein and Vondelpark chapter p.127
Hotels p.210 Restaurants p.229 Bars p.238

Outside the Centre

Amsterdam's outer districts are wrapped tight round the horseshoe of canals. Just east of Museumplein is the colourful Old South district, which borders on De Pijp, so called for its narrow, pipe-like lanes. De Pijp hides a clutch of cosy bars and restaurants, as well as the famous Albert Cuypmarkt – a stretch of vibrant stalls that extends for more than a mile. During the 1920s, architects of the Amsterdam School were let loose on housing projects in both De Pijp and the residential New South, throwing wavy rooftops and bulbous stairwells into the mix. To the east lie the Oosterpark and the colourful Tropenmuseum.

Clockwise from top: Brouwersgracht, bar, Amsterdam School architecture, De Pijp.

From top: Redeveloped warehouses, dockside buildings, Nemo.

Amsterdam's waterfront is an area in flux, a site of massive redevelopment, with neglected warehouses and old industrial sites forever mutating into designer studios, showpiece offices and cultural complexes. And there are watery tourist attractions, too, such as the Scheepvaart Museum, which throws light on the city's love affair with the sea, and the ship-shaped Nemo, a museum of science and technology, which rises from egg-shaped Oosterdok. Out west, past wildly photogenic Brouwersgracht, the old road to Haarlem (Haarlemmerstraat) is now a quirky string of shops and cafés with a life all of their own.

Outside the Centre
Outside the Centre chapter p.145
Hotels p.211 Restaurants p.229 Bars p.238
Amsterdam School walk p.166

Days Out
in Amsterdam

Couples' City p.14

Amsterdammers' City p.16

BAKKERIJ
Balvert

Indoor City p.18

Outdoor City p.20

Café Culture City p.22

Architectural City p.24

COUPLES' CITY

Amsterdam is Europe's 'Venice of the North', a network of neighbourhoods linked by innumerable dainty bridges, offering a thousand peaceful trails through its pedestrian heart. It is a city without pretensions, mature in its liberalism and generally hassle-free. Waterside restaurants run the gamut of world cuisine from candle-lit French to sizzling Surinamese, and the range of cafés for a quiet beer is staggering. And there's no shortage of entertainment, with an overflow of cinemas, a world-renowned concert hall, a burgeoning range of club nights and a general love of experimentalism and the arts.

One

Start: Tram 13, 14, 17 (Prinsengracht stop).

Breakfast: **Villa Zeezicht**, with a view over the Singel canal.

Morning: A leisurely stroll along beautiful **Brouwersgracht**, then climb the **Westerkerk** tower for great views over the city.

Lunch: Enjoy a grand buffet in the splendour of the **NH Grand Hotel Krasnapolsky Winter Garden**.

Afternoon: Visit the floating **Bloemenmarkt** (flower market) on the Singel canal, then hunt for antiques in the **Spiegelkwartier**.

Dinner: French cuisine near an old almshouse courtyard at **Het Begijntje**.

Evening: A classical concert at one of the world's best concert halls, the **Concertgebouw**.

Night: Finish off with a drink at traditional 'brown café' **Café Welling**, behind the Concertgebouw.

Two

Start: Tram 1, 2, 5 (Spui stop).

Breakfast: Coffee and pastries at **Pompadour**, a renowned *chocolaterie*.

Morning: Spend the morning pedalling your way around the Grand Canals on a floating **canal bike** or sit back and relax on a **canal boat tour**.

Lunch: Under the trees at **Moko**, on one of the calmest canalside squares in town.

Afternoon: Pick up a few tips at the **Sex Museum** or, if that sounds just a little crass, head out to the sands of **Zandvoort** for a walk among the dunes.

Dinner: Atmospheric **De Compagnon**, down an alley in the Red Light District, filled with antique bric-a-brac and with views across the little harbour on the Damrak.

Evening: Dance the night away at **ToNight** at the Arena Hotel.

AMSTERDAMMERS' CITY

Cars are frowned upon here and any self-respecting Amsterdammer has long since joined the traditional flurry of two-wheelers – it's the only way to travel. But for a top lesson in Dutch temperament, explore the city's myriad cafés – particularly the neighbourly 'brown cafés' of Jordaan. Otherwise pass an afternoon sifting through the city's many market stalls and nose about a few *hofjes* (almshouse courtyards), or explore the newly hip hinterland of old docks and islands on the River IJ.

Three

Start: Lindengracht (5–10mins on foot from Centraal Station).

Breakfast: Coffee at neighbourhood café **De Kat in de Wijngaert**, in Jordaan.

Morning: Wander the labyrinth of streets and *hofjes* in the old working-class **Jordaan** district (for a structured route, follow the *Hofjes and Hidden Markets* walk).

Lunch: **De Blaffende Vis**, a traditional brown café in Jordaan.

Afternoon: Head south towards the De Pijp district and explore the stalls of the **Albert Cuypmarkt**, then take in the nearby **Heineken Experience**, to learn about and taste the local brew.

Dinner: Top-quality traditional Dutch cuisine at **Piet de Leeuw**.

Evening: Round off the evening at **Greenhouse** in De Pijp, widely rated as Amsterdam's top coffeeshop.

Four

Start: Schreierstoren (5mins on foot from Centraal Station).

Breakfast: Wake up with a coffee at **VOC Café** in the 15th-century Schreierstoren fortification.

Morning: Hire **bikes** and explore the **Grand Canals** and cobbled lanes Dutch-style, stopping off at the **Woonbootmuseum** for an insight into the lives of Amsterdam's houseboaters.

Lunch: **Surinam Express**, a tiny place with truly authentic Surinamese food.

Afternoon: The antique shops of the **Spiegelkwartier** deserve exploring,

or get your skates on and tackle the frozen canals in mid-winter, if it's cold enough.

Dinner: Join the commuters on the free ferry across the IJ, then dine at **Wilhelminadok**, a popular neighbourhood restaurant with views over the river.

Evening: Dance the night away at **De Melkweg**, a long-standing club and music venue.

INDOOR CITY

Amsterdam crams in more than forty museums, and enough covered markets and cafés from which to watch a week of rains pass by. The institutions of Museumplein house a priceless crop of painted master-pieces and many lesser-known works that will keep you holed up for hours. There's a warming jenever (Dutch gin) waiting at any of the city's *proef-lokaals* (tasting houses), and a crisp beer or two on offer at the Heineken Experience.

Five

Start: Tram 1, 2, 5 (Keizersgracht stop).
Breakfast: **The Metz Café**, in the glass cupola on top of one of Amsterdam's poshest department stores, with a great view.
Morning: Spend some time at the **Anne Frankhuis**, then visit a few of the city's old churches: **Westerkerk** (*photos above*), the not-so-new

Nieuwe Kerk (*photo right, middle*) and the 14th-century **Oude Kerk**.
Lunch: Famous **Dolores** – organic snacks in a former police hut.
Afternoon: Explore a wide range of modern and contemporary art at the **Stedelijk Museum**, or admire the works of the 'father of modern art' at the **Van Gogh Museum**.
Dinner: Oysters and foie gras at **De Ondeugd**.
Evening: Opera or ballet at the state-of-the-art **Muziektheater**, or peer out over the waters of the Oude Schans from leaning **Café De Sluyswacht**.

Six

Start: Noordermarkt (10mins on foot from Centraal Station).

Breakfast: **Hein**, in the 'Negen Straatjes'.

Morning: Explore some of the city's quirky indoor markets, such as **De Looier Indoor Antiques Market** in the Jordaan neighbourhood.

Lunch: Art Deco splendour at the **Café Américain** on Leidseplein.

Afternoon: Visit the Philips Wing at the **Rijksmuseum** (housing high-lights of the museum during renovation) or take in a movie at the beautiful **Tuschinski**.

Evening: Trendy **De Ruimte**, a bar and restaurant that doubles as an exhibition space for contemporary art, with mellow jazz tones playing in the background.

OUTDOOR CITY

With the seductive glint of canal water never more than a few yards away, there's no real urge to venture far from the centre on a sunny day. Nevertheless, warm weather sees a minor exodus of Amsterdammers to the parkland that borders the Grand Canals. The most popular spot is Vondelpark, a far cry from your run-of-the-mill patch of scrappy urban greenery, with sweeping ponds, an outdoor theatre, a flock of noisy parrots and troupes of outlandish street performers. Other outdoor highlights include the courtyard havens of the old *hofjes*, the tropical oasis of the Hortus Botanicus, the Waterlooplein fleamarket and the boating lakes of Amsterdamse Bos.

Seven

Start: Tram 1, 2, 5, 13, 17 (Nieuwe Kerk stop).
Breakfast: **Cobra Café**, on Museumplein.

Morning: The calm oasis of the **Begijnhof** (*photo above*) off Spui, an ancient courtyard that once served as a commune for single women, then try your hand at chess on the huge outdoor board in **Max Euweplein** or window-shop along chic **P.C. Hooftstraat**.
Lunch: **'t Ronde Blauwe Theehuis** in the centre of Vondelpark.
Afternoon: Spend the afternoon in **Vondelpark** (*photo above left*), the centre's only major green space – it's a great spot for rollerblading, or simply dozing under a tree. If you get bored, head for the **Albert Cuypmarkt** and mooch between stalls.
Dinner: **Eetcafé Van Beeren**, with a secluded garden courtyard.
Evening: If it's summer, head back to Vondelpark for theatre and live gigs at the open-air theatre. Or try **Café Vertigo** attached to the nearby Nederlands Filmmuseum, with an enormous balcony terrace.

Eight

Start: Metro Nieuwmarkt; tram 9, 14.

Breakfast: Coffee beneath the medieval turrets of **De Waag Café**, in the centre of the Nieuwmarkt market stalls.

Morning: Beat the hordes to the **Waterlooplein fleamarket**, then head over to the **Grand Canals** for some gable-spotting.

Lunch: **Moko**, tucked behind the Amstelkerk, with one of the few terraces in central Amsterdam where the traffic doesn't hurtle between you and the canal.

Afternoon: The revamped **Artis Zoo**, or catch tram 5 out to 2,000-acre **Amsterdamse Bos** for a splash in the boating lake or a walk in the forest.

Dinner: Jump back on the tram to Centraal Station and dine over the waters of the IJ at **Pier 10**.

Evening: **Café Hoppe** on the Spui, dating from 1670, standing room only on the terrace in summer.

CAFÉ CULTURE CITY

Legend has it that the first Amsterdam café opened its doors around the year 1200 when two men and a dog ran dry on the muddy banks of the IJ. Since then Dutch publicans have never looked back, installing a café for every mood: the famous smoke-stained 'brown café', the grand Parisian-style café and that smoky space unique to Amsterdam – the 'coffeeshop' – where you can order from a menu of choice marijuana buds and cannabis. To delve deep beneath the skin of the city, track down one of the old *proeflokaals* and sling back a *kopstoot* (beer with a Dutch gin chaser, literally 'knock on the head'), then sit back and enjoy that blend of conviviality and cosiness known as *gezelligheid*, the very stuff of the Dutch temperament.

Morning: A cosy Dutch breakfast at **Ricky's Koffiehuis** in the red-light district, then head for **Het Hok** for a quiet game of chess.

Lunch: A coffee and roll at **De Jaren**, a famous grand café overlooking the waters of the Binnenamstel.

Afternoon: Pay a visit to the **Hash, Marijuana, Hemp Museum**, then relax in the hemp-furnished museum coffeeshop, or enjoy people-watching from the balcony of **De Kroon Royal Café**, overlooking Rembrandtplein.

Dinner: The Art Deco **Café Schiller** on Rembrandtplein.

Evening: Listening to jazz in the dreamy confines of **Het Molenpad**, a brown café on the Prinsengracht.

Nine

Start: Tram 4, 9, 14, 16, 24, 25 (Muntplein stop).

Ten

Start: Metro Nieuwmarkt; tram 9, 14.

Breakfast: Beside the waters of the Oude Schans at quaintly leaning **Café De Sluyswacht**.

Morning: Relax with a range of international papers at **Café Luxembourg**.

Lunch: **Café Américain** (*photo second left*) in the celebrated American Hotel, an Art Nouveau grand café, once the hangout of Amsterdam's literati.

Afternoon: Soak up a bit of local atmosphere at the daily **Albert Cuypmarkt** in De Pijp, stopping in at the spacious café **De Engel** for a break. Finish off at the **Heineken Experience**, to see how Dutch beer is brewed.

Dinner: Eat exotic kebabs at the comparatively new lounge-bar-style **Local** in Jordaan, then track down **Café Chris**, which by contrast lays claim to be Amsterdam's oldest brown café.

Evening: Change beer for wine at **De IJsbreker**, a sophisticated bar and music venue on the banks of the Amstel.

Night: Head for the famous **Paradiso**, housed in a 19th-century church, and regarded by many as the best club venue in Amsterdam; or venture to **iT**, Amsterdam's largest and most well-known gay club, with a number of high-profile nights.

ARCHITECTURAL CITY

Don't just think gables (although you'll learn to love gables after a weekend here) – Amsterdam has far more to offer than 17th-century canal houses, from the bulbous, rippling homes by the Amsterdam School to Postmodern designer flats out on the Eastern Islands. From the days before fires made brick the only way forward, there are just two medieval wooden houses left in the city. Fortifications and churches linger from the days before the Golden Age boom. The Golden Age meant architecture in Amsterdam would never be the same again, with rich merchants demanding delicate neck gables galore. Later names such as P.J.H. Cuypers and H.P. Berlage brought Dutch architecture into the 20th century, leaving monuments including Centraal Station, the Rijksmuseum and the Beurs.

Eleven

Start: Tram 1, 3, 5, 6, 12.

Breakfast: A quick coffee in the **Hollandsche Manege Café**, over-looking one of Amsterdam's best-kept secrets, the arena of the elegant 19th-century riding school.

Morning: Take a stroll along the **Grand Canals**, lined by gabled homes, and peep in at some of the canal-house interiors. Get a close-up view of a 17th-century interior at the **Willet-Holthuysen Museum**.

Lunch: Walk up to **Brouwersgracht**, the most photogenic canal, and lunch at **Grand Café Restaurant Eerste Klas**, the former first-class waiting room at Centraal Station.

Afternoon: Wander eastwards along

the IJ, getting a taster of various periods of Amsterdam's architecture: the monumental 19th-century **Centraal Station** (*photo far left*); **In 't Aepjen**, one of the two remaining wooden houses in Amsterdam; **Scheepvaarthuis** (*photo above, top*), an Amsterdam School masterpiece; and Renzo Piano's boat-shaped **Nemo** building. Over in the Eastern Islands, spot some trendy new architecture on **Borneo-eiland** or **KNSM-eiland**, with its striking ironwork gates and bridges.

Dinner: **De Gouden Reael**, for French provincial cuisine in a 17th-century house in the Western Islands.

Evening: Take in an opera at the **Muziektheater**, one of Amsterdam's most controversial buildings of recent times, or if it's summer head off for a 'beach party' beside Renzo Piano's **Nemo** building.

Twelve

Start: Tram 3, 5, 12, 24 (Roelof Hartplein stop).

Breakfast: **Wildschut** (opens 11am), with an Art Deco interior and great views of Roelof Hartplein, conceived by the Amsterdam School.

Morning: Follow our **Amsterdam School walk** (*photos above*) around the De Pijp district, where buildings are sculpted into organic shapes, with bulging bay windows and stairwells, waving or pleated tilework and odd-shaped windows.

Lunch: Take the tram over to **'t Ronde Blauwe Theehuis** in Vondelpark, an odd piece of 1930s New Functionalist architecture.

Afternoon: Compare P.J.H. Cuypers' grand Gothic **Vondelkerk** and his nearby **Rijksmuseum**, then wander over to **Roemer Visscherstraat** for 19th-century houses illustrating seven different national styles. Head north to the **American Hotel** (*photo below*), for jutting Art Nouveau balconies, and then to the **Tuschinski Cinema**, built in 1921 and a hot contender for the world's most beautiful cinema .

Dinner: Visionary food at **De Silveren Spiegel** in a 1614 building complete with Delft tiles.

Evening: See a show at the **Koninklijk Theater Carré**, in a lively Classical building designed for a circus.

Night: Finish up with drinks at **Café Schiller**, with its Art Deco interior.

Food and Drinks

De Gouden Reael, p.232
Grand Café Restaurant Eerste Klas, p.222
Hollandsche Manege Café, p.229
't Ronde Blauwe Theehuis, p.238
De Silveren Spiegel, p.220
Wildschut, p.239

Sights and Activities

In 't Aepjen, p.90
American Hotel, p.124
Amsterdam School walk, p.166
Borneo-eiland, p.160
Brouwersgracht, p.150
Centraal Station, p.97

Grand Canals, p.118
KNSM-eiland, p.159
Nemo, p.156
Rijksmuseum, p.130
Roemer Visscherstraat, p.144
Scheepvaarthuis, p.155
Tuschinski Cinema, p.100
Vondelkerk, p.144
Willet-Holthuysen Museum, p.118

Nightlife

Café Schiller, p.236
Koninklijk Theater Carré, p.242
Muziektheater, p.242

Roots of the City

1000–1317: Watery Beginnings

A 17th-century English pamphleteer scoffed that the Dutch were 'bred and descended from a horse turd which was enclosed in a butter-box'. Our knowledge of the origins of the first Amsterdammers is only a shade more enlightened. For much of its early history Amsterdam was a swamp. The River Amstel petered out in the vast tidal flats of the IJ. There was a Roman settlement in the dunes near Leiden (Pliny was miserable there in AD 50), but they weren't too keen on the marshes to the north. The first inhabitants of the area we now call Amsterdam were probably intrepid adventurers who came floating down the Rhine in hollowed-out logs around AD 1000, looking for better land. Luck was certainly not on their side, but they made the best of a boggy lot, built huts on muddy mounds and drained the land around them, creating the first polders.

In the 12th century a local bigwig, **Gijsbrecht**, built himself a castle at the spot where the River Amstel was dammed (on the site of the present-day square known as the Dam). He called himself the first Lord of Amstel and laid claim to the countryside emerging from the water around him. The Lords of Amstel were answerable to the Bishops of Utrecht, and rather resented it. In the late 13th century **Gijsbrecht IV** felt he was powerful enough to rebel, but he didn't reckon on his neighbour, **Floris V**, the Count of Holland, joining in the fray. Floris had wooed popular support in 1275 by granting special toll privileges to the people who lived beside 'the Aemstelle Dam'. Floris defeated Gijsbrecht, but later Gijsbrecht murdered him. The Bishop of Utrecht took advantage of

the confusion and confiscated Gijsbrecht's land. In 1300 he granted the town of 'Aemstelledamme' its first charter. When he died in 1317 he ceded Amsterdam and the surrounding countryside to his nephew, **William III**, the new Count of Holland. The people of Amsterdam took full advantage of their toll privileges and of William's wide influence and settled down to serious trading and money-making.

1317–1500: Growing Prosperity

The growth of Amsterdam as a trading post owes itself to **herring and beer**. In 1323 the Count of Holland granted Amsterdam the sole right to import beer from Hamburg – at that time northern Europe's largest brewing town and a prominent member of the powerful alliance of Baltic trading ports, the Hanseatic League. As most people drank beer rather than the poisonous local water, Amsterdam merchants began to get rich. Then in 1384 one Willem Beukels hit upon a way of preserving herring more efficiently – by gutting them before salting. This meant that ships could stay out at sea even longer and travel further afield. At about the same time, as if obeying some cosmic plan, the herring moved their spawning ground from the Baltic to the North Sea. The industry prospered. It needed salt (from Portugal) and wood for the barrels (from Germany and Scandinavia). Amsterdam merchants had no qualms, as they moved further into the Baltic, about breaking in on the Hanseatic League's trade and developing new routes. Soon the city's ships were also carrying furs, iron ore, cloth, wine and grain to feed Europe's growing population (bread was still the staple diet). Wily merchants built warehouses all over the city to store goods until the best price could be fetched. Amsterdam became a thriving commercial centre and a nexus for European trade. It fought a bitter **trade war** with the Hanseatic towns, but, by the mid-15th century, was indomitable.

1000–1317
Amsterdams Historisch Museum, for displays on the city's growth and early history, p.98
Oude Kerk, with a tower dating from 1300, p.84

During medieval times the town remained small – a cosy cluster of wooden houses stretching along the banks of the Amstel. In 1300 Amsterdam had one church (the Oude Kerk) and two streets – the present-day Warmoesstraat and Nieuwendijk. The town was razed by great fires in 1421 and 1452. Wooden buildings were forbidden after the second blaze, and only two remain today. By the 15th century the boundaries extended as far as Oudezijds Voorburgwal, Nieuwezijds Voorburgwal and Spui. There was a new church as well as a clump of monasteries, chapels and inns built to cope with pilgrims who were now flocking to the scene of the **Amsterdam Miracle**.

In 1345 a dying man had vomited up the host after his last communion. It was thrown on a fire but didn't burn. Later it developed healing powers, and would transport itself overnight between churches. A chapel of its own seemed to make it stay in one place and, though this burnt down, the host survived. It became an object of worship, and is still honoured today in the Stille Omgang (Silent Procession). One of those healed by the magic wafer was **Maximilian I**, Emperor of Austria (later Holy Roman Emperor). Amsterdam had further earned his gratitude by supporting his faction, the Kabeljauwen (Codfish), against the conservative Hoeken (Hooks) in the struggle for domination of the Low Countries. In 1489 he upped Amsterdam's prestige by granting the city the right to use his royal insignia in its coat-of-arms. Trade flourished, and by 1500 Amsterdam had become a town that bustled with 9,000 inhabitants.

1500–1600: Reformation and Revolt

At the beginning of the 16th century Europe was firmly in the grip of the Roman Catholic Church. But on 31 October 1517 **Martin Luther** calmly walked up to the chapel of Wittenberg Castle and nailed his '95 Theses' to the door. The 'Theses' condemned superstition in the Church and the practice of indulgences. Luther's act marked the beginning of the **Reformation** – theologians everywhere, from Erasmus in Rotterdam to Calvin in Geneva, became braver and more audible in their criticism. The Catholic Church responded swiftly and thousands were tried for heresy.

Trade ships carried new ideas quickly to Amsterdam. The revolutionary theology caught on, and there were many heresy trials, but the city fathers were traditionally tolerant and didn't always carry out sentences they were obliged to impose. In fact, Calvin's austere doctrines and the notion of civil power rather appealed to a number of wealthy merchant families. The city became ruffled only when the lower-class sect of **Anabaptists** began to jostle the status quo. In 1534 Melchior Hoffman became convinced that mankind was on the brink of a new world order. Münster in Germany was to be the New Jerusalem. He styled himself 'King of Münster' and sat back to await the Second Coming. Fervent crowds of believers joined him. Soon he was sending 'prophets' to Amsterdam, where people were easily convinced that they too lived in a chosen city. The city fathers were at first benign, but on 11 February 1535 a frenzied handful of Anabaptists stripped naked and cavorted about the Dam. Then, on 10 May, 40 members of the sect took advantage of the celebrations of the feast of the Guild of the Cross and occupied the *stadhuis*, while the councillors were 'far gone in drink'. It took the (probably inebriated) Civic Guard until the following morning to get them out. Heresy was bad enough, but civil unrest was intolerable. Normally mild Amsterdam came up with horrible death sentences for the usurpers: 'The chest is to be opened up while they are still alive, the heart removed and thrust into their faces, whereupon they are to be beheaded and quartered.' Pictures were commissioned of the Anabaptists' acts of 'raving insanity', and were hung in the *stadhuis* as a warning to anyone else. The lax city fathers were replaced.

At this time the Netherlands was ruled by **Philip II of Spain** (later husband of Mary Tudor). Philip was head of the mighty Austro-Spanish Catholic house of Habsburg which dominated much of Europe, owned most of South America and even laid claim to the English crown. Unlike his reassuringly named predecessors (Philip the Good, Charles the Bold and Philip the Fair), Philip II was a cruel and fanatical despot. He also took ages to reach decisions, so his subjects spent most of their lives in a terrified limbo. Action was dangerous, no orders came from above and political situations had the habit of deteriorating around the protagonists. This was particularly aggravating in territories as far flung as the Netherlands. Even Dutch Catholics, outraged by the Inquisition and this distant monarch's cruel repression, became antagonistic. Opposition to Philip began to grow along nationalist as well as religious lines. Philip took a quiet step back, leaving his sister, **Margaret of Parma**, to deal with any unpleasantness. Angry city regents persuaded her to sign the '**Moderation**', which implied some measure of religious tolerance. Calvinist preachers came to Amsterdam, where Protestant services were permitted outside the city walls. During the summer of 1566, hundreds of people left the city's churches to listen to these open-air 'hedge-sermons'.

A crop failure the previous winter had caused a famine which gave an even sharper edge to the religious rancour being stirred up in the polders outside Amsterdam. On 30 August sailors brought back fragments of marble statues smashed by Puritans in Flemish churches. This sparked off a frenzy of

> ## 1500–1600
> **Amstelkring Museum**, a clandestine Catholic church, p.85
> **Bijbels Museum**, for the history of the Dutch Bible, p.119

destruction. The iconoclasts smashed the windows of the Oude Kerk and battered or burnt all popish treasures and artworks. A brave group of women encircled the chapel of the Heilige Stede (where the miraculous host was kept) and fended off furious attackers, but the violence spread. The rabble was diverted by the discovery of the wine cellars at the friary of the Friars Minor, but was only subdued when the city fathers offered up the Franciscan church for Protestant worship.

Even Protestant Amsterdammers, suddenly brought face to face with a wrathful populace, were shaken. Philip II was livid. He sent an army of 10,000 men under the **Duke of Alva** – the 'Iron Duke' – to punish the heretics. Most of the Protestant leaders, sensing what was coming, hastily left the country. He moved in style into a house on the prestigious but desolate Warmoesstraat and borrowed vast amounts of money to pay his army (including 14,000 guilders from his landlord). A reign of terror began. So many people were executed by his **Council of Blood** that the city was nicknamed 'Murderdam'. In 1568, the date taken as the beginning of the Eighty Years' War with Spain, the exiled **William of Orange** attempted a campaign against Alva. Terrified local Protestants gave him little support and the invasion was a failure. William didn't have enough money to pay his soldiers and had to creep away from them in the night. He wandered around France gathering another army, and by 1572 was meeting with a little more success. He was assisted by the Sea-beggars, a rough and ready bunch of quasi-pirates, who were later to form the basis of the Dutch navy. Soon William controlled all the towns around Amsterdam. Meanwhile, the populace was turning against Alva – less as a result of his vicious persecutions than because of the 10th penny tax he had imposed (which diverted 10% of all citizens' income into the Duke's coffers). Alva slipped away one night in 1573, just a few hours before he was due to face a meeting of angry creditors.

In the winter of 1575–6 William laid **siege** to the city. The town officials were so worried about infiltrators that they banned skating on the canals and even stood guard at important gates themselves. Priceless silver was melted down and minted into coins in an attempt to keep business ticking over. After a long siege, it became clear that William was going to win the war, so, in 1578, the city fathers judiciously swapped allegiance and made peace with William. This signalled the virtual end of Spanish dominion over the Netherlands (though they were to retain sovereignty for another 70 years). Exiles streamed back into the city and on 26 May all the Catholic officials and most of the clergy (who had expected retaliatory executions) were bundled into a boat and cast off to find their way to more hospitable climes. A Protestant city government was set up by members of leading Calvinist families. With characteristic Amsterdam grace, the events of 26 May were tactfully referred to as the '**Alteration**'.

In 1579 the southern, Catholic and largely French-speaking provinces signed the **Union of Arras** and declared their allegiance to Spain. This gave Spain a base for attacks on the north (most notably the punishing Siege of Antwerp in 1584–5). Seven northern provinces responded with the **Union of Utrecht**, a Protestant military federation with The Hague as the centre of power. The Union upheld the 'freedom of religious belief': this meant that you could be a Roman Catholic, but still weren't allowed to worship openly. Amsterdam, however, turned a blind eye to the clandestine churches that opened up in attics and behind domestic façades all over town.

Amsterdam was now by far the most economically powerful city in the federation. The siege of Antwerp had not only wiped out

a major trade rival, but had despatched droves of refugees who made straight for the haven in the north. Amsterdam's tolerance paid off. The newcomers brought skills, like diamond-cutting, that fired the city's industries into new life. Through much of its history Amsterdam seemed to operate on the principle that 'if we didn't supply the enemy, we couldn't afford to fight them'. Arms dealers would support entire wars all over Europe, and brokers of marine insurance (introduced in the late 15th century) had no qualms about insuring both sides in a battle. Amsterdammers excelled at making money. At the end of the 16th century they were on the brink of the most resplendent era of their history.

1600–50: The Golden Age

A map worked into the floor of Amsterdam's 17th-century *stadhuis* (town hall) places the city at the centre of the universe – and for much of the century that must have seemed true. Goods flowed into the port from around the world, guilds flourished, and even the lowliest workers earned nearly twice as much as their English counterparts. The **Beurs** (Exchange) thronged with merchants from countries as far away as India and Turkey. Isaac le Maire had the idea of trading in blanco – dealing on paper with goods he didn't yet own – and the first futures market was begun. In 1609 the city council founded the **Amsterdam Wisselbank** (Bank of Exchange) in the cellar of the town hall. It drew up bank drafts to replace coins (which could be clipped, melted down or stolen), gave quick mortgages and lent at a good rate of interest (an encouraging 3.5–4%; England dragged behind at 6%).

People flooded into the city and by 1650 the population had shot past the 200,000 mark. As early as 1613, far-sighted town planners had begun an extension of three **new canals** around the perimeter of the city. Initially the Herengracht (Gentlemen's Canal), Keizersgracht (Emperor's Canal) and

Prinsengracht (Princes' Canal) went only as far as the present-day Leidsegracht, but further construction in 1662 gave Amsterdam its familiar half-moon shape. Malodorous industries and the poor were banished to the fields beyond, to the area now known as the Jordaan. Merchants built mansions along the new canals and the city built a *stadhuis* that was proclaimed the eighth wonder of the world. The arts and intellectual life flourished. **Rembrandt**, **Vermeer** and **Frans Hals** kept busy, and lesser painters churned out 20 million pieces of work during the first part of the century. Books rolled off Amsterdam's **uncensored presses** – and in the cafés you might find Spinoza or Descartes.

The city's economy was solidly based on the Baltic grain trade (it filled four-fifths of the warehouses), but the spirit of the Golden Age shines clearest in the romance, daring and glamour of the trade with the East. Initially Amsterdam hadn't bothered to send ships further than Lisbon, relying on intrepid Portuguese sailors for booty from the Spice Islands. In 1580, however, Philip II conquered Portugal and closed its ports to his arch-enemy. It was clear that Amsterdam would have to send her own ships to the East. In 1595 Cornelis Houtman set off with four ships and 200 men on a voyage of discovery. Only 99 men limped back in battered ships on 23 August 1597, and investors just managed to break even, but the port buzzed with excitement. When a second voyage realized a profit of 400%, merchants exploded into action. In 1597 the romantically named 'Compagnie van Verre' (Far Away Company) began direct trade with the East Indies. Everybody wanted to get in on the act. So many new companies were formed that they looked likely to put each other out of business before they'd really started. On 20 March 1602 they all united to form the **Verenigde Oostindische Compagnie** (United East India Company, VOC). All of Amsterdam seemed greedily caught up in the spirit of adventure. Domestic servants and seamstresses were among the thousands of early shareholders. The company had the monopoly of Dutch trade from the Cape of Good Hope to Cape Horn, and at the peak of its influence it had over 150 merchant vessels protected by 40 fighting ships and its own army of 10,000 soldiers. It sailed all over the East Indies and also to India, Ceylon, China, the South Pacific Islands and South Africa. For nearly two centuries it was the most powerful trade organization in the world. It could even establish colonies, sign treaties and declare war.

In 1624 the **West India Company** was formed, a smaller and less prosperous copy-cat venture, which had the trade monopoly over the seas between Africa and the Americas. Its main claim to fame was that it administered the American colony of New Amsterdam – later captured by the British and renamed New York. The trading companies' economic clout gave Amsterdam tremendous sway over the rest of the Netherlands. Eight of the Chamber of Seventeen, the powerful governing body of the VOC, had to be Amsterdam citizens, and managers were appointed by the *burgemeester*. Power in the city itself was grasped by a handful of patrician families. The

Catholic clique ousted during the Alteration was replaced by a Protestant oligarchy that became known as the **Magnificat**. Family names like Hooft, Pauw, Bicker, van Beuningen and Six can still raise an Amsterdammer's eyebrow. Wives and daughters sat on the boards of charities and almshouses (housed in confiscated monasteries) and sons would serve in the civil guard on their way up to becoming *burgemeesters* or magistrates. The city was ruled by the Heren (Lords) XLVIII, a council of four *burgemeesters*, a sheriff, seven jurists and 36 advisors. These 'regents' often came into conflict with national government. After the Union of Utrecht, the Netherlands was governed by the States General, a body of representatives that met at The Hague. Each province was headed by a *stadhouder* (an ancient title that was previously used for the king's deputy). In practice, all the provinces chose William of Orange as their *stadhouder*. Successive generations elected heirs to the House of Orange, so the title became all but hereditary. William's son, Maurits, was called 'Prince', and soon the family was grand enough for a match with an English princess.

The *stadhouder* was commander-in-chief of the country's armed forces, and this brought him into conflict with the regents. Peace was better for business than war and, after the final defeat of the Spanish in 1648, the Amsterdam merchants wanted to cut back on military spending. **William II** wanted to keep his armies. The traditional unease between Amsterdam and the House of Orange bristled into tension. On 23 June 1650 the *stadhouder* visited Amsterdam and demanded an official reception. The regents refused, and condescendingly invited him for dinner instead. 'If we are to wine and dine together,' sniffed William, 'then we would have to be better friends than we are at present.' He left the next day, gathered troops and sent them to take Amsterdam by surprise. Civil war was narrowly averted. The invading army had got lost in a fog and was spotted by a postman on his way over from Hamburg who warned the city. When

William died of the pox, the States General passed a law forbidding anyone from the House of Orange ever to become *stadhouder* again – a resolution that lasted only a few decades.

1650–1814: The Decline

In the first half of the 17th century Germany was battling through the Thirty Years' War, the Roundheads and Cavaliers were roughing each other up in England, and France had been left rather limp by the war with Spain. Around 1650 the dust began to settle, and the pugnacious neighbours turned their attention to the prosperous little country in their midst. The conflicts of the late 17th and 18th centuries drained the United Provinces' (and especially Amsterdam's) coffers and gave the warfaring House of Orange a useful step-up back to power.

Squabbles over herring and punitive anti-Dutch import laws led to **wars with England** in 1652 and 1664. Rather unwillingly, the Provinces found themselves fighting France in the **War of the Spanish Succession** (1701–14). There was another war in 1780 when England discovered the Dutch had been trading with rebel American colonies. London and Hamburg began to take over as mercantile centres, while Amsterdam's old trade routes were threatened. **England's increasing sea power** began to erode the East Indies trade, and in 1791 the VOC went into liquidation. Antwerp was back on the map as an important port and trade became a less important part of the economy: while Amsterdam focused its attention on banking, the early Industrial Revolution passed it by.

As the money business boomed, the Amsterdam oligarchy became increasingly corrupt and complacent. The rich got ostentatious, and the poor got angry and subversive. On 24 June 1748 an Amsterdam merchant noticed a 'shameless slut' in the buttermarket who turned her back on a guard and 'several times raised her skirt, smacking her bare buttocks saying "that's for you'". The guard shot her ('in her bare funda-ment') and she later died. This was all that was needed to spark off some well-organized street violence. Armed with lists of tax collectors' addresses, a mob stormed the grand canals and sacked the houses. The **Tax Farmers' Riot** was swiftly suppressed, but the civil guard had to beat drums below the scaffold to drown out the slogans shouted by the ringleaders as they went to the gallows.

Vociferous bands of volunteers, heady with Rousseau's ideas, began to roam the country-side spreading the gospel of democracy. They had the support of some patricians, such as Hendrik Hooft (affectionately known as 'Father Hooft'). Soon these **Patriots** had taken over the governments of many smaller towns, and on 27 April 1787 they staged a coup in Amsterdam. The Prince of Orange had had enough. With the armies of his brother-in-law, the King of Prussia, he sent the Patriots packing. Many fled to France, where they were just in time for the Revolution. In 1795 a French Republican army, with the support of exiled Patriots, crossed the frozen Rhine and advanced on Amsterdam. There was, by this time, strong pro-French feeling in the Netherlands. The invading armies were seen as liberators, and the regents were bloodlessly deposed in what became known as the **Velvet Revolution**. A 'Freedom Tree' was erected on the Dam and Amsterdammers danced around it celebrating the newly declared Batavian Republic (the Batavians were the ancient tribe of the Netherlands). Amsterdam got its first elected city govern-ment, but the *liberté*, *égalité* and *fraternité* were not to last for long. In 1806 Napoleon appointed his younger brother, **Louis Bonaparte**, King of the Netherlands. Louis converted Amsterdam's *stadhuis* into a palace and demolished the ancient weigh-house on the Dam because it spoilt his view. The city wasn't consoled by the fact that it was now the new capital.

On his first day in the new job Louis announced to his ministers, in heavily

> **1650–1814**
> **Felix Meritis**, built in 1778 to house an arts and scientific society, p.120
> **Koninklijk Paleis**, converted into the royal palace in 1808, p.94
> **Van Loon Museum**, a 1672 canal house, p.121

accented Dutch, '*Ik ben uw Konijn*' ('I am your rabbit') rather than '*Ik ben uw Koning*' ('I am your king'). But though he started off on the wrong foot, Louis soon endeared himself by visiting the stricken during smallpox epidemics, actively supporting the arts and sciences and foolishly standing up to his older brother. (He allowed Dutch smugglers to break Napoleon's blockade of British ports.) Napoleon hadn't expected his young sibling to be such an upstart, so in 1810 he deposed him and incorporated the Netherlands into the French Empire. But Waterloo was just around the corner. Even before that battle, in 1813 (after Napoleon's retreat from Moscow), the French garrison withdrew from Amsterdam and the Netherlands was proclaimed a constitutional monarchy under the House of Orange. The **1814 Congress of Vienna** united all the Netherlands provinces (north and south) for the first time – though this lasted only until 1831, when Belgium became an inde-pendent kingdom.

1814–1939: From Gloom to Light

Historian Jan Romein describes 19th-century Amsterdam as 'drabness piled on drabness'. After months of bickering with The Hague, Amsterdam had become the capital of the new Dutch Republic and home to the Netherlands Bank, but it was a stuffy and threadbare town. The city's coffers were empty. Napoleon's blockade of English ports and the British occupation of Dutch colonies during the Napoleonic Wars had strangled trade, the money market had slipped across the Channel to London, and Amsterdam's entrepreneurs had disdained the inventions of the Industrial Revolution. The trading companies' dainty sailboats were soon to be eclipsed by heavy steamships, too bulky to negotiate the Zuider Zee. In 1824 the North Holland Canal (between Amsterdam and Den Helde) was given a festive opening, but the bravado was misplaced: the bends and locks compelled such creeping progress that it was hardly worth the merchants' while.

The sagging city almost collapsed under the burden of a population that doubled in the last half of the 19th century. Areas like the Jordaan and De Pijp became squalid, overcrowded slums, ravaged by cholera. Amsterdam had fallen far from the glory-days of the Golden Age. In 1838, with deft symbolism, the piles under the Stock Exchange gave way and the building met its end in spectacular fashion.

As the disconsolate city limped through the early decades of the 19th century, a few valiant paladins of the new industries tried to revitalize her. The king set up the Nederlandse Handelsmaatschappij (Netherlands Trading Company) to perk up the drooping trade in tropical products. In 1825 **Paul van Vlissingen** started running regular steamship services to London and Hamburg and built an engineering works on Oostenburg island in east Amsterdam. Almost single-handedly he nudged the city into the industrial age. But the man most personally responsible for rousing Amsterdam from her torpor was the peppy doctor and philanthropist **Samuel Sarphati**. With his motto '*Amsterdam Vooruit!*' ('Amsterdam Advance!'), he was bent on pushing the town headlong into another Golden Age. He founded a commercial college, several banks, a construction company, the city's first hygienic bread factory, the Amstel Hotel (still one of the best in town) and an efficient and profitable refuse-disposal service (the city's stinking waste was shipped out in sealed barges, composted and sold to farmers). He founded the Vereniging voor Volksvlijt (Industrial Society) to knock new life into the city's

manufacturers and to inject new technology into the factories. His sparkling glass Palace of Industry rose up on Frederiksplein and was home to countless displays, exhibitions and concerts until it burnt down in 1929.

Towards the end of the century Amsterdam began to thrive once more. **New industries –** even a motorcar factory – flourished. The opening of the Suez Canal in 1869 meant easier access to the Orient, and in 1876 the **North Sea Canal** was cut through the dunes to give proper access to bigger ships. Amsterdam became the main supplier to a newly unified Germany, and manufacturing and shipbuilding industries revived. The discovery of diamonds in South Africa led to a boom in the diamond-cutting trade, with workers becoming deliriously rich overnight. In 1839 the first **railway** in the Netherlands ran from Amsterdam to Haarlem, and fifty years later the city had a grand new railway station that obliterated the view of the harbour. During the 1880s the first trams and bicycles appeared. (Lady cyclists had to attend special riding schools, as it was thought undignified, if not lewd, for them to be seen wobbling along.) The Vondelpark was laid out on the edge of the city and the élite scurried to live around it. The **arts** blossomed. The Rijksmuseum, Concertgebouw, Carré Theater, Amsterdamse Schouwburg and Stedelijk Museum sprang up in the last two decades of the century, and in 1883 Amsterdam hosted the **World Exhibition**.

1814–1939

The 19th century saw an increase in parliamentary democracy in the Netherlands. The 1848 revolts in the rest of Europe made King William II nervous. Amsterdam was tense – the slum area of the Jordaan, in particular, regularly erupted into violence. In 1848 the king set up a **reform committee** under the liberal Rudolph Thorbecke and changes were hurried through after a mob stormed around the Dam in 1849, with the alarming proclamation that 'All men are brothers'. As the franchise was extended, support grew for the socialist movement. In 1902 Henri Polak took up the first seat for the **Social Democratic Labour Party** (SDAP) on the city council. By 1915 the SDAP was the largest party in Amsterdam, housing associations had been formed, a 1901 Housing Act had stipulated minimum living conditions, and council houses all over the city relieved the pressure on areas like De Pijp and the Jordaan.

Amsterdam entered the 20th century on the crest of a boom. The Netherlands remained neutral in the **First World War**. Amsterdam happily traded in arms with both sides, and emerged comparatively unscathed – though the rest of her trade had taken a blow and food shortages in 1917 had provoked the Jordaaners into riots. The city's population was again growing fast. Canals were filled in to cope with burgeoning road traffic and in 1920 two converted De Havillands, carrying two passengers apiece, began to fly regularly to London. The world's first air-travel booking office opened at Schiphol in the following year. In 1928 Amsterdam hosted the **Olympic Games**, but the 1929 Wall Street crash slid the city into an **economic depression**. Gangs of unemployed were set to work creating the Amsterdamse Bos (Amsterdam Forest) outside the city, and when, in 1934, the council tried to lop 25c off the dole pay, the Jordaaners again rioted. The 1930s also saw the growth of a small but vociferous Dutch Nazi Party (NSB).

1939–45: The Second World War

The Netherlands hoped to remain neutral in the Second World War, as they had in the first. But on 10 May 1940 the Germans attacked Dutch airports and military barracks. **Queen Wilhelmina** and the Dutch government skipped across the Channel to the relative safety of England. They left **Supreme Commander Winkelman** to deal with the advancing Germans. He held out for five days, during which Rotterdam was mercilessly bombed from the air. On 15 May the German army occupied the Netherlands and Hitler declared the Austrian Nazi **Arthur Seyss-Inquart** Rijkscomissaris (State Commissioner).

At first life in Amsterdam carried on much the same as before, with citizens exercising their indefatigable capacity to turn a blind eye to anything that threatened to ruffle the smooth flow of daily business. However, when Seyss-Inquart's early softly-softly attempt to *Nazificeren* ('Nazify') Holland met with stolid Dutch inertia, he became more brutal. Jews, especially, were the butt of systematic oppressive decrees. The wearing of **yellow stars** was compulsory and Jews were banned from driving or from using trams. They had to hand in their bicycles, be indoors by 8 o'clock (not even out in their own gardens), were allowed to shop only in Jewish shops between 3 and 5 o'clock in the afternoon, and couldn't visit theatres, cinemas or sports grounds. Soon they were forbidden to visit Christians, had to go to separate schools and were fenced off in ghettos. On 22 February 1941, German trucks rumbled into the Jodenhoek (Jewish Quarter) and the first **round-up of Jews** began. In the years that followed, nearly all of Amsterdam's Jews (10% of the city's population) were transported, along with Romanies and homosexuals, to concentration camps in Germany. Hardly any survived.

The February *razzia* (raid on Jews) sparked off a spontaneous Amsterdam-wide **strike** that was viciously put down. Right through the occupation, heroic **Resistance** fighters sabotaged German munitions and supplies stores, attempted to assassinate Nazi leaders, spawned batches of false documents and reeled off secret newspapers to keep the public properly informed. Nazi retaliation was diabolical. If they couldn't dig out the ringleaders, whole groups of innocent people would be shot in reprisal for any Resistance activity. Opposition also went on in quieter, but no less courageous ways. Many non-Jews wore yellow stars in sympathy, and thousands gave shelter to *onderduikers* ('divers') – members of the Resistance, or Jews (like the Frank family), who went into hiding around the city. On **Prince Bernhard's birthday,** thousands imitated his habit of wearing a white carnation, much to the confusion of the Nazis, who didn't know quite what to legislate against. Queen Wilhelmina broadcast cheering messages to her people from the security of a BBC studio.

By the winter of 1944 – '**Hunger Winter**' – the fabric of the city had collapsed. Everybody was starving (especially those sharing ration books with *onderduikers*), as the Germans had restricted the flow of food in retaliation for a Dutch railwaymen's strike. Walking was the only means of transport and rubbish bins and sewers overflowed. Fuel was impossible to come by, so Amsterdammers stole any wood they could lay their hands on. Sleepers were torn from the tram tracks, parks thinned out mysteriously overnight, and any empty houses were stripped of furniture, beams and floorboards. The Jodenhoek began to crumble.

On 5 May 1945 the Netherlands was liberated. On 7 May jubilant crowds crammed the streets of Amsterdam to greet the **Canadian liberation force**. In a final lash of malice, German soldiers opened fire on the crowd, killing 22 people.

1945 Onwards: Post-war Amsterdam

The Netherlands was devastated by the war. Its transport system was paralysed, industrial production had slumped by 30% and the Germans had broken dykes, flooding much of the countryside. Despite chronic shortages of almost everything, Amsterdammers bounced back with a lively resilience. They even managed city-wide street parties in 1948 to celebrate **Queen Juliana**'s coronation and Dutch victories in the Olympic Games. Tropical trade declined, but Amsterdam soon got down to the more mundane business of keeping the hungry new **Ruhr industries** fed. After the widening of the North Sea Canal and construction of the new **Amsterdam–Rhine Canal** in 1952, regeneration was meteoric. Garden-city suburbs sprang up around Amsterdam, and the 1960s vision of air, light and towering concrete gave birth to the **Bijlmermeer** (vast stretches of concrete dotted with towerblocks that nobody wanted to live in).

Old patterns began to emerge. The solid Calvinist burgers were still very much in control, but the city's traditional tolerance soon made space for a new phenomenon of dreamy hippies and tatty youth. In the 1960s Amsterdam became a mecca for the blossoming **youth culture**. Troupes of long-haired young people hung out and slept around Centraal Station, the new Nationaal Monument (a war memorial) on the Dam and in Vondelpark. In 1969 **John Lennon and Yoko Ono** staged their week-long 'Bed-in' for world peace in the Hilton Hotel. An old church near Leidseplein was converted into the **Paradiso** – a place to puff away on marijuana without fear of arrest, and have your ears blasted by the latest music. Homosexuals began to join the party, and soon

Amsterdam was known as the **gay capital of Europe**.

At the centre of the Amsterdam counter-culture was a group of flamboyant jesters, the **Provos** (from '*provocatie*', 'provocation'; *see* p.158). Philosophy student Roel van Duyn and magician and one-time window cleaner Robert Jasper Grootveld, with a motley gang of accomplices, staged 'happenings' on the Dam and around the statue of the *Lieverdje* ('*Little Darling*') on the Spui. The Provos were against capitalism, traffic and tobacco, and for free bicycles and free sex. However, when **Crown Princess Beatrix** married a German in 1966, the mood soured. The royal family was, to the Provos, the distillation of the Establishment. Not only the Provos were angry. Ratepayers resented having to foot the bill for the celebrations and the older genera-tion – still raw from the Occupation – were appalled that their princess could marry a German. Demonstrators lined the route of the wedding procession waving banners demanding 'Republic' and 'Give me my bike back' (the Nazis had confiscated bicycles during the war). Although the day passed without serious incident, discontent bubbled on through the spring. One hot June day a minor industrial dispute over construction workers' holiday pay erupted into violence. During a scuffle with the police in the Jordaan (as always), one worker died of a heart attack. Rumour spread that the police had killed him, and a full-scale riot spread right across the city, sucking in Provos, Nozems (youth gangs) and anyone who enjoyed a fight. By nightfall the *burge-meester* was about to call in the army, but Chief Commissioner van der Molen of the Amsterdam police took the matter in hand. He donned full dress uniform, called for his sword and strode out bravely into the midst of a bemused crowd. He didn't entirely defuse the situation, but the disruption fizzled out after two days.

Later that year, violence broke out again over proposals to build a huge bank on Frederiksplein. Amsterdammers felt that big money was destroying the heart of the city by denuding it of anything but banks and offices. Concerned burghers held a 'Teach-In' at the Hotel Krasnapolsky to debate the issue. In putting the case for the objectors, Dr W.F. Heinemeyer, a local academic, hit upon what, for many people, is Amsterdam's charm: '...most Amsterdammers want a closely mixed-up network of streets and squares...where there's a great variety of possibilities for doing things one doesn't have to do, shopping, going to films and plays, sitting on terraces, in cafés, looking around, wandering about...a place where one can be out and at the same time at home, where it's a pleasure simply to be...One can call it the "forum" nature of the inner city, and this is something so precious that no administration must be indifferent about it.' But three days later the city regents debated the proposal and voted in favour of the bank by 30 to 14.

Meanwhile, the crowds camping out, especially those around the Nationaal Monument, had begun to test the patience of upright citizens. In 1967 off-duty Marines had descended on unsuspecting hippies outside the Centraal Station and cut off their hair. The mess left by the impromptu camp-sites was an affront to the obsessively neat Amsterdammers and a bye-law passed in 1969 banned sleeping around national monuments. In 1970, after violent clashes with the police had failed to oust the Dam dropouts, the Marines once again decided on unofficial unilateral action. Bands of strap-ping lads belted down the Damrak, and frightened the hippies away forever. Amsterdam's youth culture survived the attack, but was more formally accommo-dated in hostels and sleep-ins.

The Provos had broken up in 1967 'in order to avoid bloodshed', but Roel van Duyn went on to establish the **Kabouters** ('helpful gnomes') – a whimsical party of idealists with odd flashes of common sense. In May 1970 they gathered, wearing pixie hats, on the Dam, planted an orange tree and issued a proclamation. They declared an Orange Free State (with van Duyn as its ambassador) that would soon link up in a fairy circle with other socialist elf cities around the world. Theirs was no longer to be the 'socialism of the clenched fist, but of the intertwined fingers, the erect penis, the escaping butterfly'. They wanted more trees, fewer banks and polluting industries, a ban on traffic in central Amsterdam, free white bikes for all – and improved psychiatric services. In the summer election they polled 11% of the vote and won five seats on the city council. As the decade wore on, they lost their appeal and were finally disbanded in 1981.

Though the Kabouters were on the wane, the late 1970s and early 1980s saw some spectacular battles. The council's plan to build a **Metro** – largely to serve the outer suburbs – met with outrage. It was expensive, and meant pulling down more houses in the inner city. Many refused to move and, on 25 March 1975, '**Blue Monday**', there were violent demonstrations when officials tried to clear the first houses for demolition. The ferocity of the opposition increased until 1978, when the council agreed to build new homes and renovate areas of the inner city. Skirmishes went on right up until the opening of the Metro in 1980.

In 1980, 13% of the city's population was on the housing list. **Squatting** had become a popular solution to the chronic shortages. A lot of work went into the renovation of

squatter homes, and the building of accompanying studios and cafés. The network became highly organized and, with 10,000 members by 1982, was a force to be reckoned with. Police attempts to evict squatters were heavy-handed (they used tanks on a squat in the Vondelstraat) and not always successful. But by 1984 the last of the big squats had fallen: on others a compromise had been reached – the council bought up the property, renovated it and let it back cheaply to the inhabitants.

Ed van Thijn, Amsterdam's (socialist) *burgemeester* for most of the 1980s and the early 1990s, was tough on squatters when he first came to office, but then initiated a strong programme of *stadsvernieuwing* (urban renewal) to help ease the severe housing crisis and to transform the city's image. Every few decades, the city fathers get it into their heads that Amsterdam is backward and old-fashioned and needs to be promoted as a modern metropolis. This usually leads to big new buildings in the centre of town. In the 1890s the Centraal Station, a temple to the new railways, blocked off Amsterdam's view of its harbour forever; in the 1920s the enormous Nederlandse Handelsmaatschappij (Chamber of Commerce) building pushed aside rows of historic gabled houses near Rembrandtplein; during the 1960s concrete and glass monstrosities appeared all over town, the most controversial being the Nederlandse Bank on Frederiksplein. The 1970s and early 1980s saw the arrival, amidst violent protest, of the Metro and the 'Stopera', a combined city hall and opera house on Waterlooplein (*see* 'Opera and Stopera', p.107). In the 1990s Burgemeester Van Thijn began to emphasize Amsterdam's role as a tourist, banking and congress metropolis. (It is now Europe's fourth tourist city after London, Paris and Rome, and in the world's top ten as a congress venue.) Vast new development went on in the area around Centraal Station, a glittering casino complex was built alongside Leidseplein, and business parks bristling with skyscrapers appeared on the outskirts of town.

Van Thijn's successor, **Schelto Patijn**, assumed office in 1994. Amsterdam's mayors are not elected by the citizenry, but appointed (ostensibly by the Queen). Yet they wield extraordinary civic power. Patijn's efforts at giving Amsterdam a more upmarket, businesslike image resulted in such moves as towing away some of the old houseboats (seen as illegal and messy), and attempting to close down a number of café terraces (thwarted by rousing local opposition). **Job Cohen** was appointed as *burgemeester* in 2001. For a while it was thought he might ease up a little on Patijn's strict approach, but if anything he has proved even tougher, stymieing attempts to reinstate Koninginnenacht (revels on the night before Queen's Day), moving swiftly to close night clubs after drugs raids, and threatening an end to 'hash cafés' (coffeeshops that stretch tolerance even further by selling alcohol as well as marijuana).

Now the city's notorious **drugs problem** does seem more under control. Heroin dealers have been cleared out of the tourist areas around Zeedijk and Nieuwmarkt and now hole out in the south of the city. The *stadswacht* (modern-day equivalents of the civil guards in the Old Masters' portraits) wander about, unarmed, in smart uniforms with red trimmings, keeping an eye on public behaviour and making sure that buskers don't sing too loudly. Tourist figures over the past few years have risen steadily. Amsterdam is enjoying a quiet, rather comfortable moment in its history, but its age-old tolerance of mischief remains the finest antidote to complacency. Amsterdam's flourishing gay community, the bustling Red Light District, the newest wave of immigrants (from Turkey, Morocco and Eastern Europe), the Kabouters' legacy of environmental awareness and the Amsterdammers' nose for disruptive politics keep the cafés alive and the old port rough beneath its smooth veneer.

Art and Architecture

DUTCH PAINTING

Sacheverell Sitwell wrote that painting and architecture are as endemic among the Dutch as poetry is among the English. During the 17th-century Golden Age (a high-water mark for painting, as well as an economic boom) an estimated 20 million paintings were executed. Even the humblest homes had the odd oil tacked up on the wall. A 17th-century English traveller observed that 'many times blacksmiths, cobblers etc. will have some picture or other by their forge or in their stall. Such is the general notion, inclination and delight that these country natives have to painting'.

These days Amsterdam is still the centre of a flourishing art trade, with nearly 150 commercial galleries that sell anything from Picasso to post-artschool hopefuls. There's an enormous annual art fair at the RAI Congress Centre (usually in June) and open-air art markets spring up around town in the summer. Here you often find inspired work nestling among more predictable ceramics and watercolours – but never the sort of kitsch and tat that's draped on the railings of London's Hyde Park on a Sunday afternoon. Artists' ateliers are everywhere: in the Red Light District, on boats, stretched out in glass-walled grandeur in the posher parts of town. Clusters of studios in the same area have open days from time to time, when (clutching a rough, photocopied map) you can wander in and out, look at work in progress and chat with the artists. Sunday afternoons are the favoured time for 'openings'. These affairs seem less overdressed, tense and poseur-ridden than is usual in other parts of the world.

And, of course, there are all the Old Masters in the Rijksmuseum, a whole building full of Van Goghs, and the go-getting Stedelijk Museum. Even in the Stedelijk, however, you're likely to find something by the latest American whizz-kid or the Dutch boy-next-door tucked in among the Chagalls and Mondriaans. In Amsterdam there's a feeling that art matters, is part of everyday life, and that even the zaniest of new painters belongs to a long continuum of artists working in Holland.

1300–1600: Before the Golden Age

It is important to draw a distinction between Dutch and Flemish art. In 1579 the Netherlands polarized into a Flemish, predominantly Roman Catholic south, and an alliance of seven Dutch, Protestant northern provinces. Eugène Fromentin, the 19th-century art critic, observed that 'Holland had never possessed many national painters... While she was blended with Flanders, it was Flanders that took upon herself to think, invent and paint for her.' Early Flemish art resounds with familiar names like Breughel, Bosch and van Eyck, while Holland musters **Cornelis Ketel**, a portrait painter who grew bored with his craft and, as a ruse to liven up his technique, started painting with his toes, with no noticeable loss in quality. However, in the 17th century migrations of prominent painters to the Protestant north, a blossoming national confidence and snowballing economic prosperity stimulated a new Dutch School. This exclusively Dutch painting was influenced by Flemish artists, but also by Italians and a small heritage of local painters less disgruntled with their lot than Cornelis Ketel.

In his *Book of Famous Men*, the 15th-century humanist Barolèmmo Fayio lists only two Flemish artists: Jan van Eyck and Rogier van der Weyden – painters we still consider pivots of the period. Both had a strong influence on later Dutch painting. **Jan van Eyck** (1385–1441) and his shadowy brother, Hubert (some say they collaborated; some say that Hubert never existed), are credited with the discovery of oil paint. In reality, they merely perfected a technique that northern European painters had been using for some time. Oil paints, which can be applied in layers, give a rich, deep tone which was much favoured by artists who were fascinated by appearances – the glowing colours of objects as they were touched by light. Italian artists, on the other hand, tended to be more concerned with structure, bodies and movement: they worked in tempera (egg-based paint), which rendered sharper, brighter colours – but soon latched on to the practical and artistic merits of oils.

Early Netherlandish art was mainly devotional. Static groups of bodies crowded pictures crammed with detail and heavily symbolic bric-a-brac. **Rogier van der Weyden** (1399–1464) swept the canvas clean. He focused tightly on a few figures and injected a passionate, authentic emotional intensity into his work. This was rare in religious art of the time, and had a powerful impact on later Dutch painters.

Albert Ouwater (active 1450–80) was the man who took these ideas north. He settled in Haarlem around the time that a book by the Florentine Leon Battista Alberti was being passed around painters' studios. Alberti argued that *historia* (narrative) was crucial to good art. Dutch painting became less static; small dramas and conflicts began to emerge from the canvas. **Geertgen tot Sint Jans** (c. 1460–95) was much influenced by Ouwater. He painted bright, beautiful pictures, still laden with symbolic references but with a much freer arrangement of figures. The figures themselves, however, were still rigid, with little real eloquence of movement. **Lucas van Leyden** (1489–1553), a child prodigy who was already engraving in his native Leiden at the age of nine, burst onto the scene with sparkling, dynamic, densely peopled paintings that revolutionized Dutch art. As these various strands combine we can see, in the work of painters like Van Leyden and **Jan Mostaert** (1475–1555), the first signs of a separate Dutch school of painting.

In 1604 Karel van Mander, a painter and theorist working in Haarlem, published *Het Schilderboek* – a collection of biographies and a theoretical handbook for artists. It was the first full-scale work of art theory to delineate Dutch and Flemish traditions. Van Mander exalted Haarlem as the cradle of Dutch art. The school of painters working there was developing its own style of Italian Mannerism. The Mannerists believed their work shouldn't slavishly imitate Nature, but improve upon it with imagination and Art. Paintings (even those with innocent titles such as *John the Baptist Preaching*) swarm with lumpy nude musclemen and elongated female figures. They sport about in exotic settings in which piled-up fragments of Roman art, stylized plants and fabulous beasts abound.

The first Dutch painter to travel to Renaissance Italy (it later became *de rigueur* for any artist who wanted to be taken seriously) had been **Jan van Scorel** (1495–1562). He passed through Germany and Venice on a pilgrimage to Jerusalem. On his way back he visited Rome, and was given the job of curator of the massive papal art collection by Hadrian VI, the only Dutch pope in history. This experience changed his painting style completely, and he returned to Haarlem (as Van Mander puts it) as 'the lantern-bearer and road-paver of the Arts in the Netherlands'. Others would claim that honour for Lucas van Leyden, but Van Mander thought that Van Leyden was a show-off – and, besides, he didn't come from Haarlem. Van Scorel's pupil **Martin van Heemskerck** (1498–1574) also travelled to Italy and was one of the main propagators of Mannerist ideas in Holland.

Mannerism made Dutch painting far more lively and flexible, but painters began to tire of its ornament. A move to greater realism and narrative clarity – more Nature, less Art – can be seen in the works of **Hendrik Goltzius** (1558–1616), another member of Van Mander's Haarlem mafia.

By the 1620s another school of painters had sprouted, this time in Utrecht. Artists such as **Hendrick Terbrugghen** (c. 1588–1629) and **Gerrit van Honthorst** (c. 1590–1624) were followers of the Italian painter Caravaggio, whose chiaroscuro technique (strong contrasts of light and shadow) influenced successive waves of Dutch painters all the way through to Rembrandt and Vermeer. Terbrugghen was the first Dutch Caravaggist to return to Holland (after a 10-year stay in Italy), but he was self-effacing and a bit of a misfit – he wasn't even elected to office in the Utrecht guild. The flattering and flamboyant Van Honthorst, on the other hand, ran up impressive lists of patrons wherever he went and became the best known of the Dutch Caravaggists. His beautiful nocturnal scenes – candlelight and shadow playing over huddles of faces – earned him the nickname 'Gherardo delle Notti'.

1600–1700:
The Golden Age

France has shown a great deal of inventive genius, but little real faculty for painting. Holland has not imagined anything, but it has painted miraculously well.

Eugène Fromentin, art
critic, writing in 1875

In 1565, mobs stormed through the Netherlands breaking church windows and destroying religious paintings and statues. In their enthusiasm to eliminate idolatry, these iconoclasts wiped out much of the country's artistic heritage. There seemed little call to replace it. The austere Calvinists who took control of the northern provinces after 1579 whitewashed the insides of churches and had no time for papish decoration. Italy and its art went out of fashion. The rising merchant classes seemed suspicious of unprofitable aristocratic foibles like patronage of the arts. Artists were in a dilemma: what were they to paint, and who would pay them for it? Eugène Fromentin comes right to the point:

The problem was this: given a bourgeois people, practical, not inclined to dreams, very busy withal, by no means mystic, of anti-Latin tendency, with broken traditions, a worship without images, parsimonious habits – to find an art to please [them]... there remained nothing for such a people to propose to themselves but a very simple and daring thing... to paint its own portrait.

And so the Dutch set about painting 'the portrait of Holland, its external image, faithful, exact, complete, life-like, without any adornment'. In the Golden Age that followed, you find few flamboyant devotional paintings or pompous, heroic battle scenes. Instead, you are given portraits of merchants, town squares, street scenes, glimpses of daily life, breakfast tables, brothels, taverns, the countryside, or moments in history. No other nation has managed a more intimate and beautifully executed chronicle of its life and times.

Genre Painting

Early English critics called the pictures of scenes from everyday life 'drolleries' – nowadays we refer to them as genre paintings. By the mid-17th century, genre was one of the most popular art forms in Holland, and the cheapest to buy. These were straightforward, unembellished paintings of taverns, brothels and family life, but they often contained a covert moral message. Sometimes the signal was crude – wildly copulating dogs in a doorway behind a flirting couple refer to the saying 'As with the woman, so with her dog'. Sometimes complex allegorical references and obscure symbols were knitted into the apparently simple pictures. Unravelling these was, for an educated 17th-century viewer, half the fun of genre paintings.

There are examples of genre work in the paintings of the Caravaggists Hendrick Terbrugghen and Gerrit van Honthorst, and in the work of some Mannerists, but it was the writing and painting of **Willem Buytewech** (1591–1624) in Haarlem, and the short visit to the town of Flemish painter **Adriaen Brouwer** (1605–38), that really established the style in Holland. Brouwer was a disorderly bohemian and a popular painter. Both Rubens and Rembrandt went to great lengths to add his work to their collections, though Haarlem society took some time to recover from his high spirits. He was strongly influenced by his compatriots Breughel and Bosch, and would sit about in pothouses knocking off cruelly realistic sketches of the

Finding Amsterdam's Art

clientele. The grotesque portrayal of peasants appealed to his Haarlem pupil **Adriaen van Ostade** (1610–85), and this became a feature of one strain of Dutch genre painting. (As Van Ostade grew older and richer, however, his work became calm, cosy and far more respectable.)

Another style of genre grew up in Leiden around the painter **Gerard Dou** (1613–75). His meticulous, highly finished, almost slick work was widely imitated and gave rise to the school of Leiden *fijnschilders* ('fine painters'). The paintings, often of genteel middle-class interiors, have subtle chiaroscuro lighting effects and some very abstruse symbolic references. Leiden seemed to enjoy especially difficult allusions, maybe because it was a university town. Dou's pupils **Gabriel Metsu** (1629–67) and **Frans van Mieris** (1635–81) excelled in elegant genre work.

In faraway Deventer **Gerard ter Borch** (1619–81) was developing his own style – highly attentive to detail and with an especially fine touch in painting fabrics. In Delft **Jan Vermeer** (1632–75) was painting the hushed, softly lit interiors that have earned him the reputation (with Rembrandt and Frans Hals) of being one of the three great painters of the age. Vermeer produced eleven children, and only three times that many paintings in his life. In the midst of his tumultuous household, he would lock himself away and work painstakingly on tranquil portraits of Dutch homes without a single child in sight. The reticent, and poor, painter would even hide from influential art dealers when they came to call.

The best recorder of riotous domestic uproar was tavern-keeper **Jan Steen** (1625–79). He paints the lewd, sozzled and wanton inhabitants of his sitting rooms, taverns and brothels with such verve and good humour that it's difficult to judge just what his moral attitude really is. The paintings of **Pieter de Hooch** (1629–after 1688) and **Nicholaes Maes** (1629–93), on the other hand, are closer to the subdued interiors of Vermeer. De Hooch is especially known for his sensitive portrayals of mothers and children. His paintings of the dark interiors of burgher homes with, somewhere in the picture, a door opening onto the bright outdoors, set a pattern for many other genre painters.

Historical and Biblical Painting

The 16th-century Mannerists had used biblical and historical subjects as a pretext for fanciful flights of imagination, an excuse to adorn paintings with naked bodies and elaborate ornamentation. But there was no place for this in respectable 17th-century merchants' sitting rooms, and the austere Calvinists proscribed art in churches. Most artists were launched into an open market of more acceptable styles – portraits, landscapes and genre scenes – but a few soldiered on in the grand old style. Many of these painters were simply out of touch with the spirit of the new age, but others came up with an innovative, more realistic style of historical painting.

The Dutch Caravaggists (*see* above) were prime movers in the new direction. Their bold realism appealed to painters in this Age of Reason. The new style of historical painting leant on experience, rather than invention, and had a much clearer narrative. Unlike the Mannerists, who had indulged themselves in flashy virtuoso performances without any deference to period, 17th-century artists painted scenes from the Bible or from history (especially banquet scenes or intimate group studies of Christ with the apostles), attempting to portray clothing, buildings and utensils with some sort of historical accuracy (they were, however, usually quite spectacularly off the mark).

The Amsterdam painter **Pieter Lastman** (1583–1633) was the spearhead of the new generation of history painters. It was to study as his pupil that **Rembrandt van Rijn** (1606–69) went to Amsterdam in 1624. Rembrandt clearly wanted to be part of the modern movement of realism. Kenneth Clark calls him 'the great poet of that need for truth and that appeal to experience which had begun with the Reformation'. His quest was for naturalness and authenticity. He used his neighbours in the Jewish Quarter for biblical paintings, and infused his pictures with a powerful psychological realism. By the 1640s he was undoubtedly the best history painter in Holland, but it was a lonely mission, as the style remained unpopular during his lifetime. Only one of his pupils, the last, **Aert de Gelder** (1645–1727), concentrated exclusively on history painting. He worked in a lighter, more sentimental style than Rembrandt would ever have allowed himself to fall into.

Portraiture

Portraiture is the most conservative of all the categories of visual art. Painters commissioned to record the wealthy, pompous and important for posterity usually opt for well-tried, acceptable forms. The Golden Age brought some exciting innovators – especially with double and group portraits – but the changes were subtle and the style soon hardened once more into an emptier, more formalized genre.

Anthonie Mor (1519–74), who Italianized his name to Antonio Moro, spent some time in the court of Emperor Charles V, and introduced the fashionable classical style of Italian portraiture to the Netherlands. It was taken up by **Michiel Miereveld** (1567–1641). He had a comfortable job in the court of Frederick Henry in The Hague, churned out competent, formal pictures and became the leading portraitist of the early Dutch Republic.

It was **Frans Hals** (1585–1666) who brought verve to portrait painting. His acute psychological perception, comic wickedness and lightness of touch give his portraits an unprecedented vibrancy. For the first time the sitters seem unconstricted, even friendly. Though his work became very dark towards the end of his life, his early group portraits are exuberantly stage-managed and really capture the high spirits and optimism of Holland's new-found freedom.

Rembrandt's portraits are more introspective, with subtle nuances of light and mood, but portraiture was, for him, primarily a source of income. The earlier 'jugs on a shelf' approach to sitters had been corrected by Hals, but it was Rembrandt who gave canvases real vitality, particularly in larger works. His dynamic arrangement of the guardsmen in *The Night Watch* (1642; *see* p.131) revolutionized group portraiture. Although he brings his full artistic weight to the task, he reserves any radical experimentation for pictures of himself and his family.

Govert Flinck (1615–60) and **Ferdinand Bol** (1616–80), both students of Rembrandt, are admired as portraitists. Bol followed Rembrandt so slavishly that even art historians can't always tell them apart. Flinck had the awkward honour of being commissioned to paint for Amsterdam's new town hall after his teacher's preliminary sketches had been turned down. He died before completing his sketches, and Rembrandt was one of the painters employed to finish the job.

Frans Hals and Rembrandt gave portraiture a fresh burst of life, but by the middle of the century other artists were cementing their innovations into a new repertory of poses and gestures. Dutch society was becoming grander and more pompous, and the artists it commissioned to paint its picture – like **Bartholomeus van der Helst** (1613–70) – thought Hals' and Rembrandt's work too plain. Once again the portraits lost spontaneity and, though often stylish, became formalized and rhetorical.

Landscape Painting

In his *Natural History*, Pliny marvels at the exactness with which some ancient painters could imitate Nature: birds would crash into a wall on which Zeuxis or Apelles had painted a still life. Early Netherlandish painters were impressed by this idea and paid loving attention to background landscapes – so much so that Sir Henry Wotton, a 17th-century English ambassador to the Low Countries, could marvel at their 'Artificiall Miracles'. (Michelangelo, however, is reputed to have scoffed at the literalness of this Netherlandish style, saying it was fit only for young or very old women, monks, nuns and certain tone-deaf members of the aristocracy.) This interest in realism did mean that landscape established a sturdy niche for itself in Dutch art during the Golden Age.

The 16th-century Mannerists used natural scenery, laced with fantastical creatures, as an exotic backdrop to biblical and classical scenes. The well-travelled **Gillis van Coninxloo** (1544–1607) painted very much in the Mannerist style, but is generally regarded as the first Dutch landscapist. Mannerist pictures were usually painted from a high viewpoint. It was **Esaias van de Velde** (1591–1632) who, quite literally, brought things down to earth. He painted dry, rather matter-of-fact country scenes from a low, more naturalistic viewpoint – a style that was adopted by practitioners of what

became known as the tonal phase of Dutch landscape painting.

Paintings of the tonal phase, which lasted until the 1640s, are delicate, almost monochromatic, and are animated by the atmosphere they create. The 17th-century poet and critic Constantijn Huygens praised the school for its ability to evoke 'the warmth of the sun and the movement caused by a cool breeze'. The first tonal painter was Esaias' pupil **Jan van Goyen** (1596–1656). Although he began painting in the bolder colours of his master, he was soon producing translucent worlds of hazy greens, browns and greys. **Salomon van Ruysdael** (1600–70) painted refined, spacious landscapes and is considered the second major tonal painter. **Hercules Seghers** (b. 1590) painted some inspired and original scenes of waterfalls, valleys and stormy mountains. Although he worked at the same time as the tonal painters, his unique style evoked the power of a much grander Nature. He had a reputation for being drunk and depressed, and disappeared in 1633. **Rembrandt** was a great admirer of Seghers, and owned eight of his paintings. His small oeuvre of landscapes strongly reflects Seghers' influence.

From the 1650s a new generation of landscape painters started producing rugged, grandiose works with more solid forms and stronger contrasts of light and colour than the rather pale pictures of the tonal-phase artists. Leaders of this new classical phase were **Jacob van Ruisdael** (1628–82; Salomon's nephew, though they spelt their names differently) and **Albert Cuyp** (1620–91). Ruisdael is acknowledged as the greatest Dutch landscapist and is especially admired for his stormy skies. Cuyp combined clarity and a firm classical structure with (especially in his late work) Italianate lighting that suffuses his pictures with a soft glow. Ruisdael's pupil **Meindert Hobbema** (1638–1709) produced paintings very much derivative of his master's work before marrying the *burgemeester*'s kitchen maid and becoming a wine gauger in the

Amsterdam customs house, abandoning painting almost entirely.

Cuyp, like many other Dutch landscapists, fell under the spell of Italy. Many Hollanders were drawn south by the warmth and shimmering light. Right from the beginning of the century Italianate landscapes existed alongside the more typically Dutch pictures. (The term, however, refers more to the subject matter than to the influence of Italian art.) The escapist, rather nostalgic paintings by artists such as **Jan Both** (*c*. 1618–52) and **Nicolaes Berchem** (1620–83) were very popular with the Dutch public. By the 19th century the style was beginning to lose favour: the English painter John Constable, in a lecture in 1836, berated Both and Berchem as specious painters whose reputation was propped up by dealers demanding high prices. When, reeling from the vehemence of the attack, an avid collector remarked that he had better sell his Berchems, Constable replied, 'No, sir, that will only continue the mischief – burn them.'

Still Life

The English term 'still life' comes from the Dutch '*stilleven*', the word that began to be used around the 1650s to describe a theme in Dutch painting that was very typical of the 17th-century taste for the domestic and realistic. The stylistic development of still-life painting parallels that of landscapes. Early works are 'tonal' – suspended against a plain background, suffused by a transparent, dull light. The objects painted are simple everyday things. The *ontbijtje* (breakfast piece) with bread, cheese and pewter mug is a favourite subject. Later, *vanitas* still lifes, reminding us of the ephemerality of life and earthly pleasures, became popular. Fruit is seen at its *toppunt*, the point of ripeness just before it goes bad, and darker symbols like skulls and snuffed-out candles make an appearance. As the Golden Age society prospered, the simple *ontbijtjes* were replaced by *pronkstilleven* ('*pronk*' means ostentation). The style of these luxurious pieces is similar to that of the classical phase of landscape

painters. Colours are brighter and each object seems sharply picked out, as if by spotlight. Gold, silver, china, expensive seafood and exotic fruit replace the simpler fare of earlier work.

Paintings of flowers were a specialized branch of still life. Real blooms were often cripplingly expensive, and short-lived. The 17th-century Dutch preferred pictures of flowers in their houses. The paintings were often complete fantasies – exotic blooms from all over the world, that flowered at different times of the year, would all be arranged in one vase. They were painted with an exacting and extravagant realism. Samuel Pepys enthuses in his diary over a 'little flower pott' done by **Simon Verelst** (1644–1721), marvelling that it was 'the finest thing that ever I saw in my life – the drops of Dew hanging on the leaves, so as I was forced again and again to put my finger to it to feel whether my eyes were deceived or no'. (Verelst was asking 70 guilders for the painting. The notoriously mean Pepys 'had the vanity' to offer 20 guilders, which wasn't accepted.) **Ambrosius Bosschaert the Elder** (1573–1621) and his three sons were the most prolific flower painters of the period. By the time he died, Bosschaert could command 1,000 guilders a painting.

Sea, Buildings and Animals

Despite Holland's reliance on the sea, marine painting doesn't occupy an important position in its art. Early painters such as **Jan Porcellis** (1584–1632) seem primarily concerned with the atmosphere of the sea and sky, while later artists such as **Willem van de Velde the Younger** (1633–1707) begin to reflect the nation's pride in the ships themselves. Of the architectural paintings, **Pieter Saenredam**'s (1597–1695) exquisitely executed church interiors are the most pleasing – and so accurate that they are still used as blueprints for restoration work. The most interesting animal painter is **Paulus Potter** (1625–54), whose bulls and cows have an intense reality that is almost nightmarish.

1700–1900: Through Romanticism to Symbolism

After decades of entrepreneurial adventure, Amsterdam settled back to enjoy its wealth, and seemed to lose the drive that had propelled it through the Golden Age. Society began to look to France as a model of graceful living, and associations for the promotion of French ideas and culture sprang up.

With the deaths of Frans Hals (1666), Rembrandt (1669) and Vermeer (1675), the Golden Age of Dutch painting also came to an end. The achievements of the 17th century were so great that they seemed to haunt 18th-century painters, who didn't dare do anything new. Paintings became over-refined and uniform in their imitation of French styles and reworking of old ideas. Much 17th-century painting had reflected the stern ethics of Calvinism, but the 18th century began to shed the moral sobriety that had been the dominant humour of the previous age. The freshest painting of the period comes from the few artists who reflected this change in mood and worked playfully with the established Dutch styles. The most impressive of these lighter-hearted painters was **Cornelis Troost** (1697–1750), whose delicately composed satires have earned him the title of the 'Dutch Hogarth'.

Much work was to be had painting the ceilings of grand mansions and decorating the interiors of new public buildings. **Gerard de Lairesse** (1640–1711) was the market leader in this field. His somewhat over-enthusiastic admirers dubbed him the 'Dutch Raphael'. His successor, **Jacob de Wit** (1695–1754), excelled as a trompe l'oeil artist and a decorator of churches. Protestant churches were still bare, but Catholicism was tolerated provided that (a 1730 decree cautioned) care was taken 'that the meeting places of the Catholics do not have the appearance of churches or public buildings, nor should they strike the public eye'. There were no such restrictions, however, on interiors, and De Wit made his fortune on commissions from wealthy parishes.

During the 19th century, painting became more documentary – any allegorical meaning or high moral purpose disappeared entirely. Romantic painters such as **Jozef Isradls** (1824–1911) and **A.H. Bakker Korff** (1824–82) did imbue their work with emotion, but it was of the sober, cosy Dutch variety rather than anything explosive or passionate. Landscapists ploughed on in a Neoclassical or grand Romantic manner, though in the world of **A.G. Bilders** (1838–65) you can see the beginnings of a simpler naturalism. In place of the distant, artificially constructed views found in previous paintings, the landscape is seen from close to. This radical change, which gave paintings the sort of perspectives seen in photographs, characterized much work later in the 19th century. This is particularly evident in the city scenes of the Amsterdam Impressionist **G.H. Breitner** (1857–1923). The landscapes and seascapes of **Johann Barthold Jongkind** (1819–91), drawn from the 17th-century tonal tradition, influenced later French Impressionists and the Dutch artists of the Hague School.

The Hague School was active between 1870 and 1890, an Art for Art's Sake movement made up of an enthusiastic group of Impressionistic painters. They became famous for their grey skies and paintings of the long flat beaches and rainswept polders (reclaimed land) around The Hague. Subject matter was less important than personal feelings and style. **Anton Mauve**'s (1838–88) gently coloured landscapes are the best known. **Hendrik Mesdag** (1831–1915) was a skilled seascapist, and painted the impressive *Panorama* in The Hague (see p.193). The **brothers Maris** – Jacob (1837–99), **Matthijs** (1839–1917) and **Willem** (1844–1910) – contributed fine landscapes and nature studies to the movement.

Undoubtedly the greatest painter of the 19th century was the man that a director of the Stedelijk Museum called 'the lowliest, most human', **Vincent van Gogh** (1853–90). During his short, troubled painting career, Van Gogh produced work quite unlike any other Dutch artist; his work also takes its own individual course in the stream of Postimpressionist painting in general (*see* 'Vincent van Gogh', p.139).

Jan Toorop (1858–1928) trailed along with the stylistic changes of the century, from Pointillism to Expressionism. His best work, like that of his contemporary **Johan Thorn Prikker** (1868–1932), was in a delicate, almost fairy-tale Symbolist style that begins to point towards Art Nouveau.

1900 Onwards: De Stijl to Diversity

The individualism of the late 19th century undermined the supportive strength of the great painting traditions of the past. Twentieth-century Dutch artists were left not only with the question that had dogged their 17th-century forebears (what to paint), but also by a new problem: how to paint. There was no longer a framework of assumptions within which they could make their decisions. Twentieth-century art fragments into splinter groups trying to find their way through the dilemma.

The artists of De Stijl ('The Style', or 'The Way') came up with a new set of assumptions, a theory they believed would take the place of the old traditions. This theory was propounded in a series of polemical articles in the periodical from which they got their name (published from June 1917 to January 1932). They claimed that they were getting rid of all the inaccuracies, obscurity and casual accidents of individualism, and had discovered the essence of art – a Platonic ideal that the world could understand. The best-known visual expression of this great universal principle is the straight black lines and blocks of primary colours in the work of **Piet Mondriaan** (1872–1944; he dropped the second 'a' in his name in order to appear more French – a pretension that most Dutch museums ignore). Mondriaan gives us a one-

man lesson in the development of abstract art. Even in early, recognizable landscapes you can see the germs of his fascination with horizontal and vertical lines. Gradually the figurative images dissolve and you're left with the dashes and crisscross lines of what is aptly known as his 'plus-minus' period. Then the lines get straighter and bolder, and the colours resolve into bright, flat reds, yellows and blues. Mondriaan claimed he was aiming for the 'lucid tidiness' that the new age demanded. In this he is, paradoxically, very much part of a Dutch tradition of stillness and quiet, careful composition. As Kenneth Clark suggests: Mondriaan is Vermeer without the light.

The prime motivator of De Stijl, and editor of the periodical, was **Theo van Doesburg** (1883–1931). His paintings were more dynamic than Mondriaan's, and caused a rift between the two artists. The work of a third member of the group, **Bart van der Leck** (1876–1958), is instantly recognizable – coloured triangles scattered on a white canvas. Van Doesburg was the real energy behind the movement. When he died, the magazine ceased publication and formal contacts between members dissolved. Though De Stijl lasted only 15 years, its impact was felt all over the world, not only in painting, but also in architecture, interior design, typography and even literature and music. The images are still plagiarized by trendy designers for company logos, coffee mugs and T-shirts.

Most of the major art movements of the early 20th century seemed to pass Holland by. There were, however, two Dutch schools of Expressionists active before the Second World War. The Bergen School centred on the recalcitrant work of **Charley Toorop** (1891–1955; daughter of the 19th-century painter Jan Toorop). De Ploeg ('The Plough') was led by **Jan Wiegers** (1893–1959) and influenced by Van Gogh and the German Expressionists. They painted angular and explosively coloured pictures, often of the countryside around Groningen.

The hard, nightmarish quality of the Dutch Magic Realists is reminiscent of Salvador Dali's Surrealism, but their scenes are not as hallucinatory. **Pyke Koch** (1901–91) painted alluring, pithy works with awe-inspiring prowess. He is shamefully little-known outside Holland. **Carel Willink** (1900–83) and **Raoul Hynckes** (1893–1973) were two other prominent Magic Realist painters, if not quite as inspired.

The most exciting movement to emerge after the war was COBRA (made up of artists from **CO**penhagen, **BR**ussels and **A**msterdam). These painters were inspired by primitive art and children's paintings to develop a *volwassen kinderstijl* ('grown-up child style'). Their key words were vitality and spontaneity. **Karel Appel** (b. 1921) remarked 'I just mess about' and 'I paint like a barbarian in a barbarous age'. The gaudy, vibrant and topsy-turvy paintings of COBRA appear to represent a purposeful effort to wipe out any vestige of classical tradition.

During the 1960s, minimalistic monochrome canvases and white reliefs made an appearance. Work by **Jan Schoonhoven** (1914–94) was influenced by the German Zero/Nul movement, which was trying to create a new beginning for art by reducing individual influence to nothing. **Ad Dekkers** (1938–74) and **Edgar Fernhout** (1912–74; Charley Toorop's son) produced similar work, but were more in the abstract geometrical tradition of Mondriaan.

The technological revolution has had its impact on Dutch art. **Peter Struycken** (b. 1939) began very much in the vein of Dekkers, but since 1968 has been using a computer to generate the colour and patterns of his work. **Jan Dibbets** (b. 1941) uses montages of photographs geometrically arranged on clean white canvases, in a way that seems to link him to Mondriaan and Saenredam (the 17th-century painter of church interiors). Nowadays, the club scene and the computer revolution is spawning exciting multimedia art. Colourful pieces by **Dadara** (b. 1969; a.k.a. Daniel Rozenberg), rather in the manner of Keith Haring, are proving commercially very popular, and finding their way onto T-shirts and mouse pads.

Among contemporary artists, keep an eye open for witty sculptures by **Servaas**, innovative painting by **Ido Vunderink** and **Robert Geveke**, **Raimond Wouda**'s stylish, perceptive photographs, ground-breaking work by **Marlene Dumas**, and beautifully shaped ceramics by **Wouter Dam**. In the early 1990s **Seymour Likely** made an appearance on the art scene. Likely was the creation of three Amsterdam artists. He berated gallery directors and collectors in long letters, and produced works that tweaked at the Art Establishment with a refreshingly cheeky iconoclasm. Before his demise he lent his name to a trendy Amsterdam bar, which way past the millennium continued to top up the original artists' coffers.

ARCHITECTURE

The delights of Amsterdam's architecture are small-scale, domestic ones. It's a city of little corners and quiet surprises. Wealthy merchants over the centuries have built some grand mansions, but they're not gargantuan. Though you're unlikely to be bowled over by the sheer magnificence of some glittering edifice, you're sure to be stopped in your tracks, suddenly captivated by an ornamented gable, a witty façade decoration or a neat, perfectly poised little house.

Amsterdam is built on treacherously soft soil. Buildings are prevented from gracelessly subsiding into the bog by a centuries-old method, perfected around 1700 and little changed since. Rows of piles are sunk, in twos, along the line of a proposed wall, right down to one of two hard sand levels (at 37ft/12m or 61ft/20m below the surface). Nowadays concrete piles are used in preference to wood, and some skyscrapers have piles that reach down to a third hard layer, 152ft (50m) underground. Planks are fastened to the piles, and the walls are built on top. As old piles rot or sink, so buildings lean, bulge, crack or collapse. You can see houses listing at precarious angles, propped up by wooden beams. Over the gap left by the demise of one structure, two others will incline towards each other until they're stoutly pushed apart (by more wooden beams). There are a few sad cases where owners have had to make do with propping up the first floor and amputating the rest.

1000–1600: In the Beginning...

The first houses in Amsterdam were made of **wood**, but after fires nearly destroyed the city (in 1421 and 1452), people began building in brick. At first this only applied to the lower walls: the gables (which formed the outer walls of attics and were often shaped to give more interesting definition to steep triangular roofs) were still wooden. The shapes of early brick gables, called **spout gables**, are a direct reflection of their wooden ancestry. Wooden constructions were built with each successive storey sticking out a little further than the previous one, so that rainwater would drip onto the street and not seep back into the body of the building. Early brick gables leant over for the same reason, which is another contributing factor to Amsterdam's cityscape of tilting façades.

Most of the pre-17th-century buildings still standing belonged to the city **fortifications**, built in stone in the 15th century to deflect the impact of newly invented gunpowder. These include the Schreierstoren and St Antoniespoort. Amsterdam's oldest building is the Oude Kerk, dating back to 1300 but now a hotchpotch of styles covering three centuries.

1600–70: New Ideas

Towards the end of the 16th century, architectural pattern books from Italy made an appearance in Amsterdam. The Dutch architects who pored over translations of these books were inspired both by the classical

system of proportion, and by the ornamental designs. In the buildings these architects subsequently produced, the simple spout gable gave way to the more decorative **step gable**, and red-brick façades were lavishly decorated with plaster scrolls, escutcheons, vases and masks. The ornamentation reached a high point in the playful work of **Hendrick de Keyser** (1565–1621).

It took until the end of the 17th century for people to stop building in the Renaissance style, but the adventurous were already experimenting with a purer form of **Classicism** in the 1620s. Proponents of this new wave reacted against lavish ornament, and were far more intrigued by the strict lines and proportions of Classical design. Fruit, flowers, animals and human figures do join the line-up of gable adornments, but not in such profusion. The larger houses begin to resemble temple fronts, with garlands and festoons under windows. Smaller buildings sport **neck gables**. Simpler and more suitably Classicist than the cascading step gables, neck gables are often topped off with a purely Classical fronton and are a compromise between a vision of architecture that imitates the buildings of Greek and Roman antiquity, and the practicalities of building for a rainy climate. (The tall 'necks' mask steep roofs, something a conventionally Classical straight cornice could not do – it was only in the 19th century that reliably leak-proof flat roofs could be built, and straight cornices became more widespread.) Notable architects of the period are **Jacob van Campen** (1595–1657), who built the *stadhuis* on the Dam (now the Koninklijk Paleis), and **Philips Vingboons** (1607–78) and his brother **Justus** (1620–98), famed for their domestic architecture.

1670–1800: Decoration and Decline

Towards the end of the 17th century austerity set in, and architects began to emphasize simplicity and harmony. **Adriaan Dortsman** (1625–82) is the master of the school of '**Restrained Dutch Classicism**'. Windows were made larger and façades became simpler and more rhythmical in design.

In the 18th century, as the economy picked up, many merchant families gave their homes a facelift during which brick façades were plastered over or replaced by sandstone. But more money to spend also meant more decoration. The century is marked by a fascination with the **French style**. Gables became draped with acanthus leaves (Louis XIV), encrusted with asymmetrical fripperies

(Louis XV) or strung with modest garlands (Louis XVI). Sometimes buildings were crowned with excessively ornate **balustrades** – a nifty way of hiding a steep roof with what appeared to be a Classical straight cornice. The 18th century also saw the advent of the standardized, **pre-fabricated gable** – a sort of architectural mix-and-match. Unfortunately, plot widths were inconveniently irregular, so little disguises to hide the shortfall in the gable width – like vases on corners – were introduced.

1800–1900: Public Pomp

Amsterdam was a poor and sorry city for most of the 1800s. Little building went on until money began to dribble back into the coffers in the last decades of the century. The city's first social housing estates went up in areas like De Pijp and the Jordaan, but the period is remembered more for public buildings than domestic.

The driving force behind 19th-century Dutch architectural innovation was **P.J.H. Cuypers** (1827–1921), the designer of the Centraal Station and Rijksmuseum. He based his work on indigenous brick and wood architecture, but was easily lured towards **neo-Gothic** extravagance. His belief that the entire building, from basic structure to the smallest detail of decoration, should be governed by a single coherent principle became the basis for modern Dutch architecture. Two other styles dominated 19th-century building: the upstarts of the **Architectura et Amicitia** society went in for idiosyncratic fantasies that outdid even Cuypers' ornamentation, while the more conservative members of the **Maatschappij ter Bevordering der Bouwkunst** (Society of Architects) favoured an eclectic approach, resulting in a mixture of diluted styles. Most of the interesting 19th-century buildings in Amsterdam today come from the boom period of the latter part of the century, and reflect this divergence of taste. On the one hand you'll see buildings like **A.N. Godefroy**'s Adventskerk (Keizersgracht 676), which manages to lump together a Classical rusticated base, Romanesque arches, Lombardian moulding on the façade and imitation 17th-century lanterns. On the other hand, there are also wildly ornamented buildings like **J.L. Springer**'s Stadsschouwburg. In the last decades of the century architects began to reject eclecticism and work in a neo-Renaissance style. This led to a revival of indigenous Dutch brick architecture.

1900 Onwards: Modern Times

H.P. Berlage (1856–1934), the designer of the Beurs, is known as the father of modern Dutch architecture. Like Cuypers, he used traditional Dutch materials. He relished displaying a building's structure with graceful brickwork, but was never tempted into frivolous ornamentation. The most exciting 20th-century school of Dutch architecture arose as a reaction to Berlage's homespun, rational buildings. Younger architects, many of them in the employ of the city's housing department, began experimenting with decorative folds and turrets of brickwork shaped around a more solid inner skeleton of concrete. These modern, quirky brick fantasies of the **Amsterdam School** (active from around 1912 to 1924; see 'The Amsterdam School', p.167) have, until recently, been neglected, but an exhibition of photographs and architects' drawings at the Stedelijk Museum in the 1980s shot them back into fashion.

But the work of the Amsterdam School stands beside the mainstream of Dutch architecture. A second modern movement, which emerged as an extension of rather than a reaction to Berlage's work, was to prove more influential. Under the influence of De Stijl (see p.137), Bauhaus in Germany, Frank Lloyd Wright in the USA and Le Corbusier in France, a new style of building emerged – all sharp edges, concrete, steel and glass. Like Berlage, the architects of what became known in the Netherlands as **Nieuwe Zakelijkheid** (New Functionalism) believed that they should use their materials to emphasize, not disguise, the basic structure of their buildings. Nieuwe Zakelijkheid dominated the middle decades of the 20th century. Though it produced some neat and attractive buildings, such as 't Ronde Blauwe Theehuis in the Vondelpark (1937), and some fine domestic architecture by **Gerrit Rietveld**, it must also take the blame for the thinking behind high-rise 1960s horrors, such as the estates at Bijlmermeer.

Amsterdam has suffered more than its fair share of architectural atrocities in recent years – tacky façades of insensitively used modern materials and buildings hugely out of scale. Notable exceptions are the monumental Stopera in Waterlooplein (1986) and the NMB Bank Headquarters (1987). This extraordinary brick building in Bijlmermeer has hardly a right-angle in sight, mineral water fountains instead of air-conditioning, a system that warms the building by recycling the heat generated by computers, and installations of mirrors and stone that play light tricks at the solstices.

Amsterdam's most impressive contemporary architecture is in the business parks sprouting around the edges of town, most notably in Sloterdijk and Amsterdam South East. Dutch architects are encouraged to take chances, and the result is a series of sparkling high-rise blocks – many of them European headquarters of multinationals – that show

A Short Glossary of Architectural Terms

attiek (stress the second syllable – 'teak'): not the same as English 'attic', but the line of ornaments above a *cornice* (see below) that hides the roof from the street.

bel-étage: the floor above the *souterrain* (see below), reached by a short flight of steps, but functionally the ground floor.

cartouche: elaborate sandstone ornamentation often seen around small oval windows or *hoist beams* (see below).

claw-piece: the ornamentation that fills in the right-angled step made by the side of a neck gable and the wall below.

console: a supporting bracket (rather like a shelf bracket), often ornamented and supporting a *cornice* (see below).

cornice: a moulded projection which crowns a façade and runs the width of the building. It may be simple and flat, or ornamented.

festoon: ornament in the form of a garland – usually with fruit or flower motifs.

fronton: triangular (though sometimes rounded) piece that crowns a façade. It runs the width of the gable only (not the whole building, like a cornice). In some Classical designs the fronton is very large, often supported by pillars and running almost the full width of the building – this is called a tympan.

gable: the Dutch word *'gevel'* refers to the whole façade, but technically this is just the part of the wall that covers the triangular end of the roof.

gable stone: stone tablet, with a picture or symbol carved on it, embedded in the façade. In the 17th century it acted as a house number.

hoist beam: beam sticking out from the top of a façade. It has a hook on the end through which a block and tackle can be hung to hoist goods to the upper floors.

œil-de-bœuf ('bull's eye'): small oval windows, often with an elaborate sandstone framing, seen in the tops of façades.

pilaster: flattened pillar that projects slightly from a façade. May be decorative or have a structural function.

pothouse: an extension of the kitchen with a separate entrance slightly below street level. Originally used to store pots, and later used as workshops for craftsmen.

souterrain: the part of the house below street level. Because of Amsterdam's high ground-water level, the souterrain is not as low as a conventional cellar, and is usually reached by a door under the *stoop* (see below).

stoop: the steps leading up the front of a building to the front door (which is usually a little above street level). In most houses the steps rise across the façade, rather than extending frontally from the door down to the street. The landing is sometimes big enough for a few chairs, and there is occasionally a small bench built into the railings.

volute: scroll-like whorls which form part of *claw-pieces* (see above), or fill in the 'shoulder' of a gable.

bravura and flair. Foreign architects invited to work on projects in the city have also made their mark – especially in new housing estates such as the Oranje Nassau Kazerna (converted 19th-century barracks combined with a row of new buildings commissioned from various architects), and in the rejuvenation of derelict islands (notably KNSM-eiland and Borneo-eiland) in the Oosterdok (Eastern Docks). The most exciting contemporary-style addition to the city's skyline in the 1990s has been the Nemo building, designed by **Renzo Piano** (co-architect of the Centre Pompidou in Paris). Shaped like the prow of a giant ship, it thrusts out into the harbour beside Centraal Station.

Travel

GETTING THERE

By Air

In 1921 the world's first air-travel booking office opened at Amsterdam's Schiphol Airport. The dashing Captain Jerry Shaw would fly intrepid passengers, two at a time in a fragile De Havilland, across the Channel to Croydon near London (Heathrow and Gatwick were still meadows). These days Schiphol enjoys a reputation as one of the world's sleekest and most user-friendly airports. It serves direct flights from London, Manchester, New York, Los Angeles, Toronto, Vancouver and Sydney as well as many other airports around the UK and Americas (*see* also 'Arrival', p.62).

From the UK

In 1984 the British and Dutch governments passed legislation that broke the monopoly held by KLM and BA over the Amsterdam–London route, and the number of airlines offering flights rocketed. A browse through the travel ads in the British press (such as *Time Out* or London's *Evening Standard*) will divulge any number of return flights priced below £100, even on scheduled airlines. Flights from London take about 45 minutes.

Scheduled Flights

British Airways, *UK (reservations)* **t** *0870 850 9850, UK (travel shop)* **t** *0845 6060 747, Amsterdam* **t** *(020) 346 9559,* **w** *www. britishairways.com*. Regular flights from Heathrow, Gatwick, Birmingham and Manchester. Fares start at £78 return (inc. tax).

British Midland, *UK* **t** *0870 6070 555; Amsterdam* **t** *(020) 346 9211,* **w** *www. flybmi.com*. Eight flights daily from Heathrow; four daily from East Midlands. Fares from £90 (inc. tax).

KLM, **t** *08705 074 074,* **w** *www.klm.com*. Regular flights from airports all over the UK. From £70 return (inc. tax).

ScotAirways, **t** *0870 606 0707,* **w** *www.*

Flights on the Internet

The best place to start looking for flights is the Web – just about everyone has a site where you can compare prices (*see* the airlines listed below), and booking online usually confers a 10–20% discount.

In the UK and Ireland

- **w** *www.airtickets.co.uk*
- **w** *www.cheapflights.com*
- **w** *www.flightcentre.co.uk*
- **w** *www.lastminute.com*
- **w** *www.skydeals.co.uk*
- **w** *www.sky-tours.co.uk*
- **w** *www.thomascook.co.uk*
- **w** *www.trailfinder.co.uk*
- **w** *www.travelocity.com*
- **w** *www.travelselect.com*

In the USA

- **w** *www.air-fare.com*
- **w** *www.airhitch.org*
- **w** *www.expedia.com*
- **w** *www.flights.com*
- **w** *www.orbitz.com*
- **w** *www.priceline.com*
- **w** *www.travellersweb.ws*
- **w** *www.travelocity.com.*
- **w** *www.smarterliving.com*

In Canada

- **w** *www.flightcentre.ca*
- **w** *www.lastminuteclub.com*
- **w** *www.newfrontiers.com*

scotairways.co.uk. Seven daily flights from Southampton. From £120 return; your stay must include a Saturday night.

Low-cost Airlines

The cheap no-frills low-cost carriers can offer astonishingly low prices if you book well in advance (usually two months at peak travel times). You can book directly over the Internet and a discount is usually offered if you do. Prices go up the closer you get to your leaving date; fares booked last minute are, in fact, not much cheaper than those of the major carriers. Each ticket has various conditions attached: for example, whether you can get a refund or whether the date of the flight can be changed. All services may be less frequent in the winter.

EasyJet, t 0870 600 0000, **w** www.easyjet.com. Five daily flights from Luton, plus daily flights from Gatwick (4), Liverpool (5), Edinburgh (2), Glasgow (1) and Belfast (2). From £50 return, plus tax.

Charter Flights

These can be incredibly cheap, and offer the added advantage of departing from local airports. Check out your local travel agency, the Sunday papers and TV Teletext. In London, look in the *Evening Standard* and *Time Out*. Remember that there are no refunds for missed flights.

Airtours, t 0870 238 7788, **w** www.airtours.co.uk.

Thomson, t 0870 165 0079, **w** www.thomson-holidays.com.

Unijet, t 08706 008 009, **w** www.unijet.com.

From the Republic of Ireland

Aer Lingus, UK **t** 0845 084 4444, Ireland **t** 0818 36500 **w** www.aerlingus.ie. Five daily flights from Dublin.

Ryanair, UK **t** 0871 246 0000, Ireland **t** 0818 303030, **w** www.ryanair.ie. From various airports to London Stansted for connecting flights.

From the USA and Canada

Direct flights from New York take about 8 hours. Prices start at about US$200 for special deals and go up to around US$800 for more conventional fares – American travellers thinking of stopping over in London might find it cheaper to buy a ticket to Amsterdam in the UK. KLM, the Dutch national airline, operates in partnership with the American company Northwest Airlines. Together they offer a service that takes in most major US cities (*see* below).

Scheduled Flights

Air Canada, USA/Canada **t** 1-888 247 2262, **w** www.aircanada.ca. No direct flights, but connections in London and Frankfurt.

American Airlines, USA **t** 1-800 433 7300, **w** www.aa.com. For UK connections.

Delta Airlines, USA **t** 1-800 241 4141,

> ### Airline Offices in Amsterdam
> **Aer Lingus: t** 517 4747.
> **Air Canada: t** 346 9539.
> **American Airlines: t** 201 3610.
> **British Airways: t** 346 9559.
> **British Midland: t** 346 9211.
> **Delta Airlines: t** 201 3536.
> **EasyJet: t** (023) 568 4880.
> **KLM: t** 474 7747.
> **Martinair: t** 601 1222.
> **United Airlines: t** 201 3708.

w www.delta.com. Daily flights from New York and Atlanta direct to Amsterdam.

KLM, USA **t** 1-800 447 4747, **w** www.klm.com. Regular, direct flights from New York, Boston, Detroit, Minneapolis, San Francisco, Los Angeles, Toronto, Montreal and Vancouver. Fares from New York start at US$350 return.

Martinair, USA **t** 1-800 627 8462, **w** www.martinairusa.com. Regular, direct flights from Los Angeles, Miami, Orlando, Newark, Toronto, Calgary and Vancouver.

United Airlines, USA **t** 1-800 538 2929, **w** www.ual.com. Daily flights from Washington, DC.

Charter Flights

Major charter companies and consolidators include:

STA Travel, 205 East 42nd St, New York, NY 10017, **t** 1-800 329 9573, **w** www.statravel.com.

Courier Flights

Courier companies include:

Global Courier Travel, w www.couriertravel.org. A search engine that finds courier flights departing from New York.

Now Voyager, t (212) 459 1616, 315 West 49th Street, Plaza Arcade, New York, NY 10019, **w** www.nowvoyagertravel.com.

By Train

The most convenient method of travelling by train to Amsterdam from the UK is going through the tunnel with **Eurostar**. Although there are plans to extend the Eurostar service to Amsterdam, for the moment you will have to take the Eurostar train to Brussels and make a platform change for a local train to Amsterdam. Standard return fares are £83 (including a Saturday night, if booked 14 days in advance) or £99 (including a Saturday night, if booked 7 days in advance); first class return fares are £163/£185.

Stena Line offers combined rail and ferry tickets from London to Amsterdam, departing from Liverpool Street via Harwich and the Hook of Holland. The total journey time is about 8 hours, and standard fares start at £79 return, although there are often promotional fares on offer that can bring the price down to a mere £50.

Travelling around Holland by rail is cheap. You don't have to book as services are frequent, and you can hop off a train to explore towns en route to your destination without paying extra. The information desk at Centraal Station can give you details of the various cheap tickets and passes offered by the network – a good idea if you're planning a lot of day trips.

Contact:

Eurostar, *UK t 08705 186186, USA t 1-800 EUROSTAR, w www.eurostar.com.*

Rail Europe, *178 Piccadilly, London W1 or by post to 34 Tower View, Kings Hill, West Malling, Kent ME19 4ED, t 08705 848 848, w www.raileurope.co.uk; USA t 877 257 2887, Canada t 1-800 361 RAIL, w www.raileurope.com.* For rail tickets to Amsterdam from England, or vice versa. Take your passport when you book.

Stena Line, *t 08705 455 455, w www.stena line.co.uk.*

By Coach

This is the cheapest way to go, but it can also be the nastiest, with a journey time of between 9 and 12 hours. Overnight journeys, in particular, seem planned so that you're woken at a border crossing every few hours.

Eurolines, *w www.eurolines.com,* offers departures from London's Victoria Coach Station. Most services go via the Channel Tunnel, although there are two that travel by ferry (on Fridays and Sundays). Tickets are £35

return if you book 7 days in advance, or £47 if you book within 7 days of departure, and there are discounts for anyone under 26, senior citizens and children under 12.

Netherlands: *Rokin 10, Amsterdam, t 560 8787, w www.eurolines.nl.*

Republic of Ireland: *Bus Eireann, t (01) 836 6111, w www.buseireann.ie.*

UK: *Eurolines/National Express, 4 Cardiff Rd, Luton U1 1PP, t 0870 514 3219, w www. nationalexpress.com.*

By Car

To bring your car into the Netherlands you'll need a valid insurance document (such as the EU 'green card'), current registration and road safety test certificates, an international identification disc and an EU or international driving licence. Speed limits are 50kph (31mph) in built-up areas, 80kph (50mph) on the open road, and 100kph or 120 kph (62mph or 75mph) on motorways. Drive on the right, and give way to traffic approaching from the right, except where you have clear right of way. In Amsterdam be wary of sightseeing pedestrians, give way to cyclists and remember that the yellow trams give way to no one.

The shortest ferry crossing is Harwich–Hook of Holland on the **Stena Line**, though, depending on where you're setting off from, you might find other lines more convenient: **P&O Ferries** (Dover–Calais, Hull–Rotterdam and Hull–Zeebrugge), *t 08705 202020, w www.ponsf.com.*

Stena Line, *t 08705 455 455, w www.stena line.co.uk.*

TOUR OPERATORS

A good place to start looking for a tour operator is the official Netherlands Tourist Office nearest you (*see* 'Tourist Offices' in the 'Practical A–Z' chapter, p.77). The following offer city breaks to Amsterdam, some catering to a special interest.

In the UK

ACE Study Tours, *Sawston Road, Babraham, Cambridge CB2 4AP,* **t** *(01223) 835055,* **f** *837394,* **w** *www.study-tours.org.* Cultural and garden tours.

Bridge Travel, *Bridge House, 55–9 High Road, Broxbourne, Herts EN10 7DT,* **t** *0870 191 7272,* **w** *www.bridgetravel.co.uk.*

British Airways Holidays, **t** *0870 243 4224,* **w** *www.british-airways.com; BA Travel Shop, 156 Regent St, London W1N 9DL,* **t** *0870 240 0747,* **w** *www.batravelshops.com.*

Compass Agencies, *669 Honeypot Lane, Stanmore, Middlesex HA7 1JE,* **t** *0870 444 3580,* **f** *0870 444 3581,* **w** *www.compass agencies.com.*

Drive Alive Holidays, **f** *0114 292 2971,* **w** *www.drive-alive.co.uk (bookings through website only). Self-drive holidays.*

Driveline, *Greenleaf House, Darkes Lane, Potters Bar, Hertfordshire EN6 1AE,* **t** *0870 756 7562,* **f** *0170 649 1261,* **w** *www.driveline.co.uk.*

Eurobreak, *Inghams Travel, Gemini House, 10–18 Putney Hill, London SW15 6AX,* **t** *(020) 8780 7700,* **f** *8780 7705,* **w** *www. eurobreak.com.*

Eurodestination, *12th floor, Alexandra House, Alexandra Road, Swansea SA1 5ED,* **t** *0870 744 2211,* **w** *www.eurodestination.com.*

Great Escapes, *27–31 West Street, Storrington, West Sussex RH20 4DZ,* **t** *0870 160 5742,* **w** *www.greatescapes.co.uk.*

Leisure Direction, *Image House, Station Rd, London N17 9LR,* **t** *0870 442 8955,* **f** *(020) 8324 4030,* **w** *www.leisuredirection.co.uk.*

Skyflights, *13 Ravenings Parade, Ilford, Essex IG3 9NR,* **t** *0870 747 2111,* **f** *0870 747 3112,* **w** *www.skyflights.com.*

Sovereign, *First Choice House, London Rd, Crawley, West Sussex RH10 9GX,* **t** *0870 366 1634,* **f** *(01293) 588680,* **w** *www.sovereign.com.*

Thomson Holidays, *Greater London House, Hampstead Rd, London NW1 7SD,* **t** *0870 165 0079,* **w** *www.thomson-holidays.com.*

Travelscene, *11–15 St Ann's Rd, Harrow, Middlesex HA1 1LQ,* **t** *0870 777 9987,* **f** *(020) 8861 4154,* **w** *www.travelscene.co.uk.*

Travelsphere, *Compass House, Rockingham Rd, Market Harborough, Leics LE16 7QD,* **t** *(01858) 410818,* **f** *461956,* **w** *www.travel sphere.co.uk.* Single travellers and special-interest trips.

Worldwide Holiday Breaks, **t** *0845 458 8909,* **w** *www.worldwide-holiday -breaks.co.uk.* Booking by phone and Internet only.

In Ireland

Go Holidays, *28 North Great George's St, Dublin 1,* **t** *(01) 874 4126,* **f** *872 7958,* **w** *www. goholidays.ie.* City breaks.

In the USA

Contiki Travels, *801 East Katella Av (3rd floor), Anaheim, CA 92806,* **t** *888 CONTIKI,* **f** *(714) 935 2579,* **w** *www.contiki. com.* Bus tours for 18–35-year-olds.

Europe Through the Back Door, *130 4th Ave N, Edmonds, WA 98020,* **t** *(425) 771 8303,* **f** *771 0833,* **w** *www.ricksteves.com.* Fully guided and budget bus tours, and more independent 'bus, bed and breakfast' tours.

Jet Vacations, **t** *1-888 205 3315,* **w** *www. vacations.net.* Independent travel packages and customized group packages specializing in Europe.

Kesher Tours, *347 Fifth Av, Suite 706, New York, NY 10016,* **t** *(212) 481 3721,* **t** *1-800 847 0700,* **f** *(212) 481 4212,* **w** *www.keshertours. com.* Fully escorted kosher tours.

Trafalgar Tours, *11 East 26th St, New York, NY 10010,* **t** *(212) 689 8977,* **w** *www.trafalgar tours.com.*

ENTRY FORMALITIES

Passports and Visas

EU nationals and citizens of Australia, Canada, New Zealand and the USA need only a valid passport to visit the Netherlands if your stay is for less than three months. If you intend to stay for longer than three months you should get your passport stamped on entry, and you will need a residence permit (*see* 'Working and Long Stays', p.79).

Thanks to the Schengen Agreement, the Netherlands, Austria, Belgium, France, Germany, Italy, Luxembourg, Portugal and Spain have effectively eliminated passport control at their common borders. They do, however, have the right to make random passport checks, and as a general rule it is always wise to carry both passport and national identity card.

Customs

Since July 1999, duty-free goods have been unavailable on **journeys within the European Union**. However, this doesn't necessarily mean that prices have gone up – shops at ports, airports and the Channel Tunnel do not always choose to pass on the cost of the duty. It does mean that there is no limit on how much you can buy, as long as it is for your own use. Guidelines are issued (e.g. 10 litres of spirits, 800 cigarettes, 90 litres of wine, 110 litres of beer) and, if they are exceeded, you may be asked to prove that it is all for your own use.

Non-EU citizens flying from an EU country to a non-EU country (e.g. flying home from Amsterdam) can still buy duty-free. US citizens can take home 1 litre of alcohol, 200 cigarettes and 100 cigars, etc. Canadians can take home 200 cigarettes and 1.5 litres of wine or 1.14 litres of spirits or 8.5 litres of beer.

If you've bought goods **tax-paid** within the EU then there are no restrictions, within reasonable limits.

You should leave any meat, fruit, plants, flowers, illegal radio transmitters and offensive weapons at home. If you bring in your dog or cat it must be accompanied by a certificate stating that it's been inoculated against rabies. The exporting of flower bulbs is permitted to the UK, but you need an inoculation certificate for the USA. It's best to have bulbs posted home to avoid border hassles. Most reputable dealers will do this, and the necessary paperwork, for you.

ARRIVAL

Schiphol Airport

Schiphol is built around a central 'Plaza', where you'll find dozens of shops, restaurants, cafés, snack bars and even a branch of the Rijksmuseum, with ten old masters. Upstairs is a mall of 'duty-free' shops. There's a brown bar in the West Lounge; a children's playroom with toys, slides, computer games and baby-care facilities off the corridor between Gates E and F; and a 'clothes-on' massage room, also between Gates E and F. There's a communications centre above the Central Lounge (**open** 6am–11pm), with Internet access on 28 terminals as well as fax and phone facilities. Information counters can be found in Schipol Plaza, in Arrivals 2 and 3, and between Departures 2 and 3. Medical attention is available 24 hours a day on the top floor of Departures 2, above counter 16 (follow the signs or call **t** 0900 109 1096). The airport also provides a Quiet Room for prayer or meditation (off the corridor between Departures 2 and 3; **open** 6am–11pm). Lost property is located in the basement between Arrivals 1 and 2 (**open** Mon–Fri 7.30am–5.30pm, Sat–Sun 9am–5pm, or call **t** 601 2349, **e** *lost_found@schiphol.nl*).

For more information about the airport, contact: t 0800 72 44 74 65, **w** *www.schiphol.nl*.

Getting to and from Schiphol Airport

By Bus

You can swan into town on the plush **Airport Shuttle Connexxion Hotel Bus** (**t** 653 4975). The service is available to anyone, even if you sneaked over on a bucket flight and intend sleeping in the Vondelpark. Buses leave at 20min intervals from 5am to 8pm and tickets cost €10.50 from the city centre. Route A stops include the Pulitzer, Krasnapolsky, Jolly Carlton and Okura (i.e., mainly central Amsterdam). Route B focuses more on southern Amsterdam, stopping at such hotels as the Hilton, the Beethoven and the Apollo.

By Train

Trains (**w** *www.ns.nl*) leave for Centraal Station every 15mins (until 1am, then hourly until 5am). They depart from beneath the airport: look out for the escalators in the centre of Schiphol Plaza. The journey takes about 20mins and tickets cost €3.10 one way.

By Taxi

Taxis will cost you at least €35–40, and hardly seem worth it given the ease, frequency and price of public transport. They leave from outside Schiphol Plaza; call **t** 653 1000, **w** *www.schipholtaxi.nl*.

By Car

All three main **car parks** (P1, P2, P3) have disabled spaces. There's a luxury car park (P7) directly beneath the terminal for credit-card holders. Car park P3 offers a free **shuttlebus** service. **Car rental** companies are situated in Schiphol Plaza (**open** 7am–11pm).

GETTING AROUND

Amsterdam is a sedate, compact and intimate city. Pedestrians and cyclists set the pace, and you'll find most places you want to visit within comfortable walking distance. If your legs are tired, or you're in a hurry, yellow trams will whisk you to almost anywhere you want to go. A car is a liability: parking is expensive (when it's possible), and driving in the narrow streets, which throng with bicycles and jaywalking tourists, is something of a nightmare. Public transport, on the other hand, is efficient, safe and cheap, and to be recommended.

By Tram

Trams run Mon–Fri 6am–midnight, Sat 6.30am–midnight and Sun 7.30am–midnight. They hurtle about, bells clanging, scattering cyclists and pedestrians and forcing passengers to hang on for dear life. On some trams you can get on or off through any one of three doors (which open if you press the adjacent metal button) though increasingly lines have conductors, who sit at the back. On these trams you can get on only through the rear door. The newest trams have a conductor in the middle. If it looks as if you're the only person due to get off, you'll need to tell the driver to stop by pushing one of the bell nipples inside (on older trams these are unmarked and can be quite obscure). Tram stops have yellow boards showing the numbers of the trams they serve and listing further destinations along the route. Information on door-to-door public transport (even to or from private addresses) is available from **t** 0900 9292. You'll hear an electronic voice when you first get through, but if you stay on the line a real person will answer. Information is also available on **w** *www.gvb.nl*. There's a tram map at the back of this guide.

By Bus

Buses work on the same system as trams, though you board at the front door. You're much less likely to use them, unless you need a night bus. A black square with the bus number printed on it is shown on the board of night-bus stops. By some inscrutable logic the night buses decrease in frequency at about the time the bars close (2am). After this time there is only one bus an hour on some routes, and none at all until 4am on others. So your alternatives are a very late night out, a taxi or walking home.

By Metro

The metro is used mainly by commuters from the eastern and southeastern suburbs. There are only two lines, both terminating at Centraal Station. Running times and ticketing are the same as for trams.

Tickets and Travel Information

Once you've grasped the quirky logic behind it, the ticketing system seems quite sensible. Although you can buy single tickets on boarding a tram or bus, it's cheaper and easier to buy a **strip ticket** (*strippenkaart*; €6.20). This is valid on the metro and on all buses and trains throughout Holland. The *strippenkaart* is divided into 15 units. Each time you make a journey allow 1 unit for 'boarding', then one more for each zone you travel through: a journey in one zone needs 2 units, through two zones needs 3 units, and so on. Fold the card over at the appropriate unit and slip it into the slot of the stamping machine (on board buses and trams and at the entrance to metro stations). Your card is then stamped with the zone and time and is valid for an hour, even if you swap lines. Most tourist sights are within the central zone, but there are maps at all stations and stops, should you be in any doubt. *Strippenkaarten* are valid for a minimum of 12 months. You can buy them from stations, newsagents and the GVB (*see* below).

Bus and tram drivers can also sell you a **single ticket** (*enkeltje* – pronounced 'enkil-chya') for €1.60 which allows you to travel anywhere in Amsterdam within an hour of its validation. If you intend to use a lot of public transport, the most economical ticket will be a **day ticket** (*dagkaart*). This allows unlimited travel in Amsterdam and costs €6 for one day. You can buy *dagkaarten* from drivers or the GVB. Weekly, monthly or annual **season tickets** (*abonnement*) are also available from the GVB, starting from €9.30.

Uniformed and plain-clothes inspectors will spot-fine you €29.40 if you travel without a valid ticket. Playing the confused foreigner will get you nowhere.

Maps, information (on all forms of transport anywhere in Holland) and tickets are available from the **GVB** (Amsterdam Municipal Transport Authority), Stationsplein 15, opposite Centraal Station, **t** 0900 9292 (**open** Mon–Fri 7am–9pm, Sat and Sun 8am–9pm, **w** *www.gvb.nl*). In the summer there's often a mobile branch on Leidseplein.

By Taxi

Theoretically, you can hail an Amsterdam cab in the street, but you're unlikely to have any luck at all. Your best bet is to pick one up at a rank, or telephone the 24-hour central control, **t** 0900 677 7777. The main ranks are at Centraal Station, Rembrandtplein and Leidseplein. Cafés, restaurants or nightclubs will usually phone a cab for you, and one will arrive within minutes. The city has its share of grumpy male cabbies, but on the whole taxi drivers are friendly and honest – though make sure at busy ranks at night that the meter is displaying the correct minimum charge. Even short journeys are expensive, with a flat rate of around €2.90 for starters, then €1.80 a kilometre (€2 a mile) and increasing after midnight.

Amsterdam also has a '*Wielertaxi*', a **tricycle rickshaw** (with multiple gears so the driver doesn't have to sweat too much) – a fun and environmentally friendly way of getting about the city centre. The initial charge is €2.50, followed by €1 for every three minutes.

By Bicycle

Cycling is the perfect means of transport in Amsterdam. It's convenient and gets you about at just the right speed to enjoy the city to the full. It's also a very Dutch way to travel. There are 700,000 people living in Amsterdam, and 550,000 bicycles. Hundreds end up dumped in the canals, and from time to time a dredger with a massive iron claw floats round to fish them out. A curious crowd invariably gathers to watch.

The city has an excellent network of cycle-lanes, and motorists are either considerate or outnumbered and intimidated. (Amsterdam drivers have a saying that it would be better to run over a queue of old ladies at the bus stop than one cyclist.) Bicycles are cheap to hire, though it can often be more economical to pick up a second-hand one. This you can do from markets or cycle shops for around €100 (*see* 'Shopping', p.248).

Hire charges vary according to season, but start at around €6.50 a day. You'll need to take your passport, and a deposit. This ranges from €25 to €90, but you can usually get around it by leaving an imprint of your credit card. Try:

Bike City, *Bloemgracht 68*, *t 626 3721*.
Macbike, *Mr Visserplein 2*, *t 620 0985*.
Rent-A-Bike, *Pieter Jacobsdwarsstraat 11*, *t 625 5029*.

Bicycle theft is endemic in Amsterdam. Never leave your bike unlocked. The best way to secure it is with a solid metal U-shaped lock (thieves go armed with clippers that cut through chains in seconds). Lock the front wheel and the frame to a railing or high post. It's a good idea, when you're hiring a bike, to check on your liabilities under the rental firm's terms of insurance.

By Water

If you have the time for the leisurely journeys, canal trips can give you an eye-opening perspective on the city. The moment you step on a boat you seem to cross a mysterious boundary. People on shore carry on with their lives – nicking bicycles, arguing – apparently oblivious of you sailing past only a few feet away.

The **Canal Bus** (**t** 623 9886, **w** *www.canal.nl*) takes you on a gentle cruise along some fine stretches of canal. There are three routes – two through the city centre and one around the eastern part of town – covering 14 stops. Routes are circular, beginning and ending at Centraal Station, and there's a 'bus' leaving roughly every 20 minutes (around two an hour on each route) from 10am until between 5pm and 6pm. Buses leave at 45min intervals between 10am and 6pm. A day ticket costs €15. The All Amsterdam Transport Pass is a day pass that includes all public transport as well as unlimited use of the Canal Bus and costs a mere €19.

A **Museum Boat** will chug you pleasantly along the canals between 16 of Amsterdam's museums. Tickets valid for a day (€14.25) also entitle you to discounts on some admissions. Boats leave every 45mins, 10am–3.15pm daily, from one of seven stops: Centraal Station (main boarding point and office, **t** 622 2181), Prinsengracht/Egelantiersgracht (Anne Frankhuis), Singelgracht (Van Gogh, Stedelijk, Rijksmuseum), Herengracht/Leidsegracht (Bijbels, Amsterdams Historisch, Allard Pierson), Amstel/Zwanenburgwal (Rembrandthuis, Joods Historisch), Oosterdok/Kattenburgergracht (Tropenmuseum, Kromhout Museum); for information see **w** *www.lovers.nl*.

Water taxis can be great fun if you're in a party mood – the company will even lay on a guide, food and drink for appropriate extra charges. If you're lucky you can hail an empty water taxi as it putters past (they can stop anywhere along the canalside). You can also order them from Water Taxi Centrale (Stationsplein 8, **t** 535 6363; **open** daily 9.30am–6pm, Fri and Sat 9.30am–10pm; major credit cards accepted). Fares are metered – an 8-seater boat works out at around €75 for the first half an hour, irrespective of the number of passengers, and €60 for every subsequent half-hour.

The **Grachtenmusea Watertaxi** takes you to eight different canalside museums and monuments. The initial starting point is Smits Koffiehuis on Stationsplein, but you may board anywhere along the route. There are five boats a day, starting at 10am, and tickets (which include entrance to the museums) may be bought at the Watertaxi office on Stationsplein, or on board. A day ticket costs €24.50 (child €12.25) or €19.50 (child €9.75) for a half-day.

If you're feeling energetic you can hire a **Canal Bike** (a pedalboat that seats up to four people) at a cost of €8 per person per hour, or €7 for more than two people; (deposit €50; no credit cards; **t** 626 5574, **w** *www.canal.nl*). Explore the canals for a while, then drop it off at any one of the hire company's four moorings – at Leidseplein (between the Marriott and American Hotels), at the Rijksmuseum, at the Anne Frankhuis, and on the

Keizersgracht near Leidsestraat. Remember to keep to the right, and keep an ear open for warning hoots from long canal boats as they approach sharp corners or narrow tunnels.

By Car

If you do find yourself lumbered with a car in Amsterdam, you can find covered **car parks** (indicated by a white P on blue background) at De Bijenkorf (on Beursplein), Byzantium (Stadhouderskade, opposite Leidseplein), Europarking (Marnixstraat 250), RAI (on the Europa Boulevard) and under the Stopera (Waterlooplein). Charges are around €3 an hour. **Street parking** (also around €3 an hour) works by the 'pay-and-display' method. You put your money into a machine (often cunningly concealed), estimate your time of return, then leave the ticket it prints out on your dashboard. If you park illegally, your car will be towed away before you've had a chance to buy an ice cream. It will cost you at least €350 to get it back from the pound (Daniël Goedkoopstraat 7, **t** 553 0333), and they won't take credit cards. If you overstay your time in a parking bay, your car will be clamped. A yellow sticker on the windscreen tells you where to pay the fine (which will be at least €60). Some meters are free after 7pm and on Sundays, but in the city centre you have to pay up to midnight, Sunday inclusive. It's always best to check before abandoning your car to the clampers.

Particularly useful is the **parking card**. The cost varies according to zone; a day card covering the inner area and museum quarter costs €18 (9am–7pm) or €27 (9am–midnight), and weekly and monthly cards are also available. These can be obtained from the Dienst Stadstoezicht (Weesperstraat 105A, Beukenplein 50, Ceintuurbaan 159, Kinkerstraat 17, J.P. Heijerstraat 94; **t** 553 0333). A **park-and-ride** system (known to the Dutch as a *transferium*) operates from the Amsterdam ArenA, in Amsterdam Southeast.

The national emergency **car-repair service** is ANWB Wegenwacht (**t** 0800 0888; **open** 24 hours). The most convenient 24-hour **petrol stations** are at Marnixstraat 250 and Sarphatistraat 225.

For **car hire**, the international companies are well represented. Local companies often charge less than half the price. An EU or international driving licence is valid; you'll also need your passport and a credit card (to pay a deposit). Try:

Budget: *Overtoom 121,* **t** *612 6066.*
Diks: *Van Ostadestraat 278–80,* **t** *662 3366.*
Drive Yourself: *Cruquiuskade 5,* **t** *627 4001.*
Hertz: *Overtoom 333,* **t** *612 2441.*
Kuperus: *van der Madeweg 1,* **t** *668 3311 175.*

Guided Tours

On the jetties around Centraal Station you'll find a cluster of boat companies offering canal tours, candlelight cruises and dinner cruises. Prices and standards are almost uniform, but **Lovers Rondvaarten** (Prins Hendrikkade opp. 25–27, **t** 530 1090) has the best reputation.

The **Amsterdam Tourist Board** (*see* 'Tourist Offices', p.77) not only takes bookings for canal cruises, but constantly comes up with new ideas for touring the city – its staff can suggest all sorts of walking and cycling routes in and about town. **Yellowbike** (NZ Kolk 29, **t** 620 6940) offers guided cycle tours around the city and surrounding waterlands.

More rewarding than the commercially organized tours are the informal walkabouts with old Amsterdam residents offered by **Mee in Mokum** (**t** 625 1390; **open** Mon–Fri 1–4pm). The guides aren't professional, but give a homely, resident's touch that you're unlikely to find elsewhere. The tours are usually done in Dutch, but since the groups are small (about eight people), it's often possible to arrange an English alternative. **Archivisie** (**t** 625 8908) offers specialist architectural tours.

Practical A-Z

Addresses

Houses on the main canals are numbered from west to east, even numbers on the outer circumference. The Dutch write the house number after the street name, and follow it by Roman numerals indicating the storey: Bloemstraat 56 II would be an apartment two floors above street level at No.56 Bloemstraat. An apartment at street level is shown by the letters 'hs' ('*huis*', house).

Amsterdammers seem to have run out of imagination when naming their streets. If they think they've hit on a good name they'll use it again and again – so you get not only Eerste/1e (1st) Helmersstraat but also Tweede/2e (2nd) Helmersstraat and Derde/3e (3rd) Helmersstraat. Transverse streets get the epithet '*dwars*', and also appear in multiples, so Tweede Egelantiersdwarsstraat will be the second street off Egelantiersstraat.

The Oudezijd (old side of the city, east of Damrak) and the Nieuwezijd (new side, west of Damrak) are abbreviated in addresses to OZ and NZ – Oudezijds Voorburgwal, for example, is usually written OZ Voorburgwal. Postcodes are written before the word 'Amsterdam'. Postcode directories are available in post offices.

Climate

The songs, and all the clichés, about tulips and the spring are right. It's a heady time to be in Amsterdam. The city looks sharp and fresh in the clear light that glints off the canals, café-owners tentatively put out a few tables and chairs to catch the new sun, there are flowers everywhere, and everyone seems to be in a good mood. In summer, the atmosphere becomes almost feverish. Tourists crowd the streets and bars, the air gets heavy and humid, and mosquitoes breed abundantly on the canals. Gable-spotters enjoy autumn and early winter, as long lines of canalhouses reappear from behind the summer foliage. Brick, cobblestone and leaves mingle in a subtle spectrum of browns. January and February can be punishing. As you teeter along the slippery pavements, icy blasts of wind howl down the narrow streets and lash round corners. But as the door bangs behind you in a warm café or *proeflokaal*, you'll discover the true meaning of the Dutch word *gezelligheid* ('cosiness' and 'conviviality' are about as close as English can get; *see* '*Gezelligheid*', p.86). The one thing common to all seasons is rain – sudden showers more frequently than the monotonous drenching sort.

Average daily temperatures in °C/°F

Jan	April	July	Oct
2 (35)	8 (47)	17 (63)	10 (52)

Crime and the Police

Contrary to received opinion, **soft drugs** are not legal in Holland, though an official blind eye is turned to the possession of under 28g (1oz) of cannabis. The tolerance goes as far as allowing some coffeeshops to sell marijuana over the counter (*see* 'Nightlife', p.235); here people smoke marijuana on the premises. But this is not true of all coffeeshops and cafés. Anyone found in possession of **hard drugs**, such as heroin or cocaine, can expect swift prosecution.

As far as big cities go, Amsterdam is comfortably safe. You need have little fear of serious street crime at any time of day or night (though women walking alone would be well advised to avoid the Red Light District after midnight). At one time the area around Zeedijk in the city centre prickled with drug dealers and junkies and was quite creepy to walk through. A massive police clean-up has made the area safer, but despite council efforts to encourage shops and galleries to move there, it can still seem seedy and tense.

Bicycle theft, theft from cars and pickpocketing are something of a problem. You'll often see quite abusive signs on car windows informing all who might be tempted that there is nothing at all inside to steal.

Useful Numbers

American Express: *stolen cheques* **t** *0800 022 0100, stolen cards* **t** *504 8000 (* **t** *504 8666 after 6pm).*

Amsterdam Tourist Assistance Service: **t** *625 3246.* Offers support and advice if you're the victim of a crime.

AUB Uitburo: **t** *0900 0191 (Mon–Sat 10am–6pm).* Gives entertainment information and sells advance tickets (booking fee €1).

Central Medical Service: **t** *592 3434 (24 hours).* Will refer you to a duty practitioner if you're ill or need a dentist or chemist.

Diners Club: *stolen cards* **t** *654 5501.*

Directory enquiries: **t** *0900 8008.*

De Eerste Lijn (The First Line): **t** *613 0245 (24 hours).* If you're a victim of rape or sexual abuse.

International directory enquiries: **t** *0900 8418.*

MasterCard: *stolen cards* **t** *0800 022 5821.*

Operator (also for collect calls): **t** *0800 0410.*

Opvang Seksueel Geweld: **t** *613 0245.* Help and advice for victims of sexual harassment.

Police, ambulance, fire brigade: **t** *112 (the operators speak English).*

Student information line: **t** *444 5000.*

Tourist information: **t** *0900 400 4040 (costs around €0.50 a minute and you have to be prepared to be kept for ages in an electronic queue).*

Visa: *stolen cards* **t** *660 0611.*

Amsterdammers sometimes spend more on a lock than on their bicycle ('And I'd just bought a new lock!' is a common wail after a bike has been stolen). A favourite trick of **pickpockets** is to sidle up close and offer to sell you something illicit. In your annoyed efforts to get rid of them (or keenness to see what they've got), you don't notice that your wallet is being gently removed.

Sensible vigilance is the only way to avoid these petty crimes: don't leave valuables in your car, always lock your bike securely, and don't carry a wallet in your back pocket or leave it on top of a shop counter when

paying. Keep traveller's cheques and stubs separate and don't carry large amounts of money in one pocket.

Amsterdam's **police** generally keep a low profile and are a relaxed and sympathetic lot. If you do need them, the emergency number is **t** 112; for non-emergencies **t** 0900 8844. Main police stations are at Lijnbaansgracht 219 and Beurstraat 33. Report any theft immediately, and get a written statement for your insurance claim.

The Amsterdam Tourist Assistance Service (ATAS; Nieuwezijds Voorburgwal 114–8, **t** 625 3246) offers victim support, should you have been shaken up by your experience, or feel at a loss as to what to do. If, on the other hand, you find yourself in trouble with the police, phone your consulate as soon as you can (but remember that Dutch police are under no legal obligation to allow you a phone call, and can detain you without charge for up to 24 hours). If you are a victim of rape or sexual abuse contact De Eerste Lijn (The First Line) on **t** 613 0245 (24 hours).

Disabled Travellers

Amsterdam's cobbled streets and tiny houses with narrow doorways and steep stairs pose problems for those with limited mobility. Older **trams** have high steps, and are not accessible at all, though newer models are more wheelchair-friendly. There is, however, a special **taxi service** for wheelchair-users (**t** 613 4134), and the **metro** is accessible. In addition, **Netherlands Railways** publishes timetables in Braille and a detailed booklet, *Rail Travel for the Disabled*, available at Centraal Station, or through their London office (**t** 01962 773646).

The **Red Crosser** is a tram with facilities for wheelchairs and staffed by Red Cross volunteers that offers two tours daily of the sights of Amsterdam (information and bookings via Tours and Travel Services, Draaierweg 24, **t** 635 3118).

The Dutch government takes an enlightened and constructive view of the problems faced by disabled people. You'll find nearly all museums, cinemas and churches have wheelchair access and many have facilities for the visually impaired and hard of hearing. In our **museum** entries throughout this book, we use the term 'wheelchair accessible' for those places that are most accessible for disabled travellers, but calling ahead to get the full picture is the safest bet. In our 'Eating Out' chapter we list those **restaurants** with wheelchair access – but, as before, there's no substitute for calling ahead.

Web Sites

w *www.accesstourism.com*. Information on hotels and specialist tour operators.

w *www.disabilityworld.com*. Specialist information for disabled travellers.

w *www.emerginghorizons.com*. Travel newsletter for disabled people.

w *www.geocities.com*. Network with information and links on travel guides for disabled travellers.

w *www.sasquatch.com/able-info*. A Webzine with travel tips for the disabled.

Organizations in the Netherlands

Accesswise, *Postbus 532, 6800 AM Arnhem*, **t** *(026) 370 6161,* **f** *377 6753,* **w** *www.access wise.org*.

Amsterdam Tourist Board, *Stationsplein 10 (near Centraal Station), New Side,* **t** *0900 400 4040*. They offer brochures and information on accessibility and disabled facilities in the city. Also available from the London branch of the Netherlands Board of Tourism (18 Buckingham Gate, SW1, **t** (020) 7828 7900).

AUB Ticketshop, *Leidseplein 26*. Brochures and information.

Nederlands Instituut voor Zorg en Welzijn, *Catharijnesingel 47, Utrecht,* **t** *(030) 230 6603*.

International Organizations

Accessible Europe, *Sfoglia Viaggi, Viale Londra 16, 00142 Rome,* **t** *(+39) (06) 504 2134,* **f** *715 8294/5,* **e** *info@accessibleurope.com,* **w** *www.accessibleurope.com*. A network of specialist European travel agencies who can provide detailed information on major sites

and transport, as well as organizing assistance for disabled travellers.

Organizations in the UK

Holiday Care Service, *7th Floor, Sunley House, 4 Bedford Park, Croydon, Surrey CR0 2AP,* **t** *0845 124 9971,* **f** *0845 124 9972,* **w** *www. holidaycare.org.uk*. Up-to-date information on destinations, transportation and suitable tour operators.

RADAR (Royal Association for Disability and Rehabilitation), *Unit 12, City Forum, 250 City Rd, London EC1V 8AF,* **t** *(020) 7250 3222,* **f** *7250 0212,* **w** *www.radar.org.uk*. Publishes several books with information on everything travellers with disabilities need to know.

Royal National Institute for the Blind (RNIB), *105 Judd St St, London WC1H 9NE,* **t** *(020) 7388 1266,* **f** *7388 2034,* **e** *helpline@ rnib.org.uk,* **w** *www.rnib.org.uk*. Its mobility unit offers a 'Plane Easy' audio cassette which advises blind or partially sighted people about travelling by plane. They also advise on accommodation.

Royal National Institute for the Deaf (RNID), *19–23 Featherstone St, London EC1Y 8SL, infoline* **t** *(020) 7296 8000, textphone* **t** *(020) 7296 8001,* **f** *7296 8199,* **e** *information-line@rnid.org.uk,* **w** *www.rnid.org.uk*. Their information line has advice on travelling.

Tripscope, *The Vassall Centre, Gill Ave, Bristol BS16 2QQ,* **t** *08457 585641,* **f** *(0117) 939 7736,* **w** *www.tripscope.org.uk*. Practical advice and information on travel and transport for elderly and disabled travellers. Information can be provided by letter or tape.

Organizations in the USA and Canada

American Foundation for the Blind, *11 Penn Plaza, Suite 300, New York, NY 1001,* **t** *1-800 AFB LINE (1-800 232 5463),* **f** *(212) 502 7777,* **e** *afbinfo@afb.net,* **w** *www.afb.net*. The best information source in the USA for visually impaired travellers.

Disability Info.gov, **w** *www.disability info.gov*. Comprehensive online resource specifically designed to provide people with information on matters of easy access for those with disabilities.

Federation of the Handicapped, *211 West 14th St, New York, NY 10011, t (212) 747 4262.* Organizes summer tours for members; there is a nominal annual fee.

Mobility International USA, *PO Box 10767, Eugene, OR 97440, t (541) 343 1284, f 343 6812, w www.miusa.org.* Offering information, advice and tours; there is a US$35 annual membership fee.

MossRehab ResourceNet, *MossRehab Hospital, 1200 West Tabor Rd, Philadelphia PA 19141-3099, w www.mossresourcenet.org/ travel.htm.* Good resource providing advice and information on all aspects of accessible travel.

SATH (Society for the Advancement of Travel for the Handicapped), *347 5th Av, Suite 610, New York, NY 10016, t (212) 447 7284, f 725 8253, w www.sath.org.* Advice on all aspects of travel for the disabled, for a US$3 charge, or unlimited to members (US$45, concessions US$30). Their Web site is a good resource.

Organizations in Ireland

Irish Wheelchair Association, *Blackheath Drive, Clontarf, Dublin 3, t (01) 818 6400, f 833 3873, w www.iwa.ie.* They publish guides with advice for disabled holidaymakers.

Electricity, Weights and Measures

The voltage in the Netherlands is 220 AC, which is compatible with the UK, but you'll need a transformer for American electrical equipment. Wall sockets take rather flimsy two-pronged plugs.

Holland uses the metric system; below is a conversion chart for quick reference.

1 cm = 0.39 inches
1 metre = 3.09 feet
1 kilometre = 0.62 miles
1 kilogramme = 2.20 pounds
1 litre = 0.22 gallons (imperial)
1 litre = 0.26 gallons (US)

1 inch = 2.54 centimetres
1 foot = 0.30 metres
1 mile = 1.61 kilometres
1 pound = 0.45 kilogrammes
1 liquid pint = 0.47 litres
1 gallon (imperial) = 4.55 litres
1 gallon (US) = 3.79 litres

Embassies and Consulates

In the Netherlands

Canada: *Sophialaan 7, The Hague, t (070) 311 1600.*

Ireland: *Dr Kuyperstraat 9, The Hague, t (070) 363 0993.*

UK: *Koningslaan 44, t 676 4343; tram 2.*

USA: *Museumplein 19, t 575 5309; tram 3, 5, 12, 16.*

For the telephone numbers of other consulates consult the Amsterdam Tourist Board (*see* 'Tourist Offices', p.77), or one of the listings magazines.

Abroad

Canada: *Constitution Square Building, Suite 2020, 350 Albert St, Ottawa, Ontario K1R 1A4, t (613) 237 5030, w www.netherlands embassy.ca.*

Ireland: *160 Merrion Rd, Dublin 4, t (01) 269 3444, w www.netherlandsembassy.ie.*

UK: *38 Hyde Park Gate, London SW7 5DP, t (020) 7590 3200, w www.netherlands -embassy.org.uk.*

USA: *4200 Linnean Ave, NW Washington, DC 20008, t (202) 244 5300, w www.nether- lands-embassy.org.*

Etiquette

Queuing at supermarket delicatessens, some banks and public institutions is controlled by an electronic ticketing system. You tear off a ticket as you enter and wait for your number to flash up on a screen. At cash machines and bank and post-office counters, the rest of the queue keeps a polite metre or so's distance from the person transacting business. Sometimes there's a boundary line painted on the floor. Step over this mark and the atmosphere turns icy.

English is spoken almost as a second mother tongue in Amsterdam. Some Hollanders seem to resent this, but many (especially those working in restaurants, bars and shops) seem insulted if you ask 'Do you speak English?' One way round this is to open with a cheery 'Dag!' ('darhg', good day) and then speak English. 'Dag' – called out with a friendly upward lilt in the voice – is used at all times of day or night, entering and leaving shops, when speaking to barmen, policemen, cabbies and tram drivers. When you meet a Dutch person for the first time, it's polite to shake hands and say your name clearly.

If you are used to slick New York **service**, or even to the slightly less brisk British style, you are in for a sad surprise when you visit Amsterdam. Bring a bottle of Valium to help keep calm and a pack of cards to while away the time, or you will find your holiday intensely frustrating. It is not unknown for customers to sit for 20 minutes to half an hour in a café before there is even a whiff of a waiter, though when they do come they are so full of shiny-eyed friendliness that it's difficult to be angry. Expect to wait at least half an hour to 40 minutes for your dinner to arrive once you have ordered it. The knowledge that everything is being prepared fresh rather than subjected to the microwave is scant consolation to a rumbling stomach.

The maxim that the customer is always right does not hold true in the Netherlands. If you dare to complain, it will be pointed out to you in no uncertain terms that it is in fact you who is at fault. Inform the receptionist that something has been stolen from your room, and rather than being offered sympathy you will be told off for not putting it in the hotel safe – and will probably have to pay for the phone call to the police. Dare to order a meal 15 minutes before the advertised closing time of the kitchen (usually astonishingly early anyway) and you'll have a strip torn off you for eating so late. Even situations where it seems self-evident that you are in the right – such as a complaint about

the lack of a shower curtain – can lead to a brush-up with the management that leaves you feeling you are to blame. Paradoxically, service in Amsterdam is cheery, relaxed and friendly. Just be prepared to wait... and don't complain.

Health, Emergencies and Insurance

Police, ambulance, fire brigade: t 112 (the operators speak English).

The most useful place to ring if you are ill or need a dentist is the Central Medical Service on **t** 592 3434. This 24-hour service will refer you to a duty practitioner. The most central hospital with an outpatients department is Onze Lieve Vrouwe Gasthuis, 's Gravensandeplein 179, **t** 599 9111. Chemists (*drogisterij*) sell non-prescription drugs and toiletries. If you need a prescription made up you should go to an *apotheek*. The Central Medical Service can also advise you on this.

If you've crushed your contact lenses or dropped your specs in a canal, try York Optiek, Heiligeweg 8, **t** 623 3295 (**open** Mon–Wed and Fri 10am–5pm, Thurs 10am–8pm, Sat 9.30am–5pm; appointment advisable, major credit cards accepted). If your dentures take a crunch try Accident, Amstelveenseweg 51, **t** 664 4380 (**open** 24 hours). There's a free and confidential VD clinic at Groenburgwal 44, **t** 555 5822 (**open** Mon–Wed and Fri 8–10.30am and 1.30–3.30pm, Thurs 8–10.30am, 1.30–3.30pm and 7–8.30pm; arrive before 10.30am for first consultation; appointment not necessary). The Polikliniek Oosterpark, Oosterpark 59, **t** 693 2151 (**open** Mon–Fri 9am–5pm), offers contraception and morning-after pills, but its services are not free.

It is always advisable to take out **travel insurance** before any trip abroad – and to do so as soon as you buy your tickets. Specially tailored travel-insurance packages cover medical expenses, lost luggage and theft, and also offer compensation for cancellation and delayed departure. Check before you buy insurance what excess applies, requiring you to pay the first £50 or so of every claim.

The cost of travel insurance is steadily rising, but is still insignificant when compared to the potential costs of a serious emergency, or even the value of your tickets should you have to cancel your trip. Consult your insurance broker or travel agency. In the event of needing to make a claim, be sure to check the small print of your policy to see what documentation (police report, medical forms, invoices, etc.) is required by the insurance company.

That said, **EU nationals** are entitled to receive free or reduced-charge medical treatment in the Netherlands: British visitors will need a form E111 (fill in application form SA30, available from post offices in the UK). Theoretically you should organize this two weeks before you leave, though you can usually do it in one visit. The E111 does not insure personal belongings.

It's a good precaution to e-mail yourself (to an account that can be accessed from any internet point) details of your travel insurance policy together with other important numbers and a scanned image of the main page in your passport, so if you lose everything, you can still pick up the vital details.

Internet

Internet Cafés

There are Internet cafés dotted all over town. Try one of the following:

ASCII, *Jodenbreestraat 24*, **w** *www.squat. net/ascii*; **tram** *9, 14*; **metro** *Waterlooplein*. **Open** *daily 2–7pm*.

EasyEverything, *Reguliersbreestraat 22 and Damrak 33*, **t** *320 6289*, **w** *www.easyevery thing.com*; **tram** *9, 15, 16, 24, 25*. **Open** *daily 7.30am–11.30pm (Damrak branch), 8am–9pm (Reguliersbreestraat branch); from €1/hour*. The Reguliersbreestraat branch is the first EasyEverything to open outside the UK and has more than 250 terminals. All terminals have Webcam and Internet telephony. The Damrak branch has 144 terminals.

Freeworld, *Nieuwendijk 30*, **t** *620 0902*; **tram** *1, 2, 5, 13*. **Open** *Sun–Thurs 9am–1am, Fri and Sat 9am–3am; from €2/hour*.

M.A. Internet Café, *Tweede Van Der Helststraat 15*, **t** *471 2353*: **tram** *12, 25*. **Open** *Mon–Sat 11am–11pm, Sun 2–11pm, €1.50 per half-hour, €2.50 per hour*. Functional but friendly neighbourhood Internet café near the Albert Cuyp market with good, fast equipment.

Web Sites

The following Web sites give information on visiting Amsterdam:

w *www.amsterdam.nl*

w *www.amsterdamhotspots.nl*

w *www.amsterdammuseums.nl*

w *www.amsterdampromotion.nl (site of the Amsterdam Promotion Foundation for business-orientated information)*

w *www.amsterdamtourist.nl*

w *www.channels.nl (virtual tour through Amsterdam)*

w *www.dinnersite.com*

w *www.goudengids.nl (Yellow Pages)*

w *www.holland.com*

w *www.hotelned.com (general hotel information)*

w *www.iens.nl (local restaurant tips)*

w *www.museumserver.nl*

w *www.nbt.nl/nbt-amst-index.html (tourist office site)*

w *www.ns.com (railway services)*

w *www.theater.nl*

w *www.uitlijn.nl (entertainment calendar)*

w *www.visitamsterdam.com*

w *www.9292ov.nl (public transport information)*

Lost Property

There are lost property offices at Centraal Station, GVB Head Office, Prins Hendrikkade 108–114 (**open** Mon–Fri 9am–4pm; for items lost on public transport), or the police at Stephensonstraat 18 (**open** 9.30am–3.30pm, **t** 559 3005). You'll need to allow a day or two for your property to filter through the system before trying to reclaim it.

Media

Don't be surprised if you find yourself chatting over a coffee with an Amsterdammer about the previous night's BBC TV soap opera. Amsterdam gets BBC1 and 2, Radio 4 (198kHz longwave) and the World Service (6045 kHz AM). Even on Dutch television, British and American shows tend to be subtitled rather than dubbed. Most homes and hotels are connected to cable. You can get about 20 stations (including CNN) and can decide what to watch by flicking through to Infokanaal – two alternating screens with simultaneous broadcasts of what's on offer on all channels. Non-Dutch speakers might like to tune in to Netherlands Radio 3 (96.8 mHz) for pop or Radio 4 (98.9 mHz) for classical music. There are also a number of smaller and pirate music stations – Amsterdam FM (106.8 FM) plays the hippest dance music.

International **newspapers** are available all over Amsterdam, usually on the day of publication. If you want to pigeonhole the Amsterdammer opposite you on the tram by the newspaper he/she's reading, here's a short list. *De Telegraaf* is right-wing, sensationalist press (though it has good accommodation ads on Wednesdays). It was the only paper allowed to publish during the Nazi occupation. The *NRC Handelsblad* is the favourite of intellectuals. *Het Parool* started life as a Resistance news-sheet during the war; *Trouw* also went underground, and *De Volkskrant* was banned. These three now form the nucleus of the left-wing press. *Het Financieel Dagblad* gives business news, and has an English summary.

Money, Banks and Taxes

On 1 January 1999, the euro (€) became the official **currency** of the Netherlands (at the rate of 2.20371 Dutch guilders to the euro), and guilder notes and coins became obsolete on 28 January 2002. At the time of writing, the euro was worth UK£0.70, US$0.85 and C$1.58. The flashy, this-is-the-future-of-Europe bills come in denominations of 5, 10, 20, 50, 100, 200 and 500 euros, and the bills themselves get bigger as you go up. You will have trouble using anything over €50 in most shops. One euro is divisible by 100 cents, and cent coins are issued in denominations of 1, 2, 5, 10, 20 and 50. Euro coins are issued in denominations of 1 and 2 euros.

Credit cards such as Amex, Visa and MasterCard are all widely accepted. But it's always a good policy to double-check. A number of shops will charge you extra if you pay by credit card. **Eurocheques and traveller's cheques** are a good idea. If you have appropriate identification, many establishments will accept them direct. Nowadays, hole-in-the-wall **cash dispensers (ATMs)** are the most convenient way of getting money. Check that your bank card and PIN are programmed for overseas withdrawals, and that your bank doesn't charge for the service. You can usually withdraw up to €200 a day.

The Postbank (at post offices) and GWK (Grens Wissel Kantoor – official bureaux de change) are the best places to change your money. **Banks** are open Mon–Fri 9am to 4 or 5pm (some stay open until 7pm on Thursdays). **Bureaux de change** often offer the same rates as banks, but take more commission. There are bureaux open until midnight on Leidsestraat. The GWK exchanges at Centraal Station and Schiphol (both open 24 hours daily) are a better bet than the deals offered by hotel receptions, and even many banks. If you exchange traveller's cheques at a company branch, you don't have to pay commission at all. You'll find offices of **American Express** at Amsteldijk 166, Damrak 66, **t** 504 8504 (with 24-hour cash dispenser for cardholders and automatic traveller's cheque refund service); and **Travelex** at Dam 23–5, Damrak 1–5 (**open** Mon–Sat 8am–8pm and Sun 9am–8pm) and Leidseplein 31A.

Lost or stolen credit cards can be reported on the following numbers:

American Express: *stolen cheques* **t** *0800 022 0100, stolen cards* **t** *504 8000* (**t** *504 8666 after 6pm*).

Diners Club: *t 654 5501.*
MasterCard: *t 0800 022 5821.*
Visa: *t 660 0611.*

Value-added tax is known in Holland as Belasting Toegevoegde Waarde, or BTW, and is levied at 6% on restaurant bills, 5% on hotel bills (included in the price except at very expensive places), and 19% on retail goods. Tourists from non-EU countries can claim a refund on any goods purchased in any one store whose total price exceeds €135, as long as they are taken out of the EU within three months. Request a VAT form when you buy, have it stamped by a customs official when you leave the EU, and then the official will send the stamped document back to the store, who will post you a cheque. If you want your refund immediately you leave the country, shop in places displaying the 'Tax-free for Tourists' sign. The sales-person will give you a stamped cheque that can be cashed when you leave the EU. Items excluded from the scheme are motor vehicles, boats you intend to sail to a destination outside the EU, goods for business purposes, bullion, unmounted gemstones, goods requiring an export licence and goods bought by mail order.

Opening Hours

Restaurants are generally open from 6pm to 11pm or midnight. Many are open for lunch from noon to 2.30pm. Some are closed on either Sunday or Monday. The huge variety of bars and cafés have varied opening hours, though most close at around 1am during the week, and a little later at the weekend.

Shops are generally open Monday to Saturday 9am to 6pm, though some are closed on Monday morning and others are open seven days a week. Night shops selling groceries and alcohol are widespread around town.

Most **museums** are open daily from around 10am to 5pm, though this is not strictly the case, and many are closed on Sunday morning and Monday. For bank opening hours, *see* 'Money, Banks and Taxes', above.

Public Holidays

On public holidays most things close and Amsterdam can be very quiet indeed. A fair few museums are, however, open for several hours on public holidays (with the exception of Christmas Day and New Year's Day).

1 Jan	New Year's Day
March/April	Good Friday
March/April	Easter Sunday
March/April	Easter Monday
30 April	Queen's Day (Koninginnedag)
4 May	Remembrance Day
5 May	Liberation Day
April/May	Ascension Day
June	Whit Sunday
June	Whit Monday
25 Dec	Christmas Day
26 Dec	Boxing Day

For **post-office** opening hours, *see* 'Post and Fax', p.76.

Packing

It's a good idea to pack an umbrella at any time of the year. The temperature can drop suddenly, even in summer, so a few warm clothes are a wise precaution.

Amsterdammers are not ostentatious dressers. The dress code seems to be that, if it feels good, it looks good. Nightclubbers are less self-conscious about fashion than in other cities. You'll find bank clerks wearing jeans to work, and there are T-shirts as well as black bow ties at the opera.

English-language books are readily available, though expensive, so it's better to buy your holiday reading before you go.

Photography

Camera film is widely available in Amsterdam, though not particularly cheap. There are places to develop film all over town.

Try the Albert Heijn chain of supermarkets for a cheap option. For other reliable places track down any of the following:

Foto Amsterdam, *Rokin 22*, **t** *624 4000*.
Heno Fotostudio, *Vijzelstraat 3*, **t** *623 4934*.
Quick Print, *Rijnstraat 58B*, **t** *673 0357*.

Post and Fax

Post offices are generally open Mon–Fri
8.30am–5pm. Larger branches may also open
Sat 9–noon. Here you can buy stamps, and
send letters, express letters and telegrams
(get in the right queue – sometimes counters
are labelled for certain functions only).

The main post office is at Singel 250 (**t** 330
0555; **open** Mon–Wed and Fri 9am–6pm,
Thurs 9am–8pm, Sat 10am–1.30pm) and, as
well as the usual facilities, has phones,
photocopiers, a gift shop and a philately
counter. Parcels can be sent only through
this office.

Stamps (*postzegels*) can also be bought
from tobacconists. At the time of writing, a
letter to the UK costs €0.59 priority; to the
USA it costs €0.75 priority. The slot for overseas mail on postboxes is marked '*Overige*'.

A **poste restante** service is available. Letters
should be addressed to: Poste Restante,
Hoofdpostkantoor TPG, Singel 250, 1016 AB
Amsterdam. You'll need a passport to claim
your mail.

Smoking

Smoking (cigarettes) is widespread in
Amsterdam, whether at the theatre during
the interval, or in restaurants. Public transport and taxis are non-smoking, but there
are smoking carriages on trains. Smoking
weed is allowed in some bars and cafés –
not all of them. *See* also 'Crime and the
Police', p.68.

At the time of this book going to print,
legislation was being put before the Dutch
parliament to ban smoking in restaurants
and cafés. While this news comes as a relief
to those tired of choking on the fumes
emitted by an early Dutch diner lighting up a
post-prandial cigar, just as other diners' delicately flavoured starters are arriving, the

possibility of a ban is causing much wheezy
outrage.

An added factor to the opposition is that
the 'coffeeshops' selling marijuana will
suddenly become a contradiction in terms, as
they will also fall into the category of public
places where people are not allowed to
smoke.

True to the Dutch tradition of careful argu-
ment and compromise, discussion on the
smoking ban looks likely to be a long drawn-
out affair.

Students

Amsterdam has a large student population
(around 30,000). The main university is UVA
(Universiteit van Amsterdam), which has
buildings dotted about the centre of town.
The big student nightclub is Dansen Bij
Jansen (Handboogstraat 11, **t** 620 1779,
w *www.dansenbijjansen.nl*).

If you're looking for somewhere to stay
and want to seek out your own kind,
Amsterdam's hostels are well-endowed with
travelling students. The best university bookshop is VU Boekhandel (De Boelelaan 1105,
t 644 4355). The main library is UVA Main
Library (Singel 425, **t** 525 2266). Information
for students can be gleaned from the UVA
Service and Information Centre
(Binnengasthuisstraat 9, **t** 525 8080); otherwise call the VU Student Information Line:
t 444 5000.

The CJP (Cultureel Jongeren Passport) costs
€12.50 and entitles anyone under the age of
26 to discounts at museums, theatres and
cultural events. It's available from the Tourist
Offices (*see* opposite) and theatres and
museums or via cjp.nl (Leidseplein 26,
t 621 1211).

Telephones

Phoning direct from **hotel rooms** is usually
very expensive. Amsterdam's **telephone
boxes** are green, with a white 'KPN' logo.
Most payphones accept credit cards, and all
operate with **phonecards**, which you can buy

at post offices, railway stations and newsagents. Instructions in phone boxes are clear, but don't be confused by the local ringing tone – a long continuous sound rather like the British 'engaged' signal. A busy line in Holland is indicated by rapid tones.

Another surprise is the Dalek voice you get when phoning popular numbers such as airports or taxis. You're told: '*Er zijn nog drie* (three)/*twee* (two)/*een* (one) *wachtenden voor u*' – an indication of how many people are patiently waiting ahead of you in an electronic queue.

All numbers given in this book that are not preceded by a bracketed **code** are Amsterdam numbers (*see* below for direct dialling codes). Numbers preceded by 0800 are free, and those beginning with 0900 are charged at a special rate (a recorded voice will tell you how much you are forking out).

Directory enquiries: *t 0900 8008.*

International directory enquiries: *t 0900 8418.*

Operator (also for collect calls): *t 0800 0410.*

International calls are cheaper between 8pm and 8am, but calls to other European countries don't count as international. International direct dialling codes:

From Amsterdam to USA: *t 00 1 + area code (without 0).*

From USA to Amsterdam: *t 011 31 20.*

From Amsterdam to UK: *t 00 44 + area code (without 0).*

From UK to Amsterdam: *t 00 31 20.*

Time

Amsterdam is 2 hours ahead of Greenwich Mean Time in the spring and summer, and 1 hour ahead in winter and autumn. It is 6 hours ahead of Eastern Standard Time.

Tipping

Restaurant and bar bills in Holland are inclusive of tax and service, so a tip isn't really necessary. It's customary, though, to round the amount up to the nearest euro. If the service has been exceptional, it's quite acceptable to add a little more. Don't leave money on the bar counter by way of tip after buying your drink. Amsterdammers will either think it a little vulgar. Taxi drivers expect 10% – especially if they've helped with luggage.

Toilets

Amsterdam is dotted with rather attractive but foul-smelling, curved green metal *urinoirs*. These are right on the pavement, and blot out only the mid-torso from public gaze. All passers-by see is a pair of feet and a face trying desperately to look nonchalant. In the 1970s, feminists – less out of *pissoir*-envy than anger at the lack of facilities for women – bound up a few of the offending privies in swathes of pink ribbon. The protest had no effect. Apart from those at railway stations, there are still no normal public toilets in Amsterdam. For women, or men who balk at the idea of peeing alfresco, the best option is to duck into a café. This is perfectly acceptable practice, though bars in some of the busier tourist areas discourage it. The better hotel foyers provide classier options, but this takes a certain amount of poise, as you have to stroll through the lobby as if you're a resident, all the time darting your eyes about for the relevant sign – not easy if you're caught in a last-minute dash. Station loos – and sometimes those in larger cafés – are guarded by fierce women, who require you to drop at least 25c into a saucer before passing.

Tourist Offices

Abroad

For tourist office Web sites, *see* 'Internet', p.73. The Netherlands Board of Tourism offices have details of hotels and events:

Canada: *25 Adelaide St E, Suite 710, Toronto, Ontario M5C 1Y2,* **t** *1-888 2 465526,* **f** *(416) 363 1470,* **e** *info@goholland.com,* **w** *www.holland.com.*

UK and Ireland: *PO Box 30783, London WC2B 6DH,* **t** *0906 871 7777 (recorded*

Discount Cards

Amsterdam Pass (€26 for a 24-hour pass, €36 for 48 hours and €46 for 72 hours – it can pay for itself within a few days). Entitles you to all sorts of concessions: free access to over 20 museums and attractions, as well as free use of public transport and restaurant discounts. Available from the Amsterdam Tourist Board (see 'Tourist Offices', p.77). You'll need a photograph.

Museumkaart (Annual Museum Card; €25 plus €4.95 administrative charge; under 25s €12.50 plus €4.95 administrative charge). Museums in the Netherlands are seldom free, but this gets you into most museums in Holland for nothing, or at a substantial discount. Buy one at museum ticket offices. You'll need a photograph.

Cultureel Jongeren Passport (CJP; €12.50). If you're under 26 the CJP entitles you to discounts at museums, theatres and cultural events. It's available from the Amsterdam Tourist Board offices and many museums and theatres. You'll need a photograph and proof of age.

information), *f* 7539 7593, *e* information@ nbt.org.uk, *w* www.holland.com,

USA: *355 Lexington Av, 19th Floor, New York, NY 10017,* *t* *1-888 GO HOLLAND,* *f* *(212) 370 9507,* *w* www.holland.com; c/o Northwest Airlines, 11101 Aviation Boulevard, suite 200, Los Angeles, CA 90045, *t* (310) 348 9339, *f* 348 9344, *e* info@goholland.com, *w* www.holland.com.

In Amsterdam

The Amsterdam Tourist Board has English-speaking staff who can change money and (for a €1.50 fee) arrange hotel and theatre bookings. They sell a range of maps and brochures and can suggest tours and walks. Offices include:

Opposite Centraal Station, Stationsplein 10. **Open** *daily 9am–5pm.*

Leidseplein 1. **Open** *daily 9am–7pm.*

Platform 2, Centraal Station. **Open** *Mon–Sat 9am–8pm, Sun 9am–5pm.*

VVV-Schiphol (HTI), Schiphol Airport Plaza. **Open** *Mon–Sun 7am–10pm.*

There is a central information telephone number, *t* 0900 400 4040, but it costs around €0.50 a minute and almost invariably you are kept for ages in an electronic queue.

Other useful resources include:

AUB Uitburo, *Leidseplein 26,* *t* *0900 0191.* **Open** *Mon–Sat 10am–6pm.* Gives information and sells advance tickets (booking fee €1) for the city's theatres and concert halls and for many other cultural events. It also distributes leaflets and listings magazines.

GVB (Amsterdam Municipal Transport Authority), *Stationsplein 15,* *w* www.gvb.nl. **Open** *Mon–Fri 7am–9pm, Sat and Sun 8am–9pm.* Has extensive information about public transport.

Women Travellers

Amsterdam is one of Europe's safest cities for women, with little street harassment and an unquestioned recognition of the equality of the sexes. However, the seedier corners of the Red Light District can be intimidating, especially for women, so it's probably not advisable to explore this area alone.

There is a large range of support groups and other sources of information for women in Amsterdam:

IIAV (International Information Centre and Archives of the Women's Movement), *Obiplein 4,* *t* *665 0820.* A centre for women's studies, with feminist literature and information regarding the contemporary status of women in Holland.

Meldpunt Vrouwen Opvang Amsterdam, *t* *611 6022.* General advice, and information about the full range of women's groups.

Opvang Seksueel Geweld, *t* *613 0245.* Help and advice for victims of sexual harassment.

Xantippe Unlimited, *Prinsengracht 290,* *t* *623 5854.* The city's best women's bookshop, with many titles in English.

Het Vrouwenhuis, *Nieuwe Herengracht 95,* *t* *625 2066.* Provides information about women's activities and events, along with a library of related books.

Working and Long Stays

If you're considering living and working in Amsterdam, you'll need all the energy, imagination and cunning you can muster to find an apartment and a job. Traditional options for English-speakers – such as language teaching – barely exist in Amsterdam because the locals speak English so well. It's a small city, and reasonably priced accommodation is very hard to come by – though, of course, once you cross the magic boundary into the world of company lets and luxury rents, problems vanish.

Long-term Residence and Finding a Job

Neither EU nor American citizens need a visa for stays of under three months. If you want to stay longer than that you will need some proof of financial independence – usually that means a job in the Netherlands.

The situation for EU citizens is not straight-forward. The first thing to do is to get your passport stamped when you enter the country. This won't be done automatically, and sometimes you have to be quite insistent. A stamped passport is the only proof of duration of residence that most authorities will accept. Then within five days you should report to the Bevolkingsregister section of the City Hall (on Waterlooplein) to register your address and get a residence permit. To do this you must have a permanent address. Hotels and sub-let apartments do not count – and, as everyone in the Netherlands has to register their address, the computer will find you out if you are fibbing. If you are staying 'permanently' with friends, you must have a signed letter from them (and this renders them liable to extra taxes).

Armed with a residence permit, you now need a work permit. You cannot legally take on a job unless you have one. You won't get a work permit until you have a residence permit, and you are highly unlikely to find a permanent place to stay if you don't have a job. This is just the first of many catch-22s waiting to ensnare you. If you are lucky enough to have a signed contract or firm offer of a job before you enter the country, your employer should be able to organize a work permit for you. If not, then hold tight. You will (eventually) get a work permit from the Vreemdelingenpolitie (literally, 'Strangers' Police'; Johan Huizinglaan 757, t 559 6300). Be prepared to queue from around 6am in order to get a ticket (when the office opens at 8am) that will place you in an electronic queue. Don't leave the building. Bring all the documentation you can think of, including passport, passport photos (all exactly the same), proof that you are medically insured and your residence permit. Even if you have no offer of a job, the Vreemdelingenpolitie are obliged to give you an 'EU Letter' that allows you to register with an employment agency. This letter is valid for three months, after which you have to visit the Vreemdelingenpolitie again in order to get a work permit for one year. You might be lucky enough to swing an appointment for this second visit, rather than having to queue. A year later, if you have all the valid documents and haven't been anywhere near the Social Security office, you are eligible for a five-year permit.

American citizens are the only non-EU citizens permitted to apply for a residence permit once they're already in the country, rather than before they leave home. The procedure once you arrive is the same one outlined above for EU citizens. The place to start looking for a job is an *uitzendburo* (employment agency) or in newspapers such as *De Volkskrant* (which has a very good jobs section on Saturday). But be warned: unless your Dutch is excellent you're up against very stiff competition from multilingual locals.

Useful employment agencies are:

Manpower, *Heiligeweg 9*, *t 622 7081*. General office/secretarial.

Tempo Team, *Rokin 118*, *t 523 6110*. Academic/catering/medical/secretarial/technical.

Finding Somewhere to Stay

Shared accommodation is not as common in Amsterdam as in other large cities. The *De Volkskrant* or *De Telegraaf* (Wednesdays) newspapers have 'Rented Accommodation Offered' columns (*Woonruinte te huur aangeboden*), and the weekly freebie *De Echo* is also a good bet. The noticeboards in libraries, supermarkets and tobacconists' windows are a good source of medium-term accommodation. Word of mouth is really the best way. Just be prepared to be a bore at parties until you finally find someone who has a friend whose neighbour is moving out.

As a last resort, try one of the accommodation agencies (*see* 'Apartments', p.213). Be prepared to fork out a whacking fee, plus a month's rent as deposit and a month's rent in advance. Consider yourself lucky if you're offered something for under €700 a month. Sometimes you're also expected to pay *overnamekosten* (literally, 'taking-over costs') for whatever tatty carpets and fittings the previous tenant has left behind. *Overnamekosten* can run into thousands of euros. Haggle a little, but too much quibbling could lose you the apartment.

The Centre:
Old Side

The Centre: Old Side

The original settlement of Amsterdam grew up in the early 13th century along Kerkstraat ('Church Street', later renamed Warmoesstraat) on the right (east) side of the river. Towards the end of the 19th century the village expanded along Windmolenstraat (Windmill Street) on the left (west) bank. The Church Side and the Windmill Side soon became known as Oude Zijd (Old Side) and Nieuwe Zijd (New Side), and the corresponding sides of Damrak are still called that today. The Old Side still has its canals, the Oudezijds Voorburgwal and Oudezijds Achterburgwal, and remains the city's heart, spilling over with energy, shops, cafés, markets and museums, as well as the brazen strip of porn shops, video booths and peep shows which make up the city's infamous Red Light District.

1 Lunch

Het Karbeel, *Warmoesstraat 58*, **t** *627 4995;* **tram** *4, 9, 16, 24, 25.* **Open** *daily 10am–11pm.* **Inexpensive**. An upmarket café on the edge of the Red Light District. It started life in 1534 as an inn and is still connected to the Damrak by a secret smugglers' passage. Good sandwiches, snacks and fondues.

2 Tea and Cakes

De Waag Café, *Nieuwmarkt*, **t** *422 7772;* **tram** *51, 53, 54;* **metro** *Nieuwmarkt.* **Open** *daily 10am–5pm and 6–10.30pm.* The medieval city gate and weigh-house is now a café with long communal tables, plenty of reading material and a terrace on the Nieuwmarkt.

3 Drinks

In 't Aepjen, *Zeedijk 1;* **tram** *4, 9, 14, 16, 24, 25.* **Open** *daily 3pm–1am.* Fills the tiny ground floor of a 15th-century seamen's lodging house. It's a '*rariteitencafé*' crammed with antiques, leather armchairs and barrels. The painted wall-panels were rescued from a 1920s travelling dance hall.

Highlights

Romantic City: The Schreierstoren, or 'weepers' tower', where sailors' wives used to wave goodbye to their husbands, p.89

Amsterdammers' City: The Hash, Marijuana, Hemp Museum, a shrine to the hemp plant (but it will, of course, be filled with other tourists), p.87

Indoor City: The lovely light-filled Amstelkring Museum, p.85

Outdoor City: Wandering the alleys and canals of the eye-opening Red Light District, pp.84–8

Architectural City: In 't Aepjen, one of the last two wooden houses in Amsterdam, p.90

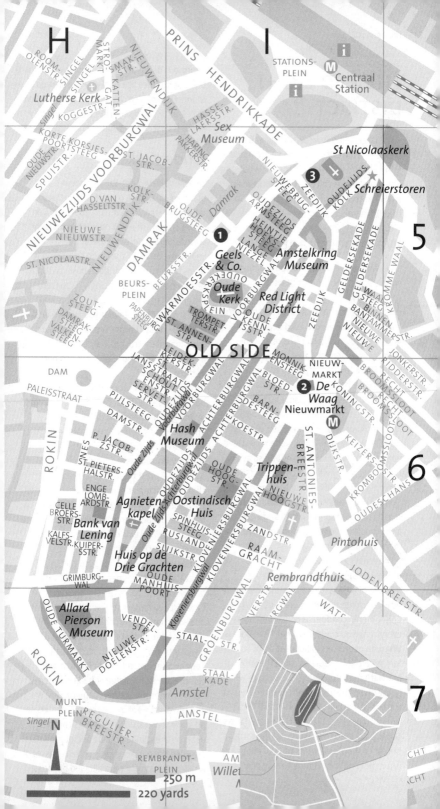

H

ROOM-OLENSTR-SINGEL
SINGEL
STROOGAT-MARKT
SMAKKATTEN-STR.
NIEUWENDIJK
PRINS HENDRIKKADE

Lutherse Kerk

KOGGESTR.
Singel

KORTE KORSJES-POORTSTEEG
OUDE NIEUWSTR.
SPUISTR.
ST. JACOB-STR.
NIEUWENDIJK
D. VAN HASSELTSTR.
KOLK-STR.
BRUGSTEEG
OUDE BRUGSTEEG
Damrak
HASSE-LAERSTR.
HARING-PAKKERSTR.

Sex Museum

NIEUWE NIEUWSTR.
NIEUWEWEG-STEEG
ZEEDIJK
OUDEZIJDS ARMSTEEG
OUDEZIJDS KOLK

❸

St Nicolaaskerk

✠

Schreierstoren ★

I

STATIONS-PLEIN
ℹ
Ⓜ Centraal Station
ℹ

5

ST. NICOLAASTR.
ZOUT-STEEG
DAMRAK-STEEG
VALKEN-STEEG
BEURS-PLEIN
BEURSSTR.
WARMOESSTR.
PAPENBURGSTEEG
ST. ANNEN-STR.
WARMOESSTR.
TROMPETTERSTEEG
OUDEKERKSPLEIN
HENTJE HOEKSTEEG
LANGE NIEZEL
OUDEZIJDS VOORBURGWAL

❶

Geels & Co.

Oude Kerk

Amstelkring Museum

Red Light District

VOORBURGWAL
OUDE KENN.-STR.
ZEEDIJK
GELDERSEKADE
GELDERSEKADE
KROMME WAAL
WAAG-GSTEEG
BINNEN BANTAMMERSTR.
NIEUWE RIDDERSTR.
JONKERSTR.
RECHT BROOMSSLOOT

✠

OLD SIDE

DAM
PALEISSTRAAT
LEIDEKERSTR.
JANSSTRAAT
SCHOUT-ENSTR.
SERVET-STEEG
OUDEZIJDS VOORBURGWAL
OUDEZIJDS ACHTERBURGWAL
MONNIKENSTEEG
BLOED-STR.
BARN-DOESTEEG

❷ *De Waag*

NIEUW-MARKT
Nieuwmarkt
Ⓜ
KONINGSTR.
BROOMSSLOOT
KEIZERSSTR.
KROMBOOMSSLOOT
OUDESCHANS

6

PIJLSTEEG
DAMSTR.
P. JACOB-ZSTR.
SNEES
ST. PIETERS-HALSTR.
ROKIN

Hash Museum

OUDEZIJDS VOORBURGWAL
OUDEZIJDS ACHTERBURGWAL
BARN-DOESTEEG
ST. ANTONIES-BREESTR.

Trippenhuis

NIEUWE HOOGSTR.

ENGE LOMBARDSTR.
CELLE BROERS-STR.
KALFS-VELSTR.
KUIPER-SSTR.

Agnieten-kapel

Bank van Lening

Oostindisch Huis

SPINHUIS-STEEG
RUSLAND
OUDE HOOG-STR.
KLOVENIERSBURGWAL

✠

ZANDSTR.
RAAM-GRACHT

Pintohuis

JODENBREESTR.

Huis op de Drie Grachten

SUIJKSTR.
OUDE MANHUIS-POORT
GRIMBURG-WAL
Oude Zijds Achterburgwal

Rembrandthuis

GROENBURGWAL
VERSTR.

Allard Pierson Museum

OUDE TURMARKT
VENDEL-STR.
NIEUWE DOELENSTR.
STAAL-STR.
STAAL-KADE

Amstel

AMSTEL

7

ROKIN
MUNT-PLEIN
REGULIER-BREESTR.
Singel
N

REMBRANDT-PLEIN

Willet

AM

CHT

250 m
220 yards

THE RED LIGHT DISTRICT

The large belt of narrow streets and canals between Warmoesstraat and Nieuwmarkt forms today's Red Light District, or what Amsterdammers call De Walletjes ('the little walls') – after the city walls that once ran through here.

Warmoesstraat I5

Warmoesstraat is Amsterdam's oldest street. Originally a cluster of wattle and daub cottages, it was by the 16th century a row of prosperous merchants' houses and powerful banks. The Duke of Alva lived here in 1574 during his reign of terror (the rest of the street was understandably empty at the time) and left without paying his rent. Vondel (the 'Dutch Shakespeare') had a small hosiery business at the Dam end before he became a famous poet (see p.143); and Sir Thomas Nugent, a seasoned 17th-century traveller, recommended it as the only street where you'd find English inns and so avoid being cheated by wily Dutchmen. In 1766 Mozart senior held court in the tavern of De Goude Leeuw and sold tickets for his precociously talented son's recitals; and a century later Karl Marx pondered and scribbled away in the inn next door.

These days Warmoesstraat is the first layer of the Red Light District, and a strange mixture of past respectability and the seediness which lies beyond. Here you'll find the **Condomerie** (condom as consumer item – everything you could imagine). Next door is **W139**, an enormous gallery, set up by squatters, where you're sure to catch the very latest (though not always the best) of what's going on in Amsterdam art. Further up, past a string of leather fetish bars, you'll find Amsterdam's best tea and coffee specialists, **Geels & Co**, at No.67. Just round the corner a butcher's shop lays out its trays of chops and drumsticks right next door to a display of enormous dildos and little plain-covered books with titles like *Pent-up Pleasure* and *Mom's Donkey Urge*. It's a grubby, dishevelled street, but no one seems to take it seriously enough for it to be sordid.

Oude Kerk I5

Oudekerksplein, **t** *625 8284,* **w** *www. oudekerk.nl;* **tram** *4, 9, 14, 16, 24, 25.* **Open** *daily 11am–5pm; closed 1 Jan, 30 Apr, 25 Dec;* **adm** *€4. Admission and opening hours may vary during special exhibitions.*

Only the tower of the Oude Kerk actually dates from 1300. The original basilica disappeared behind an increasingly haphazard outgrowth of side chapels, transepts and clerestories. Most of what you see today is lofty early 16th-century Renaissance, but even that has a crust of warden's offices, choir rooms and houses, built over a period of three centuries.

The interior has survived frequent bouts of heavy-handed restoration, an engulfing coat of Prussian blue paint in the 18th century, and violent attacks by iconoclasts. In August 1566, roused by the sight of fragments of statuary from smashed-up churches in Antwerp, Protestant mobs stormed the church, breaking windows and destroying all graven images. A local girl, Lange Weyn, threw her shoe at a picture of the Virgin Mary in the excitement, and was later drowned in a barrel on the Dam for the outrage.

After what is discreetly called the 'Alteration' of 1578, when the Protestants finally took control of the city, the new Calvinist city fathers stripped the church of its dedication to St Nicholas (patron saint of sailors and so, aptly, of Amsterdam) and the popular title of Oude Kerk became official. They also set about turning it into a more sombre place of worship. It had become a hearty communal gathering place. Dossers and travellers slept in the corners, pedlars set up stalls in the aisles, merchants clinched deals on the square outside and dog-owners crowded the entrance (only certain classes of Amsterdam society were allowed big dogs,

Working Girls

A 1629 law closed all taverns between St Annenstraat and the Oude Kerk because of the 'great acts of insolence and wantonness' going on there. The taverns have since reopened, though little else has changed. In those days the women nailed up romanticized portraits of themselves outside the doors. Nowadays they display themselves live, barely clad and deeply bored, perched on bar stools in the windows. Catch someone's eye and immediately there's a bright smile and a sparkle which disappears the moment you look away. If business is bad, or if you walk with eyes downcast, you'll hear the windows being rapped noisily. The rooms are functional cubicles, though from time to time you'll see one decked out in lace, knick-knacks and potted plants – a quaint parody of a Dutch bourgeois sitting-room.

In the mornings, the little alleys, some narrower than a doorway, are inhabited only by the desperate (on both sides of the glass) and the area has a feeling of secrecy and expectancy, rather like an empty theatre. Off-duty prostitutes join friends to go out shopping, or wander off in groups to the clinic for a check-up. In the afternoons it all seems too blatant and seedy, but later a wild festivity sets in as the lanes fill with the merry, the lecherous and the plain curious. Phalanxes of Japanese businessmen troop about aching to take photographs, drunken schoolboys gawp and try to pluck up courage, while tight clutches of Dutch families from the provinces ooh and aah and snicker at all the wickedness.

and if your mutt couldn't squeeze through the special iron hoop at the church door, its days were numbered). These days the church plays host to travelling exhibitions and the occasional concert (such as World Press Photo, with prize winners from the world's biggest photo-journalism competition).

Inside you can see the **tomb of Rembrandt's wife**, Saskia van Uylenburgh (near the Weitkoperskapel on the north side); some beautifully restored and remade **stained glass** (especially the windows depicting the Annunciation in the Mariakapel); and the **secret door** (once covered by plaster, 16ft above the ground in St Sebastiaanskapel) to the IJzeren Kapel (Iron Chapel), a hiding place for important city documents until 1892.

Oudezijds Voorburgwal

H6–I5

Oudezijds Voorburgwal was the canal immediately inside (*voor*, 'in front of') the first city wall. Today it's a brash, brazen strip of porn shops, video booths and peep-shows, though some stylish gables and façades poke out above the lurid layer at street level. Look out for: the **diving dolphins** opposite the Amstelkring; a **mask- and bust-encrusted house** by Hendrick de Keyser opposite the Oude Kerk; Africans and Indians relaxing on tobacco bales on the neck gable at **No.187**; and an elegant neoclassical building by one of the three great 17th-century domestic architects, Philips Vingboons, at **No.316**. Halfway down the canal the sleaze shops suddenly come to an end and you find yourself in a leafy nook of old Amsterdam.

Amstelkring Museum I5

Oudezijds Voorburgwal 40, t 624 6604, w www.museumamstelkring.nl; tram 4, 9, 14, 16, 24, 25; metro Nieuwmarkt. Open Mon–Sat 10am–5pm, Sun and hols 1–5pm; closed 1 Jan, 30 April; adm €6.

One of Amsterdam's most charming small museums, the Amstelkring Museum, also known as Ons Lieve Heer op Solder (Our Lord in the Attic), was a *schuilkerk* – a clandestine church. During the 17th and 18th centuries Roman Catholic services were illegal, but ever-tolerant Amsterdam turned a blind eye to what was going on behind domestic façades. The attic of the little spout-gabled house joins up with two others in the houses behind and was consecrated as a church in 1663. Inside the museum you can wander

Gezelligheid

Dictionaries translate the Dutch word *gezellig* as 'convivial' or 'cosy'. A 1970s historian defined it, in the idiom of his time, as 'partly a sort of cosiness and partly a living togetherness'. *Gezelligheid* is the stuff of the Dutch temperament, and Amsterdammers pride themselves that their town bulges with it.

A café with nicotine-stained walls and scuffed leather chairs is *gezellig*; when you move into a new apartment you hang a few pictures, buy in some pot plants, adjust the lighting and make the flat *gezellig*; the mood in a neighbourhood bar on a cold winter's afternoon is *gezellig*; the behaviour of British lager louts in the bars of Leidseplein is definitely not. Sometimes *gezelligheid* seems subconscious. During the street riots of the 1960s the police were equipped, not with aggressive-looking anti-riot gear, but with large round wicker shields. It must have been almost impossible to hurl a missile at a policeman who was sheltering behind something resembling a dog basket. In its extreme forms *gezelligheid* becomes oppressive – the lace window screens, shelves of knick-knacks and safe respectability of a stolid burgher

sitting room. At worst, *gezelligheid* inhabits a trim, embroidered world somewhere between kitsch and twee. A nice, *gezellig* family hotel in a small seaside town would probably be the last place you'd choose to spend your summer holiday.

The up-side of *gezelligheid* is to be felt in the warm conviviality that suffuses Amsterdam cafés and even markets and squares. Living in cramped houses in a small-scale city has honed Amsterdammers' social behaviour to a fine edge. They seem to have discovered that the best way of getting on when your neighbours are at such close quarters is by developing a frank, easy-going tolerance – a subtle decorum. Rules are clear, universally understood and sometimes broken if the occasion demands. In 17th-century Calvinist Amsterdam, Roman Catholics were allowed to worship freely, provided that their churches were discreetly hidden behind domestic house-fronts. Today Amsterdam authorities turn a blind eye to the sale and smoking of marijuana (technically still illegal) in certain cafés. Centuries of reasonableness have produced a culture that, perhaps more than any other in Europe, deserves the epithet 'civilized', and at its core are the virtues of *gezelligheid*.

about an 18th-century reception room, into a classic 17th-century Dutch *sael* (living room) with symmetrical black and white marble flooring and a monumentally grand walnut fireplace, up through bedrooms with quaint box-shaped cupboard beds, higher and higher to a small wooden staircase. Turn the corner at the top of the stairs and suddenly you're in what seems an enormous church with two galleries, light streaming in, an abundance of carving and painting and a voluptuous organ that must have been audible throughout the neighbourhood. The church is filled with treasures and mementoes of oppressed Catholicism (you can get an explanatory pamphlet downstairs). Try to get there early in the day, when you can appreciate the dream-like atmosphere in relative solitude.

Bank van Lening H6
Oudezijds Voorburgwal 300; tram 4, 9, 14, 16, 24, 25.

At No.300 is the Municipal Pawn Broker – the Bank van Lening, euphemized as 'Ome Jan' (Uncle John's). For the past three hundred years it has been a more sympathetic alternative to professional moneylenders – interest is fixed at a rate that corresponds to your ability to pay. Vondel, bankrupted by his playboy son, spent his septuagenarian years here as a clerk, going to work each day through a gateway that had one of his own poems inscribed in the arch. It's still there, advising the rich to hurry past, as they have no business inside.

Agnietenkapel H6

Oudezijds Voorburgwal 231, t 525 3339; tram 4, 9, 14, 16, 24, 25. Open by appointment; adm free.

This is a 15th-century convent church housing some 17th-century paintings and a specialized and not particularly captivating collection of prints, photographs and ephemera centring on academic life. The chapel has been part of the university since 1632.

Allard Pierson Museum H7

Oude Turfmarkt 127, t 525 2556, w uba.uva.nl/apm; tram 4, 9, 14, 16, 24, 25; wheelchair accessible. Open Tues–Fri 10am–5pm, Sat and Sun 1–5pm; closed 1 Jan, Easter, 30 April, 3 June, 25 Dec; adm adults €4.30, children €1.40.

Round the corner from the southern end of the canal is this superb archaeological collection, though it's poorly presented. There are finds from Ancient Greece, Rome, Egypt and the Middle East, as well as scale reconstructions of the pyramid complex at Giza and the Temple of Zeus at Olympia. Temporary exhibitions focus on specific elements of the Ancient World, such as music or trade. There are few English texts, but children like the Roman chariot.

Oudezijds Achterburgwal H6–I5

The Oudezijds Achterburgwal canal was just outside (*achter*, 'behind') the first city boundary. Most of the buildings in this area are now part of the University of Amsterdam, but they were once (in the words of a 17th-century visitor) a collection of 'almshouses which look like princes' houses, hospitals for fools and houses where beggars, frequenters of taphouses, women who feign great bellies and men who pretend they have been taken by Turks were confined and set to hard work'.

These institutions, a product of prosperous and Calvinistic Amsterdam, were considered far-sighted and revolutionary by the rest of Europe. Beyond the **Huis op de Drie Grachten** (House of the Three Canals – the only one in the city with this qualification) is a gateway on the corner – copied from a Michelangelo design – which leads to the **Gasthuis** (hospital). A little further down you come to another elaborate arch, the entrance to the **Oudemanhuis**, an old men's almshouse. These days glass doors slide back as you approach and you find yourself in a dim arcade of second-hand bookstalls with medieval-looking proprietors. A shaft of light halfway along comes from a door that leads to the elegant almshouse courtyard. It's a private court belonging to the university, but nobody will stop you if you want to have a look.

Spinhuis I6

Oudezijds Achterburgwal 28; tram 4, 9, 16, 24, 25; metro Nieuwmarkt.

The Spinhuis was a place where 'incorrigible and lewd women' were made to spin cloth for the poor. A rather alarming relief above the door shows the poor women being whipped with a cat-o'-nine-tails. Underneath is the not entirely convincing inscription:

Schrik niet, ik wreek geen quaat maar dwing tot goet.
Straf is mijn hand, maar Lieflijk mijn gemoed.
Cry not for I exact no vengeance for wrong, but force you to be good.
My hand is stern but my heart is kind.

The altruism of successive custodians seems to have been directed more towards passing gentlemen. For a small fee they were given access to the wicked inmates.

Hash, Marijuana, Hemp Museum I6

Oudezijds Achterburgwal 148 (planned to move to Achterburgwal 120), t 624 0386, w www.sensiseeds.com; tram 4, 9, 16, 24, 25; metro Nieuwmarkt. Open daily 11am–10pm; adm €5.70.

After years of battling with the authorities, this museum (aptly located in an old tobacco warehouse) appears to have come out on top

– though you won't find it in any of the tourist brochures. As well as tracing the history of dope, the museum is a kind of shrine to the hemp plant, explaining its medicinal qualities and its uses as an alternative energy source. There's a small reference library, a grow room full of bud-laden plants, and a shop selling books, magazines and hemp products. If you're lucky (and willing) you can have a go on the recently invented 'vaporizer', which allows you to inhale the THC chemical from the resin without the usual lungful of smoke.

NIEUWMARKT AND AROUND

Metro Nieuwmarkt.

Nieuwmarkt is an open, brick-paved square that marks the eastern boundary of the Red Light District, connecting some of its more sinister alleys. Furtive men pop out of side streets, blink uncertainly in the bright light, then slip away. The police have cleared out the junkies and dealers who used to hang about the square, and it's been given a facelift. Now that the underworld is banished, Nieuwmarkt has moved into limbo. Cafés are opening in the area, and the once-barren square is beginning to fill up with terraces and regain some of its old liveliness, but it retains an edge of seediness. On Sundays in the summer months there's a bustling **antiques market**, and on feast days you can sometimes find a **fairground** or one of the old Dutch travelling dance halls.

De Waag 16

Nieuwmarkt 4.

A ring of modern streetlamps, like giant mauve praying mantises, seems about to devour the solid medieval St Antoniespoort which huddles, flanked by dumpy towers, in the middle of the square. St Antoniespoort began life in 1488 as one of the main gates in

the city wall. It was a popular spot for public executions. If you have a look on the south side you can see the rectangular holes (now bricked up) where the support beams of the scaffold slipped in. In one of the octagonal towers was a *galgekamertje* (little gallows room). From here the hapless prisoner got a foretaste of what was to happen to him. A small window looked out on the hangings, brandings and chopping off of bits going on a few feet below.

In 1617 the gate was converted into a public weighing house. As all wholesale goods had to be weighed for taxes, 'De Waag' was the centre of trading activity. Liveried porters carried produce to and fro. Fierce armed guards were posted everywhere to keep an eye on the filling coffers and to arrest defaulters. (The sewer below the square was a highway for smugglers and bandits.) In 1691 St Antoniespoort housed the dissecting room of the Guild of Surgeons (cadavers being so conveniently at hand). You can just make out their inscription above the door in the south tower. On the other side, brick-layers decorated the door to their guild room with elaborate wreaths of trowels. Today De Waag houses a trendy café (*see* p.217).

Before you leave the square, treat your nostrils to the herbalists **Jacob Hooy & Co.** at No.12. In one half of the shop, barrels and boxes of herbs are piled to the ceiling; the other half comes right up to date with a range of ecologically sound products.

Kloveniersburgwal 16–7

The Kloveniersburgwal canal, running south from Nieuwmarkt, was a fashionable address in the Golden Age. The grand classicist house at No.29 (across from the police station), known as the **Trippenhuis**, belonged to the Trip brothers. The brothers were powerful arms dealers: together with their rival, De Geer, they controlled almost all of Europe's munitions supply in the 17th century. In an ostentatious display of wealth, they clubbed together and built two sepa-

Six-Week Masters

The Dutch East India Company treated sailors well, but found recruiting seamen to be a problem – the odds on ever returning from a voyage were pretty low. 'Soul merchants', employed by the company, would ensnare Amsterdam's (often foreign) poor by paying their board and lodging. When the drums and trumpets announced enlistment day, the soul merchants stopped paying the rent. For many, the only alternative was to sign up as indentured seamen to work off their debt (the soul merchant earning a commission on the deal).

Once at sea, sailors were well paid. They were given danger money and supplements for sighting land. Most did a bit of trading on their own account – smuggled goods weighed down some ships so much that they sank. Sailors who got back home found themselves wealthy men – and in relief at having returned safely would often go on a frenzy of spending. A favourite prank was to hire three coaches, in an ostentatious display of their new wealth. The first would contain the sailor's hat and would have to drive fast enough to keep a flag constantly flying. Careering behind would be a coach with the sailor's pipe and tobacco box, and the third contained the sailor himself. These 'six-week masters' were as poor after a few weeks as they had been before the voyage.

rate houses behind a vast single façade. The chimneypots were made to look like cannons. When they were moving in, their coachman grumbled that he would be happy with a house the size of their front door. He got what he wanted, across the canal at **No.26**.

Oostindisch Huis (East India House) I6

Tram 4, 9, 14, 16, 24, 25.

The monumental red-brick building on the corner of Oude Hoogstraat and the Kloveniersburgwal is Oostindisch Huis, once the headquarters of the Dutch East India

Company. It used to fill the whole neighbourhood with the scent of spices. Nowadays it's part of the university. At first glance it seems rather austere – though if you take a peek into the courtyard you'll be surprised by the richly decorated entrance. A rather small door is surrounded by wedding-cake embellishments of volutes and scrolls.

Geldersekade I5

Bus 32, 33, 34, 35, 39; **metro** Nieuwmarkt or Centraal Station.

North of Nieuwmarkt is the Geldersekade canal, beside which the old city wall used to run. Along this stretch the wall was covered in a tangle of herbs and camomile. Centuries later Van Gogh's Uncle Stricker lived on the site of **No.77**. When Vincent was in Amsterdam studying for the priesthood, Uncle Stricker had the fairly hopeless task of supervising his lessons. The drinking houses on the right-hand side of Geldersekade were notorious. A 17th-century British ambassador to the Netherlands was horrified: 'There are tolerated in the city of Amsterdam, amongst other abuses, at least 50 musick-houses where lewd persons of both sexes meet to practise their villainies.' His moral outrage didn't preclude him from having a detailed knowledge of the prices and opening times of the 'Long Seller', a public meeting house where 'rogues and whores make their filthy bargains'. The Red Light District has moved fractionally eastward: Geldersekade is now a grimy collection of downmarket Chinese shops and restaurants.

Schreierstoren I5

At the end of the Geldersekade, the Schreierstoren (the 'Weepers' Tower', built 1480) is a dwarfish brick tower with a pixie-hat roof. It's one of the few remnants of Amsterdam's first city wall. Romantics maintain the tower gets its name because sailors' wives would gather on the battlements to see the men off to sea. Well might they weep and wave. Voyages could take up to four years and, on average, two-thirds of the men who set off never returned. More pedantic linguists point out that '*schreier*' comes from the old Dutch word for 'astride' or 'angle' and that the tower straddles two canals. The romantics win: a stone tablet on the wall depicts the wailing wives. Henry Hudson also has a plaque, as it was from here, in 1609, that he went off to discover a new route to the East Indies and found Manhattan instead, giving his name to the Hudson River. The Schreierstoren was originally a solid defence tower. The top storey, windows and doors were all added later. Nowadays it houses a café (*see* p.236).

Zeedijk I5

Bus 32, 33, 34, 35, 39; *metro Nieuwmarkt or Centraal Station.*

In the 14th century, Zeedijk, which runs parallel to the Geldersekade, marked the city limits. Modern Amsterdammers associate it with the *rode knipoog en witte kick* (the 'red wink' of prostitution and 'white kick' of heroin). A massive clean-up campaign by the council and police has got rid of the drug dealers and is turning Zeedijk into a respectable street of restaurants and galleries. The red wink is still just round the corner.

In 't Aepjen I5

The timber house at No.1 Zeedijk is one of the oldest buildings in the city and one of the two remaining wooden buildings in central Amsterdam. It was built in 1550 as a seamen's hostel. The innkeeper allowed sailors who'd drunk or gambled away their wages to leave pet monkeys in payment. The hostel became infested with apes and fleas and became known as 'In 't Aepjen': you could always spot the scratching seamen who'd slept 'in the monkeys'. The Dutch still say of someone who is in difficulty that they have *in de aap gelogeerd* (literally, 'stayed in the monkey'). You can still visit In 't Aepjen (*see* 'Nightlife', p.231).

St Nicolaaskerk I5

Prins Hendrikkade, *t 624 8749;* *metro Centraal Station.* *Open April–Oct Mon 12–3pm, Tues–Fri 11am–4pm, Sat 11.30am–2pm.*

This is a sprucely restored 19th-century neo-Renaissance building with a murky interior. A small ship set above the door at the back is the only reminder that it was a seamen's church. Every March during the Stille Omgang (Silent Procession), Roman Catholics walk silently through the streets to the St Nicolaaskerk to commemorate Amsterdam's Miracle (*see* 'History', p.29). Paintings in the left-hand transept depict the story.

The Centre:
New Side

The Centre: New Side

Immediately to the west of Damrak and Rokin, bound on the outside by the Singel canal, is the New Side. The New Side is only slightly newer than the Old Side, and certainly has its own distinct character, with quiet, leafy squares and some of Amsterdam's grander hotels. At its heart is the Dam, which isn't quiet at all but is home to three of the city's main attractions: the Nationaal Monument, the Koninklijk Paleis (Royal Palace) and the Nieuwe Kerk. Further south are the pedestrianized, café-strewn Rembrandtplein, a hang-out for artists and musicians (and, of course, tourists), and the Bloemenmarkt, or flower market.

Highlights

Couples' City: The lurid but amusing Sex Museum, p.97

Amsterdammers' City: Buying tulips in the Bloemenmarkt, p.102

Indoor City: Koninklijk Paleis, with its dazzling Burgerzaal, p.95

Outdoor City: The peaceful Begijnhof, a refuge in the city centre, p.99

Architectural City: The Tuschinski Cinema, perhaps the most beautiful in the world, p.100

1 Lunch

Helder, *Taksteeg 7,* **t** *320 4132;* **tram** *4, 9, 14, 16, 24, 25.* **Open** *Mon–Sat 11am–6pm.* **Inexpensive.** Teensy lunch venue with daily-changing menus of pastas, salads and rolls.

2 Tea and Cakes

Divertimento, *Singel 480;* **tram** *1, 2, 4, 5, 9, 16, 24, 25.* **Open** *Mon–Fri 8.30am–5.30pm, Sat 8.30am–6pm, Sun 10am–5.30pm.* In the flower market, serving enormous ice creams.

3 Drinks

De Drie Fleschjes, *Gravenstraat 18;* **tram** *1, 2, 5, 13, 17.* **Open** *Sat–Wed 3–8.30pm, Thurs and Fri noon–8.30pm.* Proeflokaal behind the Nieuwe Kerk that dates from 1650.

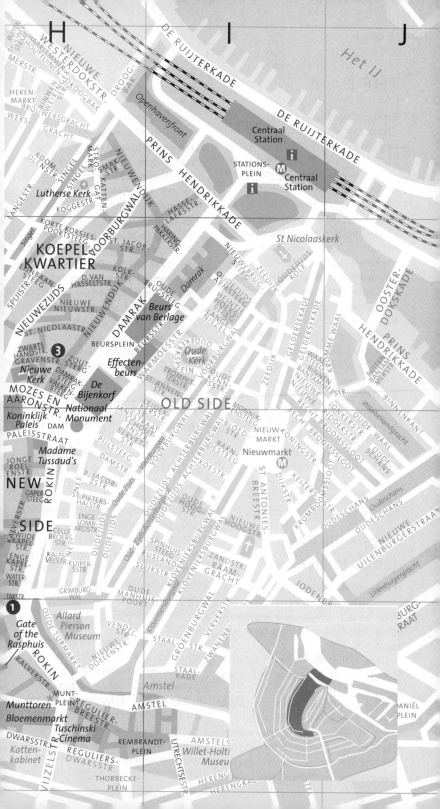

THE DAM

***Tram** 1, 2, 4, 5, 9, 13, 14, 16, 17, 24, 25.*

Traffic on the Dam these days is just as frantic as it has always been (*see* 'The Old Dam'), but the square has lost all the verve it once had. It remains the city centre and the carillon still peals out pop tunes, but the Dam is soulless, spiritless and dull.

The eastern end is dominated by the towering, phallic **Nationaal Monument**, erected in 1956 as a memorial to the people killed in the Second World War. In the 1960s it became a sort of hippie totem pole and hundreds of people would sleep around it in the summer. Police attempts to put a stop to this (such as washing it down with fire-hoses) led to protest riots, but in 1970 a marauding group of off-duty marines chased away the campers forever.

Walking around the Dam you pass the **NH Grand Hotel Krasnapolsky**, where the Winter Garden has been a chic gathering place for over a century, and **De Bijenkorf**, a run-of-the-mill department store with a grand reputation and arty window displays. The view from the roof of De Bijenkorf was filmed for montage shots of the fictive capital of Tomania for Charlie Chaplin's Hitler satire *The Great Dictator* (1940).

Koninklijk Paleis (Royal Palace) H6

t 620 4060, **w** www.koninklijkhuis.nl. **Open** *June–Aug daily 11am–5pm, Sept–May Tues–Sun 12.30–5pm, but times vary; sometimes closed for state functions;* **adm** *adults €4.50, 5–16s €3.60.*

Taking up the entire western end of the Dam, the Koninklijk Paleis was the *stadhuis* (city hall) until Louis Bonaparte decided he wanted to live there in 1808. It's been a royal palace ever since, though Queen Beatrix prefers the leafier groves of Huis ten Bosch in The Hague and never spends the night here. The area in front of the *stadhuis* was a favourite spot for theatrical public

> ### The Old Dam
>
> Riots, garrottings, camping hippies – the Dam has seen it all. Reputedly the site of the original dam across the Amstel, it hit its zenith as city centre in the 17th century. Pragmatic Amsterdam merchants wouldn't stand for any decorative open space at the heart of the city and the Dam bustled with a fishmarket, a public weighing house, a communal crane and a dock that allowed ships to sail right up into the middle of town to offload. Popular tunes rang out from the *stadhuis* carillon and, above all the racket, the town crier's horn would from time to time blast out (once for good news, twice for bad). When you needed to go home, you could ring a bell to summon a taxi. After a brief wait for the drivers to throw dice to decide who should take you, you'd set off at a reckless speed in a slide carriage (wheels presented a problem on the hump-backed bridges), accompanied by packs of sprinting boys throwing water and greased rags under the runners to make the carriage go faster, or straw to make it stop. You'd have to drop out coins at intervals to ensure your rapid progress, and a few more at the humpy bridges to the stalwart lads who hung around to give a much-needed extra push.

executions. On the right, above the entrance arches, you can still see the blocks where the scaffold slotted into the wall. The ornate streetlamps along the front were commissioned by King William Frederick in 1840. They were the city's first gas lamps, but were so expensive to run that the council secretly turned them off whenever the king was out of town.

When the *stadhuis* was built in the mid-17th century, only St Peter's, El Escorial and Venice's Palazzo Ducale rivalled it in grandeur. The poet Constantijn Huygens dubbed it 'the eighth wonder of the world', and a passing Englishman wrote of 'a most neat and splendid pile of a building'. But Sir William Temple, the British Ambassador to the Netherlands, harrumphed that it was '*una gran piccola cosa*' ('a big little thing' – he was quoting someone else's remark about the Louvre).

The architect, Jacob van Campen (designer of the ill-fated Nieuwe Kerk tower), had produced a grandiose celebration of Amsterdam's mercantile supremacy and civic might – a classicist heap of windows, pilasters and relief carving. On the front pediment, collected water deities worship an allegorical Maid of Amsterdam; at the back of the building the trading nations of the world grovel to her. Peace stands high under the dumpy dome (a cornucopia overflowing at her feet), holding not only an olive branch but also Mercury's staff (a symbol of commerce). Atlas buckles under a copper globe so heavy that it needs iron rods to prop it up. Despite all this confident symbolism, there's no grand entrance (the eight little arches along the front look more like tradesmen's gates or the way into the stables) and nowadays you are more likely to agree with Sir William Temple than Constantijn Huygens: the rather grimy palace has as much architectural impact as a main post office or magistrates' court.

The Interior

However, if you're passing during the rather restricted opening hours, don't miss the chance of popping inside to be dazzled by the **Burgerzaal** (Citizens' Hall). It's a vast space encrusted with marble carving that glints in the light pouring in from all sides. Rows of chandeliers drip from the distant ceiling, and brass inlaid maps on the floor show the heavenly and terrestrial worlds (with Amsterdam very much at the centre of things and the enthroned maid of Amsterdam proudly surveying it all). The few chairs around the edges, even a grand piano for the inevitable recital, look like doll's house furniture.

Scattered throughout the building are delicate and often witty **marble reliefs** (Icarus takes a tumble outside the Bankrupts' Court, caryatids look bored with holding up the cross-beams). Most of them are by Artus Quellinus, the noted Golden Age sculptor who also carved the pediments outside. The city fathers, however, blundered when it came to commissioning the wall paintings: they sent Rembrandt packing after he had presented his preliminary sketches.

The **Empire furniture** dispersed around the building was left behind by Louis Bonaparte. When he took over the *stadhuis* he carpeted the marble floors, boarded up the galleries, turned the virtually empty upper storey into living accommodation and also had the weighing house on the Dam demolished because it spoilt his view. His wooden-partitioned upstairs apartments lasted well into the 20th century and were such a fire risk that whenever Queen Wilhelmina used the palace everyone was instructed not to smoke and to sleep with the doors open. A fireman in gym shoes would creep about at night to catch offenders.

Nieuwe Kerk H5

t 638 6909, w www.nieuwekerk.nl. Open daily 11am–5pm, but times and admission vary according to exhibition.

The construction of the Nieuwe Kerk actually began nearly 600 years ago. It's a soaring Gothic heap without a steeple. (In the 17th century, Oude Kerk parishioners, who had always been jealous of the flash rival church, were delighted when the city council stopped construction of the tower because it was going to be higher than the town hall.) Like most of Amsterdam's large churches, the Nieuwe Kerk is now used mainly for exhibitions and concerts. Even if you can't catch a recital on the sumptuous **Great Organ**, the instrument itself, fluttering with angels and cherubs and surrounded by soft-painted shutters, is worth a visit. **Admiral de Ruyter**, the Dutch naval hero, is buried in the choir. (His invasion of the River Medway in England caused Sir William Batten, Surveyor of the British Navy, to explode to Samuel Pepys: 'I think the devil shits Dutchmen.') There's a memorial to the poet **Vondel** near the west door. Before you leave, have a look also at the richly carved pulpit and ornate copper choir screen.

Madame Tussaud's H6

*Peek & Cloppenburg department store, Dam
20, t 522 1010, e madame.tussauds@
scenarama.com, w www.madame-tussauds.
com. Open mid-July–Aug 9.30am–8.30pm,
Sept–mid-July 10am–6.30pm; last entry 1
hour before closing; adm adults €17.50,
4–15s €10.*

Here you can see some rather good reconstructions of 17th-century life and a perfectly
horrible personified Europe (in a frock made
of national flags) who rises from the centre
of a tulip to the strains of Beethoven's *Ode to
Joy*. Madame Tussaud disdainfully floats
away from it all on a painted cloud.

DAMRAK

Stretching north from the Dam to Centraal
Station is Damrak, once a busy port built
along the Amstel, but these days a street
lined with the fast-food joints, rip-off
bureaux de change, tacky restaurants and
tackier hotels that usually cluster around
tourist inlets. The only remaining patch of
water is a tiny dock filled with the glass-
covered boats that bus you around on
hour-long canal trips (*see* 'Travel', p.65).

Hurry past the gaudy signboards and
flashing neon lights, but keep an eye open
for the four baboons and twenty-two owls
that stare down at you from the façade of
Nos.28–30. These are the work of the
Expressionist sculptor J. Mendes da Costa. He
was lodging opposite the zoo when he
submitted the design.

Beurs van Berlage H–I5

*Beursplein 1, t 530 4141, w www.beursvan
berlage.nl; tram 4, 9, 14, 16, 24, 25. Open
Tues–Sun 11am–5pm; closed 1 Jan, 24 Dec; adm
€5, including visit to tower.*

Halfway up Damrak is the Beurs van
Berlage museum. The first Beurs (Exchange)
was built by the prolific 17th-century architect Hendrick de Keyser in 1608. The city

council thought it necessary to confine all
the outdoor wheeling and dealing that took
place along Damrak and around the Oude
Kerk to one (warmer and drier) venue. The
result was deafening. As international trade
expanded, Turks, Indians and Hungarians
joined the locals packed around the pillars
and arcades of the small hall on the Rokin,
bargaining madly for silks, shares, tobacco
and tulips – or anything the boats brought in.

De Keyser's Beurs held out for 200 years.
The building that replaced it (on the site of
the present De Bijenkorf department store)
was universally unpopular and in 1874 the
city held a competition for a new design.
When it was revealed that the winner had
cribbed the façade from a French town hall,
H.P. Berlage (who had come third) smartened
up his original plans and landed the prize.
Many revisions later, he came up with a
building that has become an Amsterdam
landmark and earned him the reputation of
being the father of modern Dutch architecture.

The Beurs van Berlage (completed in 1903)
is all clean lines and functional shapes.
Berlage allows himself some gently
patterned brickwork, but there's not one
extraneous twirly bit nor a glimmer of 19th-
century Gothic fantasy. The pillars and
arcades inside are an echo of the original
Beurs. The **clock tower** (also a quote from De
Keyser's building) displays the mottoes '*Duur
uw uur*' and '*Beidt uw tijd*' ('Last your hour'
and 'Bide your time'), apt maxims given the
seven years Berlage took to come up with a
final design. These days part of the Beurs is
used for concerts, while the rest is a **museum**
(comprising a modest display on the history
and design of the building) and exhibition
hall. A visit to the museum gives you access
to the clock tower and a view over the oldest
part of town. In the smaller of two **concert
halls** you sit and listen to the music in an
enormous glass box which has solved the
problem of abysmal acoustics without
defacing the original interior. You can get a
glimpse inside by popping into the café at
the south end.

Beursplein H5

Tram 4, 9, 14, 16, 24, 25.

Here you'll find the dainty neoclassical **Effectenbeurs** (Commodities Exchange), where the real trading now happens. Across the square, a row of silently chewing, blank faces stare out at you from behind a sheet of plate glass. These are exhausted shoppers propped up along a snackbar in the back window of De Bijenkorf, though they look as if they're for sale.

Sex Museum I5

Damrak 18, t 622 8376; tram 4, 9, 14, 16, 24, 25; wheelchair accessible. Open daily 10am–11.30pm; adm €2.50.

This museum is lurid evidence that the pornographer's imagination has changed remarkably little over the centuries. This is not a place that takes itself too seriously. There are erotic cartoons, prints, early examples of pornographic film, and phallic chairs for those in a swoon to rest their feet.

KOEPELKWARTIER

Aptly nicknamed the Montmartre of Amsterdam, it's easy to see where the Koepelkwartier (Dome Quarter) gets its name. The enormous copper dome of the old **Lutherse Kerk** (Lutheran Church) towers over the narrow lanes and pavement cafés west of Damrak. The church (also known as the Ronde Lutherse Kerk – Round Lutheran Church) was built in 1668 by Adriaan Dortsman, a leading light of the appropriately named Restrained Dutch Classicists. A careless plumber caused a fire which burnt it down in 1822; it was rebuilt the following year and was used as a church until the early 1930s, when dwindling congregations resulted in its closure. After some years of disuse, the church was converted into a conference hall for the hotel across the road, but in 1993 it burnt down again. The gutted building cost nearly €2 million to restore and opened for business again in 1995. The round brick walls look impenetrable (conference delegates reach it through an underground tunnel).

In 1614 Laurens Spiegel, a wealthy soap-manufacturer, built the dainty **twin step-gable houses** next door to the Koepel as an investment. He seemed to rather enjoy punning on his surname (which means mirror). He called his own house (in a classier part of town) 'De Drie Spiegels' (The Three Mirrors), and the two houses on the Kattengat (possibly in view of the profits he hoped to make by letting them out) were called 'De Goude Spiegel' (Golden Mirror) and 'De Silveren Spiegel' (Silver Mirror).

STATIONSPLEIN

Stationsplein is wildly and happily chaotic. Traditional Dutch barrel organs compete bravely with 10-piece South American bands and the 1970s rock-music repertoires of buskers with portable amplifiers. Pedestrians stream in all directions, oblivious of the battalions of trams which, bells clanging, seem intent on converging on one particular spot in the centre. Rent-boys eye you from the arches, junkies droop against the walls, smart businessmen stride purposefully past, and backpackers picnic on the concrete, propped up against their rucksacks. For the next few years the area in front of Centraal Station is going to be one big building site – but the plans are that a tranquil pedestrianised area will emerge from this, with major transport links going underground.

Centraal Station I4

Built between 1884 and 1889 atop thousands of wooden piles on an artificial island, the Centraal Station is such an elaborate and sustained exercise in 19th-century ornament that it can almost be forgiven for screening off Amsterdam's view of the old harbour. The architect P.J.H. Cuypers (also responsible for the Rijksmuseum) succumbed to every temptation to gild bits of his red-brick extravaganza, so that it sparkles in the sunlight like a Walt Disney palace. Its twin towers are adorned not only by a clock, but also by a wind-rose, a delightfully super-fluous instrument that rotates languidly showing the frequency of winds blowing from the various leading points of the compass. The roof bristles with stone and iron spikes and the central section sports classically inspired reliefs showing allegories of sailing, trade and industry. There's a large section over the entrance depicting the peoples of the world paying homage to the maiden Amsterdam. The building seems very much in the tradition of the triumphal arch or elaborate city gate and is indeed a grand place to arrive in Amsterdam. The city is laid out like a semi-circular spider's web with the Centraal Station in the middle. As you step out of the main entrance you get the full impression, across the shapeless open space of Stationsplein, of the spires, gables and cupolas of Amsterdam's delicate skyline.

KALVERSTRAAT

Tram 1, 2, 4, 5, 9, 16, 24, 25.

Kalverstraat is the busy pedestrianized shopping street that links the Spui with the Dam. Shoulder-to-shoulder consumers push in and out of high-street stores, scrabble about in the sales baskets and devour pungent fast food. A little way down, on the right (heading north to south), you can seek sanc-tuary behind the lost-looking Gothic door of **De Pappegaai** (The Parrot), a 19th-century Catholic church which gets its name from the fierce-looking polly carved on the archway.

Burgerweeshuis H6

Kalverstraat 92; tram 1, 2, 4, 5, 9, 16, 24, 25.

Walk up the yellow cobbled path to a rather lopsided gateway. At one time all houses on public roads had such cobbles in front of them to stop night-time travellers veering off the highway into the gutter. The

gate was designed by Joost Jansz Bilhamer, who designed the main extensions to the Oude Kerk. The old Burgerweeshuis was a home founded in 1520 for orphans from the top ranks of Amsterdam society.

Having passed through the Bilhamer gate, you find yourself immediately in the quiet loggia and courtyard of the boys' section, now the terrace of In de Oude Goliath café, but with the boys' wooden lockers still visible in the wall. Through the next arch, the girls' courtyard is even quieter and emptier. It's a sober red-brick court with sensible Ionic pilasters. The girls had their own gate, on the right side of the courtyard. The thrifty governors transferred it stone by stone from a building that was being demolished nearby and had a mason carefully alter the date stone from 1571 to 1634. Boys and girls were effectively kept separate by an open sewer that ran between their respective dormitories. The sewer has since been covered and the resulting passageway converted into a promenade gallery for civic guard portraits which are too big to hang anywhere else, but which don't make particularly riveting viewing.

Amsterdams Historisch Museum H6

t 523 1822, w www.ahm.nl. Open Mon–Fri 10am–5pm, Sat, Sun and hols 11am–5pm; closed 1 Jan, 30 April, 25 Dec; adm adults €6, under-16s €3.

On the far side of the Burgerweeshuis is one entrance to the Amsterdams Historisch Museum, a compact and accessible introduc-tion to the city's history. The exhibition is arranged chronologically from Amsterdam's foundation up to the 20th century, with ample English labelling. You can skim round quickly or stop to pick up details about periods that interest you. Along the way are some intriguing diversions, such as a recon-struction of 't Mandje, the café belonging to local legend Bet van Beeren, and one of the first in town openly to welcome gay clien-tele; and a section tracing the lives of 14 children, the first born in 1863, the last in

1987, through photos, letters and other personal paraphernalia.

A map on the ground floor lights up in sections showing different phases of **Amsterdam's growth** over the last millennium. There's a sudden expansion in the Golden Age and an even bigger one in the late 20th century, after which all the lights go out with an alarming thud. You can get a bird's-eye view of early Amsterdam from a medieval painting (quite a feat of imagination for an artist who had never been higher than the top of the Oude Kerk tower); see a collection of the surprisingly basic **navigational instruments** that guided the Dutch East Indiamen all over the world; and push buttons that make period music come out from behind **models and paintings**. There's a whole room of paintings, banners and relics connected with the **Amsterdam miracle** (*see* 'History', p.29). Up a spiral staircase you can listen to recordings of the city's various **carillons** and even have a go at playing the one taken from the medieval Munttoren (*see* p.101) – though if you get too carried away an attendant clambers up to glower at you. The museum also stages excellent **temporary exhibitions** on specialist aspects of Amsterdam's history.

THE SPUI

Tram *1, 2, 4, 5, 9, 16, 24, 25.*

Some of Amsterdam's most enduringly popular cafés skirt the Spui. At the southern end, the diminutive **statue of Het Lieverdje** ('The Little Darling', an impish Amsterdam rascal) was the focal point of provocative 'happenings' in the 1960s (*see* p.158). You can either stay on the Spui for a quiet coffee, or nip down Voetboogstraat for a look at the outrageous **gate of the Rasphuis**, the male equivalent of the Spinhuis (*see* p.87), where men had to saw wood into a fine powder used for dye. Carved figures are tied down by real chains. A castigating Amsterdam raises her hand high, but someone has pinched her

flail. The Calvinist custodians of the Rasphuis thought up a most ingenious method of compelling the inmates to good soul-saving work. A 17th-century British consul in Amsterdam was much impressed: 'They are beaten with a bull's pissel (penis) and if yet they rebel and won't work, are set in a tub, where if they do not pump, the water will swell over their heads.'

Begijnhof H7

A short passage lined with Delft wall tiles leads from the Spui out into the Begijnhof, which has the atmosphere of a quiet village square. You can hardly believe, in the leafy calm walled in by its neat gables, that the busiest parts of the city are only a few metres away. The Béguines were an order of lay nuns, founded in the 15th century, who, through self-effacement and powerful family connections, remained undisturbed by the religious upheavals of the following centuries. Sister Antonia, the last of the order, died in the house at **No.26** in 1971. The small **mound** near the gate (covered by flowers in the spring) is the grave of another Béguine, Sister Cornelia Arens. When she died in 1654 she was buried, at her own request, in the gutter. Most of the houses were rebuilt in the 17th and 18th centuries, but at **No.34** you can see the last remaining original façade, one of only two medieval wooden houses left in Amsterdam. Next door is an old clandestine **church** which still holds weekly Mass. The church across the pathway was the original **Begijnkerk**, consecrated in 1419 and the only medieval church in the city with the tower in its original state. After a period of disuse during the Reformation, it was offered to Protestant dissenters fleeing England in 1607 and became known as the English Church. A plaque on the tower and stained glass in the chancel commemorate the fact that this group formed the core of the Pilgrim Fathers who sailed for America in 1620.

Bibliotheca Rosenthaliana G7

Singel 425, t 525 2366; tram 1, 2, 5. **Open** *Tues–Fri 1–5pm; closed public and Jewish holidays.*

If you're interested in Judaica you may want to visit the Bibliotheca Rosenthaliana, housed in the University Library, the modern building to the south of the Spui. This priceless collection of over 100,000 volumes, dating from the 15th century, disappeared during the Second World War, but was later tracked down to a village near Frankfurt. As well as old Hebrew manuscripts, there's a large collection of Spinoza, old broadsheets, engravings and photographs.

REMBRANDTPLEIN AND AROUND

Tram 4, 9, 14.

Rembrandtplein was a butter market until the mid-19th century when a group of worthy burghers plonked a statue (Amsterdam's first) in the middle and grew some grass around it. Cafés sprang up. Variety artists from the halls along the Amstel would meet their agents at the posh **Café Kroon**, then retreat across the square to the darker recesses of the **Hotel Schiller** (*see* p.222), where they felt more at home among the artists, writers and other friends of proprietor Frits Schiller (whose paintings still decorate the walls). Nowadays the square is a favourite after-work stopover and a magnet to tourists, who come for the relaxed Amsterdam conviviality. Traffic is banished from most of the square but buskers keep the noise level high. When the sun sets, things get even livelier. The cafés change gear as the night staff come on duty. Music systems are turned on full, jazz from one corner, Dutch sing-along from another. Congas of drunken Dutchmen snake out of pubs and around bemused policemen. At one

bar the three barmen break out at intervals into a well-rehearsed dance routine. Whether you're carousing with the revellers, or just sitting and watching it all, it's a cheerful place to stop for a drink.

Otherwise, pop in to the apothecary on the corner of **Vijzelstraat**: it's stuffed to the ceiling with scents, spices and cough drops that can cure at twenty paces.

Tuschinski Cinema H7

26–8 Reguliersbreestraat; tram 4, 9, 14, 16. **Guided tours** *July–Aug on Mon and Sun 10am;* **adm** *€7. Films also showing.*

Situated on the short, tacky street between Rembrandtplein and Muntplein is the Tuschinski Cinema, which must be a contender for the most beautiful cinema in the world. Abraham Tuschinski, a Jewish refugee from Poland, saw his first film in 1910 and immediately wanted to own a cinema. His first 'bioscope' opened in 1911 in a disused seamen's church with a converted outside lavatory as the box office. But Tuschinski wanted a cinema where his 'guests' could lose themselves in another world. In 1921 he was wealthy enough to achieve his dream. You walk through a soaring Art Deco façade, with flagpoles, camp statuary and curly iron lamps, into an interior that lurches between heady luxury and high kitsch. It's a stylistic cocktail of five different colours of marble, Persian carpets, and thousands of electric lights. You can go on a guided tour or come back later and see a film. Ask for a balcony ticket in the main cinema. On the first Sunday of each month during the winter, there's a special morning screening of a silent movie, with musical accompaniment and sound effects from the original Wurlitzer organ.

The concrete and glass **Cineac** (opposite the Tuschinski) seems from another century. It's hard to believe it was built only 13 years later. The architect, J. Duiker, was a movie fanatic. The auditorium opened directly onto the street and the projectionist could be seen from outside through the glass wall on the

The Great Tulip Mania

Flowers are everywhere in Amsterdam. The tattiest houses sprout windowboxes and you'll see neat little posies on the counters of bars. People give flowers for the flimsiest reasons. Bunches hurriedly bought from canal-side barrows pass between friends like pecks on the cheek. Everyone has favourite blooms and nose-curling aversions, and to forget your loved-ones' floral preferences is like not remembering whether they take milk in their coffee.

Flowers are a national obsession. In the 17th century, when the blossoms were stratospherically pricey, painters made a comfortable living churning out floral still lifes as a substitute. Though these cost as much as the blooms themselves, the (at times regrettable) permanence of the paintings justified the expense. More recently, carnations were the vehicle for a subtle national rebellion. In the early months of the Nazi occupation, thousands of Amsterdammers wearing white carnation buttonholes suddenly appeared on the streets one morning. The Germans were taken by surprise and hadn't the faintest idea what was going on, but any Hollander knew: it was the birthday of their exiled Prince Bernhard, who always wore a carnation in his lapel. When the war ended and Queen Wilhelmina returned, people flocked spontaneously to Noordeinde Palace in The Hague and left so many offerings of bouquets that the lawn in front of the palace was completely covered

in flowers. Ever since then, the reigning monarch has had to emerge on her birthday to accept thousands of posies and shake the hands of adoring subjects as they file past.

Tulips – homely, suburban and pure – have become a national cliché. Yet behind these apparently innocent blooms lurks a past of envy, greed and intemperance almost unparalleled in Dutch history. Tulips were first spotted in Adrianople, Turkey, by Dutch diplomats at the Ottoman court. In the early 17th century the flowers made a spring début in some of French and Dutch society's best gardens. Soon, Johan van Hooghelande, a Leiden botanist, had found out how to vary the colour and shape of the blooms. Connoisseurs queued up, money pouches bulging, for the latest varieties, and by the 1620s the tulip was the flower of fashionable aristocracy.

This alchemical combination of scientific research, visual allure and the chance of profit – three great Dutch enthusiasms – incited the Great Tulip Mania. At first, the bulbs were seen as exotic rarities. The Calvinist Church even regarded them as dangerous – perhaps because the flamed petals reminded them of the ribbons, ruffs and other vanities that ministers railed against from the pulpits. The bulbs were swapped and grown by a handful of aristocratic connoisseurs who, as was their wont, imposed a strict hierarchy on the tulip world. The noblest were the roses (red and pink on white), then came the violets (lilac and purples on white) and finally *bizarden* (red or

---

first floor. Rebuilding in the 1960s and 80s all but destroyed the original concept. In the late 1990s Cineac got yet another facelift, this time emerging as a restaurant in the Planet Hollywood chain.

Munttoren H7

Muntplein; **tram** *4, 9, 16, 24, 25.*

West of Rembrandtplein on Muntplein is the Munttoren, a solitary clock tower with a polygonal base, and yet another steeple by

Hendrick de Keyser – a verticomaniac responsible for nearly every spike on Amsterdam's skyline. The base dates from 1490 and was part of Reguliersport, one of the gates in the old city wall. The structure gets its name because the guard house was briefly used as a mint in 1672–3, when the French were occupying much of the rest of the Netherlands and the Amsterdam merchants couldn't get at their usual source of Rijksdollars and ducatoons.

violet on yellow). Humble plain colours barely merited an estate. It was the irregular, flamed and striped varieties, like the red and white Semper Augustus and the Viceroy, that mattered. (The democratically minded Dutch, however, preferred to call their nobler varieties 'Admiral' or 'General' followed by the name of the grower.)

Gradually the hoi polloi began to edge in on the scene. Tulips were easily reproducible for a wider market. Delftware, an imitation of expensive Chinese porcelain, was already decorating more modest homes. The Flemish carpet industry had its foundations in copying Turkish rugs. Tulips copied themselves, so by the mid-1630s weavers, blacksmiths and bakers were able to buy the bulbs at village fairs. The fashion spread and a tulip fever gripped the nation. Prices took off, then went into orbit. An Admiral de Maan that sold for 15 guilders in 1634 went for 175 guilders three years later. At the height of the boom an 800-guilder Scipio changed hands after a few weeks for 2,200 guilders. People went to any lengths for a prized bulb. One farmer met the 2,500 guilders demanded for a single Viceroy by payment in kind: two last of wheat, four of rye, four fat oxen, eight pigs, a dozen sheep, two oxheads of wine, four tons of butter, 1,000 pounds of cheese, a bed, a suit of fine clothes and a silver beaker.

The rocketing prices were fuelled not only by demand, but by the growth of a futures market. In 1634 one bright dealer had the idea of buying in the winter for future delivery, and then selling to a new buyer before he actually possessed the stock. Soon deals were being done on negotiable pieces of paper, with the time of delivery as an expiry date. A quick turnover meant a quick paper profit. Dealers were selling bulbs they didn't yet possess, for amounts they couldn't possibly raise. As the delivery date drew closer, the danger of actually having to pay up increased, but so did the possibility of making an huge profit as prices rose by the hour. At the bottom of the pile, and in danger of ending up with a heap of worthless bulbs if the market collapsed, were the growers. (The actual tulips would be the last thing on the mind of a merchant facing bankruptcy and trying to settle his paper debts.)

And collapse it did. By 1636 this *windhandel* ('trading in the wind') was beginning to worry the city magistrates and outrage the Church. Whether it was the rumour of intervention that caused the panic, or the panic that caused the intervention, is unclear. But on 2 or 3 February 1637 a warning whisper shot round Haarlem and dealers went all-out to sell. Prices plummeted, the bubble burst and the magistrates had to intervene with special legislation to rescue the innocent growers from the debris of bankrupts. It wasn't until spring 1638 that the market found a normal level, but the passion for tulips was there to stay. As the scandal subsided they quietly assumed their place alongside clogs, cheese and blue and white china as part of the nation's iconography.

Bloemenmarkt H7

*Singel canal, near Muntplein; **tram** 1, 2, 4, 5, 9, 14, 16, 24, 25. **Held** daily 9am–5pm. Cash only.*

Flowers are a national obsession in Holland (*see* 'The Great Tulip Mania', p.101) and Amsterdam's floating flower market can be a bit of a disappointment. It's not very long, not all that cheap, you can't tell from the street that it's floating, and it's full of confused tourists clutching maps and asking each other: 'Is this it?' But the buckets of cut flowers and rows of potted plants are pretty to look at, and on hot days the mingling scents of the flowers fill the whole passage. If you're a keen gardener there's a tempting variety of seeds and bulbs that can be posted home (but *see* 'Customs', p.62).

At the western end of the flower market, across Koningsplein, **Amsterdam's smallest house** (No.312) overlooks the Singel canal. In the 15th century the Singel was the city's line of defence ('*singel*' means moat). These days it's a sober business and residential canal.

Waterlooplein and the Plantagebuurt

Waterlooplein and the Plantagebuurt

The area around Waterlooplein was once a thriving Jewish Quarter. Amsterdammers nickname their city 'Mokum', from the Yiddish '*mokum aleph*', 'the best city of all', and they'll often leave you with a cheery '*de mazzel*' – 'good luck'. As early as the 16th century, Amsterdam's religious tolerance was attracting Jews fleeing persecution in other European countries. This tolerance stemmed less from the milk of Christian kindness than from sound commercial reasoning. The Sephardic Jews, who came from Spain and Portugal in the 16th and 17th centuries, brought good inside information on the opposition's colonies and trade routes. Even the poorer Ashkenazim (from Central and Eastern Europe) had skills that fuelled the Golden Age boom.

The city's trade guilds, however, refused to admit Jews, who could find work only in fields that did not present direct competition to locals. Many were physicians or apothecaries, or worked in high-risk finance and in the new trades associated with the cotton or diamond industries. But Jews could retain their religion and didn't have to live in ghettos or wear distinguishing badges. The city soon became known as the 'Jerusalem of the West'.

Jewish prayers rang out above the clamour of the market and lumber yards around Waterlooplein, where most Jews settled. Later, more prosperous families moved east, to the adjoining Plantagebuurt, a former parkland that was turned into a suburb in the 19th century. But Waterlooplein remained at the heart of the community, and there was hardly a more crowded or busier place in town. The Nazi occupation (*see* the 'History' chapter, p.36) put an end to that. Of the 130,000 Jews living in

Amsterdam in 1938 (10% of the total population), 100,000 did not survive the war. For a long time the Jewish quarter lay empty and derelict, as if the buildings themselves were in a state of shock. Recovery took decades, but the market is now back in place and the area around Waterlooplein is as lively as ever, though the Jewish community itself is all but invisible.

Highlights

Couples' City: Hunting for bargains in the Waterlooplein fleamarket, p.108

Amsterdammers' City: The Verzetsmuseum, for an insight into the Resistance movement and the lives of Amsterdammers during the war, p.114

Indoor City: The Joods Historisch Museum, for a look at Amsterdam's Jewish life, p.111

Outdoor City: The Hortus Botanicus, with one of the biggest botanical collections in the world, p.112

Architectural City: The once controversial but now well-loved Stopera, p.106

1 Lunch

Plancius, *Plantage Kerklaan 61A, t 330 9469; tram 9, 14. Open daily 10am–4.30pm. Amex not accepted. Moderate.* An ultra-trendy converted garage that appeals to arty types. An excellent international menu.

2 Tea and Cakes

Café De Sluyswacht, *Jodenbreestraat 1, t 625 7611; tram 9, 14; metro Waterlooplein. Open daily 11am–3am.* Café in a 17th-century lock-keeper's house, which these days rivals the tower at Pisa for tilt.

3 Drinks

Café Dantzig, *Zwanenburgwal 15, t 620 9039; tram 9, 14; metro Waterlooplein. Open Mon–Sat 9am–1am, Sun 10am–1am.* Part of the Stopera complex. Deeply trendy and postmodern.

WATERLOOPLEIN

Tram 9, 14; metro Waterlooplein.

Waterlooplein, the centre of the Old Jewish Quarter, has had its highs and lows over the years. The square was originally the man-made island of Vlooyenburg, so named because the Amstel flooded it with monotonous regularity (*vlooyen* means 'flow', and also 'fleas', which seems rather more appropriate these days). Vlooyenburg was built on a sandbank in the Amstel in 1593, and soon became a popular neighbourhood for Jews arriving from Portugal. In the mid-17th century they were joined by the Ashkenazim, and Vlooyenburg became the heart of the Jewish quarter.

Despite its sogginess, it was at first quite well-to-do. Prosperous Sephardim lived along the water's edge but, with the great influx of Ashkenazim, buildings were constantly subdivided and more and more people were crammed into less and less space. The economic decline of the 18th and 19th centuries made conditions even worse. A contemporary traveller complained that everywhere there were 'horrible piles of excrement and offal, the walls around drenched with urine'. Later in the 19th century, however, the economy boomed and conditions improved. In 1882 the council reclaimed more land, and filled up two canals to create a large market square to replace the squalid, crowded network of alleys. In 1886 the clusters of market traders who had overrun the side streets were moved to the newly created Waterlooplein. There was much grizzling because it was so open and windy (an objection you're sure to sympathize with if the weather is bad) but soon the market had the reputation of being the busiest and most cheerful in Amsterdam.

The district was devastated during the Nazi occupation. Convoys of trucks would rumble into the market and cart away hundreds of people at a time. The empty houses they left behind were stripped of anything burnable during the freezing winters. For decades after the war, the square was silent and deserted. A few squatters in the 1960s began to revive the old spirit, but they were evicted to make way for the Stopera, and consequently Waterlooplein ceased to be a residential square. However, the Stopera builders' rubble has long since been cleared away, and the hotchpotch market stalls have crept around the square, reclaiming the old space and rekindling something of Waterlooplein's old liveliness.

Stopera (Muziektheater) 17

Waterlooplein 22, t 625 5455.

When the city council announced plans (in 1979) to build a combined city hall and opera house on Waterlooplein, there was public outrage (*see* 'Opera and Stopera' opposite). The city hall was ugly, the opera house seemed unnecessary, and the few people still living in the neighbourhood would have to be evicted. The giant pink building was nicknamed the 'Stopera' – from *stadhuis* (city hall) and opera. The new Muziektheater (the opera house) opened in 1986, followed two years later by the *stadhuis*. The city hall is indeed bland, but most Amsterdammers grudgingly admit to the beauty of the Muziektheater. Its glass walls, sweeping stairways, soft pink colour scheme and marble coliseum-like shell look their best in the early evening. As the light fades, the whole building seems to glow. The artists themselves are delighted with the state-of-the-art equipment and huge dressing rooms. But acoustics experts from around the world took years to solve the (severe) problems in the auditorium and there were some massive architectural blunders backstage – the ballet rehearsal rooms had ceilings so low that dancers couldn't practise lifts, the orchestra didn't have a rehearsal room at all, and the scenery lifts were at the opposite end of the building from the loading entrances. Both the Netherlands Ballet and Opera are resident, and the programme is

Opera and Stopera

The early Calvinist Church regarded opera with horror. It was not only an invention of the devil, but (perhaps even more damning) was most extravagantly un-Dutch. Conventional drama was bad enough. In 1655 one Reverend Witterwrongel railed against stage performances 'because they are generally lecherous and wanton, full of indecency, cruel, bloody, usually taken from the heathen comedies and tragedies which are filled with superstitions, shameful idolatry, blasphemy and embellished fables and lies'. Anything so solely committed to entertainment as the opera, which added profane music and 'enjoyable dancing' to this list of wrongs, was intolerable. Amsterdam's first opera house survived just 53 weeks.

Dirk Strijker was the son of the Consul of Holland in Venice. He grew up feeling more Italian than Dutch, changed his name to Theodoro, and returned to Amsterdam around 1679 filled with a missionary zeal. Opera was the driving passion of his life, and he was determined that his fellow Hollanders should see the light. Despite the disapproval of the Church elders, the general populace of Amsterdam was already developing a taste for opera. Amsterdam did have a theatre, on the Keizersgracht. The Calvinist Church (which seemed to have learnt accounting practice from its Roman Catholic predecessor) was willing to turn a blind eye to the existence of this house of sin, provided that certain 'charity levies' were made to Church concerns. Almost the entire box-office receipts from the theatre on the Keizersgracht went to the Orphans' Home and the Men's Home for the Aged. On the evenings when nothing was scheduled,

itinerant Italian and French opera companies would sometimes stage performances.

Strijker, however, was determined that the city should have a purpose-built opera house. In 1680, after complex negotiations with the Church and the city fathers, and substantial donations to the orphans and aged men, he was finally granted permission to build a theatre on the Leidsegracht for (in the words of the uninitiated council secretary) 'silent performances and fine music'. But this was the beginning rather than the end of the battle. When he finally set the opening night for Saturday 28 December 1680, the Church objected that it was the night before a Holy Communion celebration and would brook no competition. The opera house eventually opened on New Year's Eve.

Over the next few months, audiences flocked over from the theatre on the Keizersgracht, and its box office takings dropped to such a sad level that the Orphans' Home and Men's Home for the Aged began to complain. The large chunk of Strijker's profits that was destined to placate these worthy concerns never materialized: opera is an expensive business, and his theatre ran at a loss. Deprived of this income, the Church began to exert pressure for the closure of the opera house. Strijker got no help from a blandiloquent city council, and after a year and a week he was forced to abandon his venture and retreat 'in slechten en miserabelen stand' ('in a sorry and deplorable state') into obscurity. Today there is no sign of the old opera house on Leidsegracht. No one even knows what happened to it and not a single picture of the building exists. The Church must have been determined to obliterate every trace.

Strijker's audience, however, had had their appetites whetted. Gradually the Church's

varied, with many international visitors (*see* p.242).

In a passageway connecting the *stadhuis* and Muziektheater, three **water columns** show the tides at IJmuiden and Vlissingen (below knee-level) and the sobering sight of the level reached during the 1953 Zeeland

flood (way above your head). You can walk down a flight of stairs, below sea level, and touch the bronze knob (its position was calculated in the 17th century) which represents the **zero point** from which heights in much of Europe are calculated.

attitude began to soften. The theatre on the Keizersgracht, which had been churning out moralistic dramas, began to stage operas again, and the first Stadsschouwburg (Municipal Theatre) opened on Leidseplein in 1774. Here you were subjected to operas of a rather questionable standard – good singers were thin on the ground and all the female leads were taken by the director's wife. The middle years of the 19th century were boom years, with a good local opera company resident at the Stadsschouwburg, but by the turn of the century interest had dwindled dismally. A plan in the 1920s to build a national opera house across from the Concertgebouw on Museumplein was vetoed by the city council.

After the Second World War, however, there were murmurings in the corridors of power about the need for a national opera house. Plans for a building on the Museumplein, and for one further to the south on Allbéplein, were abandoned when someone suggested Frederiksplein. At just the same time, the council committee responsible for the building of a new city hall was also attracted to the idea of Frederiksplein. There followed a sort of architectural musical chairs, during which opera house and city hall pursued each other about Amsterdam, claiming for themselves in turn the few choice sites available and preventing each other's plans from materializing.

By 1969 the council had decided to build the new city hall on Waterlooplein. An Austrian architect, Wilhelm Holzbauer, won the competition to design the new *stadhuis*, but in 1972 the provincial authority vetoed the funding because his building was going to be too expensive to run. One afternoon in 1979, with the authorities still locked in negotiation, Holzbauer was standing looking glumly over Waterlooplein when he had the brilliant idea of combining the *stadhuis* and opera house into one complex. This seemed to solve everyone's problems, and a plan was finally passed. But the idea caused a furore among the burghers of Amsterdam.

Many of the objections seemed to follow the old Calvinist pattern. Opera was unnecessary. Amsterdam didn't need an opera house. But it was the choice of the site that caused the greatest ill-feeling. Waterlooplein had been the heart of Amsterdam's large Jewish neighbourhood, and had been a sad and derelict scar since the Nazis had all but obliterated the Jewish population. Many people thought an opera house to be an inappropriate building to occupy a location with such poignant associations. The few people still living on Waterlooplein after the war had already been evicted in the 1960s to make way for the proposed *stadhuis*; they had then looked on as their empty homes were occupied by squatters while the council dithered over the cost of the proposals. Now they had no intention of giving up their homes to what they saw as a temple of élitist entertainment. A vociferous 'Stop the Stopera' campaign erupted. Police attempts to evict squatters met with the strongest public resistance the city had seen since the street fighting of the 1960s and 70s. Opposition raged right up until the day the Muziektheater opened in 1986. At the opening ceremony Queen Beatrix and Prince Claus had to be smuggled in through the stage door to avoid the angry throngs around the main entrance. But today the dust has settled and most Amsterdammers will admit that the elegant Muziektheater has become an attractive city landmark.

The Fleamarket 17

Held Mon–Sat approx. 10am–4pm.

Bang up against the back wall of the Stopera, and creeping around the edges, reclaiming the space it has occupied for over a century, is the famous fleamarket. There's a wonderful lack of logic in its layout and a pervasive air of bargain-hunting and money-making. Antiquarian booksellers rub shoulders with purveyors of used porn. Lines of Peruvians, Balinese and Surinamese sell bright national clothing and jewellery. There are heaps of mildewy second-hand overcoats and racks of precision-selected designer classics, tables of used kitchenware and haphazard conglomerations of expensive antiques. The rows of oddities and exotica are punctuated by more down-to-earth stalls selling bicycle parts, underwear or cleaning equipment. In one corner a muttering clump of old men surreptitiously flash watches and bits of gold to each other. A relentless stream of collectors, Amsterdammers looking for bargains, tourists and the openly curious flows up and down between the stalls.

Mozes en Aäronkerk J7

In 1649 this was the site of a clandestine Roman Catholic church, named after the gable stones (one depicting Moses and the other Aaron) on the two house fronts that hid it. The present somewhat heavy-looking neoclassical church (with its wooden towers painted to look like sandstone) was built in the 19th century, but you can still see the original gable stones round the back. The church was famous for its choir and even the local Jews would come in for the music on Christmas night. The Jewish philosopher Spinoza lived in the house next door to the original church. The Sephardic community excommunicated him for his secular beliefs, but regretted their haste when he went on to become one of the most lauded intellectuals of his time.

Holland Experience I7

*Waterlooplein 17, t 422 2233 w www.holland -experience.nl. **Open** daily 10am–6pm (last show 5.30pm); duration 30mins; **adm** adults €8.50, under-12s €7.25.*

This is a multimedia show and exhibition on Holland's top sites, offering 'scent and sound effects' as well as 18,000 gallons of water, which crash towards you in a simulated dyke collapse.

Rembrandthuis I6

*Jodenbreestraat 4–6, t 520 0400, w www. rembrandthuis.nl; **tram** 9, 14; **metro** Waterlooplein. **Open** Mon–Sat 10am–5pm, Sun and hols 1–5pm; closed 1 Jan; **adm** €7.*

Rembrandt lived here for nearly twenty years (*see* 'Rembrandt', p.132) and his old house is now a museum. It has been carefully restored to its original state, using plans and descriptions to ensure authenticity. In the adjoining modern wing, you can see the pick of Rembrandt's etchings, including a series of tiny self-portraits of the painter pulling funny faces. Rembrandt used himself as a model more than any other 17th-century painter. He even slips into crowd scenes on some of his larger canvases. There's a slide-show on Rembrandt's life, in English, in the basement (hourly on the hour until 3pm).

ST ANTONIES-BREESTRAAT

St Antoniesbreestraat, the westernmost stretch of the Old Jewish Quarter, links the district to the city centre. At the southern end of the street is **St Antoniessluis** (St Antony's Lock), once the site of a busy second-hand clothes market, before the move to Waterlooplein. The common Dutch surname Sluis or Sluys can often be traced back to Ashkenazi families who worked here. Beyond the lock, lined with apartment blocks, the street itself is unremarkable, though there are a couple of sights worth exploring.

Zuiderkerk I6

*Tram 9, 14; **metro** Waterlooplein or Nieuwmarkt. **Open** Mon 11am–4pm, Tues, Wed, Fri 9am–4pm, Thurs 9am–8pm; **tower open** June–Sept Wed–Sat 2–4pm; **adm** €2, free on Thurs.*

Off St Antoniesbreestraat, through a sculpted gate embellished with a macabre skull motif, stands the Zuiderkerk, built between 1603 and 1614. It was the first Protestant church to be built after the Reformation, and is a triumph of Amsterdam's great steeple designer, Hendrick de Keyser. The soaring spire with its decorative Ionic columns and its clusters of slightly oriental pinnacles was much admired by Christopher Wren, and inspired the designs of his City of London churches. During the harsh winter of 1944–5 more people died in the neighbourhood than the authorities were able to bury, and the church had to be used as a temporary mortuary. Today it's a deeply uninteresting information centre for urban development.

Pintohuis I6

69 St Antoniesbreestraat; tram 9, 14; metro Waterlooplein or Nieuwmarkt. Open Mon and Wed 2–8pm, Fri 2–5pm, Sat 11am–4pm; adm free.

This great slab of a house belonged to the wealthy 17th-century banker Isaac de Pinto and was the envy of the neighbourhood. The poorer inhabitants of the surrounding alleys would mutter that someone was 'as rich as de Pinto'. These days it's a public library, so you can nip in for a look at the odd bits of gilding and the brightly painted birds and cherubs which fly all over the ceiling.

MR VISSERPLEIN AND AROUND

Tram 4, 9, 14; metro Waterlooplein.

Mr L.E. Visserplein (*Meester* is the Dutch title for a lawyer) is named after the Jewish Dutch President of the Supreme Court dismissed in 1940 for refusing to co-operate with the occupying forces. He later refused to wear a Star of David and worked for *Het Parool*, the illegal Resistance newspaper that developed into a popular Amsterdam daily. The square is a turmoil of traffic hurling in and out of the IJ Tunnel.

Portuguese-Israelite Synagogue J7

Mr Visserplein, t 624 5351, w www.esnoga. com. Open April–Oct Sun–Fri 10am–4pm, Nov–March Sun–Thurs 10am–4pm, Fri 10am–3pm; adm €5.

There was little love lost between the Sephardim and Ashkenazim. Even today old Sephardic Jews can remember being warned off '*vrotte Tedesco*' (filthy Germans) with: '*Je kan nog beter met een Goya trouwen dan met een Tedesco*' (Rather marry a gentile than an Ashkenazi). The Sephardim were a smaller but more powerful community, with a class of wealthy professionals, and were happily welcomed into Dutch society. Their Portuguese-Israelite Synagogue (or 'Snoge' after the Spanish *esnoga*) was built between 1671 and 1675 as a showpiece.

It was more than twice the size of the Ashkenazi temple completed the year before on the site next door. Only in Amsterdam could Jews make such an open display of their place of worship. There was no established building style for synagogues, and the architect, Elias Bouman (who had also designed the Ashkenazi building), claimed he was creating an imitation of Solomon's temple following descriptions in the Old Testament. However, the building he produced, with its mahogany pews and brass chandeliers, bears a remarkable resemblance to the larger Christian churches of the period. It's an imposing brick block that dwarfs the buildings around it. The Hebrew letters of the name 'Aboab' are worked into the text above the door (which translates as 'And I – in Thy great love – shall enter Thy House') in acknowledgement of Rabbi Isaac Aboab de Fonseca's efforts to get the synagogue built.

Jonas Daniël Meijerplein J7

Round the other side of the synagogue from Mr Visserplein is the relative peace of another square, Jonas Daniël Meijerplein.

Jonas Daniël Meijer (1780–1834) whizzed through his school years and was a doctor of law by the time he was 16. He was the first Jew admitted to the Bar and one of the first to fight for and get full Dutch citizenship. As a favourite of the potty but enlightened Louis Bonaparte and under William I, Meijer did a lot to improve the legal position of Jews.

During his brief spell as a theology student in Amsterdam, Van Gogh could be seen 'with his books clamped under his arm, holding snowdrops in his left hand in front of his chest, his head stooped forward slightly', crossing this square to the third floor of the house at No.13, where he studied classics with Mendes da Costa. The original house has been demolished.

De Dokwerker

In the middle of the square, standing stalwartly, his sleeves rolled up and chin cocked defiantly – ready for a fight – is Mari Andriessen's bronze statue *De Dokwerker* (*The Dockworker*; 1952). Every year on 25 February people lay flowers at its feet to commemorate the resistance to Nazi occupation. This is the anniversary of the general strike which swept through a shocked Amsterdam in a matter of hours as an expression of solidarity with the Jews after the first Nazi round-ups.

Joods Historisch Museum (Jewish Historical Museum) J7

Jonas Daniël Meijerplein 2–4, t 626 9945, w www.jhm.nl; wheelchair accessible. Open daily 11am–5pm; closed Yom Kippur; adm adults €6.50, 6–12s €2, 13–17s €3.

The museum is a complex of four old Ashkenazi synagogues (*see* 'The Ashkenazim') with displays of art, memorabilia and artefacts aimed at explaining Jewish life. The museum diffuses a positive energy from the delicately embroidered prayer shawls, photographs of bar mitzvahs

The Ashkenazim

The Ashkenazim, fleeing pogroms in Poland and massacres in Germany, arrived in Amsterdam in the mid-17th century. They soon outnumbered the Sephardim (who had begun arriving half a century earlier) by ten to one, but were pitifully poorer. They really had to struggle to build themselves a synagogue. Just as they were about to begin, their attention was diverted by Sabbatai Zvi, a false Messiah who claimed he would lead them back to the Holy Land. They waited for four years before giving up on him and building the Grote Sjoel (Grand Synagogue) in 1671.

As the congregation expanded, more temples were built on adjacent plots. The Obbene Sjoel (Upstairs Synagogue; 1686) was followed by the Dritt Sjoel (Third Synagogue; 1700). The Neie Sjoel (New Synagogue; 1752) opened with great ceremony. Tickets were sold at an outrageous 10 guilders (though crowds of poor were let in for free). Ashkenazi congregation records revel in the pomp of the occasion and bristle with anti-Sephardic rivalry: 'An orchestra pit has been placed next to the bima [raised central platform], where the musicians took their places with their music. Below that there was an uncircumcised musician playing a contrabass and for the rest only Jews who played for free and even one Portuguese Jew.' The complex was gutted during the Second World War and remained empty until the 1980s, when the temples were restored and reopened as the Historisch Museum.

and overwhelmingly extravagant silverware on show. The 'Jewish identity' displays in the New Synagogue explain aspects of tradition, Zionism and the reaction to persecution. Most of the Great Synagogue is given over to expositions of Judaism itself – the rituals, festivals and rites of passage. You can see the original mikveh (ritual bath) unearthed during the renovations, a cute circumcision set and some stylish modern temple silverware. In the galleries of the Great Synagogue, paintings and old documents illustrate the history of Jews in Amsterdam. The connecting walkways house temporary exhibitions and work by Jewish artists (look particularly for Jaap Kaas' fierce, funny bronze monkeys). The museum also has a library and media centre, a kosher café and a good bookshop.

Oudezijds Huiszittenhuis J7

Onderwijzerhof.

Across the alley from the Jewish museum is the Oudezijds Huiszittenhuis (the rather Dickensian-sounding 'Old Side Home for the Domiciled Poor', built in 1654). The Alms Board wardens would enter through a rather grand private staircase on the other side of the building. Paupers could come in through a gate opposite the Dritt Sjoel and huddle for hours in the courtyard waiting for handouts of bread, cheese and peat.

The peat was stored next door in the Arsenaal (built 1610). The road down the side of this warehouse is still called Turfsteeg (Peat Alley).

Amstelhof J7

Entrances on Weesperstraat, Nieuwe Herengracht and Nieuwe Keizersgracht.

South of J.D. Meijerplein, across the Nieuwe Herengracht canal, is the long, rather austere two-storey brick building known as the Amstelhof, which originated as a 17th-century almshouse. The severe walls enclose a luscious garden courtyard with fountains, arbours and choruses of birds, where you can sit and rest if you're discreet.

Over the next few years the elderly inhabitants will be moving to more modern premises, and the Amstelhof will become a branch of the celebrated Hermitage museum in St Petersburg.

THE PLANTAGEBUURT

The elegant, wide streets of the Plantage district, the 'Plantation', were a bushy parkland where Amsterdammers would lounge about on feast days, or go on long evening walks. At the end of the 19th century it was flattened by rows of showy neoclassical houses with outrageous colonial embellishments (pineapple pinnacles, exotic festoons, African figurines propping up the beam ends). Many of the wealthier Jews moved into the grand new houses and by the 1920s it was the suburb of the Jewish élite.

Hortus Botanicus J7

*Plantage Middenlaan, **t** 625 8411, **w** www.dehortus.nl; **tram** 9, 14; **metro** Waterlooplein. **Open** April–Sept Mon–Fri 9am–5pm, Sat and Sun 11am–5pm; Oct–March Mon–Fri 9am–4pm, Sat and Sun 11am–4pm; closed 1 Jan, 25 Dec; **adm** €6.*

The Hortus Botanicus was originally an apothecaries' herb garden in a marshy corner of the Plantage. It was later inundated by tropical plants pillaged by the Dutch East India Company, and has ended up with one of the biggest botanical collections in the world. A coffee shrub cultivated at the Hortus was presented to Louis XIV in 1714. Its seeds were used to initiate the cultivation of coffee in South America. A century later the gardens narrowly survived Louis Bonaparte's attempt to turn them into a zoo. The animals arrived before any cages had been built and the orangery became a volatile dormitory for wolves, lions, monkeys and porcupines. Tranquillity was restored when, after the king's untimely departure from the Netherlands, a relieved directorate put the animals up for auction.

During the first half of the 20th century, the gardens' biggest attraction was the massive **Victoria Amazonica** water lily. People would queue for hours on the one night of the year when it flowered, and reputedly could stand, three at a time, on the broad lily pads. The sturdy plant survived this abuse, but not the demolition of its greenhouse in the 1960s. For decades there was no *Victoria Amazonica* here, but in the 1990s a new greenhouse was built, and the giant lily once more has pride of place. The Hortus is a tranquil spot, a pocket-sized patch of green that's not really part of the tourist circuit. It won't take you long to nip in and see the ancient varieties of tulip, visit the world's oldest pot plant, warily observe the cabinet of flesh-eating plants, enjoy the tropical climes of the glass-domed palm house or the balmy air in the new three-climate hothouse. Then you can cool off with a fruit juice in the Orangery.

Wertheimpark J–K7

Open *daily;* **tram** *9, 14.*

The tiny Wertheimpark is the last remaining patch of the old Plantage gardens. At the entrance, two sphinxes with lanterns on their heads glower from the top of disproportionately large gateposts. Most of the park seems taken up by a **fountain in memory of A.C. Wertheim** (1832–97), a philanthropic banker who lived out his motto, 'Be a Jew in the synagogue and a human being in society', by being available in his office for an hour every morning to anyone, Jew or gentile, who needed to appeal to his charity. In one corner of the park, built over an urn of ashes brought back from Auschwitz, is a **monument** to Jews who perished in the concentration camps. Smashed mirrors lie flat on the ground: a symbol that Earth can no longer reflect Heaven without distortion.

Hollandse Schouwburg K7

Plantage Middenlaan 24, **t** *626 9945;* **tram** *7, 9, 14.* **Open** *daily 11am–4pm, closed Jewish holidays;* **adm** *free.*

In 1897 the Hollandse Schouwburg (Holland Theatre), after a false start as an operetta theatre, became the home of the Nederlandsche Toneelvereeniging (Dutch Drama Society) – the company that propelled Dutch theatre into the 20th century. Because of the large number of Jews in both the audience and the theatre group itself, the occupying forces during the Second World War renamed it the Joodsche Schouwburg (Jewish Theatre). In 1942 it was designated an assembly point for Jews waiting to be deported. People were kept in the darkened building for days and then (apart from a few children who had managed to escape through the crèche across the road) were herded onto trains bound for Westerbork, a transit camp in the Dutch province of Drenthe. In Amsterdam, Jews spoke of Westerbork as 'the first circle of Hell'. From there trains left weekly for the death camps at Auschwitz and Sobibor. Understandably, after the war no one much wanted to use the Hollandse Schouwburg as a theatre again. In the 1960s it was declared a memorial to the deported Jews who never returned.

Today only a secluded **memorial garden** lies behind the façade. Every year on 4 May (Remembrance Day) the city keeps a two-minute silence to commemorate those who died in the war. Just before 8pm people from the neighbourhood start to arrive at the Hollandse Schouwburg (as they do at similar monuments all over the city). Trendy young things, children, people old enough to have lived through the war – all quietly join the swelling groups converging on the theatre. Most carry small posies of flowers. At 8 o'clock the trains stop, cars switch off their engines, people still in cafés put down their drinks and the whole city goes quiet.

De Burcht Vakbondsmuseum (Trade Union Museum) K7

Henri Polaklaan 9, **t** *624 1166,* **w** *www. deburcht-vakbondsmuseum.nl;* **tram** *7, 9, 14.* **Open** *Tues–Fri 11am–5pm, Sun 1–5pm;* **adm** *€2.30.*

This museum is worth a diversion for the building alone. The father of modern Dutch architecture, H.P. Berlage, designed it in 1900 for Holland's first trade union, the mainly Jewish General Netherlands Diamond Workers' Union (ANDB). Wedding-cake layers of brick arches create a light and airy entrance hall. An ornate Jugendstil lamp hangs through the depth of two storeys in the centre of the room. Upstairs there is a cosy panelled boardroom with more metal lanterns, and murals by the Dutch Impressionist Roland Holst. However, you'll have to be severely interested in the Dutch labour movement to appreciate the small exhibitions of photographs, clippings and documents (all in Dutch) in the other room.

Verzetsmuseum (Museum of the Resistance) K7

*Plantage Kerklaan 61A, **t** 620 2535, **w** www. verzetsmuseum.org; **tram** 6, 9, 14. **Open** Tues–Fri 10am–5pm, Sat–Mon and hols noon–5pm; closed 1 Jan, 30 April, 25 Dec; **adm** adults €4.50, under-18s €2.50, free 5 May.*

Newspaper clippings, photographs, tape-recordings and makeshift secret equipment give insight into the 1940s Resistance movement. As well as inspiring admiration for the ingenuity and resourcefulness of Resistance workers, the museum gives a true sense of the plight of ordinary citizens during occupation. Interactive exhibits illustrate the workings of the Resistance movement in the attempt to keep a quarter of a million inhabitants in hiding, while temporary exhibitions explore present-day parallels.

Artis Zoo K7–8

*Plantage Kerklaan 40, **t** 523 3400, **w** www. artis.nl; **tram** 6, 9, 14. **Open** daily summer 9am–6pm, winter 9am–5pm; **adm** adults €14, under-12s €10.50.*

It's green and quite attractive, as zoos go, with some interesting outcrops of 19th-century architecture. The complex includes a planetarium and an aquarium. *See* also p.259.

Grand Canals
and Jordaan

Grand Canals and Jordaan

Amsterdam's population increased tenfold between 1550 and 1650. In the early 17th century the far-sighted city fathers were already planning to push the city boundaries outwards with three grand concentric canals. The Herengracht (Gentlemen's Canal – rather than 'Kings'', a nice move by bourgeois Amsterdam), the Keizersgracht (Emperor's Canal) and the Prinsengracht (Princes' Canal) were intended for rich merchants who wanted to live away from the smells and noise of the harbour. The shops and industries there were banished to poorer parts of town. The city hall parcelled out the land in 30ft, rather than the usual 20ft, lots (though wily speculators would buy up two adjacent plots and split them into three and the really opulent merchants would combine two into a single house).

1 Lunch

Nielsen, *Berenstraat 19*, **t** *330 6006*; **tram** *1, 2, 5, 13, 14, 17*. **Open** *Tues–Fri 8am–4pm, Sat 8am–5pm, Sun 9am–4pm*. **Inexpensive**. Homey, relaxed, with an edge of hip, and some extraordinarily good apple pie. Tasty sandwiches and lighter meals with vegetarian options. A Sunday breakfast favourite.

2 Tea and Cakes

Café Américain, *American Hotel, Leidseplein*, **t** *556 3032*; **tram** *1, 2, 5*. **Open** *daily noon–12.30am*. Art Nouveau grand café. Once the hangout of Amsterdam's literati, it's now visited mainly by tourists, but is just the right environment for a pot of fresh coffee and an extravagantly gooey cake.

3 Drinks

De Blaffende Vis (The Barking Fish), *Westerstraat 118*; **bus** *18, 22*. **Open** *Sun–Thurs 9am–1am, Fri and Sat 9am–3am*. A busy Jordaan café frequented by traditional Jordaaners and the new generation of young artists.

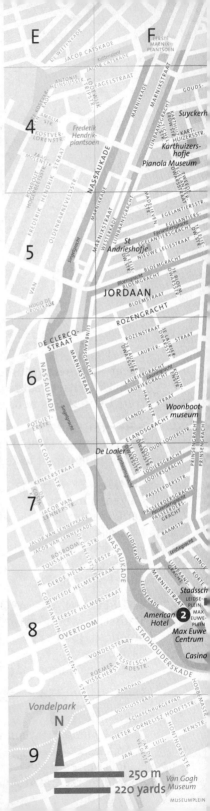

Nowadays the canals look at their best in the early evening. On summer nights the stateliest stretches are floodlit, and the bridges twinkle with fairy-lights.

Just south of the three canals is Amsterdam's tourist vortex, Leidseplein, while to the west, bordering Prinsengracht, are the inviting side streets, *hofjes* (almshouse courtyards) and intimate canals of the Jordaan, lined with cosy cafés, curious shops and good restaurants, all luring you to ferret about in your own way.

For a walk through Jordaan, *see* 'A *Hofjes* and Hidden Markets Walk', p.162.

Highlights

Couples' City: Kattenkabinet, the only museum in the world devoted to cats – for cat-lovers only, p.119

Amsterdammers' City: Wandering through the *hofjes* and markets of the traditional district of Jordaan, p.125

Indoor City: The Anne Frankhuis, home of the legendary *onderduikers*, p.123

Outdoor City: Gable-spotting on the Grand Canals, pp.118–23

Architectural City: Herengracht 475, considered by many to be Amsterdam's most beautiful house, p.119

HERENGRACHT

Fashion has claimed each canal, at one time or another, as Amsterdam's best address, but it was the Herengracht that was really built to impress. It's more grand than pretty, a little ravaged by centuries of ostentation. Subsequent occupiers have (until recently) thought nothing of pulling down old buildings to make way for bigger and better displays of wealth, but the survivors have an endearing, if worn, panache. Some extraordinary gables poke up out of the trees that line the canal.

The Narrow Tax Band

Space was always at a premium in Amsterdam and you were taxed on the width of your house, so wealth was often expressed by height rather than by boastful decoration, which was applied to the inside, or to the gables. Narrow houses mean winding stairways, uncongenial to four-poster beds and heavy carved dressers, hence most Amsterdam buildings have a hoist beam poking out from the gable so you can winch your furniture up the outside. Many lean dangerously over the street, not necessarily because they're about to subside into the city's soggy soil, but because this shows off the gables to passing pedestrians and makes the building more imposing. It also stops rising furniture from crashing into the wall. Angles became so alarming that a bye-law was introduced in 1565 to put a stop to the more adventurous tilts.

Willet-Holthuysen Museum 17

Herengracht 605, t 523 1822, w www.ahm.nl; tram 4, 9, 14. Open Mon–Fri 10am–5pm, Sat and Sun 11am–5pm; closed 1 Jan, 30 April, 25 Dec; adm €4.

At the southern end of Herengracht, near Rembrandtplein, is the Willet-Holthuysen Museum, set in a 17th-century canal house. For two centuries it was occupied by a succession of Amsterdam glitterati. The last, Sandrina Holthuysen, had spent most of her life married to Abraham Willet, an avid collector of paintings, art books, glass, ceramics and silver. When she died in 1895, alone, riddled with cancer and surrounded by cats, she left the house and contents to Amsterdam as a museum. The city then filled it with pickings from a number of similar bequests. Most of the rooms are now reconstructed as 18th-century period pieces. There's a magnificent dining room and ballroom, a similarly grand kitchen, salons and boudoirs as well as a crisp formal garden. It's a good place to get an insider's view of one of the more stately canal houses.

From Utrechtsestraat to Leidsegracht

Along this stretch of the canal, monumental sandstone frontages seem to push aside the traditional dainty gabled brick façades. Cornices curled with acanthus leaves, strung with garlands and surmounted by urns lord it over the modest step gables, though the odd defiant bell or neck gable might reply with an extravagant claw-piece. At **No.502**, though, you'll find an austere, late 18th-century building with only the slightest flutter of exuberance in the three raised *œils-de-bœuf* along the roof-line. This has been the official residence of Amsterdam burgemeesters since 1927. Nearby (**Nos.504–10**) is a little stretch of wildly decorative claw-pieces. Tigers, dolphins and seagods curl about the gables and for once upstage the grander buildings.

The bit of the Herengracht canal between Vijzelstraat and Leidsestraat is known as the **Golden Bend**, perhaps more for the wealth of the inhabitants than the refinement of the architecture. There are clusters of more gorgeous and more graceful dwellings further up the canal that better deserve the epithet, though the elegant Louis XIV building with curved balustrades at **No.475** does have the reputation of being Amsterdam's most beautiful house.

Kattenkabinet (Cat Museum) H7

Herengracht 497, t 626 5378, e info@katten kabinet.nl, w www.kattenkabinet.nl; tram 4, 9, 14, 16, 24, 25. Open Mon–Fri 9am–2pm, Sat and Sun 1–5pm; adm adults €4.55, children €2.30.

Housed in a 17th-century canal house, Kattenkabinet is the only museum in the world devoted solely to cat-related works of art. The extensive collection of feline *objets d'art* includes drawings by Rembrandt, Picasso and Rudyard Kipling. Most people enjoy making friends with the museum's cats, who vigilantly guard the collection in their own quiet way.

From Leidsegracht to Brouwersgracht

On the right-hand side of the canal, just beyond Leidsegracht, **No.401** manages to lean in three different directions at once. Across the canal is a pretty little 17th-century house with a simple festooned neck gable (**No.394**). The outrageous confection at **Nos.380–2** is a late 19th-century imitation of a French Renaissance château scrunched down to city mansion size. The more dignified row of four houses (**Nos.364–70**) with clean lines, stately neck gables and quieter decoration are by the famous 17th-century domestic architect Philips Vingboons.

Bijbels Museum (Bible Museum) G7

Herengracht 366, t 624 2436, w www.bijbels museum.nl; tram 1, 2, 5. Open Mon–Sat 11am–5pm, Sun and hols 1–5pm; closed 1 Jan, 30 April; adm €5.

This is worth a visit only if you are interested in models of Solomon's temple and the history of the Dutch Bible over the past millennium – though the interior does preserve ceiling paintings by the 18th-century design supremo Jacob de Wit. The original kitchen is also on show.

Nederlands Theater Instituut G5

Herengracht 168, t 551 3300, e info@tin.nl, w www.tin.nl; tram 13, 14, 17. Open Mon–Fri 11am–5pm, Sat and Sun 1–5pm; adm adults €4.50, 7–17s €2.25.

The Bartolotti House at Nos.170–2 was built in 1617 by Hendrick de Keyser (who designed most of Amsterdam's spiky towers) for West India Company director Van den Heuvel. (It was paid for by Van den Heuvel's mother-in-law, who stipulated the house be called after her late husband.) Its enormous neck gable is all but invisible under the encrustation of pilasters, pinnacles and decorative reliefs. Part of the building houses the Nederlands Theater Instituut, which always has good exhibitions, usually of the sort where you push buttons or pull levers and make things happen. If there are three of you, you can raise a storm with the wind, thunder and lightning machines on the ground floor.

The white sandstone house next door (known as the **White House**), built in 1668, was Philips Vingboons' first. If you walk up towards the end of Herengracht you'll pass **No.120**, one of the smaller 17th-century houses to have kept its façade free of later additions and amendments.

KEIZERSGRACHT

From Reestraat to Huidenstraat

The Negen Straatjes (nine little streets), the short alleys that lead off from both sides of this stretch of Keizersgracht, offer the most intriguing shopping and gallery-gazing in Amsterdam. Furniture from antique shops tumbles out into the streets, and it's worth ducking down each street in turn to find trendy art galleries, second-hand clothes stores or shops crammed with lamps and light fittings – from original Art Nouveau to bright and bulbous 1960s products. **Haartenstraat** holds clothes shops and a store that sells vintage electronic equipment. **Reestraat** has a *poppendokter* (dolls' doctor). Puppets hang from the ceiling and a disconcerting catalogue of dolls' faces hangs on the wall. **Wolvenstraat** is a good starter for the interiors shops and second-hand clothes boutiques for which the Negen Straatjes are renowned.

Berenstraat, across the bridge, is home to some of the younger, trendier art galleries. At the Third World Charity shop in **Huidenstraat** you can buy all sorts of cheerfully coloured clothes and Zulu weaponry, while Pompadour at No.5 sells impossibly tempting handmade chocolates. Across the bridge in **Runstraat** is the Witte Tanden Winkel (White Teeth Shop) for nothing but the tooth – psychedelic and electric toothbrushes, pastes

galore, curious aids and sound clinical advice. Just the place to expiate your sins after Pompadour.

Felix Meritis G6
*Keizersgracht 324; tram 1, 2, 5. **Open** daily 9am–7pm (foyer café), or according to evening functions.*

This imposing building was built in 1778 to house an arts and scientific society founded in the spirit of Voltaire and Rousseau. With an observatory, library, laboratories and a small concert hall, the Felix Meritis Foundation became the cultural centre of the Dutch Enlightenment. When Napoleon made his triumphal entry into Amsterdam, he was punted up the canal and ushered with pride into the building. He got no further than the foyer, spat on the floor, said the place stank of tobacco smoke, and strutted back to the boat. Towards the end of the 19th century the society went into terminal decline.

The building was later used as the Communist Party headquarters, but won back its cultural prominence in the 1970s when it housed the Shaffy Theatre, in the forefront of the European avant-garde. The theatre lost some of its significance and impact during the 1980s, but the Felix Meritis Society has been revived. As an arts complex and the home of Amsterdam's Summer University, the building is once again playing host to artists and intellectuals from around the world.

One of Vingboons' early houses can be seen at **Keizersgracht 319** (built 1639), the façade virtually untouched. It's the first one in which he combined classic elements (the Doric pilasters) with the traditional Dutch style.

From Huidenstraat to Reguliersgracht

The startlingly large windows of the public library at **No.440** (built 1897) originally lit a clothing design studio and factory. It must have been the world's most gracious sweatshop. The bank at **No.452** was once a private residence. Designed by Outshoorn in 1860 it is one of the last of a series of grand canal houses, influenced by French and Italian architecture, that were built by the three great domestic architects – Vingboons, van Campen and Outshoorn – over a period of 200 years.

Metz Department Store G7

Keizersgracht 455; tram 1, 2, 5.

This pompous building at the intersection of Keizersgracht and Leidsestraat was built on the site of Van Gogh's uncle's art shop for an insurance company in the late 19th century, but is now a refined department store. Inside, you can mount stairs, passing racks of tasteful kitchenware and mounds of Liberty prints. As you climb, the atmosphere becomes increasingly rarefied and the floors emptier and emptier. By the time you're nearing the top, there's hardly anything for sale at all. The few pieces of designer furniture scattered about look more like museum pieces than anything you could put in the dining room. At the top is a **café** designed by Gerrit Rietveld. Gazing through its glass cupola, you have a rare opportunity to view Amsterdam's spider's web from on high.

On the opposite side of Keizersgracht, the **ornately decorated building** that cuts the corner with Leidsestraat is German inspired – the Dutch were more into solid right angles at corners. A frieze of fat naked babies, lurking in shrubberies and grumpily pushing carts and canoes, runs around the wall. The bust commemorates the 17th-century poet Pieter Cornelisz. Hooft. Further along Keizersgracht, at **No.546**, nothing of the façade, except the windows, has changed since the house was built in 1760, while the bell gable is a good example of playful cake-icing Louis XV decoration.

Van Loon Museum H8

Keizersgracht 672, t 624 5255; tram 16, 24, 25.
Open *Fri–Mon 10am–5pm; adm €4.50.*

Designed in 1672, the building was home to Ferdinand Bol, a pupil of Rembrandt who married into wealth. The Van Loon family

owned the house from 1884 to 1945 and have kindly left leering portraits of their dynasty about the walls. The interior has been restored to its faded 18th-century grandeur and gives a good impression of the style in which the movers and shakers of Amsterdam once lived.

PRINSENGRACHT

Prinsengracht, the outer ring of the three grand concentric canals, borders the Jordaan neighbourhood and stretches south past Leidseplein to the Amstel River. The Prinsengracht is the site of the perennially popular Anne Frankhuis and the Westerkerk, whose tower is one of the most enduring symbols of Amsterdam.

Magere Brug (Skinny Bridge) I8

Spanning the Amstel River at the eastern end of the Prinsengracht, you can see this slim bridge built in the 17th century for two spoilt young maidens who were too lazy to walk the long way round from their house in Kerkstraat to their stables across the river. A public outcry prevented its being replaced by a steel bridge in 1929, but the old structure was rotting and today's delicate white wooden swing bridge is a replica.

Carré Theater J8

Amstel 115–25, t 0900 252 5225; tram 6, 7, 10.

Across the Amstel river, at the start of Nieuwe Prinsengracht, you will see a lively classical building with a cornice of jesters and grinning clowns. This is the Carré Theater, built as a circus for Oscar Carré in 1887. Until 1875, Amsterdam had held an annual fair every September. It was a three-week beanfeast that engulfed the entire city with celebrity performances, balls, sideshows and circuses. One of these was Carré's, which King William III had granted the honorary title of 'Royal Dutch' – the equivalent of a 'By Appointment' stamp. But the revels had grown a little too unleashed for the tastes of the Protestant patricians, and the city council declared that the 'Kermis' of 1875 was to be the last. Despite rioting in the streets (which destroyed much of the original mauve 17th-century glass in canal-house windows), their edict was carried out and Amsterdam lost its annual wassail.

But Carré decided he was going to stay. He built a 'temporary' wooden circus tent beside the Amstel, and when the council wasn't looking, erected a stone façade. Outraged city fathers declared that he should take it down, but Carré fought on tenaciously throughout the 1880s, and eventually got his way.

The striking building you see today was built within months as the circus's permanent home. Now it hosts mainly musicals, but the best time to see its circular plush interior is when it reverts to being a circus over the Christmas holiday.

Amstelkerk I8

Amstelveld.

Just before where Reguliersgracht crosses the Prinsengracht you pass along the side of Amstelveld, a secluded square with a white wooden church and small Monday flower market, well tucked away from the surrounding bustle. The recently restored 17th-century Amstelkerk has a popular left-wing preacher and is one of the few churches in central Amsterdam that packs in a congregation. It isn't continuously open to the public, but sometimes stages recitals of chamber music.

From Amstelveld you can stroll up Reguliersgracht to take a peek at **Nos.57–9 and 63**, with their elaborately carved façades designed by Gosschalk in the late 19th century – rather like two extravagant sisters flanking a maiden aunt. One is a wild combination of Old Dutch and German, the other a modest mingling of Old Dutch with Old English and Queen Anne.

Woonbootmuseum (Houseboat Museum) F6

Corner of Prinsengracht and Elandsgracht, t 626 1977, w www.houseboatmuseum.nl; tram 13, 14, 17. Open Wed–Sun 11am–5pm; adm €3, children under 152cm (5ft) €2.50.

A glimpse of the nitty-gritty of life in a houseboat – an unmissable Amsterdam experience, although you may be glad at the end of it that you live on dry land. There's a slideshow and models, and you can have a see the cargo hold, which is the living area.

Westerkerk G5

Prinsengracht 279 t 624 7766, w www.westerkerk.nl; tram 13, 14, 17. Open April–Sept Mon–Fri 11am–3pm, plus July–Aug Sat 11am–3pm; adm free.

The Westerkerk was consecrated in 1631. Its sober Protestant interior is brightened by large painted **organ shutters** showing a dancing King David and a voluptuous Queen of Sheba laden with gifts for Solomon.

The Amstel Sluice Gates

In the river opposite the eastern end of the Prinsengracht (and just down from the Magere Brug) is a barrier of sluice gates. Every night between 7 and 8.30, two hefty men turn the wooden wheels that close them. Far to the east of the city, on the island of Zeeburg, a pumping station starts up and forces 20 million cubic feet of water into the canals, pushing the old water out through sluices in the west. This helps stop the pong, which at one time was quite overpowering. Even when Amsterdammers stopped tipping their sewage into the canals and sent it off in covered wagons to be sold as field manure, the stagnating water still presented a problem. Not everyone seemed to mind. When in 1765 plans for better water circulation were proposed, 33,000 domestic maids petitioned against the idea as they felt that a reduction in the vile emanations from the canal would lose them cleaning work.

Anne Frank

Anne Frank, the second daughter of German-Jewish immigrants living in Amsterdam, got her diary for her 13th birthday on 12 June 1942. Three weeks later, her family were '*onderduikers*' ('divers') – in hiding from the Nazi occupying forces. They lived for two years in a small suite of rooms at the back of Anne's father's herb and spice business on the Prinsengracht. The windows had always been painted over to protect the herbs previously stored there, the entrance was hidden behind a hinged bookcase and, apart from four trusted office workers who supplied them with food, nobody knew they were there. Later they were joined by a dentist, Fritz Pfeffer (whom Anne calls 'Dussel'), and the Van Pelses ('Van Daans') and their son Peter.

For two years they were cooped up in what became known as the Annexe, and Anne wrote in her diaries about life with the petulant and demanding Mrs Van Daan and her hen-pecked spouse, of the tiresomely childish Dussel, and of moments of joy and desperation within her own family. No one knows who betrayed them, but in August 1944 German police barged into the offices, walked straight up to the bookcase and demanded entry. All the hideaways, except Anne's father, died in concentration camps in Germany.

The office cleaner found the diary in which Anne had written with astonishing lucidity about life in the Annexe and about growing up. When it was given to her father, he found that she'd already begun to edit it for publication. It appeared in 1947 with the title *The Annexe*, the one Anne herself had chosen. Now it's printed in over 50 languages and an estimated 13 million copies have been sold.

Rembrandt was buried here, but no one knows where the body is. There's a flutter of academic excitement every time old bones are found, but it's most likely that he was crunched up during the digging of an underground car park. A memorial plaque has been put up near his son Titus' grave.

If you walk around the outside of the church you can see the house where Descartes lived when he was in Amsterdam (**Westermarkt 6**); the pink marble triangles of the **Homomonument** which commemorates gays killed in the concentration camps; and a sad little **statue of Anne Frank**, who wrote her diary just round the corner.

Westertoren

*Open April–Sept Mon–Sat 10am–5pm; **guided tours** on the hour, every hour; **adm** €3.*

The church tower, known as the Westertoren, built by (you guessed it) Hendrick de Keyser, is Amsterdam's highest (280ft/85m) and contains its heaviest bell (16,500lb/7,500kg). In the 1940s a fervent engineer climbed out onto the top of the tower during a violent storm and, with the help of a theodolite, worked out that it swayed all of 1in. During the summer months you can climb up rather more sedately for a rare view of Amsterdam from high up. At the top is the gaudily painted imperial crown of Maximilian of Austria. Amsterdam's merchants gained considerable international clout when, out of gratitude for support given to the Austro-Burgundian princes, he granted them the right to use the crown in the city coat-of-arms.

Anne Frankhuis G5

*Prinsengracht 263, t 556 7100, w www.anne frank.nl; tram 13, 14, 17. **Open** April–Aug daily 9am–9pm, Sept–March daily 9am–7pm, 1 Jan noon–7pm, 4 May 9am–7pm, 25 Dec noon–7pm, 31 Dec 9am–5pm; closed Yom Kippur; **adm** adults €7.50, 10–18s €3.50.*

Well over half a million people visit the Anne Frankhuis annually. The building which housed the Frank family's hideout has been restored to its pre-war condition, giving a moving impression of what life was like for the families who hid there. In newer premises next door is an exhibition on Jews in Amsterdam and racial oppression.

LEIDSEPLEIN AND AROUND

Leidseplein, just beyond the Prinsengracht, is Amsterdam's tourist vortex, with more than the usual complement of British boys in Union Jack shorts learning the strength of Dutch lager. Fire-eaters and itinerant musicians busk while your pockets are picked, though at night the atmosphere improves a little as the square becomes the festive hub of late-night transport. As a 17th-century traveller cautioned, 'Here be sure to furnish yourself with money.'

The neon alleys leading off the square are lined with expensive and nasty restaurants and nightclubs with names like 'Cash'. Leidsestraat, the northern exit, is a welter of pedestrians, with every few minutes – bell clanging – a tram cutting a swathe through the middle. Delicatessens, designer boutiques and fast-food joints line the street, interspersed with the odd tacky souvenir shop selling clogs and Taiwan Delft.

Stadsschouwburg (Municipal Theatre) F8

Leidseplein 26, t 624 2311, w www.stadsschouwburg.nl; tram 1, 2, 5, 6, 7, 10. Open nightly.

State theatres in Amsterdam were usually out in the sticks, and kept burning down. The first one on this site was built in 1774 (when Leidseplein was on the edge of town) and, after suffering the usual fate, was replaced by the present building in the late 19th century. The new building was designed by Jan Springer, the bohemian kingpin of Architectura et Amicitia, a wickedly unrestrained artists' society. Budget cuts put a stop to his more florid decorations, yet still the public disapproved. Springer sulked and virtually abandoned his career. The building has a small stage and the Muziektheater on Waterlooplein has rather stolen its thunder,

but it continues to host local and international productions.

American Hotel F8

Leidsekade 97, t 556 3000, f 556 3001, w www.interconti.com; tram 1, 2, 5, 6, 7, 10.

The jutting balconies and odd protruding windows of the American Hotel off Leidseplein are a Dutch interpretation of an original Art Nouveau design. The architect, W. Kromhout, is considered a forerunner of the fanciful Amsterdam School (*see* p.167). The writers and artists who used the **Café Américain** inside the hotel for most of the 20th century have fled the tourist armies of the Leidseplein, but it's still well worth a visit for the glass Japanese parasol lampshades and patterned windows that filter the hard Amsterdam light into a soft and playful kaleidoscope.

Casino F8

Max Euweplein 62, t 521 1111, w www.hollandcasino.nl; tram 1, 2, 5, 6, 7, 10. Open daily 1.30pm–3am.

Escape Leidseplein by heading east down Kleine Lijnbaansgracht. This you do by taking the main road opposite the Stadsschouwburg, but keeping to the smaller left-hand fork following the canal. Just before the fork you pass Amsterdam's casino and nightlife complex.

It's a colourful heap of postmodern design – an architectural style ideally suited to the wry, up-front Amsterdam temperament. What other city would allow, in its centre, a massive colonnade topped with a frieze bearing the inscription '*Homo sapiens non urinat in ventum*' (Wise men do not pee in the wind)?

Max Euwe Centrum F8

Max Euweplein 30, t 625 7017, w www.max euwe.nl; tram 1, 2, 5, 6, 7, 10. Open Mon–Fri and first Sat of the month 10.30am–4pm; adm free.

This centre was set up by Max Euwe, chess world champion before his death in 1983. There's a small permanent exhibition on the origins of chess and the life of Max Euwe himself, with a collection of memorabilia. A number of chessboards and computer terminals allow visitors to play the game themselves, against either machine or man. Outside in the little Max Euweplein a **huge chessboard** is painted on the pavement, with chess pieces the size of toddlers. It was the idea of an inspired five-year-old, who proposed his little vision to the authorities in the early 1990s.

SPIEGELKWARTIER

The Spiegelkwartier, centred on Spiegelgracht, is one of the two quarters in Amsterdam dedicated to one particular business (the other one being the Red Light District) – the business in question here is antiques and fine art. The Spiegelkwartier has gone upmarket in recent years – these days even museums buy here for their collections – but it hasn't lost its charm, and the prices are still lower than in most other major cities. Here you'll find shops crammed with elaborate clocks, solemn rows of carved wooden dressers and ornate gilded furniture. Enormous chandeliers hang at eye-level, and gold, silver and colourful gems shine at you from all sides. Tucked amongst all this grandeur, you can still find idiosyncratic little shops, obviously the domain of a single collector. **Aalderink** (Spiegelgracht 15) has a sparse but expertly selected range of oriental pieces and Africana. **Anneke Schat** (No.20A) makes delicate, sculpted jewellery inspired by spiders' webs and butterflies and much favoured by Dutch glitterati and the royal family.

Nieuwe Spiegelstraat, which dissects the three Grand Canals, is where the price tags begin to get serious. If your souvenir budget runs to multiple noughts you could pop into **Elisabeth den Bieman de Haas** for a little

Chagall litho or bright modern oil from COBRA, the post-war Expressionist movement (*see* p.51). **H.C. van der Vliet** (No.74) has one of those shops you could potter about in for ages – everything from 18th-century slippers to antique African masks. **Kramers** (No.64) has tangles of old jewellery and trinkets, barrels of clay pipe bowls and a roomful of Delft tiles ranging from the 15th to 20th centuries.

JORDAAN

Jordaan comes from the French '*jardin*', but during the housing crisis in the 19th century this 'garden' on the outskirts of the city disappeared under rows of working-class housing. The houses were small, dark and close together and all the smellier industries (such as tanning) were banished to the Jordaan from the posher areas of town. Naming the streets after flowers didn't cheer things up much. Conditions were appalling, but the Jordaaners developed a pride and a culture akin to London's cockneys. The true Jordaaner is born in the small patch bound by Prinsengracht, Brouwersgracht, Lijnbaansgracht and Looiersgracht, in the shadow of the Westertoren (*see* p.123). The church tower is the symbol of the Jordaan.

Jordaaners have their own accent and are renowned for a wry sense of humour and for being adept pigeon-fanciers. Everyone over the age of forty is known as '*ome*' or '*tante*' – uncle or aunt. (Until a decade or so ago, you could still be woken by Ome Hein, a professional 'waker-up', as he made his early morning rounds with a pet goat.) They're a rebellious lot. There have been a number of historic riots, including one in 1886 when police tried to put a stop to the gory-sounding pastime of 'eel-jerking'; and another when the council threatened to reduce the dole in 1934. Recently, traditional Jordaan life has been given a new edge by an influx of artists and music students. You're quite likely to be accompanied on your walk by strains of Mozart, and will probably encounter odd art objects suspended over the street.

For a walk through Jordaan, taking in *hofjes* and markets, *see* the 'Walks' chapter, p.162.

De Looier Indoor Antiques Market F7

Elandsgracht 109; tram 7, 10, 17.
Open Sat–Thurs 11am–5pm.

This is a collectors' and dealers' market pitched halfway between fleamarket junk and Spiegelkwartier splendour. Furniture, glass, old lace and even older Delftware can be unearthed from the honeycomb of little stands. Stallholders have a lively commercial spirit – they even have their own newspaper and weekly bridge drives. There are regular specialist fairs.

St Andrieshofje F5

Egelantiersgracht 107–14; tram 13, 14, 17.

Hofjes, the courts of almshouses, are magically quiet garden courts, often completely hidden from the street. You reach this one (built 1616) through a door that looks like any other front door along the Egelantiersgracht canal and down a passage lined with Delft tiles. Most *hofjes* are private residences, but as long as you're sensitive to that, residents don't mind you popping in for a few calming moments.

Tweede Egelantiersdwarsstraat, nearby, is a narrow road of shops and cafés typical of the Jordaan's quirky charm. **Bloemgracht**, just south, is well worth a look.

Pianola Museum F4

Westerstraat 106, t 627 9624; tram 13, 14, 17.
Open Sun 11.30am–5pm; adm €3.75.

Here pianolas and player-pianos which date from the beginning of the 20th century are demonstrated using part of a massive hoard of music rolls. Regular pianola concerts are held.

Noordermarkt and Around G4

Tram 3, 10; metro Centraal Station then 10mins walk. Markets held Mon 7.30am–1pm and Sat morning.

You will find this quiet square at the northern end of Jordaan. It's usually empty, but if you come early on a Monday morning you'll find a crush of trendies, students and down-and-outs at Amsterdam's cheapest clothes market, while Saturday sees local organic farmers come to town for a busy Farmers' Market. The **Noorderkerk** was Hendrick de Keyser's last church and, as befits an old man, is solemn and austere with only the teeniest of spires. You could relax with a quiet coffee in one of the cafés around the square, or cross the Prinsengracht canal to two more *hofjes*: '**De Ster**' at Prinsengracht 89–133 (one of the best, though now closed to the public) and '**Zons Hofje**' at Nos.159–171. Or you can seek out nearby **Lindengracht**, which makes a rewarding wander.

Museumplein
and Vondelpark

Museumplein and Vondelpark

The city's greatest cultural institutions border Museumplein – the Rijksmuseum and Concertgebouw at either end, the Van Gogh and Stedelijk Museums up one side. The Rijksmuseum contains pre-20th-century paintings, sculpture, applied arts and artefacts, including the classics of Golden Age painting. The Stedelijk Museum picks up the trail with modern art. The Van Gogh Museum needs no explanation. Note, however, that threats of lengthy closures during renovation works hang over both the Rijksmuseum and the Stedelijk Museum.

A short walk west of the square is Vondelpark, a large irregular mass of lakes and ponds, lawns, canals, ornate bridges, trees and gardens. There are even a few cows and sheep. During summer weekends, Amsterdammers flock here to stroll around, picnic and enjoy the theatre performances, buskers and assorted festivities which stretch into the night. In the area between Vondelpark and Museumplein are the diamonds and designer clothing of Amsterdam's most chic shopping streets.

1 Lunch

Honderdtien *Johannes Verhulststraat 110,* **t** *771 8660;* **tram** *2, 16.* **Open** *Mon–Sat 11am–11pm.* **Moderate.** Designer décor and cuisine for demanding palates. The menu changes as the day progresses, and has an Italian lilt, with good vegetarian options.

2 Tea and Cakes

Café Vertigo, *Vondelpark 3,* **t** *612 3021;* **tram** *1, 3, 6, 12.* **Open** *11am–1am.* This smart café-bar is attached to the Filmmuseum. It has an enormous balcony terrace.

3 Drinks

't Ronde Blauwe Theehuis, *Vondelpark;* **tram** *1, 2, 5, 6.* **Open** *Sun–Thurs 9am–1am, Fri and Sat 9am–3am.* 'The Round Blue Teahouse' is an odd piece of 1930s New Functionalist architecture in the middle of the Vondelpark. It is now a trendy watering hole.

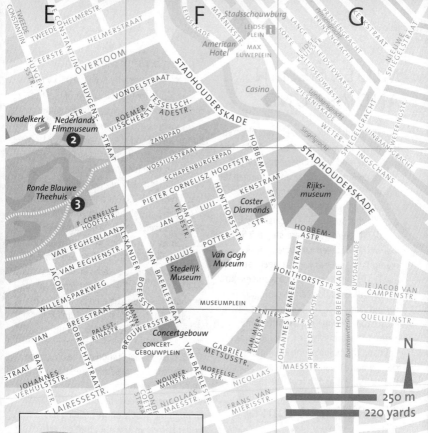

Highlights

Couples' City: The Van Gogh Museum, for an overview of the troubled painter's life and works, p.138

Amsterdammers' City: Catching a silent classic at the Nederlands Filmmuseum, p.143

Indoor City: Depending on your mood, either the Rijksmuseum, for the Golden Age art, p.130, or the Stedelijk Museum's De Stijl collection, p.136

Outdoor City: Window-shopping along chic Pieter Cornelisz. Hooftstraat, p.142

Architectural City: Roemer Visscherstraat, for houses illustrating seven national architectural styles, p.144

MUSEUMPLEIN AND AROUND

Until recently, Museumplein was bisected by a busy road nicknamed 'Europe's shortest motorway', and was windswept, deserted and nasty. But dramatic relandscaping in the late 1990s created a green and stylish spot with a long pool, a café and underground garages that suck up all the cars. As you wander through the square, stop briefly to look at the **Vrouwen van Ravensbrück memorial**, a series of vertical steel slabs erected to commemorate the women who died in concentration camps during the Second World War. The text translates as 'For those women who until the bitter end refused to accept Fascism'. The flickering light and thumping sound emanating from the sculpture are intended to call people to the monument and to continue the fight.

The Rijksmuseum G9

*Stadhouderskade 42, **t** 674 7047, **e** info@ rijksmuseum.nl, **w** www.rijksmuseum.nl; **tram** 2, 5, 6, 7, 10; most rooms wheelchair accessible, special facilities at East and West entrances. **Open** daily 9am–6pm; closed 1 Jan; **adm** €9, under 18s free. **Closed for massive renovations until probably 2008 – though Philips Wing will remain open. Check the website or with the tourist office for news of temporary exhibition spaces around town.** The following gives a taste of what the museum holds, listed according to the room arrangement before closure.*

The Rijksmuseum (pronounced 'reyks-museum') was completed in 1885 to house the national collection of paintings and sculpture. The collection evolved from a hoard of 200 paintings confiscated from the exiled Prince William V in 1798. Today the museum's rooms hold 5,000 paintings, 30,000 sculptures and works of applied art, 17,000 historical objects, 3,000 works of Asiatic art and a million prints and drawings.

> ### What's on Temporary Show in the Rijkmuseum's Philips Wing
>
> The closure for refurbishment of most of the Rijksmuseum is disappointing news for many visitors, but the silver lining is that during this period at least some of the treasures will still be on show in the Philips Wing. This is set to remain open for the entire period with an exhibition entitled 'The Masterworks'. It includes not only highlights of Golden Age painting, such as Rembrandt's *The Night Watch*, but also the pick of other collections, such as the 17th-century doll's houses and some outstanding Delftware. It adds up to some 400 pieces in all, so it is still well worth a visit. There will also probably be temporary venues scattered around the city which will draw from the museum's collections: ask at tourist offices for details.

Like the Centraal Station on the other side of town, the Rijksmuseum was designed as a grand entrance to the city. (When it was built there were only fields beyond it.) A walkway through the middle of the building has bright bathroom acoustics that attract anything from opera-singing accordionists to steel bands.

Gallery of Honour

Because of the walkway through the middle of the building, the museum's important halls are on the first floor. If you climb the stairs to the museum shop on the first floor you'll see an archway leading to the Gallery of Honour. If your time is really tight, this is the one place to visit. It gives a good introduction to Golden Age painting, and houses the Rembrandt for which the museum is famous. At the far end, taking up the full wall, is Rembrandt's *The Night Watch* (see p.131), which, together with *The Syndics* (see p.134), is considered the prize of the Rijksmuseum's collection.

Frans Hals' happy and rather cheeky-looking *Wedding Portrait of Isaac Abrahamsz. Massa and Beatrix van der Laen* (1622), and the florid *Merry Drinker* (1628–30), seemingly dashed off with swift brushstokes and

De Rijks

The original collection of paintings now held in the Rijksmuseum had been gathered in the Huis ten Bosch palace in The Hague, and later brought to the Trip brothers' 17th-century mansion in Amsterdam (see p.88). By the 1860s it was clear that the Trippenhuis was going to be too small for the growing collection. The quest for a new temple for the nation's art sparked off a conflagration of chauvinism, in-fighting and intrigue that would have impressed the Borgias. When the winners of an anonymous competition for a new museum design turned out to be German, the plan was rejected as 'non-Dutch'. Once a suitable Dutch architect was found in P.J.H. Cuypers (of Centraal Station fame), a new scandal emerged. The architect, project co-ordinator, government advisor and decorator were all Roman Catholics. Protestant Holland scented nepotism and popery. The building Cuypers produced was thought altogether too extravagant, too churchy and too foreign to house the treasures of Dutch culture. What made it worse was that Cuypers, having had a more sober Romanesque plan accepted, managed, while building was in progress, to slip in more fantastical bits of a previously rejected Gothic plan. Good patriotic Calvinists found this mish-mash of foreign styles deplorable. One critic railed: 'For two million guilders we now have the most sorry spectacle of a building that anyone could have thought to call a museum.' In response to the gilding and plethora of sculptures, portraits and tiling depicting Dutch artists that adorns the outside walls, another critic compared the museum to 'a garishly decorated house of a rich parvenu'. Even the king pleaded a prior engagement on the day of the opening ceremony.

Ironically, Cuypers thought his red-brick and wood building with its clean, simple lines to be quintessentially Dutch, and today one would be inclined to agree with him. Though not as magical as the Centraal Station, 'De Rijks' is one of Amsterdam's most conspicuous landmarks, and has become a cultural icon. When it reopened after the Second World War the waiting queue of pallid, underfed Amsterdammers in slightly shabby formal dress stretched all the way down Stadhouderskade.

In the years following the completion of the Rijksmuseum in 1885, so many people left their complete collections to the museum that it had, almost immediately, to embark on a programme of expansion. Not all the additions have been happy ones. In 1906 a committee of artists and architects spent months fiddling about in a life-sized model of a hall intended to show off Rembrandt's *The Night Watch*. They finally decided that light from the left, tempered by carefully placed curtains, would be ideal. It wasn't. The room was a disaster, ended up being used for minor exhibitions and earned the monicker 'De Puist' (the pimple). All of Cuypers' ornate interior decorations have been removed and today the museum is a maze of whitewashed rooms.

scratches in the wet paint, testify to his greatness as a portrait painter. Other paintings in the Gallery of Honour may change from time to time, but you can probably see **Nicholaes Maes'** delicately detailed *Old Woman at Prayer* and work by one of Rembrandt's better-known pupils – **Ferdinand Bol**. Massive *penschilderijen* ('pen paintings', rather like etchings) of naval battle scenes by **Willem van de Velde I** are also on show.

The Night Watch

The Night Watch was commissioned in 1642 by the militiamen of the Kloveniersdoelen (the Arquebusiers' Guildhall) to hang in their banqueting room alongside five other portraits of companies of the civic guard. It's officially called *The Company of Captain Frans Banning Cocq and Lieutenant Willem van Ruytenburch* and got its present title in the 19th century because ageing layers of varnish made it dim and murky. For years it's had the reputation of being the work that

Rembrandt

Rembrandt Harmensz. van Rijn (1606–69) was the son of a Leiden miller. When the poet Constantijn Huygens, who was also something of an art critic, visited Leiden in 1628, he went into raptures over Rembrandt's paintings (though he reprimanded the then unknown youth for his puniness and lack of manly exercise). A few years later Rembrandt upped sticks for the big city. He had made his mark in Leiden, and as the *burgemeester* wryly remarked: 'His portraits and other pictures pleased the citizens of Amsterdam, who paid him well for them.'

And indeed they did. Wealthy burghers, trades guilds and companies of the civic guard all spent handsome sums to be painted by the fashionable young artist. His unromanticized portraits hit just the right note in rationalistic, post-Reformation Holland. Even his biblical and historical paintings have a truth and psychological rigour, especially in the faces, that seem to suggest direct experience of the world he's depicting. In 1634, already a rich and celebrated painter, he married heiress Saskia van Uylenburgh and five years later felt confident about paying a swingeing 13,000 guilders for a house in the Jewish quarter. This was where he had always wanted to live – he found Hebrew culture fascinating and preferred Jewish models for his religious paintings.

Saskia died in 1642, having just changed her will to leave everything to their infant son Titus, with the estate to be held in usufruct by Rembrandt for as long as he didn't remarry. The painter got round this by having a clandestine affair with Titus' nurse, Geertghe Dircx. Then, in 1649, he fell in love with a younger servant, Hendrickje Stoffels. Geertghe sued successfully for breach of contract. This came at a bad time. Rembrandt was receiving fewer commissions now – perhaps because of gossip about his domestic affairs, perhaps because he was becoming increasingly uncompromising in his work, or maybe he was just going out of fashion. He'd also spent far too much on paintings and the house. In 1656 he was declared bankrupt. The property that had been his home for some 20 years was sold, and he moved out to live on the Rozengracht with Hendrickje and Titus. They were going to try to revive his flagging fortune by working as his agents, but Hendrickje died within two years, followed by Titus in 1669, only months after he had married. Rembrandt was so hard up that he had to sell Saskia's tomb to pay for Hendrickje's funeral. When he himself died, he was buried in an unmarked grave in the Westerkerk.

signalled Rembrandt's decline. This is ill-deserved – he still had some of his most important commissions ahead of him. It is true though, that the 17th-century public didn't like it very much, and when it was moved to the *stadhuis* in 1715 the city fathers thought nothing of lopping a bit off the left-hand side so that it would fit on the wall: two of Captain Cocq's militiamen disappeared forever.

It was usual to paint group portraits in fairly static compositions, giving each member equal prominence. Rembrandt, however, paints the company in a flurry of movement, as if about to set off on a march. Rich clothes and a wonderful collection of plumed and pointed hats all add to the sense of grandeur and motion (this is all pure invention – the guards' uniforms were in reality rather dull, and they never marched). A little girl in a luminous gold dress, possibly the company mascot, looks bewildered by all the activity. (The rather surreal touch of a dead chicken tied to her waist is an allusion to the militia's coat-of-arms.) The captain and his lieutenant, in fine clothes, dominate the scene. The rest of the company look far less important – which is possibly why the painting was initially unpopular: they had after all each paid their 100 guilders, and deserved the same billing.

Rooms 201–6: Dutch Middle Ages and Renaissance

You'll probably want to save your energy for the Golden Age, but as you pass through the early rooms have a look at **Geertgen tot Sint Jans**' brightly detailed *Holy Kinship* (1485), crammed with emblems and symbolic references, and his *Adoration of the Magi* (1480), set against an intricate backdrop of ruined landscapes, processions and misty forests. *The Seven Works of Charity* (1504), instructive panels by the **Master of Alkmaar**, have survived attacks by iconoclasts and creeping damp, and still preach their cata-logue of worthy acts. **Lucas van Leyden**'s *Adoration of the Golden Calf* (1530) is suitably riotous and a good example of the way Dutch Renaissance painters introduced real-istic landscape settings for mythological scenes. The youth trying hard not to break the egg on the tavern floor in **Pieter Aertsen**'s *Egg Dance* (1557) prefigures the scenes of everyday life that were to be such a feature of the Golden Age. The Dutch Mannerists, who worked in Haarlem between 1580 and the 1620s, get a good showing. **Cornelis Cornelisz.**'s enormous *Fall of Man* (1592) teems with animals mythical and domestic. In **Karel van Mander**'s *The Continence of Scipio* (1600), the 3rd-century BC Roman hero nobly refuses the offer of a beautiful captive for his slave and returns her to her betrothed.

Rooms 207–36: Dutch Golden Age

These rooms are filled with paintings from the 17th century, the 'Golden Age' not only of Dutch art but of the Netherlands' political and economic might. Intense realism and the naturalistic rendering of domestic and everyday life are the hallmarks of the Golden Age. There are precise, calm interiors, minutely detailed still lifes, wild taverns and salacious brothel scenes. Homely Dutch mothers and their *onnozele schaapjes* (inno-cent lambs) take the place of the Madonna and Child, and you'll see businessmen and civic guards rather than generals and fantas-tical battle scenes. As you walk around the collection you'll see more of Rembrandt and his pupils, but there are a number of other artists particularly worth searching out.

Pieter Saenredam's church interiors are so still, and he pays such close attention to architectural shapes, that they seem almost abstract. **Pieter de Hooch** – especially in *Woman and Child in a Pantry* (1658) and *Women beside a Linen Chest* (1663) – is a master of quiet family scenes. Light from the busy outside world streams in through a door or window in the background, while in the spotless rooms with their symmetrical black and white floor tiles all is order and calm – though the impish children seem just on the verge of disrupting it.

A somewhat sadder *schaapje* can be seen in **Gabriel Metsu**'s touching, yet unsenti-mental *Sick Child*. **Jan Steen** gives quite another idea of family life. He used his expe-riences as a tavern-keeper to create scenes of such jolly domestic upheaval – as in *The Merry Family* (1670) – that the Dutch still use the expression 'a Jan Steen household' for any chaotic but cheerful home. You'll also find still lifes which, at the beginning of the century, are sober arrangements of herring, bread and cheese, but later overflow with ornate tableware, full-blown flowers and juicy fruit at its *toppunt* (literally, 'top-point') – the last moment of perfection before decay. **Abraham van Beyeren**'s 1665 painting shows fat peaches, seafood, leaking melons and a toppled silver candlestick in meticu-lous detail. Look out also for **Gerard ter Borch**'s exquisite fabrics – poor little *Helena van der Schalke* (1648) is weighed down by her fine silk dress, and in *Gallant Conversation* the young woman's silver gown shimmers. (The conversation wasn't really that gallant – the man holding up his hand in gentle admonition was originally offering her a coin. A pious owner painted it out.)

In Room 217, keep an eye open for three of **Rembrandt**'s paintings: *Isaac and Rebecca*, better known as *The Jewish Bride* (1667), a glowing, tender portrait of a couple, no longer all that youthful, but very much in love; a rather depressed, world-weary *Self-portrait as the Apostle Paul* (1661); and *St Peter's Denial* (1660), showing a very troubled, down-to-earth apostle.

Also in Room 217 at the time of writing was *The Syndics*. The story behind it is that, when the controllers of the Drapers' Guild (the 'Staalmeesters', or 'Syndics') commissioned Rembrandt to paint their portrait in 1662, they were determined not to make a similar mistake to that of the Kloveniersdoelen (*see* p.131), and stipulated a more traditional composition. Rembrandt obeyed, yet still managed to create a work that brims with life. The Syndics look up from their table, and the viewer has the odd sensation of having just walked into the room and disturbed them at work. It's one of the finest group portraits ever painted – Kenneth Clark goes as far as acclaiming it 'one of the summits of European painting' – and seems to be the image picture librarians most reach for to evoke old Holland.

Skim as fast as you like through the rest of the collection, but don't miss the Vermeers (Room 218). Only thirty works by **Johannes Vermeer** (1632–75) exist; the Rijksmuseum has four of them. He had a passion for light and his paintings seem translucent. Light from a window reflects off a white wall, a jug, or softly glowing fabric. The tranquil *Kitchen Maid* (1658) and *Woman Reading a Letter* (1662/3) are totally without stylistic artifice, yet come close to perfection. In quiet, everyday scenes, Vermeer captures a sense of eternity.

Sculpture and Applied Art

The museum's collection of sculpture and applied art includes ceramics, china, glass, furniture, costumes, lace, tapestries, jewellery and silver from the Middle Ages to the 20th century, and can be utterly overwhelming. On a first visit the best idea is to give yourself a gentle overview. In the rooms leading off the entrance hall on the first floor (Rooms 238–42), you'll find some of the best pieces in the collection. Ten **15th-century bronze**

figures, poised in graceful attitudes of mourning, have been filched from the tomb of Isabella de Bourbon in Antwerp. There's a tiny **portable altar**, carved in gold and encrusted with enamel, that some lucky nun used for her private devotion in the Abbey de Chocques in France in the 16th century. Look out also for **Adriaen van Wesel**'s busy and energetic oak carving of *The Meeting of the Three Magi* (1475–7). A little further on, in Room 245, you can see **late Gothic German carvings** of *Christ and the Last Supper*, still with some original polychrome and gilding.

If you have a taste for camp, head straight for Room 251A and **Wenzel Jamnitzer**'s extraordinary *Table Ornament*, made for the city of Nuremberg in 1549. Mother Earth stands, one hip cocked, in a rockery of flowers, lizards and shrimps (all silver casts of real specimens) and supports on her head an enormous birdbath of cherubs rampant, scrolls, snakes and more flowers. All this is surmounted by yet another posy of enamelled silver foliage. Its ornate gilded wood and leather carrying case is displayed alongside.

The collection of **Delftware** (Rooms 255–7) has some prize polychrome as well as more traditional blue and white pieces. The people of Delft started making cheaper imitations of the Chinese porcelain brought back by the Dutch East India Company in the 17th century. (Things have turned full circle. Now souvenir shops sell imitation Delftware made in Taiwan.) Among the usual plates and cups you can see a functioning Delftware violin and towering tulip pagodas with space for forty stems (which, in the 17th century, would have cost a fortune to fill).

Back downstairs (in Room 164) you can see two exquisite early 18th-century **dolls' houses** – collectors' pieces assembled by the lady of the house, rather than toys. The museum is full of choice life-size furniture too, but it's rather coldly presented and not that fascinating unless you have a specialist interest – though do keep an eye open for the rich **Gobelin tapestries** (Room 165) and an ornate **oak table-leaf** veneered with tortoiseshell and inlaid with a mass of birds, monkeys, fruit and putti worked in copper, brass and mother-of-pearl. If you appreciate good porcelain, the **Meissen collection** (Rooms 170–71) is one of the best in the world. An alchemist in the German town of Meissen, near Dresden, discovered the secret of Chinese porcelain manufacture while trying to make gold for the king, and the pieces subsequently produced in the area have been collectors' items for centuries.

Rooms 102–12: Dutch History Collection

The history collection comprises paintings, documents and memorabilia dating from the Middle Ages to the Second World War. There's an understandable emphasis on ships and sea battles, but the presentation is not very exciting. If you have the time, pop in for a look at some of the more amusing curiosities – like a deceptively gorgeous **copper crown** with glass jewels sent as a trade bribe to an African king by the 17th-century Duke of York (via the Dutch naval hero Admiral de Ruyter), or the grand but diminutive **jackets** worn by the toddler Prince William V.

Room 248: Italian Collection

Here you'll find some chubby pink **Rubens**, **Carlo Crivelli**'s elegant tempera *Mary Magdalene* (1485/90) and **Piero di Cosimo**'s warts-and-all portraits of a Florentine architect and his cauliflower-eared father (1485).

Rijksprentenkabinet (Print Room)

Near the café entrance you'll find the Rijksprentenkabinet exhibition hall where you can see temporary exhibitions from a vast collection of prints, drawings and watercolours by the likes of **Rembrandt**, **Dürer**, **Goya** and **Canaletto**. To see works from the collection not on view, you need written permission (from the Director, Jan Luykenstraat 1A).

The South Wing
18th- and 19th-century Paintings

On the top floor the South Wing houses a small but carefully selected **costume and textile collection** (in Room 15, near the door to the walkway) and 18th- and 19th-century art, including bright, ethereal pastels by the Swiss artist **Jean-Etienne Liotard** (1702–89) – mostly of aristocrats and socialites. The best 19th-century work is by painters of two movements from the second half of the century. The three **Maris brothers** were leading artists of the Hague School (nicknamed the 'grey' school after its heavy, cloudy skies). Jacob painted beaches and townscapes, Matthijs portrayed romantic fairy-tale scenes, and Willem seemed preoccupied with ducks. **Anton Mauve**'s pearly-grey *Morning Ride along a Beach* (1876) is characteristic of the movement. The Amsterdam Impressionists are well represented by **George Breitner**, who liked to paint Amsterdam in the rain, and **Isaac Isradls**, whose brighter pictures are closer to the work of the French Impressionists.

On the walkway between the South Wing and the central staircase you pass a series of **four-poster beds**: the first is peppermint-green with embroidered birds, the second hung with rich tapestries, the third sparkling gold and silver – each is more alluring and sumptuous than the last, like the temptations in a fairy tale.

The Asiatic Art Collection

Downstairs is the Asiatic art collection. Three hundred years of Dutch trade connections have resulted in a glittering stash of treasures from the East. You can see lacquerwork, ceramics and textiles from Japan, Javanese sculptures, and religious works from China and India. A small, bronze dancing **Lord Shiva** (the Hindu god of creation) from the 12th century and an elegantly relaxed Chinese Buddhist saint, the **Bodhisattva Avalokitesharva**, from the same period, make the trip across to the South Wing worthwhile.

The Stedelijk Museum F9

Paulus Potterstraat 13, t 573 2911, w www. stedelijk.nl; tram 2, 3, 5, 12, 16; wheelchair accessible at Van Baerlestraat entrance. Due to close for renovation in 2004 and to move to a temporary site in Oosterdoksade near Centraal Station (K5); until then open daily 11am–5pm; closed 1 Jan; adm adults €7, under-17s €3.50.

The Stedelijk is due to close for renovations, but is embroiled in arguments over who should fund the work. The closure date is continually being postponed, and at the time of going to press stands at some time in 2004 – but don't hold your breath.

The museum itself is a solid 19th-century red-brick building with fussy plaster decorations and spiky gables. The widened entrance and glass box extension at the back were part of a drive in the 1950s to make art more accessible: the guiding principle was that a museum loses its sense of mystery when works can also be viewed from the street. A good idea – if the blinds didn't have to be drawn every afternoon against the damaging sunlight.

Don't be deceived by appearances. It's a bright, lively museum of modern art. You'll find not only conventional paintings, but all sorts of applied art (designer chairs, feather hats and gaudy teapots) and work by less established artists. The high point is the museum's collection of the Russian artist Kazimir Malevich and the Dutch movement De Stijl. Side by side, these two collections show how abstract art began and we see the gradual disappearance of any reference to outside reality.

The museum owes its existence to two benefactors. Sophia Augusta de Bruyn, the eccentric dowager of Jonkheer (Lord) Lopez Suasso, spent as little as possible on clothes (scandalizing Amsterdam society by wearing the same dress more than once). Instead she amassed as many jewels, trinkets, curios (and especially clocks) as she could. When she died, she left everything to the City of Amsterdam. There was so much that the council felt obliged to build a museum to display it all. At the same time the wealthy Vereeniging tot het Vormen van eene Openbare Verzameling van Heedendaagsche Kunst (Society for the Formation of a Public Collection of Contemporary Art), or VvHK, was looking for a home. The city council and the 'society with the long name' (as it was understandably nicknamed) got together and the museum opened in 1895. It wasn't until the early 1970s that the last of Sophia Augusta's bric-a-brac was dispersed to specialist museums and the Stedelijk became devoted exclusively to modern art.

Successive directors have left their imprint on the collection, but it was the imagination, energy and skill of Willem Sandberg – 'part poet, part artist, part designer, part administrator, part magician' – that between 1945 and 1963 established the Stedelijk as one of the world's leading modern art museums. He built up an important collection and held a series of notable, usually controversial, exhibitions. In 1949 there were fisticuffs in the foyer at the opening of the first COBRA exhibition. (COBRA was a group of artists from **Co**penhagen, **Br**ussels and **A**msterdam whose colourful, childlike painting was the first to provoke the response that 'a three-year-old could do better'.) Though that's not happened again, daring new acquisitions still spark off public uproars.

Space is limited, so only a small portion of the collection is shown at any one time. Outside the summer months (May–September) you may even find that much of the museum is taken over by a special exhibition, though present museum policy is to show the core of the permanent collection on a more stable, long-term basis. A plan of what is currently on view is available from the information desk (to the left of the entrance). The catalogue (a survey of the entire collection, in English) is a bargain.

The Permanent Collection

You'll find whatever is being exhibited of the permanent collection up the wide marble staircase, on the top floor.

In 1972 the large **Van Gogh** collection, which had been kept at the Stedelijk, moved next door to its own museum (see p.138). Because Van Gogh is considered so important to modern art, a few paintings were left behind. La Berceuse (The Cradle) was inspired by a story Gauguin told Van Gogh about fishermen who pinned prints of their patron saint – Stella Maris (Maria, Star of the Sea) – to the cabin wall. Van Gogh felt that a portrait of Madame Roulin (a postman's wife), holding a cord for a rocking cradle, would be ideal for such a print. He imagined the seamen 'would feel the old sense of being rocked come over them and remember their own lullabies'. It's a pity that the painting isn't hung the way Van Gogh suggested – as a triptych with sunflower paintings on either side. Don't miss the paintings by **George Breitner**, Van Gogh's contemporary and drinking partner. In The Dam, a view of the famous Amsterdam square, he captures that special Amsterdam light in a way that makes the exact time of year, even the time of day, immediately recognizable. Keep an eye open also for his highly patterned, exotic Woman in a Red Kimono (in reality a hat shop assistant).

The museum has a good collection of modern art classics. You'll probably find **Manet**'s picture of a barmaid (staring out at you saucily), a study for his famous Bar at the Folies-Bergère. There are some gentle **Cézanne** landscapes and a range of **Picassos** – from bright early collages to nudes from his Blue Period. One wall is sure to be filled by **Matisse**'s vast paper cut-out The Parakeet and the Mermaid, done towards the end of his life when his eyesight was too poor for painting, and painstakingly restored in 1996. You'll find at least one of **Kandinsky**'s vivid Improvisations – paintings in which he used colour to represent the sounds of various musical instruments – and some rather good **Chagalls**. The 1960s are well represented by **Warhol** screen-prints, **Roy Lichtenstein**'s comic strip blow-ups, and **Bruce Nauman**'s neon-light installations, and the museum comes right up to date with works by some of the best living European and American artists.

Malevich

The visionary director of the museum Willem Sandberg was responsible for tracking down the Malevich collection, unearthing a treasury of works that had been forgotten in a cellar in Germany. Malevich had left the entire contents of an exhibition for safe-keeping with a friend in Beieren, but was subsequently never allowed to leave Russia. He died in 1935, so there the cache remained (under a pile of rubble after the war) until Sandberg swooped down and bought it in the late 1950s. The museum has a complete range of his work, from early Impressionist pieces, through a Cubist period to the completely abstract – solid shapes of colour on a white background. Malevich composes these shapes at such angles that the paintings seem full of movement.

De Stijl

At around the same time as Malevich was working, De Stijl artists were coming up with very similar work. The best known is that of **Piet Mondriaan** (he dropped the last 'a' to appear French, but the Dutch prefer the original). His Compositions of vertical and horizontal black lines with blocks of primary colours, so shocking at the time, now appear on everything. When **Theo van Doesburg** (co-founder of De Stijl) after 10 years of rectilinear painting produced a Contra-composition, in which he daringly tilted his lines through 45°, Piet left the movement in a huff. They were never reconciled, though Mondriaan later took up the challenge by tilting his canvas through 45° and keeping the lines vertical.

Ground-floor Galleries

Most of the ground floor is given over to travelling exhibitions and applied art.

The small door to the left of the ticket office leads to rooms of odd-shaped **furniture**, gaudy **ceramics** and lumpy **mats**. There's a **video art** room under the stairs, and the glass box extension at the back of the building occasionally displays work (often dire) by **contemporary Amsterdam artists**. Two installations on the ground floor shouldn't be missed. The *Appelbar* (through a door to the right of the information desk), adorned with murals of colourful birds, fish and children, is the work of the COBRA artist **Karel Appel**. It was used as a café until the opening of the present restaurant in 1956. The commission was offered to Appel as a palliative after a débâcle at the *stadhuis* in 1951: a mural in the canteen, commissioned by the Building Department, had to be boarded over when the Catering Department insisted that it would put people off their food. **Edward Kienholz**'s *Beanery* is a near-life-sized version of a poky Los Angeles bar. You can wander about in the dim light, examining the bric-a-brac. Rusty music scratches away in the juke box. There's a murmur of conversation. A couple sit at the bar. Someone has passed out in the corner. A waitress clears the remnants of a disgusting meal. But all the faces of the figures are clock faces and you're the only thing that moves – it is a surreal and rather disorientating experience. Luckily, the real bar (bright and airy) is just across the corridor. Unlike the *Appelbar*, the *Beanery* is not a permanent installation, so sometimes disappears on tour.

Prentenkabinet (Print Room)

Here you could find anything from a **Toulouse-Lautrec** poster to **Mapplethorpe**'s startling close-up photographs of male nudes. Keep an eye open for the innovative work of Dutch photographer **Cas Oorthuys**, and **Roland Topor**'s blackly comic cartoons. Work not on display can be viewed by appointment in the study room.

The Sculpture Garden

Leaving the museum, turn right at the main entrance and then right again down the side of the museum. A gate leads into the small sculpture garden. You can't help noticing the American **Richard Serra**'s 40ft (13m)-high *Sight Point*. The best place to view

these three precariously balanced sheets of steel is from inside the sculpture itself.

The Van Gogh Museum F9

*Paulus Potterstraat 7, **t** 570 5200, **w** www.vangoghmuseum.nl; **tram** 2, 3, 5 or 12, then walk down Paulus Potterstraat; **tram** 6, 7 or 10, then cross the Singelgracht and walk through the walkway under the Rijksmuseum; wheelchair accessible. **Open** daily 10am–6pm; closed 1 Jan; **adm** adults €9, 13–17s €2.50, under-13s free.*

Few artists have a national museum all to themselves, but there's a sad irony in the long queue that snakes back under the simple silver lettering 'Vincent van Gogh' to one side of Amsterdam's top tourist attraction. The lonely artist, who sold just two paintings and got only one good review in his lifetime (*see* 'Vincent van Gogh'), is now the still point in a money-spinning world of multimillion-dollar picture sales, bizarre art theft, pop songs, novels, films and tacky souvenirs.

This museum has really cornered the Van Gogh market, with 200 paintings, 500 drawings, a collection of works by Van Gogh's contemporaries, the letters from Vincent to his brother Theo, Vincent's collections of Japanese woodcuts and 19th-century engravings, a press archive dating from 1899 – and publishing copyright for the lot. The museum was completed in 1973 and is based on an initial drawing by the influential Dutch architect Gerrit Rietveld (*see* p.54), who died before working the plan through. Brave efforts by later architects to realize his rather sketchy ideas produced a hard-edged and unsympathetic building. But in 1999 a new wing by renowned Japanese architect Kisho Kurokawa gave the museum the sort of proud architectural profile it deserves.

Works from the permanent collection are displayed in the old part of the museum (for a discussion of some of these, *see* 'Vincent van Gogh'). The Kurokawa wing is used for temporary exhibitions and houses the

Vincent van Gogh

Vincent van Gogh was born in 1853 in the tiny village of Zundert, near the Belgian border. We have an image of him as a wild, schizophrenic bohemian; a simpleton, out of touch with the world and reliant on his younger brother's handouts. This isn't the full truth. He came from an old Dutch family of clerics, naval officers and gallery owners. Though he was constantly at odds with his relations, and offended almost everyone he met, he was in many ways part of the Establishment. He spoke three languages fluently, had a wide knowledge of European art and had the connections needed to organize two exhibitions of friends' work in Paris. He signed himself 'Vincent' because he thought his surname, difficult for foreigners to pronouce, would be bad salesmanship (you say it with two guttural 'g's – 'fun HGoHG').

Yet all his life he was desperately lonely, dogged by a sense of failure and frustrated by how few people appreciated his art. Towards the end he was beset by bouts of madness which left him exhausted and depressed. He was acutely sensitive to his surroundings. The colours, people, light or weather in one environment would become loathsome to him and the need to move would become consuming. Suddenly he'd up sticks and go – to the sun, to the city, to the country. These moves were often reflected in a change in his work.

Vincent's first job, at the age of 16, was as an assistant with the art dealer Goupil & Cie in The Hague. In 1873 he went to work at the London branch and was impressed by Constable, Turner and especially the Pre-Raphaelite John Everett Millais. An unhappy love affair made him grumpy at work. He began to be rude to customers about their taste, was shuttled between London and Paris and,

finally, dismissed. Still obsessed by his English rose, he returned to Britain as a teacher, but was soundly rebuffed. He went back to Holland to work in a bookshop, but still didn't know what he wanted to do with his life.

But in May 1877 it all suddenly seemed clear: following in his father's footsteps, he set off for Amsterdam to study theology. Greek, Latin and algebra proved an uphill struggle, and after less than a year he went to a crammer for evangelists in Brussels. But he couldn't preach either. Yet again the family pulled strings. The Brussels Evangelist Committee sent him to work among the coalminers of the Borinage in south Belgium, but he was soon dismissed for over-zealous involvement with the poor. He stayed on in a hovel for another year, almost starving to death, and began to draw. He was 26 and had found his direction. His younger brother, Theo, rescued him and started to pay him the monthly allowance that was to be Vincent's only income for the rest of his life.

Van Gogh was largely self-taught, though he spent a brief period studying perspective and anatomy in Brussels in 1880. The following year he fell in love with his widowed cousin, Kee Vos. He stormed into her father's house on the Keizersgracht and held his hand over a candle yelling, 'Let me see her for as long as I can hold my hand in the flame.' But Kee had fled. He was thrown out of home and went to The Hague, where he met members of the Hague School of painting, a movement characterized by muddy colours and gloomy skies. He was given lessons by one of its leading members, Anton Mauve (a cousin by marriage), and was also much influenced by Jozef Isradls' earthy studies of peasants. He was especially friendly with George Breitner, who later became known as one of the best

darkened Print Room, where you can find Van Gogh's **drawings and studies**, and trace some of his influences – sketches by friends, pictures he copied and his collection of Japanese prints and magazine engravings.

The selection on display changes frequently, but you can usually follow his development through some rather conventional Dutch landscapes, with all the expected perspectives, and studies of gnarled hands and

Amsterdam Impressionists. They discovered a mutual interest in Zola and together drew the street life in the seedier parts of town. An uncle who had commissioned 12 views of the city was horrified by Vincent's unconventional approach and refused to pay up. The relationship with Mauve grew tense when Van Gogh began to reject the older painter's advice, and family relations soured on a wider scale when it became known that he was living with the prostitute Sien Hoornik 'in order to reform her'.

In September 1883 Van Gogh suddenly left The Hague for the countryside of Drenthe in the north of Holland. He had begun to paint in oils, but still with a muddy Dutch palette. The good people of Drenthe thought him a dangerous lunatic and a tramp, and refused to pose for him – so this became a period of landscapes with small figures in the distance. After a few months, loneliness drove him to a reconciliation with his parents and he went back south to live with them in Nuenen. Weavers and peasants in the surrounding Brabant farmland were his dominant motif. The period culminated in the dim glow and gravy browns of *The Potato Eaters* (1885). Van Gogh loved this 'real peasant picture' – he felt you could smell the bacon, smoke and potato steam.

In *The Old Church Tower at Nuenen*, the tower stands crooked and solitary in a flat, empty churchyard, while crows flutter against the overcast sky. Van Gogh painted it in May 1885, a few months after his father, an unpopular preacher in a declining sect, had been buried there, and just before it was demolished and all the wood – including the graveyard crosses – sold to peasants. *Open Bible, Extinguished Candle and Book* (1885) has been seen as Vincent's homage to their difficult relationship.

Margot Begemann, a neighbour, took poison after her family had refused permission for her to marry Vincent. She survived, but Vincent got the blame and the village turned against him. He went to Antwerp, studied Rubens, covered his walls with Japanese prints and enrolled in the academy – which he left a few months later without ever learning of the academy's decision to demote him to the beginners' class. He then went to Paris, and moved in with his brother, Theo. The first few canvases in Paris (such as *View over Paris*, 1886) still use the Dutch browns and greys. But when Theo introduced him to a few Impressionist friends, the shock of their fresh, bright canvases changed Vincent for life. At first the colour creeps in gradually (*Woman Sitting in the Café du Tambourin*; 1887), but soon he is copying the flat colours of the Japanese prints and painting some of the familiar bright self-portraits. He began to long for harder light and a less hectic milieu than Paris could offer. Writing to his sister Wil about *Self-portrait at the Easel* (1888), he draws her attention to his sad expression. He's had enough of Paris and wants the sun.

On 20 February 1888 Vincent escaped to the Mediterranean warmth of Arles in the south of France. Here in the famous 'Yellow House', which he shared for a while with Gauguin, his best-known works were painted. It is hard to believe that the raucous yellows and bright reds and blues of *Harvest at La Crau* were painted only three years after *The Potato Eaters*. Look closely at one of the versions of *Sunflowers*. Between the greens and yellows are bright streaks of ice blues, mauves and reds – colours you never notice in the reproductions. Portraits of the postman, Roulin, and his wife are drenched in sun and colour. Even the *Night Café* has a bright,

heavily jowled peasant faces to the wild movement of *Women Dancing* (1885). **Millet**'s *Labours of the Field* and woodcuts by **Hiroshige** and **Kesai Yeisen** clearly had an influence on some of Van Gogh's better-known oils.

The museum also has an exceptionally good **library**, where you can look at photographs of Vincent's letters to Theo. Various training courses, and artists' activities are held regularly.

steamy heat. The solitary **Sower at Arles** works under an enormous yellow orb in a green and pink sky. The most ordinary things around him evoke intense response. Vincent's **Bedroom at Arles** is filled with a brilliant light, but the smooth paintwork, the mauves and blues of the walls have a calming effect.

Van Gogh was very excited by Gauguin's arrival on 20 October 1888 and went to great pains to furnish his room comfortably. The money to do this, of course, came from Theo. **Gauguin's Chair** shows a piece Vincent bought for his friend (elaborate in comparison with his own). On the seat are novels intended to indicate Gauguin's spirituality and modernism. A candle burns as well as the gas light, to suggest Gauguin's fiery nature. Together they visited nearby towns such as Les Stes-Maries-de-la-Mer, where Vincent painted **Boats on the Beach**. The small red, green and blue boats had reminded him of flowers.

Gauguin's stay was not a happy one. The two artists had tempestuous arguments. After a particularly violent dispute on Christmas Eve, Vincent threatened Gauguin with a razor, then slashed off his own right ear and presented it to a prostitute who had complimented it. Gauguin left for Paris. Another nervous crisis followed Van Gogh's recuperation, and he was voluntarily admitted to the asylum of St-Paul-de-Mausole at St-Rémy. Paintings from this period – usually of fields around the asylum, the hospital garden or of individual trees and flowers – are in softer hues. In February 1890 Vincent painted **Branches of an Almond Tree in Blossom** for Theo's newly born son – blossom-laden branches stand out against an eggshell-blue background.

By May he felt well enough to leave the asylum, though he could only bear Paris for three days. He travelled to Auvers-sur-Oise, where an eccentric art-lover, Dr Gachet, promised to keep an eye on him. But Vincent became more and more overwrought: his colours became harder, brushstrokes more violent. In **Crows in the Wheatfields** (July 1890) it seems difficult for the birds to fly into the thick, dark sky. A path curves and goes nowhere. One of his last paintings, **Roots and Tree Trunks**, has even more disorientating perspectives and thick layers of paint in unexpected colours. The painter seems completely self-engrossed, and the viewer is quite alienated.

On 27 July 1890, Vincent went into the fields and shot himself, but he bungled even this. He staggered back to the inn where he was staying and died on 29 July, in Theo's arms. After a short illness, Theo himself died six months later, at the age of 32. The brothers are buried side by side in the churchyard at Auvers-sur-Oise.

Dedication, or desperation, drove Theo's widow – Johanna van Gogh-Bonger – to promote the works stacked all over her apartment. The art world began to take notice. In 1891 there was an exhibition in Brussels, followed by numerous others all over the Netherlands and in Paris. After Johanna's death in 1925, her son, Vincent's namesake, took over the collection and in 1931 put it on permanent exhibition in the Stedelijk Museum in Amsterdam. To prevent the break-up of the collection after his death, the Van Gogh Foundation was formed in 1960 and set about building the present museum. With three members of the Van Gogh family on the board of the foundation, there's a feeling that it's still very much a family concern – and Vincent, once the black sheep, is again part of the Establishment.

Concertgebouw F10

Concertgebouwplein 2–6, t 671 8345; tram 2, 3, 5, 12, 16. **Box office open** *daily 10am–7pm. Free lunchtime concert Wed 12.30pm.*

The Concertgebouw at the southern end of the Museumplein square was designed by A.L. van Gendt (one of the collaborators on the Centraal Station design) and completed in 1888. It is solid Dutch neo-Renaissance; no frivolity here – indeed, the few urns and obelisks he included in the design either never went up for lack of funds, or have fallen off through lack of funds. The twin staircase towers are intended to harmonize with Cuypers' Rijksmuseum across the way (more out of toadyism than artistic integrity – Cuypers headed the committee that chose the design). Busts of Beethoven, Bach and Sweelinck (Holland's one claim to musical fame) grace the façade. The gilded lyre on top is a 1960s replacement of the original (which fell off). The entrance is no longer through the front, but through a shiny glass extension built in 1988 as part of a renovation of the building, which had been subsiding. It certainly meets the manager's stipulation that, if there was to be a new front door, he didn't want to have to hang an 'Entrance round the corner' notice on the old one.

In the 1870s, Amsterdam, a city with metropolitan aspirations, found itself without a concert hall and with Brahms' admonition ringing in its ears: 'Ihr seid liebe Leute aber schlechte Musikanten' (You are lovely people but awful musicians). The government maintained that art was not its business, so it was a committee of private citizens that raised the money, bought some cheap land outside the city limits next to an evil-smelling candle factory and commissioned Van Gendt (more for his figures than his design). Van Gendt prided himself on being a salesman rather than an artist and was completely unmusical. It is ironic that he should have produced a concert hall with possibly the best acoustics in the world.

Under the baton of conductors like Mengelberg (who was sacked for his Nazi sympathies in 1945 after 50 years of service) and Haitink, the resident **Royal Concertgebouw Orchestra** has become world-famous. If you're passing on a Wednesday, pop in for a free 'lunch concert' (12.30pm, though it's a good idea to be there by noon). These are usually recitals given in the Kleine Zaal (Small Hall – a chamber music room upstairs), but if you're lucky you might catch the RCO itself in open rehearsal in the Grote Zaal (Big Hall – the main auditorium).

Coster Diamonds F9

Paulus Potterstraat 2–6, t 305 5555, w www.costerdiamonds.com; tram 2, 3, 5, 12. Open daily 9am–5pm; adm free.

Jews fleeing persecution in Antwerp set up the diamond-polishing industry in Amsterdam in the 16th century. Roaring trade with South Africa established it in the 19th century. (Diamond-cutters would light their cigars with a 10-guilder note, more than the average weekly wage.) The city is still a focus for diamond-dealing and processing. This means you can buy the gems for half the price you'd pay in London or New York. All over the city, factories invite you in to see the craftsmen at work in order to lure you into their salerooms.

Coster Diamonds is one of the biggest. The 'Koh-I-Noor' (Mountain of Light), one of the prize gems in the British crown jewels, was cut here, and there's a glassy replica in the exhibition hall. Smart, uniformed hostesses conduct you on a short tour through the cutting and polishing works (done with whizzing discs coated with diamond dust and olive oil) and then propel you past a room temptingly labelled 'Self-service' (it turns out to be a café) into the jewellery shop. It's an interesting ten minutes, though if you want to buy, it might be worth shopping around.

Pieter Cornelisz. Hooftstraat F9

This is Amsterdam's most chic shopping street, named after a 17th-century poet. It's one of the few streets in the city where you can confidently window-shop without fear of stepping in dog turds. There is a handful of smart restaurants and sleek cafés along here, but mostly it's clothes: shops for the hip toddler or the fashion-anxious adolescent. If you're of voting age then things range from well-cut classics to the outré (well, almost). Just about all the favourite names (Armani, Gucci, Hamnett, MaxMara, Stephane Kelian) can be found. Van Baerlestraat, which crosses

Hooftstraat, is home to some of the better Dutch designers – Edgar Vos, Rob Kroner and Sissy Boy.

VONDELPARK

Tram 1, 2, 3, 5, 6, 12.

During the so-called 'Second Golden Age' at the end of the 19th century, when the butter market was turned into Rembrandtplein and the neighbourhood around the museums was being developed as an upmarket residential area, some local burghers got together to commemorate the poet by creating the Vondelpark. It's a large park by Amsterdam standards and J.D. Kocher's informal English landscaping gives it calm, graceful lines and wide perspectives. Curved tree-lined avenues, irregularly shaped lakes, little paths through shrubberies, hidden gardens and wide stretches of lawn attract Amsterdammers from all over the city – especially at weekends. A lone accordionist sits on a bench and plays for the ducks. Refugee guitarists from South America play heartrending tunes. Jugglers meet to learn, practise and show off. There's a party atmosphere whenever the sun shines, and in the summer the festivities go on into the night, with concerts, theatre and an open-air cinema. On holidays (especially 30 April) enjoyment reaches carnival pitch.

There are dainty bridges, a few sculptural surprises and some odd architecture to catch your eye. Entering the park, you can see, across the pond, one of the more attractive examples of Nieuwe Zakelijkheid (Functionalist) architecture: H.J. Baanders' **'t Ronde Blauwe Theehuis** (Round Blue Teahouse), a cross between a pagoda and a flying saucer that seems to hover over the water. Across the way, **Vondel** himself, in badly fitting laurels, looks gouty, prosperous and entirely oblivious of the Muses playing at his ankles. His ornate pedestal was made in 1867 by P.J.H. Cuypers (architect of the Centraal Station and Rijksmuseum).

Joost van Vondel

Joost van Vondel (1582–1674; pronounced in the way an old English army officer might say 'fondle') is proclaimed the Dutch answer to Shakespeare. He excelled in ornate poems in celebration of public events, clocking up over a thousand lines for the opening of the stadhuis alone. The lack of action in his dramas is notorious: he went in for static pictorial representations accompanied by long flowery descriptions of anything exciting. His play Gijsbrecht van Amstel is a Dutch literary classic. It's said that one of the scenes inspired Rembrandt's The Night Watch. By all accounts the Master would have had quite enough time to paint it during the performance.

From humble beginnings in his father's busy hosiery shop on the edge of the Red Light District, Vondel built up a considerable reputation and small fortune. The former counted for little in mercantile Amsterdam when his son squandered the latter. At the age of 70 he had to go back to work in the city pawnbrokers. He was sacked after 10 years' service for writing poetry in office hours and finally, in his 80s, was granted a state pension. He died at 92 of hypothermia, and suggested his own epitaph:

Hier ligt Vondel zonder Rouw,
Hij is gestorven van de kou.
Here lies Vondel, without regret [or unmourned],
He was killed by the cold.

Nederlands Filmmuseum E8

Vondelpark 3, **t** 589 1400, **e** info@film museum.nl, **w** www.filmmuseum.nl; **tram** 1, 2, 3, 5, 6, 12; wheelchair accessible. **Shows** from the archive, details published in listings magazines. **Library open** Tues–Fri 10am–5pm, Sat 11am–5pm.

On your right as you enter Vondelpark, the museum is housed in the pavilion designed in 1881 by P.J. and W. Hamer. The first director, Jan de Vaal, was a voracious but secretive collector. He hoarded his treasures and seemed wary of the outside world. The result was that no one bothered about the film museum until the dynamic duo – director Hoos Blotkamp and film buff Eric de Kuyper – took over in the late 1980s and discovered an archive of world significance. Funding was secured, the building was revamped, the long process of cataloguing begun (unearthing such gems as hand-coloured silent movies) and the occasional screenings were boosted to three times a day. There are all sorts of special events, and films are shown in the original language. On summer Saturdays there are free screenings on the terrace (around 10pm), when you can buy a beer and giggle at the likes of Charlie Chaplin.

The **main hall** is worth a peek. Its interior is from Amsterdam's first cinema, the Cinema Parisien built in 1910. The Parisien had declined ungracefully into a porn pit when the daughter of the original owner heard, in 1987, that it was about to be gutted by the hotel next door. Armed with coffee flask and screwdriver she went to rescue the interior (still intact after a 1930s redecoration) and, aided by the Monuments Trust, the old atmosphere was bottled and transferred to the film museum. The **library**, with a good selection of magazines and reference works and a stash of posters and publicity material, is in the building alongside the pavilion.

Vondelkerk E8

In the centre of the roundabout on Vondelstraat; tram 1, 3, 5, 6, 12.

The grand 19th-century Gothic Vondelkerk (Heilige Hartkerk) fills a tiny oval in Vondelstraat. The architect P.J.H. Cuypers was highly respected for his churches, and this is acknowledged as one of his best. Unfortunately it's been converted to offices, so the interior is lost. The houses at **Vondelstraat 73–9** were also designed by Cuypers. The tiled tableaux on the wall show the architect, the mason and the jealous critic. The motto translates as: 'Jan conceives it, Piet realizes it, Claes tears it apart. Oh, who cares?'

Hollandsche Manege E8

Vondelstraat 140; tram 1, 3, 5, 6, 12. **Open** *Mon 2pm–1am, Tues–Fri and Sun 10am–1am, Sat 10am–5pm.*

Through an arch and up a long passage off Vondelstraat lies one of Amsterdam's best-kept secrets. As you walk up towards the black door at the end of the passage, you'll notice a clue – the earth and cumin musty smell of horses. Open the door and suddenly you are in the vast, light and eerily silent Hollandsche Manege (Dutch Riding School).

The architect, A.L. van Gendt (who also designed the Concertgebouw), was influenced by the Spanish Riding School in Vienna. The beautifully plastered interior, with horses' heads worked into the Classical design and elegant open iron roofing, comes as a complete surprise.

Walk up the wide staircase (to the left) past marble vases and gilded mirrors, and you come to two more doors. The one marked 'Tribune' leads to a balcony overlooking the **arena**. Sawdust muffles all sound and the occasional sharp command from the instructor is all that breaks the thick silence. The door marked 'Foyer' takes you to a **café** that runs the width of the building. It has the relaxed grandeur of a palace stables. The wooden floor is dusty; there's even an odd wisp of straw. The tall smoke-yellowed walls are encrusted with plaster flowers and Graces. An 18-stick brass candelabra hangs from the ceiling. A brass stallion shies at the clock on the mantelpiece. More gilded mirrors. You can see the horses in the arena through glass doors all up one side of the café – and the drinks are the cheapest in town.

Roemer Visscherstraat E–F8

Tram 1, 2, 3, 5, 6, 12.

Here you'll find a row of quaint 19th-century houses (Nos.20–30A) designed to illustrate seven national architectural styles: German, French, Spanish, Italian, Russian, Dutch and English.

Outside the Centre

Amsterdam is a compact city, whose outer districts begin beyond the U-shaped boundary of the canal belt. Most points of interest are easily accessible by tram, or even on foot. Just east of Museumplein is the lively De Pijp district, which boasts the Albert Cuypmarkt – a vibrant stretch of stalls that extends for more than a mile – while the secluded New South is a nook of eccentric modern architecture that few visitors know about. To the east lie the grassy stretches of Oosterpark and the colourful Tropenmuseum. And there's also the port of Amsterdam, stretched along the River IJ, with various boat- and trade-related attractions.

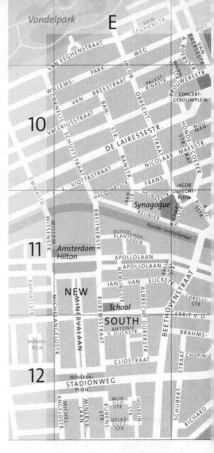

DE PIJP

The area between the Amstelkanaal and the Singelgracht is known as De Pijp (The Pipe), for the long thin passages between the 19th-century tenement houses. Once a slum, it's now a lively neighbourhood populated by artists and immigrant communities. For a walk through De Pijp and the New South, taking in Amsterdam School architecture, *see* 'Walks', p.166.

Heineken Experience H9

Stadhouderskade 78, **t** *523 9666,* **w** *www. heinekenexperience.com;* **tram** *6, 7, 10, 16, 24.* **Guided tours** *only, Tues–Sun 10am–5pm (last tour 5pm),* **adm** *€7.50.*

This brewery on the north edge of De Pijp is the birthplace of Heineken beer. It was established here in 1867 and stopped production on this site only a few years ago when Amsterdam began to drink more than the brewery could produce. Now smart guides lead you through the stables (old dray horses in situ) and past huge copper vats; the real purpose of the visit, however, seems to be the free beer at the end of the tour.

Albert Cuypmarkt H10

Albert Cuypstraat; **tram** *4, 16, 24, 25.* **Held** *Mon–Sat 9.30am–5pm.*

The streets seem to get ever brighter, busier and noisier as you close in on the Albert Cuypmarkt, where everything explodes into a cacophony of national musics, a kaleidoscope of colour and a press of eager shoppers. Between the piles of silk, gaudy modern clothes and cheap shoes, boxes of dried herbs and teas, people slip raw herrings down their throats, guzzle home-made chocolates, queue for freshly cooked waffles, taste farm cheese and stock up on fish, fruit and vegetables. Behind the stalls there's yet another layer of life – tacky clothing shops, ethnic stores and cheap Indian, Chinese and Surinamese restaurants.

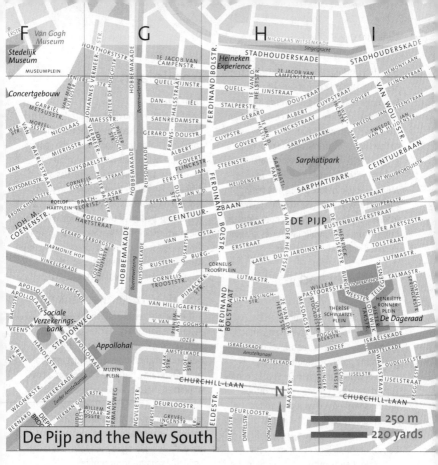

De Pijp and the New South

Sarphatipark H–I10

Tram 3.

This tiny but rather pretty park was named after Samuel Sarphati, a 19th-century philanthropist who was bent on pushing the town headlong into another Golden Age. With his motto '*Amsterdam Vooruit!*' ('Amsterdam Advance!'), he founded a commercial college, several banks, a construction company, the city's first hygienic bread factory, the Amstel Hotel (still one of the best in town) and an efficient and profitable refuse-disposal service (the city's stinking waste was shipped out in sealed barges, composted and sold to farmers). He founded the Vereniging voor Volksvlijt (Industrial Society) to knock new life into the city's manufacturers and to inject new technology into the factories. His sparkling glass Palace of Industry rose up on Frederiksplein and was home to countless displays, exhibitions and concerts until it burnt down in 1929.

THE NEW SOUTH

The Nieuw Zuid, or New South, was created by the architect H.P. Berlage (1856–1934), the father of modern Dutch architecture (*see* p.54), after a new law had revolutionized Amsterdam housing conditions. In 1915–17 he drew up a plan of wide avenues and narrow side streets that reflected the 17th-century canals. He died before he could implement it, and his work was taken on with even greater enthusiasm by Michel de Klerk and Pieter Kramer, architects of what became known as the Amsterdam School (*see* 'The Amsterdam School', p.167).

De Klerk was a working-class *wunderkind* headhunted from school to begin work with the city's leading architectural firm at the age of 14. He and Kramer set out to design buildings that were, in his words, 'sensationally shocking'. They were successful. When the New South was finished nobody wanted to live there. The area eventually became a ghetto for Jews fleeing persecution in Germany (the Frank family lived on Merwedeplein before going into hiding). In the past few years there's been a revival of interest in the Amsterdam School. Houses, bridges and even public lavatories are being declared national monuments.

De Dageraad I11

Tram 4, 12, 15.

In 1918 the housing association De Dageraad (Daybreak) gave the architects Kramer and De Klerk (*see* above) free rein to design the patch of streets and squares south of Ceintuurbaan in De Pijp. Strikingly curved staircase towers, wavy rooftops, jutting sharp-edged windows and fancy-coloured brickwork are the results of this freedom from restriction. The buildings may be wonderful to look at, but residents complain their furniture doesn't fit in the odd-shaped rooms.

The two crescents of **Burgemeester Tellegenstraat** are completely symmetrical. Look at the lettering in the doorways. You'll occasionally even find corresponding lettering on one side reflected in mirror image on the other. The barn-like houses on **Thérèse Schwartzeplein** are among the last De Klerk built – he died in the 1930s. Tiny butterfly-wing windows interrupt vast sheets of yellow brick (it must be dark in there). The houses are linked by bulbous little balconies and tall arrow-shaped chimneys. On **Pieter Lodewijk Takstraat**, on the side of the building opposite the footbridge, are powerful sculptures of rearing horses and straining figures, *De Geboorte van de Daad* (The Birth of the Deed), some of Hildo Krop's best work (*see* 'The Amsterdam School', p.167). De Dageraad is described in more detail in the 'Amsterdam School Walk', p.166.

Apollolaan D11–G12

Tram 5, 24.

The desultory **trio** on the central island of Apollolaan, at the corner of Beethovenstraat, commemorates the shooting on the spot of 29 people by the Germans in reprisal for Resistance action in 1944. There was a different kind of commotion here in 1969 when John Lennon and Yoko Ono staged a week-long 'bed-in' at the **Amsterdam Hilton**, the starting point of their world campaign for peace. For €910 a night you can stay in the same room as the late Beatle, surrounded by John and Yoko memorabilia (*see* also p.211).

Sociale Verzekeringsbank F12

The Sociale Verzekeringsbank (Social Insurance Bank; 1937–9) rises out of the surrounding domestic architecture like a huge ocean liner. It has an almost magical monumentality, but doesn't seem at all out of place. Its shape is even echoed in the curved windows of the houses towards the end of the terrace. Alas, a rather unfortunate cake-tin-shaped addition, added around the base of the building in the 1990s, has rather spoiled its magnificent profile.

Apollohal G12

The Apollohal (a sports hall) is an early example of Nieuwe Zakelijkheid (the functional concrete-and-glass style that began in the 1920s, begetter of many 1960s monstrosities). Neglected and rather sad, it's hard to judge whether it was ever pleasing to look at. The **bridge** beside it is by Kramer.

Beethovenstraat E14–F11

Tram 5, 24.

Beethovenstraat is a chic but unimaginative shopping street mainly frequented by children of diplomats and bored expatriate housewives. Look west along Gerrit van der Veenstraat and you will see the **clocktower** marking the school building used as the Gestapo headquarters during the war. The Frank family (*see* p.123) were brought here after their capture.

Churchill-laan G–112

Tram 12, 15.

Across the Zuider Amstelkanaal is the leafy stretch of Churchill-laan – an avenue where even the trams appear to run over grass. Look out for little sculptures by Krop set into the walls, Expressionist lettering and some bizarre front doors.

At the west end of the avenue is the **Amstel Boat Club**, which reverberates with the hearty shouts of boaties. They brave the vilest weather and seem to resent the occasional winter freezes when the rest of the world comes out to skate.

FAR SOUTH

COBRA Museum Off maps

Sandbergplein, Amstelveen, t 547 5050; tram 5, 51 to Binnenhof or Oranjebaan; wheelchair accessible. Open Tues–Sun 11am–5pm, closed 1 Jan, 30 April, 25 Dec; adm €6, 5–16s €2.50.

Temporary exhibitions and permanent displays focusing on COBRA, one of the most important Dutch art movements (*see* 'Art and Architecture', p.51).

Amsterdam ArenA and Ajax Museum Off maps

Arena Boulevard 3, t 311 1333, e mail amsterdamarena.nl, w www.amsterdam arena.nl; metro Strandvliet; wheelchair accessible. Museum open daily 9am–6pm; closed match days; adm for museum adults €3.50, under-13s €2.50; with tour adults €8.20, under-13s €7.20.

If you can't catch a match, take a tour of the huge state-of-the-art soccer stadium and then visit the Ajax museum. With a capacity of 51,000, the stadium looks like an enormous flying saucer. The tour includes the dugouts and the pitch itself, the top of the stands and the press room. In the museum are many of Ajax's trophies, and videos of some of the club's greatest moments.

OOSTERPARK AND THE EAST

The working-class district around Oosterpark is not high on the typical tourist agenda, with most visitors venturing no further than the **Muiderpoort**, or Old City Gate, at the end of Plantage Middenlaan. **Oosterpark** itself is a pleasant enough place to stretch your legs beyond the bustle of the centre. Like Vondelpark, its arcing pathways and slender ponds were landscaped during the 19th century in the English style.

Further afield there is really not that much to detain the visitor, with the exception of Amsterdam's cheapest general market on **Dapperstraat** (one block east of Linnaeusstraat), where you encounter members of the North African, Middle Eastern and Indonesian communities, who set up their colourful stalls alongside one another.

Tropenmuseum (Tropical Museum) L–M8

Linnaeusstraat 2, t 568 8215, w www. tropenmuseum.nl; tram 9, 10, 14; bus 22; wheelchair accessible. Open daily 10am–5pm, closed 1 Jan, 30 April, 5 May, 25 Dec; adm €7.50, under-17s €3.75.

The Tropical Museum is housed in a highly ornamented 1920s building, its façade an extravagant hotchpotch of Dutch architectural styles. Inside, the central gallery rises 72ft (24m) to its glass dome.

Reconstructions of villages, street scenes or huts in Africa, India, South America and Indonesia are the high point of the museum, complete with smells and a soundtrack. There are displays of musical instruments, tools, fabrics and jewellery, along with video documentaries dealing with Developing World issues. The affiliated bookshop is well stocked with material and makes a rewarding enough place to browse.

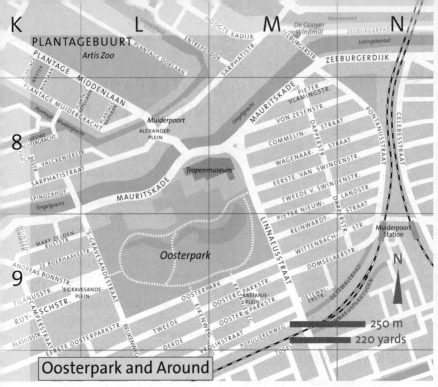

THE RIVER IJ (HET IJ)

Ferry (free) leaves landing platform 7 behind Centraal Station every 7mins 6.30am–9pm, and every 15mins 9pm–6.30am.

The grand, gilded red-brick Centraal Station (*see* p.97) so effectively blocks out the city's view of the water that the harbour on its back doorstep comes as a complete surprise. The River IJ is quite narrow at this point, so the modern docks have moved far out to the west.

Most of the *steigers* (piers) now provide mooring for tour boats and the water police. Two (free) ferries that look like floating air-traffic-control buildings work in tandem, making the journey to the opposite bank (the crossing takes only a few minutes). There, in the shadow of the towering Shell laboratory, you'll find a neat country lane of dapper wooden cottages, cheerful houseboats, gardens and trees.

The wide wooden houses found in **Buiksloterweg** date back to the 16th century

and are examples of a style that has pretty much entirely disappeared from the city centre.

SCHEEPVAART-BUURT

A brass propeller and black anchor stand on the street corners at the eastern end of Brouwersgracht, across the bridge from Koepelkwartier (*see* p.97). These mark the beginning of the Scheepvaartbuurt (Shipping Neighbourhood) to the west of Stationsplein.

Brouwersgracht G3–H4

Bus 18, 22.

The Brouwersgracht ('Brewers' Canal') is quintessential Amsterdam. Its neat, gabled houses, humped bridges and shady towpaths feature in almost every brochure intended to lure you to the city. Yet the crowds that tramp up and down the grand canals seem to pass it by. There are no neon lights or noisy cafés. It's a quiet, residential canal for the hopelessly romantic. Most of the houses are converted warehouses. In the 17th century the Brouwersgracht, right at the harbour's edge, seethed with traders and reeked of fish and beer. Stockfish warehouses and no fewer than 24 breweries crowded its banks. Amsterdam had to import fresh water from the surrounding countryside to feed its industries and populace. Most of the long flat boats carrying this water entered the city along the Brouwersgracht, so breweries sprang up along the canal that afforded them the pick of the incoming supplies.

Westindisch Huis H4

Herenmarkt; bus 18, 22.

The dumpy red-brick exterior of Westindisch Huis (West India House) dates from the 19th century, when it was rebuilt as a Lutheran orphanage. Nowadays it's an adult education college, but you can usually nip in for a glimpse of the 17th-century court-yard – the only remnant of the building's romantic past as headquarters of the West India Company. In the courtyard there's a memorial to Peter Stuyvesant, the notori-ously grouchy peg-legged Governor of Nieuw Amsterdam – the company's chief American trading post. In 1664 he surrendered the settlement to the British, who renamed it New York.

Haarlemmerstraat H4

Bus 18, 22.

Over the past few years Haarlemmerdijk and Haarlemmerstraat have developed into one of the quirkiest and most varied shop-ping quarters in town. New Age stores, junk shops, galleries, zany boutiques and ethnic gift shops all contribute to the appeal. Near the beginning of Haarlemmerstraat you'll have to look hard not to miss **De Groene Lanteerne**, which, at 4ft 2in (1.28cm) wide, claims to be the world's narrowest restaur-ant. Among the more curious attractions is

Beune's confectioners at No.156. If you take them your photograph, they'll reproduce it in icing on the cake of your choice. The result is a white slab with a sombre sepia image, rather like a Portuguese tombstone. There's a shop selling wildly coloured hand-woven Tibetan tiger rugs. A **church** by the 19th-century grandfather of modern Dutch architecture, P.J.H. Cuypers, has (like so many of his others) been converted into offices.

Along Haarlemmer Houttuinen the gaudy daubings in the arches under the railway tracks are part of Amsterdam's **longest painting**. Five hundred yards of bright colour were commissioned of Fabrice Hünd, who seems to have ended up covering up ugly concrete surfaces all over the city. (He's also responsible for the walls of the Stopera car park.) Fabrice's murals are so ubiquitous that one local outdoor artist has taken to signing his work 'not Fabrice'.

Haarlemmerplein F3

Tram 3; bus 18, 22.

Haarlemmer Houttuinen opens out into Haarlemmerplein to the west. Bewildered old men, looking for all the world like retired sailors, sit in rows on the benches, puffing pipes and staring at the traffic as it whizzes round them.

Haarlemmerpoort (a.k.a. Willemspoort), a neoclassical gatehouse built for the entrance of King William II in 1840, takes up all of one end of the square. The masons botched the rather special trompe l'oeil effect that has to be achieved to keep the perspectives right: the central columns appear to taper rather suddenly at the top. It's never been a popular structure. At a town council meeting at the start of the 20th century it was saved from demolition by only four votes. If you walk through the gate you'll see four small rectan-gles set into the second pillar on the left. They mark the position of the old *stokmaat*, the measure by which horses were judged large enough for military service. It was used right up to the First World War.

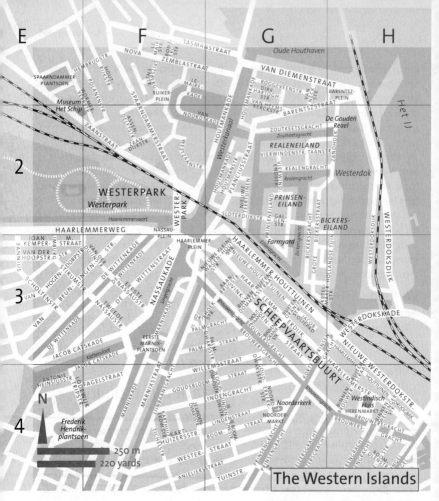

THE WESTERN ISLANDS

The Western Islands are man-made. They're close together, crisscrossed by canals and connected by little wooden bridges. There's an eerie sense of isolation, even though they are nowadays very much part of the mainland. In the 17th century, Amsterdam burst beyond the boundaries that had contained it for generations. More and more land was created by draining off water into new canals. The area of the city increased by nearly 40%. The poet Vondel wrote some histrionic verse in praise of the achievement (as was very much his wont), using the sort of hyperbole usually reserved for military victories. Travellers marvelled at the size and number of the warehouses. Buildings shot up all over the new islands, and were immediately filled with tobacco, salt, tin, wine, draperies, spices, copper, furs, gold – almost any commodity that could realize a profit.

Bickerseiland G2–H3

Tram 3; bus 18, 22, 35.

On Bickerseiland (Bicker's Island, named after the original developer), modern concrete apartment blocks with bright red and blue window frames share the space with soulless 1970s housing estates, ringed by a jumble of houseboats. Rafts, tugs, canal boats, barges – anything that floats (and some things that almost don't) have been commandeered to solve Amsterdam's

Houseboaters

In the 1950s, when the canal transport industry went into an almost terminal decline, skippers were only too pleased to offload their craft on the oddballs who wanted to live on the water. By the 1970s there were around 800 legally licensed moorings and countless illegal ones. The council outlawed all newcomers and granted an amnesty to over a thousand of the unlicensed boats that were already occupied. Recently, moves have begun again to get rid of illegal moorings.

Houseboaters are allowed to connect up to the water and electricity supplies. Arrangements for the latter are alarmingly Heath Robinson. Wonky home-made poles hold up yards of black flex as it snakes along the canalside and between the boats. Wet washing flutters from these improvised clotheslines. The electricity supply is temperamental. Anyone who wants to use a washing machine has to check that the neighbours aren't watching TV, or everyone could be plunged into darkness. There are other drawbacks to boat life – like having to get up in the middle of the night to check your moorings in a storm, or chase off drunk men who pee over the edge of the canal onto your bedroom roof.

Despite the hazards, houseboats are popular. Originally they were the domain of the weird and rebellious, but now lawyers and stockbrokers sun themselves on deck and talk for hours about waterproofing techniques. One boat even houses a community of nuns. But the old eccentrics are still there. From Bickerseiland, if the city council hasn't had its way by the time you visit, you can see the boat of a 'collector', piled high with scrap metal, rusting machines and bits of wood.

chasers whose job it was to keep the aisles free during services.

Farmyard G2

Bickersgracht; tram 3; bus 18, 22, 35.

Surprisingly, here there's a tiny urban farmyard. Fat rabbits lie stretched out in the sun next to curly-horned goats. Various fowl peck about the edge of the concrete. If you find the pong a bit much, hurry on around the corner and over the white wooden bridge to Realeneiland.

Realeneiland G2

Tram 3; bus 18, 22, 35.

Realeneiland is named after Jacob Real, the original owner. Along Zandhoek is a neat little row of 17th-century houses. Jacob Real's own, rather modest house (now a restaurant; *see* p.232) is at the end. He was a fervent Catholic. The gold-painted coin on the gable stone commemorates the treasures he saved from the iconoclasts by smuggling them out of a monastery in the nick of time. Real's surname (also the name of a coin) afforded an appropriate pun, and the house became known as '**De Gouden Reael**'. There's a tang of tar and varnish in the air. The diligent occupants of the rather stately row of boats on the dockside seem perpetually involved in maintenance.

Prinseneiland G2–3

Tram 3; bus 18, 22, 35.

Hidden in the middle of the Western Islands, Prinseneiland is perhaps the most atmospheric island of all. Its little lanes are a mish-mash of architectural styles. Tumbledown warehouses crumble quietly next to smart, sharp-edged new apartments. Tall, carefully restored façades grace the canal. The island is perfumed by freshly sawn timber from the working boatyard. There's seldom any traffic. All you hear is the sound of sawing, workmen calling to each other and (to jolt you back down to earth) pop music from their ghettoblasters.

chronic housing problem. Streetnames like 'Sailmaker's Street' and 'Blockmaker's Street' are all that's left of the shipbuilding yards for which Bickerseiland was renowned. It was also famous for its dogs. There were so many that the local church had to employ two dog-

Tesselschade

One rough night, towards the end of the 16th century, a small trading ship ran aground on one of the treacherous sandbanks around the island of Texel off the coast of North Holland. The young Dutch merchant and man of letters Roemer Visscher was one of the few survivors. That very night his wife (snug in their house on the Engelsekaai in Amsterdam) gave birth to a daughter. Although she was christened Maria, her father felt compelled to mark the coincidence and celebrate his survival by burdening her with the sobriquet 'Tesselschade' (literally 'Tessel/Texel-damage', but with gentler connotations of mischief).

Despite her nickname (and an accident involving a spark from a blacksmith's anvil) Tesselschade went on to become the one-eyed doyenne of Amsterdam salon culture. Her father made sure that Maria and her sister Anne got a sound classical education (a younger daughter, Geertruid, seemed content with embroidery) and that they picked up all the subsidiary skills required to sparkle in erudite society. By the time she was a young woman, the handsome Tesselschade could supply fluent translations of the most complex Latin, Greek or Italian texts, was an accomplished poetess, would entertain delightfully on harpsichord, lute and viol, and had a singing voice of high repute. When some of the older Chambers of Rhetoric (medieval literary societies) joined forces in 1630, it was Tesselschade who won the competition to write a poem celebrating the union.

In the first two decades of the 17th century, the house on the Engelsekaai became Amsterdam's foremost literary and philosophical salon. When their father died, the daughters were snapped up by the poet Pieter Cornelisz. Hooft to join his famous literary circle at Muiden Castle, just outside Amsterdam, where they held court until their respective marriages. The list of Tesselschade's suitors read like a *Who's Who* of Dutch letters – men like Vondel, Bredero, Constantijn Huygens and P.C. Hooft plied her with eulogistic verses. But she finally married a sea captain from Alkmaar. Anne fulfilled her merchant family's social ambitions by marrying a minor nobleman. Tesselschade returned to Amsterdam as a widow in 1640 to resume her position as a literary *grande dame*. When she died in 1649, Huygens compared her to the sun. Yet despite their obvious attributes and the frantic praises heaped upon them, the sisters never appear in any of the group portraits of the Muiden circle. It took a 19th-century painter, J.C. Kruseman, to give the Visscher sisters pride of place among the male luminaries of the Muidenkring, and today (if the painting's not in storage in the cellars) you can see the portrait hanging in the Rijksmuseum.

Galgenstraat G2

Tram 3; bus 18, 22, 35.

Galgenstraat is the narrow street that links Bickerseiland, Prinseneiland and the 'mainland', near Haarlemmerplein. 'Galg' means 'gallows'. The bridge at the eastern end of Galgenstraat used to afford a fine prospect of the city's Golgotha. The curious were not always afforded a view of the whole process. Offenders were often executed in the city centre. The heads, sometimes with the heart stuffed into the mouth, were posted on the city wall and only the discarded bits and pieces ended up on the grassy mound near the Galgenbrug.

Spaarndammerbuurt E1

Off Zaanstraat (just north of Westerpark); bus 22.

Built between the railway line and the harbour between 1913 and 1920, the dwellings in this striking housing complex were made to house dockers and railway workers. Several of the blocks – designed by De Klerk in a distinctly freer Expressionist style than the housing of De Dageraad (*see* p.148) – are often considered to be the crowning glory of Amsterdam School architecture (*see* p.167).

Museum Het Schip E1

Spaarndammerplantsoen 140, t 418 2885, w www.hetschip.nl; bus 22. Open Wed, Thurs, Sun 2–5pm; adm €2.50.

The most eye-catching of De Klerk's buildings in the Spaarndammerburt is known as 'Het Schip' (The Ship). Once a small post office, it has now opened as a museum on the Amsterdam School, with worthy exhibits on the sociological value of the movement, but it deserves a visit for a glimpse of an Amsterdam School interior.

EASTERN ISLANDS AND AROUND

Stedelijk Museum (temporary site) K5

Oosterdoksade, t 573 2911, w www.stedelijk.nl; bus 22 to Nemo (then walk over footbridge); metro Centraal Station.

At the time of writing the Stedelijk (*see* p.136) was due to move to this temporary site while refurbishment is carried out, although there was doubt as to when this will happen.

Scheepvaarthuis J5

Binnenkant; bus 22, 32, 33, 34, 35, 39.

This monumental ship-shaped shipping house was built in 1916 (on the site of the place where the first Dutch fleet set sail for the East Indies) as the offices for six big shipping companies. After serving as the headquarters of the municipal transport authority during the 1980s and most of the 1990s it was closed for renovation, and will probably reopen as a hotel.

It was the first building designed by the team of architects (Van der Meij, Kramer and De Klerk) who became known as the Amsterdam School, a sort of fantastical Dutch Art Nouveau movement (*see* 'The Amsterdam School', p.167). Nothing escapes decoration. The building comes to a prow-like point crowned by a statue of Neptune. He waves his trident while his wife Salicia takes the wheel. Four female figures represent the points of the compass. The walls are encrusted with unflattering reliefs of sea heroes. Doors, stairs, window frames and any wall space left are patterned with appropriate images – wave forms, sea horses, dolphins, anchors, seals and ship's wheels. The roof line is a *cheval-de-frise* of moulded lead. It's as if you're viewing the building in a distorting mirror: there's hardly a smooth surface in sight. Inside, the maritime motifs continue with filigreed metalwork ornamentation, beautiful stained-glass skylights and windows, and much of the original furniture (also designed by the architects). Doorknobs, lamps, wall panels and floor patterns all reflect the theme. No detail is missed.

Pop across the road for a look at the magnificent moustachios of **Prince Hendrik**, 'the seaman' (1820–79). He did a lot to promote sea trade, and the bust was erected in gratitude.

Montelbaanstoren and Around J6

Kalkmarkt; bus 22, 32, 33, 34, 35, 39.

The Montelbaanstoren is a defence tower built in 1512 when the wharves were still outside the city walls. In 1606 (when the tower was no longer used for defence) the builder Hendrick de Keyser added a wonderfully gratuitous spire. This was an activity he apparently enjoyed: he's responsible for much of Amsterdam's spiky skyline. Five years after it was built, the Montelbaanstoren began to tilt over. The good burghers of Amsterdam, unlike their more flamboyant counterparts in Pisa, would have none of it. They attached ropes to the top and pulled it straight again. Rembrandt loved to draw it, and it's still a favourite subject for visiting artists. East India Company sailors left from the Montelbaanstoren to join the large seafaring East Indiamen which were too bulky to navigate as far as Amsterdam and

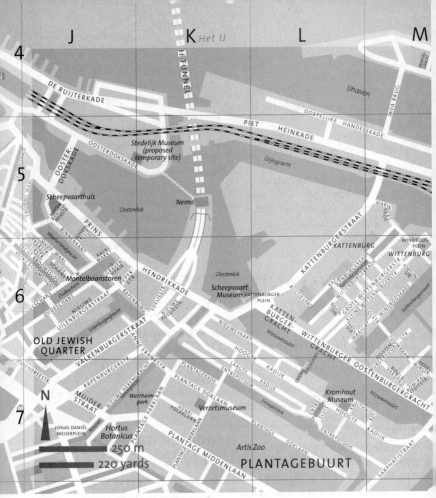

were moored far to the north. These days it houses the city water authority.

There's a delightful grotto of **antiquarian and second-hand books** in a shop opposite the tower. Nearby, sedate and calm **Binnenkant** was created in 1644 to provide more mooring. It was always a quiet spot in the harbour and retains some fine old merchants' houses. On the corner of 's Gravenhekje, over the Oudeschans, you can see the old **warehouses of the West India Company**. Their monogram is on the pediment. In its later years the ailing company gave up its head office in the western docks and moved the administrative sections in here, too. The impoverished owner of No.5, further up the street, had to sell off part of his property to the neighbours, and as they expanded they cut his house in half.

Nemo K5

*Oosterdok 2, **t** 531 3233, **w** www.e-nemo.nl;* ***bus** 22. **Open** Tues–Sun, 10am–5pm; **closed** 1 Jan, 30 April, 25 Dec; **adm** €10.*

Standing right in the centre of Oosterdok, this giant ship-shaped museum is a prominent feature. The building was designed by Renzo Piano (co-architect of the Centre Pompidou in Paris) to look like the prow of a ship. Within its gleaming green flanks are hundreds of interactive exhibits which serve to introduce children to the world of science and technology. Even if the museum doesn't appeal, it is worth climbing the broad sloping 'deck' of the building for great views over the city. In summer this becomes the highly hip 'Nemo Beach' (**w** www.nemobeach.nl), sun-trap-cum-party-space-cum-outdoor-café,

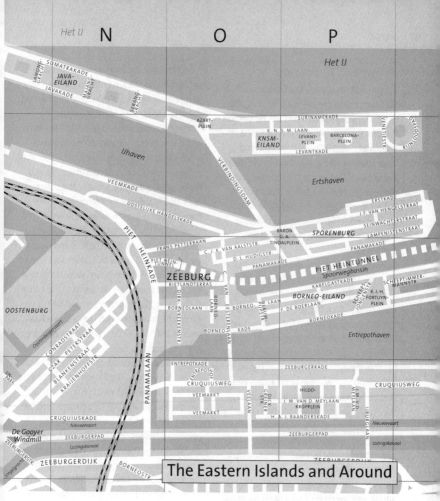

The Eastern Islands and Around

with children's activities during the day, food and drink and a DJ in the evening until 10pm.

Wittenburg, Kattenburg and Oostenburg L5–M6

Bus *22, 32.*

The Eastern Islands (Wittenburg, Kattenburg and Oostenburg) are now joined together by a wide boulevard, but were once not only separate but fiercely isolationist. There are islanders still living who remember neighbours who never once went to central Amsterdam. In 1928 the council built a public bath-house on Wittenburg and a bridge across to Kattenburg. It was a long time before anyone could be persuaded to cross the bridge and bathe on 'foreign territory'.

Scheepvaart (Maritime) Museum K6

*Kattenburgerplein 1, **t** 523 2222, **w** www. scheepvaartmuseum.nl; **bus** 22, 32; wheelchair accessible.* **Open** *Tues–Sun 10am–5pm;* **adm** *adults €7, 6–18s €4.*

Built as an admiralty warehouse in 1655, it's a wonder the building's still upright: construction workers were bribed with 'drinkgelt' (drinking money) and finished it in an amazing 9 months and 14 days. The new warehouse had a system of cisterns and sprinklers to put out fires and an army of rat-catching cats with their own office and keeper.

The museum's main attraction – a full-size replica of the *Amsterdam*, one of the East India Company's ships – is moored outside

Provos and Kabouters

If you walk east from the Scheepvaart Museum, along the avenue that now links the Eastern Islands, towards the De Gooyer Windmill, you'll notice a floating forest of scrap metal and brightly painted wood moored alongside a canalboat in the dock. These crumbling heaps of 1960s flotsam are the vestiges of water-borne sculptures by Robert Jasper Grootveld, one-time window-cleaner and self-proclaimed 'anti-smoke sorcerer and medicine man of the Western asphalt jungle'.

Grootveld and his fellow Provos were the fire beneath the cauldron of the Dutch youth revolution; their antics in the mid-1960s were to influence the course of Dutch politics for decades to come. The Provos (from the Dutch 'provocatie', provocation) began as a literary and philosophical group, but soon became a political expression of the youthful rethinking that was going on across Western Europe and the USA. In their chaotic way they captured the attention and sympathy of older Amsterdammers, and shook up the rigid structures of the Establishment. The groundwork done by the Provos, and their successors the Kabouters – especially in such areas as environmental awareness, drugs advice and squatters' housing problems – went far towards establishing the liberal attitudes prevalent in Holland today.

On Saturday nights, the Provos would gather around the *Lieverdje* on the Spui for a 'Happening'. In 1960 a tobacco company had donated the *Lieverdje* ('Little Darling' – a diminutive statue of a little boy) to the city, and it was becoming something of a landmark. Grootveld branded the statue a symbol of 'tomorrow's addicted consumer'. He and his band would subtly provoke the police with faintly ludicrous performances – like handing out raisins to passers-by while shouting out anti-smoking slogans. The police invariably rose to the bait and would bash a few heads with truncheons and make some arrests. But the Provos were nothing if not master showmen. By the time the police took action, the protesters would have a sympathetic audience on the café terraces around the Spui. At best the police appeared fools; at worst bullies.

The campaign wasn't confined to Saturday nights at the Spui. The Provos frequently met at the 'K-temple', a derelict garage near the Leidseplein, to sing the 'Ugge-ugge-song' (a 'psalm to the smoker's cough'), listen to cryptic addresses on the cigarette industry and submerge themselves in the 'post-sexual electric jesus pandemonium-language' of Arnhem poet Johnny the Selfkicker. They also daubed the letter K (for '*kanker*', cancer) on cigarette advertisements all over town. Later the words *Gnot* and *Klaas kom* ('Klaas is

(though occasionally it pays visits to other ports). You can swan about the captain's cabin and have a look at his tiny loo, then descend into the ship's murky maw, where up to 200 sailors would live for months at a stretch. From the upper deck you can look across to the East India Company warehouses on the end of Prins Hendrikkade, or back over the water to the Nemo science and technology centre (*see* p.156). Beyond that the harbour cranes poke up into the skyline. Don't be alarmed if you see a small figure hurtling off the top of one of them. It's the Amsterdam Bungee-jumping Club at play.

Back in the museum you can see a cutaway of an **1840s outrigger** and the ostentatiously gilded (and rather uncomfortable) **Royal Barge**, used for state occasions and for paddling visiting dignitaries around the canals. You can also climb up to the **Second World War room** to peer out at Amsterdam through a periscope. The rest of the museum comprises room after room of maps, navigational equipment from previous eras, and models and pictures of ships. Everything is informatively labelled in Dutch and English, giving you a good introduction to the history of Dutch seafaring. The **'Time Voyage' multimedia show** takes you a step further, portraying – with smoke machines, movies, slide shows and special effects – how unjolly it was to be a tar in the 17th century.

coming') also appeared. *Gnot* was an amalgam of God and *genot* ('delight') – nobody was ever really able to fathom out what it meant. Nor was anyone sure just who Klaas was. Perhaps it was St Nicolaas, Amsterdam's patron saint. Perhaps it was an oblique reference to Nicolaas Kroese, restaurateur of the famous De Vijff Vlieghen, who wanted to link the towers of Amsterdam's churches with gold chains to form a shield against the destructive forces of the universe.

But the Provos also had a serious side. It was they who fomented the street riots of the mid-1960s and produced the famous White Plans for a better city. Many of these were frivolous or naive, but some – like the provision of 20,000 free White Bicycles to replace cars in the city centre – were seriously considered by the sitting city council. In the 1966 council elections, the Provos polled 2.5% of the vote and won a seat on the council. By 1967, however, the Provos had lost impetus and disbanded.

In 1970 they emerged again as the Kabouters ('Gnomes' – named after a helpful character in Dutch folklore). The leading light this time was sociologist Roel van Duyn, who held the Provo (or ex-Provo) seat on the city council. The Kabouters had a lot of the playful pottiness of the Provos, but with a jot more common sense and pragmatism. In a ceremony on the Dam they proclaimed an

Orange Free State, and inaugurated their own ministers. The Minister of Public Works, for example, was to preside over the planting of more vegetables and the breaking-up of motorways; the Minister of Environment and Hygiene would battle against pollution and for 'biological balance'. The White Bicycles idea became a plan for electric White Cars that was later (unsuccessfully) piloted. They expressed widespread concern that information gathered in a forthcoming census would be correlated on computer, and were chary of the growing powers of corporate industry. The movement caught on around the country, and in the June 1970 elections the Kabouters polled 11% of Amsterdammers' votes, and sent five members to the city council.

Although they have now also largely faded from view (they were officially disbanded in 1981), you can still find the odd ex-Kabouter on neighbourhood committees, or agitating against another Amsterdam architectural ravishment. The Provos and Kabouters have had their day, but the effects of the shake-up that they gave post-war Dutch politics still remain. 'Amsterdam is known as a difficult city, and Amsterdammers are difficult people,' said the *burgemeester* in the midst of the 1965 riots. The Provos were the essence of Amsterdam: at once tolerant and far-sighted, cheeky and difficult.

The museum shop is well provisioned with books on ships, and is a treasure chest of maritime flotsam and jetsam. In an unmarked room in the cellar a man sells model kits of awesome complexity (Thurs–Sat only).

Java-eiland and KNSM-eiland L4–Q5

Track north of Kattenburg, cross the desolate main road that sweeps through the centre of the region, and across the waters of the IJhaven you'll see the former docklands – an area transformed over the last decade into a modern residential district, with beefy

apartment blocks, a series of little water channels for residents to moor their boats, and tiny bridges decorated with elaborate swirls of ironwork. The best way to get to the dockland islands is by the **Javabrug** footbridge, from where there are wide views downriver, past the towering Passenger Terminal where cruise ships offload their passengers. On the other side of the bridge is **Java-eiland**, which extends into **KNSM-eiland**, a stretch of land where design stores and cafés are popping up in numbers. Look out for **Barcelonaplein**, a circular residential block enclosed with a striking six-storey-high ironwork fence. The area is becoming renowned for its bravura contemporary architecture – the homes along Scheepstimmermansstraat on neighbouring **Borneo-eiland** being particular favourites of architecture and interiors magazines. A specialist architectural map of the islands, entitled *Eastern Docklands Amsterdam*, with background information in English and published by the architectural foundation Arcam, is available in better bookshops.

Entrepotdok K–L7

Bus 22.

Just south of the Eastern Islands is Entrepotdok, once a customs-free area where goods in transit could be stored. It was the largest warehouse complex in Europe and recently it was converted into apartments. You'll find the solid **neoclassical entrance** to the Entrepotdok at the west end of the dock. To combat the gloom, the architects created an indoor street at first-floor level, accessible via stairs marked Binnenkadijk. The long row of simple step-gabled warehouses is named in alphabetical order. There's no motor traffic: all you hear is the lap of water and the odd squawk from the nearby zoo (*see* p.114).

Near the entrance to Entrepotdok, the **Scharrenbiersbrug** – named after the cheap beer that used to be sold to smugglers and stowaways – crosses the top end of the Nieuwe Herengracht. The three bridges along this part of the canal are raised in quick succession whenever a boat passes.

Look out for the operator, who bicycles swiftly from one bridge to another, just beating the boat.

Kromhout Museum L7

Hoogte Kadijk 147, t 627 6777; bus 22. Open Tues 10am–3pm; adm €2.

Between Entrepotdok and Nieuwevaart, the Kromhout shipyard, one of Amsterdam's oldest, was one of the few to survive the 19th-century decline in shipbuilding. It had a new lease of life in the 20th century when it produced the diesel engine used by most Dutch inland craft. In the 1960s it moved to larger premises and the old yard became a museum. Some boat building and restoration still goes on, but rows of diesel engines form the bulk of the exhibits. It's very much a place for the enthusiast.

De Gooyer Windmill M7

Funenkade 5; bus 22. Sails turn first Sat of the month.

Near the brightly painted modern bridge to the Eastern Islands, central Amsterdam's last windmill is visible, poking up out of squat 1960s architecture. It was once a grain mill and is now owned by a brewery.

Walks

A *HOFJES* AND HIDDEN MARKETS WALK

The bulk of this walk takes a weaving path through the Jordaan, a fascinating district hugging the western fringe of the Grand Canals. Characterized by tight-packed housing, narrow canals and a multitude of alleyways and hidden courtyards, the Jordaan was laid out during the 17th century to house the city's less wealthy craftsmen and labourers, while the rich merchants took up residence along the spacious Grand Canals. By the beginning of the 20th century the neighbourhood had degenerated into a series of slums, crammed to saturation point with disgruntled workers. Later plans to revitalize the area were unsuccessful, and in 1972 the city council decided to lay waste to the neighbourhood and put up new housing. The plans met with wide protest from a whole cross-section of Amsterdammers, who were determined to preserve the layout and traditions of the neighbourhood. Restored and scrubbed clean, the Jordaan has attracted a wave of wealthy newcomers, along with the inevitable rush of nouveau riche

> **Start**: Lindengracht, near the Noorderkerk (tram 3, 10; metro Centraal Station then 10mins walk).
> **Finish**: Waterlooplein (tram 9, 14; metro Waterlooplein) or Albert Cuypmarkt (tram 4, 16, 24, 25).
> **Walking time**: 2–3hrs, depending on how long you loiter about the market stalls.
> **Suggested start time**: Monday for the Westerstraat market; any day but Friday for De Looier; any day but Sunday for Waterlooplein fleamarket and the Albert Cuypmarkt. Most markets don't get going until 10 or 11am and will close up at 4 or 5pm.
> **Lunch and drinks stops**: Café 't Smalle, *see* p.237; Rooie Nelis, *see* p.238; cafés in De Looier.

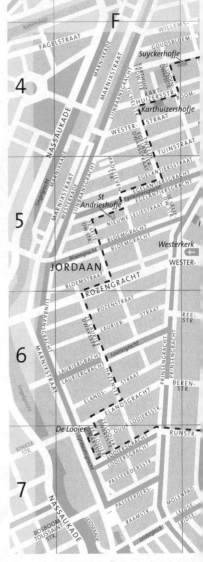

accoutrements, such as galleries, restaurants and trendy boutiques.

Hidden away behind the rows of old houses are a dozen or so *hofjes*, tight squares of housing built around a central '*hof*' or garden. These little oases of calm once served as almshouses for the city's elderly women. Today they are one of the city's hidden treasures. The doors to *hofjes* are open at the discretion of the residents, and it's advisable when visiting to be as discreet as possible. Along the way we also stop in at a number of markets, an Amsterdam tradition since its days as the world's largest port.

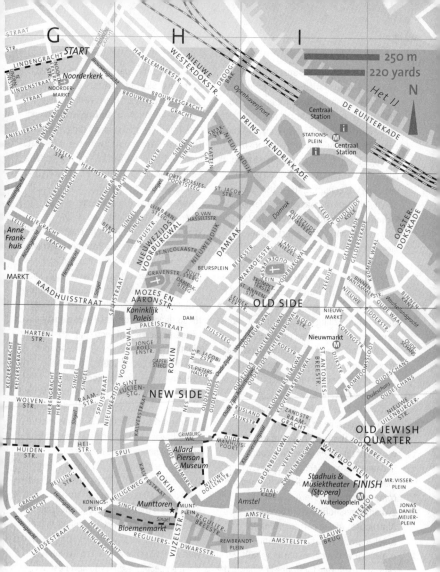

START

250 m
220 yards

N

Het IJ

Begin the walk on **Lindengracht**, just behind the Noorderkerk. This broad tree-lined street, so unlike the narrow mesh of lanes that forms the rest of Jordaan, was once the path of a murky 19th-century canal. The waters were drained after the famous 'eel riot' of 1886, when police intervened during a session of 'eel-jerking'. Find **No.186** and imagine a rope attached to the house and flung across the canal to the opposite terraces. The competition involved stringing a fat eel to the centre of the rope, then rounding up contestants who would row out to the eel and try to wrench it free (without

tumbling into the malodorous waters). When police broke up this cruel game one day in July 1886, it sparked fatal protests from belligerent locals fed up with low wages and poor living conditions. A little further down Lindengracht on the left is **Suyckerhofje** (to the right of No.147, though the house numbers are not sequential). If the door is unlocked, pass through to the tranquil court-yard of this 17th-century almshouse founded by a wealthy merchant to house a lucky bunch of elderly widows and spinsters.

Take the next left off Lindengracht onto Tweede Lindendwarsstraat and follow the street past a playground area with pyramidal-shaped shelters. Turn right onto Karthuizersstraat and you'll soon come to the long red-brick façade and black shutters of the **Karthuizershofje**, also known as the Huyszitten-Weduwenhof, built in 1650. Through the entrance corridor is a beautiful courtyard with two white-fenced gardens and twin water pumps, still in use. Continue down Karthuizersstraat and turn left onto **Tichelstraat**. This little street is pure Jordaan: very narrow, and with a direct tunnel-vision view of the Westerkerk tower half a mile to the south.

When you hit **Westerstraat**, one of Jordaan's main thoroughfares, turn left. If it's Monday this wide street will be littered with market stalls selling new and vintage fabrics as well as general market produce. Take the first right onto **Eerste Anjeliersdwarsstraat**, another pretty narrow lane, lined with second-hand clothes shops, record stores and the odd restaurant. Cross two side streets and you'll come to a brick wall covered with ivy. A tiny passage to the left of the wall leads to the **Claeszhofje** (or Anslohofje). This warren of tiny interconnecting courtyards had fallen into neglect before 1965, when the Claes Claeszhofje Foundation restored the complex, which also includes the old Zwaardvegershofje (Sword Sweepers' Almshouse). At the bottom of Eerste Anjeliersdwarsstraat is **Café 't Smalle**, a little brown bar which began life as an 18th-century *proeflokaal* for Hoppe & Jenever, the first ever distillers of gin. Stop in to sample a wedge of spicy Dutch apple cake with your beer. In Nagasaki an exact reconstruction of 't Smalle provides a touch of cosy Dutch charm.

The bar (our one) sits right on the **Egelantiersgracht**, one of Amsterdam's prettiest canals. Turn right onto the canal and cross the second footbridge. On the left at Nos. 107–14 is **St Andrieshofje**. Open the door, which is usually unlocked, and you'll pass through a passageway of Delft-blue tiles into an isolated courtyard dating from 1616. Carry on down Egelantiersgracht and turn left

onto Derde Leliedwarsstraat. As you cross the next canal, Bloemgracht, look out for the striking step-gabled houses on your left (Nos. 87–91), known as **De Drie Hendricken** (The Three Hendricks), and dating from 1642. The houses are adorned with beautiful plate glass and are identified by a carved stone tablet depicting a city dweller, a countryman and a seaman.

Walk straight on (via Tweede Bloemdwarsstraat) until you reach Rozengracht, then turn right, cross the road and head down **Tweede Rozendwarsstraat**. This road, which changes names at each junction, is lined with galleries and gift shops that bear witness to the arty, ever-upwardly-mobile types who are slowly transforming the Jordaan. Early on you'll pass a dusty **coffeeshop-cum-junkshop** supported by four great ragged tree trunks which reach out into the road. Later, on the corner with Laurierstraat, is the café **Rooie Nelis**, a Jordaan institution worth stopping in at for a drink and a bit of banter. Eventually you'll hit **Elandsgracht**, which, until 1891, was another canal. It was filled in to create easy land access to the vegetable market on Prinsengracht, and it is still a busy street, for the most part lined with parked cars. Head right down Elandsgracht and cross the road. At No.109 is the entrance to the **De Looier Indoor Antiques Market**. This quirky maze of stalls (you're sure to wind up getting lost) is a world unto itself, crammed to the hilt with the unexpected. Even if you never usually give antiques a second glance, it's worth a good half-hour's browse. Erotic etchings, 19th-century ice skates, Art Nouveau vases, over-cuddled teddy bears and stacks of quality china and silverware are some of the things you may come across. And when you fancy a rest, there's a smoky café where decrepit locals, hunched beneath tassled lampshades, chew on cigars and discuss their finds. It's a truly surreal spot.

Leave the market by the café, turning left onto Lijnbaansgracht. Shortly you'll come to Looiersgracht on the left. Walk down alongside the canal and cross Prinsengracht onto

Runstraat. This road is part of the Negen Straatjes, a famous set of 'Nine Streets' which cut across the Grand Canals and are crammed with unusual shops selling art, designer wear, antiques and much more. Towards the end of Runstraat, on the right, is **Witte Tanden Winkel**, which sells nothing but new-fangled toothbrushes. Cross each of the Grand Canals until you reach the Singel. Turn right here and you'll come to **Bloemenmarkt**, the well-known 'floating flower market' which, given its description, is invariably a bit of a disappointment. There has been a flower market on this spot since 1862, when plants and flowers were transported each morning by boat from the horticultural regions of Holland. Today the stock is delivered by lorry, and from the street it's hard to tell that the stalls are floating. There's also a touch of tackiness, with souvenirs and postcard trees poking out from behind the flowers and potted plants. Nevertheless, the short stretch of stalls confronts the passerby with a blinding wash of colour from the stacks of cut flowers, and puts on a formidable display of seeds and bulbs from places as far flung as the Easter Islands. Stallholders are happy to ship things home for you.

Once you come to the end of the market, turn left onto busy Muntplein. Walk past the **Munttoren**, a 15th-century clock tower which was used briefly as a mint, then cross the road and head up Nieuwe Doelenstraat (which runs left of Restaurant Excelsior). Turn left onto Gasthuisstraat and follow the road round past university buildings until you reach the end of Oudezijds Achterburgwal and the entrance to **Oudemanhuispoort**. This passageway was built in 1601 as the entranceway to an elderly men's almshouse – a pair of spectacles carved into the stone lintel above the entrance serves as a reminder of these origins. The passage once comprised a line of tiny shops let to raise funds for the almshouse. Since the tail-end of the 19th century the passageway has been used as a book market, and today, behind numbered alcoves, a long line of trestled tables still display stacks of old books, sheet music, prints and etchings. There's the dim antiquarian air of academia about the place. Halfway along the passage is an opening to a pretty 18th-century courtyard surrounding the bust of Minerva, goddess of wisdom, with university lecture rooms on all sides. The passage emerges under an 18th-century sculpture by Anthonie Ziesenis of a plump *Maid of Amsterdam* engaged in comforting two elderly inmates.

At the end of the Oudemanhuispoort market turn left onto the Kloveniersburgwal canal and then right onto quiet Raamgracht, the body of water that runs along beside the soaring spire of the **Zuiderkerk**. Cross the little footbridge at the end of Raamgracht and you'll drop right into the heart of the daily **Waterlooplein fleamarket**. This is Amsterdam's best-known market, a sprawling mass of stalls that hug the tall walls of the Stopera complex. Waterlooplein was originally an island built on a sandbank in the Amstel. It was a damp, windy spot that was populated by Jews, who were barred from owning shops. So they brought their trade to the streets and the Jewish quarter became the city's most lively trading centre. In 1873 the authorities filled in a couple of canals and created the present-day square, moving the market traders here from the crowded network of surrounding side streets. It became a world-famous marketplace until the Nazi occupation, and has regained some of its old composure only in recent decades. A wide mix of nationalities sell goods, new and old, from all round the globe, some flogging designer wear, others hunkered over cans of fortified lager attempting to pass on unidentifiable items of junk. It's a crowded space ripe for bartering.

If you've got the stamina left for more market stalls, you could round off the walk by heading down to the Monday to Saturday **Albert Cuypmarkt** in De Pijp, a colourful mile-long stretch that forms the country's biggest general market.

AN AMSTERDAM SCHOOL WALK

The first quarter of the 20th century saw the birth of an architectural movement in Amsterdam that would dramatically alter the residential outskirts of the city. Associations were created to provide housing for the working classes, and a group of young architects were let loose on a number of projects, scattering their aesthetic imprint across the city. Their innovation was the creation of a collective architecture in which a series of streets (comprising many thousand homes) was designed as a unified whole. By clothing the concrete skeletons of their buildings in ornate brickwork, they were able to sculpt the apartments into natural and organic shapes. Bulging bay windows and stairwells, waving or pleated tilework and odd-shaped windows are some of the characteristics, as are polychromatic bricks and the integration of sculpture into the design (see 'The Amsterdam School'). This architectural style attracted world attention and became known as the Amsterdam School. Pretty as they are, these buildings were costly and didn't make the best use of space. Later 20th-century housing focused on these problems at the expense of aesthetic appeal. In recent decades, however, the Amsterdam School has shot back into fashion, its leading exponents sometimes referred to as the 'Gaudís of the North'.

This walk explores a compact housing estate at the southern end of De Pijp which was inaugurated by the socialist housing association De Dageraad ('The Dawn') in 1923. Around this time Amsterdam School architects were often brought in to embellish the façades of housing blocks, but this complex is unusual in that the plans are also the work of the style's two principal architects, Piet Kramer and Michel de Klerk. They were obliged to satisfy various conditions, such as a maximum of four floors, but were given free rein on the exteriors, partly due to the support of alderman Wibaut (who fought off accusations of extravagance).

Catch tram 25 from the centre out to the southern edge of the De Pijp neighbourhood. It'll take about 20mins and you'll need to get out on Churchill-laan at the Waalstraat stop. Turn left off Churchill-laan onto **Waalstraat**. The houses along here are late examples of the Amsterdam School and subtle in their approach, though the projecting bay windows and multicoloured bricks are typical. Notice the patchwork brick decorations of Nos.1–5, while No.7 has curving columns of brick around its stairwell and exaggerated archer-slit windows – a hint of what's to come.

At the end of Waalstraat turn left onto **Amstelkade**. The houses along here mimic one another with their wavelike stairwells and striking chimneys. Cross the canal by the white wooden footbridge 30 yards down. Directly in front of you a series of stone sculptures blends into the façade of a large building, which was built as a **school**. Though the sculptures are a little worn, rearing horses and great mythical faces reminiscent of Easter Island heads are visible above the second floor of the building. The works are by Hildo Krop (1884–1970), the municipal sculptor whose artwork is all over De Dageraad.

Turn left off the bridge and then take the first right onto Paletstraat, which leads directly onto **Thérèse Schwartzeplein**. This pleasing square is surrounded by stout trapezoidal houses with small latticed windows and roof tiles running steeply down their flanks. At the intersection of each house are tiny round balconies, which bring to mind

Start: Waalstraat stop on Churchill-laan (tram 25).
Finish: Roelof Hartplein (tram 3, 5, 12, 24).
Walking time: 2hrs, not including lunch or drinks stops.
Lunch and drinks stops: Villa Maas, see p.231; Kong Kha, see p.231; Wildschut, see p.239.

hot-air balloon baskets, though they can't be of much use to the residents. On the north-west corner of the block is another sculpture by Hildo Krop. It's called *Sheaf-binders on the Land*, and if you concentrate on the right side of the sculpture you can see the distant outline of the city against the sky.

Head north of the square onto Thérèse Schwartzestraat, turn right onto Willem Pastoorsstraat, then right again onto **Burgemeester Tellegenstraat**. All along the right-hand side of the street the tiled roofing of this block undulates in waves. Notice also the strange little windows that protrude from the building like interlocking haircombs – eye-catching, though the space inside these houses can't get much natural light. This road converges on a tiny square that forms the centrepiece of De Dageraad. On either corner of **P.L. Takstraat** are two extravagant buildings which mirror one another, exhibiting a wide range of the characteristics of the Amsterdam School. The stairwells of these buildings rise in bulbous steps towards the brickwork lettering of 'De Dageraad'. The tops of the buildings are crenellated like battlement towers, while the brickwork sculptures on the corners are more offerings from Hildo Krop. The slug-shaped benches on the little square, and the monument to Burgemeester Tellegen (on the left face of the square) form part of the ensemble. Tellegen, who died in 1921, did much to encourage housing projects for the working classes, many of whom lived in slums during the early years of the 20th century. The unusual little clock tower which rises from behind his monument is part of the Openbare Leeszaal, which we come to next.

Follow Burgemeester Tellegenstraat round, past housing that mirrors the previous stretch of road. Round the corner is the entrance to the **Coöperatiehof**. Walk through the archway and wander round this pretty little courtyard, which harks back to the old *hofjes*, or almshouses, that pepper the centre of town. The centrepiece of the courtyard is the **Openbare Leeszaal** (Public

The Amsterdam School

In reacting against their sober, rational Dutch predecessors, the Amsterdam School produced an idiosyncratic cross between Old Dutch and Art Nouveau, which has led to some quirky and amusing, but also rather beautiful buildings. You can see why they're sometimes called the 'Gaudís of the North'. As you do this walk, a checklist of some of their innovations might help you to recognize and enjoy the style.

Shape: Their whimsical brick buildings are instantly recognizable by the curves and bulges of their façades. Entire blocks were seen as one building – waves of roofs and balconies give a delightful sense of horizontal movement. Soaring chimneys and stairways accentuate the vertical lines.

Bricks: Decorative, polychromatic, almost sculptural brickwork is used lavishly. Like Berlage, the new builders used 'honest' Dutch materials of wood and brick, but the buildings are constructed around a reinforced concrete frame, so the bricks can do what they like. The pleats and folds earned the movement's work the nickname *schortjesarchitectuur* (apron architecture). Straight edges are often softened by a frill of vertically placed roofing tiles.

Windows and doors: Odd parabolic and trapeziform windows and angulated carved doors contrast startlingly with the general symmetry of the buildings.

Sculptures: Stone and brick sculptures are integrated into the building's design, especially at corners and on bridges. In the Old South these are usually the gnome-like mythical figures by Hildo Krop (1884–1970). Krop was the municipal sculptor for many years and his chunky work is all over Amsterdam. Recently it was revealed that for much of that time he was working for the Soviet KGB, and it's even been suggested that he was involved in the recruitment of Anthony Blunt and other famous British spies.

Details: House numbers, letter boxes and hoists are all designed to fit into the larger scheme. Egyptian and oriental influences are evident in the metalwork.

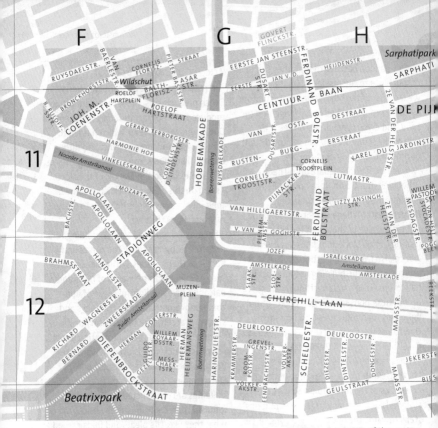

Reading Room), with its unusual belfry and clock ornamented with shells. The reading room is open to all, and a carved stone tablet above the doorway testifies to the emancipation of the working classes: a pile of books, the snake of knowledge curled round a tree, and a key.

Leave the Coöperatiehof by the same archway and walk straight on down Talmastraat past a more sober stretch of housing. Take the first right into Henriette Ronnerstraat, which leads into **Henriette Ronnerplein**. On the corner you'll pass a noseless **bust of alderman Wibaut**, the socialist dignitary who threw himself into tackling poverty and the housing problem. The houses along the right side of this square resemble those on Schwartzeplein, with the same basket-like balconies and steep tiled flanks. Cross the square and walk down to the canal via Penseelstraat. Turn left and walk alongside the canal, which is usually bobbing with ducks. On the left you'll pass a striking **doorway** of decorative brick-

work. Cross Van Woustraat, one of the main north–south tram routes, then take the first left onto Jan Lievensstraat. Continue up here and take the second right into **Smaragdplein**. Though built around the same time as the work of Kramer and De Klerk, these buildings are not part of De Dageraad. At the end of the square is a circular **bath-house** built in 1925. Turn left onto Diamantstraat then right onto **Saffierstraat**, lined with Amsterdam School housing. These large blocks are characterized by projecting bay windows above a further series of unusual elongated windows.

If you're feeling in need of a rest right now, just north of here, at Tolstraat 91, is **Greenhouse**, a coffeeshop that wins the *High Times* Cannabis Cup most years.

Back on Saffierstraat, follow the road round to the right, then head left down Smaragdstraat until you reach the River Amstel. Turn right onto Amsteldijk on the banks of the river and continue until you reach a bridge, known as **Kramerbrug**. This is

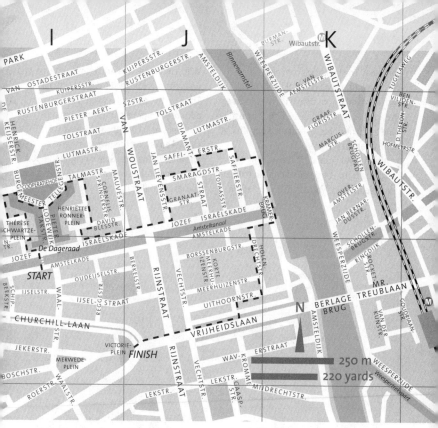

one of the finest bridges designed by the Amsterdam School and, with its over-embellished brickwork, is instantly recognizable as such. The little hexagonal buildings at either end of the bridge are flanked with brickwork that resembles organ pipes. Both have a strange needle-like appendix perched on top. The piers of the bridge are decorated with seals sculpted, once again, by Hildo Krop; these are best viewed side on from the road.

Once you've crossed the bridge take the immediate right onto Amstelkade then left onto **Holendrechtstraat**. The houses that flank the left side of the street were designed in 1922 by one of the few female architects of her day, Margaret Staalkropholler. She was much influenced by the Amsterdam School, as the extravagant stairwells and vaulted balconies of her designs illustrate. Continue to the end of the road, then turn right. You will come out into the big space of **Meerhuizenplein**. On your left, on either corner of Kromme

Mijdrechtstraat, is an extensive string of balconies and bay windows designed by De Klerk. Cut south down this road and you'll come out onto **Vrijheidslaan**, then turn right. This leafy boulevard is lined on the right with houses designed in 1922 by J. Zietsma, another architect of the Amsterdam School. At the end of this stretch is **Victorieplein**. On the western edge of the big traffic intersection is a giant **sculpture of architect H.P. Berlage**, widely known as the father of modern Dutch architecture. As well as designing the ground-breaking Beurs van Berlage building in the centre of town, he drew up the plan of wide avenues and narrow side streets that characterizes the New South neighbourhood – and it is largely as a development of and reaction to this man's architecture that the style of the Amsterdam School emerged. Behind the Berlage statue towers the severe, 12-storey **Wolkenkrabber** ('skyscraper' – the Netherlands' first), built in 1932 as a more space-efficient solution to the housing problem. The building's sober lines were a sure sign that the artistic flourish of the Amsterdam School style had come to an end. Nearby, if you're feeling peckish, is a bustling and authentic Thai restaurant, **Kong Kha**, at Rijnstraat 87.

Alternatively, round off the walk by catching tram 12 from Victorieplein to **Roelof Hartplein**, where you can rest your legs in **Wildschut**, a famous Art Deco lounge dressed up in fittings salvaged from old cinemas. Through the plate-glass windows you can admire yet more architecture from the Amsterdam School: the square was conceived during the 1920s as a grand entrance to the New South neighbourhood, and many of the surrounding buildings bear the now-familiar hallmarks of the style.

Day Trips

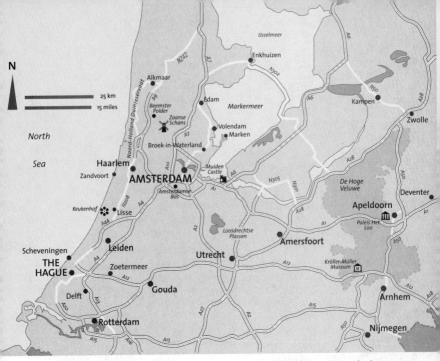

Within an hour's train journey of Amsterdam you'll find the historic towns of Haarlem, Utrecht and Leiden, each with their old quarter and fine museums. Or see cheese made and ceramics painted in the pretty towns of Gouda, Edam and Delft. For fresh air and some walking or cycling, there's the Amsterdamse Bos, the beach at Zandvoort, the villages and waterways north of Amsterdam, the bulb fields at Keukenhof, and De Hoge Veluwe National Park, with its child-friendly sculpture park. Still within an hour's rail journey, there's Holland's centre of government, The Hague, and the great port of Rotterdam.

HAARLEM

Just 15 minutes by train from Amsterdam, Haarlem has a cosy, provincial atmosphere quite different from the capital – but it's by no means dull. You'll find hordes of friendly cafés, the much-painted St Bavo's church, tiny *hofjes* tucked behind over-the-top public architecture, Holland's oldest and most intriguing museum, and an important collection of paintings by Frans Hals. Haarlem acts

as an overflow for students who have accommodation problems in Amsterdam and Leiden, and this gives the town a youthful, carefree air. Fifteen minutes on from Haarlem by train is the lively beach resort of Zandvoort.

Grote Markt

St Bavokerk

Open *Mon–Sat 10am–4pm.*

Most people arriving in Haarlem head straight for the Grote Markt (Market Square) and the imposing Gothic Grote of St Bavokerk (Great or St Bavo's Church). The interior is bright and painted white. A gleefully ostentatious Baroque **organ** upstages even the soaring Gothic arches. It was built by the Amsterdammer Christian Muller in 1738, and is said to be one of the biggest in the world. Clusters of musical putti and graceful maidens cling to the pipes. Handel, Mozart and Albert Schweitzer have all had a go on the ivory and tortoiseshell keyboard. Before you leave, have a look at the fading **tapestry designs** painted on the columns at the side of the church and the fluid lines of a **marble relief** by The Hague sculptor Xavery:

Getting There

It's a 15min train ride from Centraal Station (€3.10 single, €5.50 return) to Haarlem. Trains to Zandvoort from Haarlem run every 15 minutes, and the trip also takes 15 minutes.

Tourist Information

Haarlem: The VVV tourist office is outside the railway station, **t** (0900) 616 1600, **w** *www.vvvzk.nl* (*open April–Sept Mon–Fri 9am–5.30pm, Sat 9.30am–4.30pm; Oct–March Mon–Fri 9.30am–5.30pm, Sat 10am–2pm*).

Zandvoort: Schoolplein 1, **t** (023) 571 7947, **w** *www.vvvzk.nl* (*open April–Sept Mon–Fri 9am–5.15pm, Sat 9.30am–5.30pm*).

Eating Out

Haarlem **t** *023–*

The street behind St Bavo's, at the far end of the market, is a good place to look for restaurants and cafés – though you really need go no further than the wood panelling and hanging lampshades of the beautifully restored **Stations Restaurant** (on Platform 2).

Lambermon's, *Spaarne 96*, **t** *542 7804*. **Open** *Tues–Sat 5.30–10.30pm*. **Expensive.** Large restaurant with well-heeled clientele, renowned for its top-quality classic French cuisine, with modern touches.

Café Brinkmann, *Grote Markt 9–13*, **t** *532 3111*. **Moderate.** An elegant Art Deco establishment overlooking St Bavo's.

Jacobus Pieck, *Warmoesstraat 18*, **t** *532 6144*. **Open** *Mon 11am–4pm, Tues–Sat 11am–10pm, kitchen closes 4–5.30pm*. **Inexpensive**. Café with old lamps, huge fireplaces and modern art; a range of pastas, burgers and well-made sandwiches at lunch time.

De Karmeliet, *Spekstraat 6*, **t** *531 4426*. **Inexpensive**. Provides a cheery stopover for a simple snack or sandwich.

Poetry and Music paying homage to the town patroness. In the centre column of the **Brewers' Chapel** (near the south transept) two little lines mark the heights of past Haarlem residents: Giant Cajanus (8ft 8ins/2.6m) and Paap (3ft 1in/94cm).

Outside the church is a **statue of Laurens Coster**. Local legend has it that while he was carving his lover's name in a tree trunk, a letter fell into the sand. He was inspired by the imprint to invent printing. Though Haarlem is proud of him today, his contemporaries took him for a sorcerer and drove him out of town. He went to live in Germany – which might explain why the rest of the world believes that printing originated with Gutenberg.

The Stadhuis

The oldest part of the Stadhuis across the square is a 14th-century hunting lodge built for the Count of Holland. It's been altered and expanded over the years, and the present complex incorporates a medieval monastery. During office hours you can have a look at the old heavy-beamed Gravenzaal (Count's Hall).

Vleeshal and Verweyhal

t *(023) 511 5775; museum open Tues–Sat 11am–5pm, Sun noon–5pm; adm €4.*

On the south side of the square is the relentlessly ornamented Vleeshal (the former meat market, built in 1602). Sacheverell Sitwell remarked that we should 'regard it less as a building, than as Dutch cabinet work on a most capricious scale'. The Vleeshal and Verweyhal (former fish market) now hold a good collection of Dutch Expressionists, Impressionists and works by local contemporary artists.

Frans Hals Museum

Groot Heiligland 62, **t** *(023) 511 5775*, **w** *www.franshalsmuseum.nl*. **Open** *Tues–Sat 11am–5pm, Sun noon–5pm; adm €5.40.*

Haarlem's star attraction is housed in one of the town's grander *hofjes*, a 17th-century Old Men's Home. The museum isn't devoted entirely to Hals – there's a batch of other Golden Age painters, a wide range of furniture and applied art and an extensive modern collection. The corridors are pervaded by a steady ticking of clocks, and the displays give you some sharp surprises. In a dim 17th-century period room, you'll see an enormous drawing by the 1930s Magic Realist Pyke Koch. Bright contemporary pieces hang alongside Old Masters or in rooms displaying antique silver. All this gives the museum a quirky liveliness. Don't miss the 18th-century doll's house or the restoration workshop. (You stand behind a glass wall and watch painters work painstakingly on the tiny patch of an Old Master that will occupy them for months.) The most intriguing of Frans Hals' works in the museum are the portraits of the *Regents and Regentesses of the Old Men's Home*, painted in 1664 when Hals was in his 80s. The story that he was a bitter occupant of the almshouse is not true, but he certainly seems to be taking some sort of revenge with his brush. The Regentesses, in particular, are a sour and terrifying lot. Their expressions range from rosy stupidity to pure evil, and the white faces are thrown into stark relief by the sombre surround. You can see why Van Gogh said that Hals had at least 27 shades of black.

Teylers Museum

*Spaarne 16, **t** (023) 531 9010, **w** www. teylersmuseum.nl. **Open** Tues–Sat 10am–5pm, Sun noon–5pm (winter until 4pm); **adm** €5.*

The Netherlands' oldest purpose-built museum first opened its doors in 1784. It's the best sort of small museum – one based on the taste of an erudite, eccentric private collector, in this case the 18th-century merchant Pieter Teyler van der Hulst. A succession of astute directors have, in making new acquisitions, skilfully developed the diverse themes of Teyler's original collection. You'll find a fascinating hoard of old scientific instruments and machines, fossils, paintings and drawings (including some by Michelangelo and Rembrandt). Much of the collection is housed in beautiful wooden display cases in the original 18th-century museum building. Temporary exhibitions drawn from the superb drawing collection are held in a tasteful modern wing.

Zandvoort

Canal water can be pretty poisonous, so if the weather is hot and you feel like an outdoor swim, you can join the flocks of Amsterdammers heading for the beaches of Zandvoort. Although Zandvoort is just beyond Haarlem (another 15 minutes on the train) it has achieved the honorary status of being 'Amsterdam's beach'. It's a crowded and commercial resort, though if you wander farther up the coast you'll find a nudists' beach, a gay beach and lots of quieter spots among the dunes. On hot summer's nights Zandvoort is the scene of trendy Ibiza-style beach-party clubbing.

AMSTERDAMSE BOS

You don't have to go too far afield from Amsterdam for a healthy bit of greenery and a dose of fresh air. The wilds of the Amsterdamse Bos are only a tram ride away from the centre of town. The Amsterdamse Bos was created in the 1930s, providing jobs for hundreds of unemployed, and a new recreation space for the ever expanding city. The **Bos Museum**, Koenenkade 56, in the northeast corner of the Bos (*open daily 10am–5pm; adm free*) tells the story of how it

Getting There

You can take **bus** 170, 171 or 172 to Amsterdamse Bos, but a more picturesque means of transport is an **antique tram**, on Sunday and some afternoons from March to Sept, from Haarlemmermeer Station in west Amsterdam (every 20mins; details from the VVV; *see* 'Elektrische Museumtramlijn', p.259).

Eating Out

There are also lots of places to picnic. **Boerderij Meerzicht, *t* 679 2744,** *an old farmhouse near the museum.* ***Open*** *summer months 10am–7pm, and Nov–Feb Fri–Sun 10am–6pm.* ***Inexpensive.*** Have a pancake amongst the live peacocks on the terrace.

all happened. There is plenty to do here, whether you want to laze around or be a little more energetic. You can hire bikes at the main gate, go boating on one of the vast stretches of water, or visit a buffalo reserve.

NORTH OF AMSTERDAM

The coasts, canals and waterways north of Amsterdam make ideal day-trip destinations from the city. Even more so if you are travelling by bicycle. Provided you have sufficient puff to pedal, you can easily combine a cycling trip to Broek-in-Waterland, a friendly and likeable place, with a visit to one of the Meer towns, such as Marken, in a day. If you don't like crowds, try to avoid the area during high season as tourists can get pretty thick on the ground.

Broek-in-Waterland

Heading northeast out of Amsterdam, through a gentle landscape of fields and waterways, you come to the village of Broek-in-Waterland, a cluster of pretty wooden houses surrounded by canals and small lakes. Set in leafy gardens, some of these cottages date back 300 years and have become hot property amongst design-conscious moneyed Amsterdammers. At the heart of the hamlet is a **16th-century church** that holds the grave of one Neeltje Pater, a whizz 18th-century businesswoman who built up a fleet of 16 merchant ships, and had a nest-egg of eight million guilders stashed away in the Bank of England.

The Beemster Polder

Created in 1612 by the draining of a large lake and surrounding marshland, the Beemster Polder covers 18,000 acres (7,200 hectares) and is in places up to 15ft (5m) below sea level. Dead straight canals criss-cross the polder, dividing the emergent land into neat rectangular blocks. This emphatic symmetry is a product of the 17th-century vision of an ideal landscape, intended to reveal the harmony between humankind and nature – and it is because the original design remains intact that Beemster earned a place on UNESCO's World Heritage List in 1999. Everything obeys the diktat. Trees are planted in straight lines. Villages and farmyards are almost surreally neat. The landscape is ordered, restrained, with the same mini-malist appeal as modern Dutch interior design. Its charm lies in nuance, balance and gentle repetition. Yet on this delicate canvas, the seasons wreak dramatic changes. Winter snows create a world of stark black on white, the landscape reduced to horizontal and vertical lines of flat, frozen fields and gaunt, leafless trees. In spring, flowering bulbs turn the narrow plots into oblongs of brilliant blue, red and yellow. Summer brings irregularity – tangles of wild flowers, patches of shade, black-and-white Dutch cows, let out of their barns to graze in the sun. And autumn really is a time of mists and mellow fruitfulness, as the wetlands breathe out their stored-up summer warmth to steam the air, and piles of pears, pumpkins and rosy apples appear along the wayside. It's a wonderful place for cycling; there's organic produce on sale, a couple of good restaurants in the villages, and even a wine farm.

Getting There

Well-signposted cycle paths crisscross the whole area.

Broek-in-Waterland: Bus 110 or 111 from Centraal Station.

Beemster Polder Most easily visited by car or bicycle. Or take a train from Centraal Station to Alkmaar, then bus 127 to the main village of Middenbeemster; or a train to Purmerend then a Train-Taxi (cheap onward taxi link; buy a ticket at the same time as your train ticket and go to/phone from the taxi rank outside the station) on to Middenbeemster.

Zaanse Schans: Train from Amsterdam to Koog Zaandijk, then an 8-minute walk; or bus 88 from Zaandam station. You can hire bicycles at the entrance to Zaanse Schans for €5 per half-day.

Marken: Bus 111 from Centraal Station.

Volendam: Bus 110 from Centraal Station.

Edam: Bus 110, 112, 114 from Centraal Station.

Bergen aan Zee: Take the train to Alkmaar, then bus 160 or 162 to Bergen. Buses go every half-hour.

Tourist Information

Zaanse Schans: Visitors' Centre, Schansend 7, **t** (075) 616 8218 (open daily 8.30–5), **w** www.zaanseschans.nl.

Volendam: Zeestraat 37, **t** (0299) 363 747 (open April–Oct daily 10am–5pm, Nov–March Mon–Sat 10am–3pm).

Edam: VVV, Damplein 1, **t** (0299) 315 125 (open April–Sept Mon–Sat 10am–5pm, and Sun 1–5 July–Aug).

Bergen aan Zee: VVV, Plein 1, **t** (072) 581 2400 (open Mon–Fri 10am–5.30pm, Sat 10am–5pm, and Sun 11am–3pm July–mid-Sept).

Eating Out

Broek-in-Waterland (t 020–)

De Witte Swaen, *Dorpsstraat 11,* **t** *403 1525.* ***Inexpensive.*** An old-fashioned pancake parlour housed in a pleasantly traditional Broek-in-Waterland building, with a sunny terrace.

The Beemster Polder (t 0299-)

Het Heerenhuis, *Rijperweg 83, Middenbeemster,* **t** *682 010.* **Open** *Wed–Mon 11.30am-10.30pm.* ***Expensive.*** Chef Toon Rumphorst comes up with such delights as haddock with a creamy brandade (salt-cod purée). Much of the produce is organic, and from the Beemster itself. Over 100 excellent wines are available by the bottle, with around 30 offered by the glass.

Zaanse Schans (t 075–)

De Hoop Op d'Swarte Walvis, *Kalverringdijk 15,* **t** *616 5629.* ***Expensive.*** One of the region's top restaurants, housed in a complex of historic buildings. You can taste soup made with mustard that was ground at the windmill nearby.

Edam (t 0299–)

De Fortuna, *Spuistraat 3–7,* **t** *371 671.* ***Moderate.*** Dinky step-gabled building belonging to a family-run hotel – heavy beams, soft lighting and superb food. Try the home-smoked lamb with mint and rocket couscous.

The Dunes (t 072–)

De Kleine Prins, *Oude Prinsweg 29, Bergen aan Zee,* **t** *589 6969.* ***Expensive–moderate.*** You can tuck into such delights as grilled rabbit with calvados sauce.

De Uitkijk, *beach pavilion, Egmond aan Zee.* ***Inexpensive.*** Cheap 'n' cheerful eats.

Zaanse Schans

Attractions open *Daily 10am–5pm; **adm** free, though individual sights have own opening times and fees; parking €6/2hrs.*

A few miles west, outside the town of Zaandam, you'll find the Zaanse Schans, resplendent with 12 working windmills. This cluster of green wooden houses dating from the 17th and 18th centuries was put up in the 1950s, to help convey the impression of what a village in the area was like at a time when more than 1,000 windmills ground away at various activities along the River Zaan.

Though it throngs with tourists, the Zaanse Schans somehow manages to preserve some charm, and a visit to one or two of the **mills** is fascinating – one grinds mustard, another produces cooking oil, in a third a man makes paint from natural pigments (highly popular with Amsterdam artists). There's also a working **dairy**, a **clog maker** and a **pewterer**. You can see the first ever **Albert Heijn** grocery store (which grew into the nation's biggest chain of supermarkets), and visit the **Clock Museum**, where a timepiece from 1520 thunks away in one corner, while in another a 31-bell carillon tinkles out folk tunes. At the entrance to the village, the **Zaans Museum** (*open Tues–Sat 10am–5pm, Sun noon–5pm; adm*) offers an excellent multimedia history presentation on the district, which claims to be 'the oldest industrial area in Europe'.

Marken

Once an isolated fishing community, Marken is now crawling with tourists in the summer, who come over the causeway to snap willing locals in traditional costume. It's still a bleak and impressive place though, particularly out of season. Have a look at the island's history at the **Marker Museum** (*Kerkbuurt 44; open April–Oct Mon–Sat 10am–5pm*).

Volendam

Edging farther along the coast, you come to the somewhat larger town of Volendam. People flock here from all over the world to ogle and photograph locals in traditional dress – men in fez-like black hats and wide lapels, women in pointy lace caps and long aprons. But there is real life in Volendam too – quaint, empty side streets lined with gabled houses, the occasional real fishing boat with a catch for sale, and even its own pop-music style – palingbeat (eel beat) – which emerged in the late 1980s. If you come in midwinter, you might find the harbour frozen over, the townsfolk turned out to skate, and barely a visitor in sight.

Edam

Now almost a suburb of Volendam, Edam is perhaps best known to outsiders because it gives its name to the round, rubbery cheese that the Dutch export in large quantities. Yet despite a tacky and utterly fake **cheese market** (*held on Wednesday mornings in summer*), Edam escapes the worst toy-town excesses, and is perhaps the most pleasant and atmospheric of all the towns on this stretch of coast. Founded in the 12th century, Edam enjoyed its high point in the 16th and 17th centuries, and still bears the architectural imprint of that time. The imperious Gothic **Grote Kerk** on the edge of the town centre was largely rebuilt in the 1620s, after it had been struck by lightning, and contains some beautiful stained glass – rare in the iconoclast-ravaged north. The slender, solitary **Speeltoren** (built 1561) was also once part of a church, demolished in the 19th century. In 1970, its original six-bell carillon was augmented by another 29 bells – so many that some had to hang outside, and the tower nearly fell over from the weight two years later.

The richly decorated **Kaaswaag** on the Kaasmarkt still weighs out Edammer cheese at the statutory 1,000 or 1,600 grams, though as far as décor goes it's upstaged by the ornate 18th-century **Stadhuis** on nearby Damplein. Next door to the Stadhuis, in a step-gabled house that dates back to 1550, is the **Edams Museum** (*open mid-April–Oct Tues–Sat 10am–4.30pm, Sun 1.30–4.30pm; adm*), restored as a period merchant house but most famous for its floating cellar floor, supposedly built by a sea captain who just couldn't get to sleep on solid land.

Noord-Holland Duinreservaat

West of Zaandam, you come to the Noord-Holland Duinreservaat (North Holland Dune Reserve), one of the most beautiful stretches of coast in the country. In places the dunes are like rugged little mountains; at times they waft down into meadows. The north of the reserve is thick with forest, while the beaches are long, sandy and often quite deserted. **Egmond aan Zee** gets very overrun – the towns to head for as a base are **Castricum aan Zee** and **Bergen aan Zee**.

MUIDEN CASTLE

*t (0294) 261 325, **w** www.muiderslot.nl.*
***Guided tours** only, every half-hour, duration one hour; **open** Nov–Mar Sat and Sun 1–3pm (last tour), April–Oct Mon–Fri 10am–4pm (last tour, Sat, Sun and holidays 1–4pm (last tour); **adm** adults €6, 4–12s €4.50.*

Muiderslot (Muiden Castle) stands firmly fixed in the national psyche for two reasons. It was here in 1296 (a date as familiar to Dutch schoolchildren as 1066 is to British) that Count Floris of Holland was imprisoned and murdered. Over three centuries later, the castle was the focus of the Muiderkring (Muiden Circle), the country's most famous literary circle, centring on the poet P.C. Hooft. It was here that Tesselschade, the doyenne of 17th-century letters, sparkled (*see* p.154). For 'castle' in Holland you can usually read 'stately home'. But Muiderslot is very much in the moated, turreted, impenetrable-stone-wall mould. Most of the building dates back to the 13th and 14th centuries, though inside it has been restored in a style which rather effectively re-creates an atmosphere that

Getting There

Muiden is just 20mins' drive along the A1. Alternatively, take **bus** 136 from Amstel Station (50mins), or a local **train** from Centraal Station to Weesp, then bus 153 (45mins).

Eating Out
*Muiden **t** 0294–*
Graf Floris V, *Herengracht 72*, **t** *261 296*. **Inexpensive**. Traditional café in the village, where you can get savoury and sweet pancakes, and simple meals.

would have been more familiar to members of the Muiderkring. You can see the chamber where Floris met his fate, and the desk at which P.C. Hooft wrote his poems, standing up. The rooms are filled with such curiosities as a 'money table' (you detected counterfeit coins by clinking them on the limestone top), and a family box-bed (children in drawers underneath, parents shut into a wardrobe above, with a cord to pull that opened a vent when it all got a bit too pongy). Keep an eye open for a painting in which human figures have cabbages for heads – done a good 400 years before Magritte came up with the idea.

After visiting the castle you can wander through its attractive formal **garden**, then stroll along fortified walls beside the River Vecht into the village of **Muiden** – a cluster of dinky gabled houses along the waterfront.

LEIDEN

The plan of a Dutch town is: a bridge, a canal: under an arch into a street: pointed stepped houses; 1620: on brand new garages: a great red brick tower, then a vast church, shut up... Some frescoes on white-washed walls... all shining spick & span.
Virginia Woolf, *Diary*, 8 May 1935

Leiden fits the plan perfectly, and even throws in a couple of windmills for good measure. This was Rembrandt's birthplace and home to the Pilgrim Fathers, the site of the most famous battle in Dutch history and of the first tulips grown in Holland. Yet despite its wealthy air and historical reso-nance, Leiden is no stuffy museum piece. The local university, founded in 1581, is one of the most prestigious in the country and student life gives the town spirit and verve. Just a few minutes' journey from Amsterdam, Leiden is a popular day-trip destination. Just visiting the museums could easily consume a full day. The Molenmuseum Valk gives a fasci-nating insight into the innards of a windmill, while the collection of Japanese artefacts at the Rijksmuseum voor Volkenkunde is so

Getting There

Leiden is only half an hour by **train** from Amsterdam's Centraal Station (€11.70 return). One leaves every 15–20mins. By **car**, it's 25 miles (40km) along the A4.

Getting Around

All the main tourist sites are within easy walking distance of the centre and the railway station. They are all very well sign-posted, and there are helpful maps dotted all over the city centre (look for the *i* sign).

Bicycle rental: Behind the station, **t** (071) 512 0068; €7.30 per day. You'll need to leave €50 deposit and have proof of identification.

Boat trips: Rederij Rembrandt (dep. Beestenmarkt, **t** (071) 513 4938) offer trips through the city's canals (April–Oct).

Tourist Information

The VVV tourist office is right near the railway station at Stationsplein 2D, **t** (0900) 222 2333, **f** (071) 512 5318, **w** *www.tref.nl/ 3355/sport/vvv.htm* (open Mon 11am–5.30pm, Tues–Fri 9.30am–5.30pm, Sat 10am–4.30pm).

Festivals

Most of Leiden erupts in a city-wide party on **3 October** (as it has done for over 400 years) to celebrate the relief of its siege in 1574. Traditional white bread, herring and *hutspot* are served, and celebrations in restaurants and cafés spill out into the street.

Eating Out

Leiden **t** *071–*

The best place for cafés and restaurants is around Pieterskerkhof and Hooglandskerk.

Fabers, *Kloksteeg 13*, **t** *512 4012*. **Expensive**. Cool service, haute cuisine and a good price to quality ratio.

Het Prentenkabinet, *Kloksteeg 25*, **t** *071 512 6666*. **Moderate–expensive.** Classy, multi-roomed restaurant in a patrician townhouse near the Pieterskerk, its walls covered in old prints (the name means Print Cabinet). Excellent new Dutch cuisine and good wines.

Het Panacee, *Rapenburg 97*, **t** *566 1494*. **Moderate**. Realm of the deans and profes-sors. Tuck into such dishes as venison with forest mushrooms and honey-truffle sauce.

Burgerzaken, *Breestraat 123*, **t** *071 566 1122*. **Inexpensive**. Busy all-day eaterie, where you can sit with coffee and the papers, enjoy a lunchtime sandwich (with largely organic products), or a fuller meal in the evening. Sunday is tapas day.

Lunchroom Snijders, *Botermarkt 15*, **t** *512 2583*. **Inexpensive**. Behind a richly carved 19th-century shopfront, through a tempting patisserie, is a room with a gently fading 1930s atmosphere. Good for a quick sand-wich or gooey cake.

De Waterlijn, *Prinsessekade*, **t** *512 1279*. **Inexpensive**. Floating, angular, modern glass-walled café with a view up the canal to a windmill. Apple pie and light meals.

---

impressive that people make pilgrimages from Japan to view it, and the Egyptian antiquities at the Rijksmuseum van Oudenheden are of world renown.

Rijksmuseum voor Volkenkunde

Steenstraat 1, **t** *(071) 516 8800*, **w** *www.rmu.nl*. **Open** *Tues–Sun 10am–5pm; adm €6.50 (surcharge for special exhibitions)*.

You have barely stepped off the train when you come across one of Leiden's weighty museums, the National Museum of Ethnology. In a converted 19th-century hospital beside what was once part of the city moat, you'll find Javanese puppets, Bornean ear-jewellery made from the beaks of hornbills, a Greenlander's Sunday best and other riches from around the world.

But the real attraction is the **Siebold Collection of Japanese art and artefacts**. In 1825, Philipp von Siebold went to Japan as a doctor, under the auspices of the Dutch government. He had instructions to collect as much information as he could about what was then a relatively unknown culture. Siebold came back laden with 6,000 objects, ranging from fans to enormous 17th-century statues of Buddha. This stash forms the core of what has become one of the most noted representations of traditional Japanese culture in the world. There are rooms set out ready for a tea ceremony, cabinets of beautiful lacquerware, suits of Samurai armour and ceremonial swords. The display of prints boasts work by Ando Hiroshige (1797–1858), including the well-known *Sudden Shower over the Bridge of Atake*. Keep an eye open for the 17th-century clocks. At that time the Japanese divided the daylight hours into six equal periods, named after animals in the Chinese astrological chart. The length of these periods varied according to season. The mechanisms of these first clocks were copied from Western models, but a clockmaker had to visit every month to adjust them to follow seasonal fluctuations.

Molenmuseum de Valk

2e Binnenvestgracht 1a, **t** *(071) 516 5353.* **Open** *Tues–Sat 10am–5pm, Sun 1–5pm;* **adm** *€2.50.*

A restored 18th-century grain mill, 'De Valk' offers a rare inside view of how windmills work. You can potter about the lower storeys, where the last miller lived until the 1900s. Then leave the cosily furnished rooms to clamber past millstones and flour chutes to the grinding cogs, seven storeys high. On the way you can step out onto the reefing stage (the platform that runs around the middle of the windmill) for a view over the city.

De Lakenhal

Oude Singel 32, **t** *(071) 516 5360,* **w** *www. lakenhal.nl.* **Open** *Tues–Fri 10am–5pm, Sat and Sun noon–5pm;* **adm** *€4.*

'The Cloth Hall' was built in 1640 as the administrative centre of Leiden's prosperous cloth industry. In 1874 it was converted into a municipal museum. Much of the original interior wall panelling and stucco work is intact, and there are good collections of silver and furniture. But the star attractions are the

Hofjes

There are many *hofjes* (almshouse courtyards) around Leiden, hidden behind unassuming doors. On your wanderings, pop in for a glimpse of the rather grand 18th-century Coninckshofje (Oude Veste 15); St Stevenshof (Haarlemmerstraat 48–50), founded in 1487; and the Groeneveld-stichting (Oude Veste 41), built for the widows of clergy in 1882. All are still private residences but, provided you respect that, you are usually welcome to look around quietly. Though if you see a sign reading 'Verboden Toegang Art. 461', bear in mind that means 'Trespassers will be Prosecuted'.

paintings. Look out especially for **Lucas van Leyden**'s fine and delicately coloured triptych *The Last Judgement* (1572); works by the young **Rembrandt** and his studio-mate **Jan Levens**; **Gerard Dou**'s tiny, intense oils (which established a Leiden style); and the lecherous abandon of **Jan Steen**'s *Amorous Couple* (1660). There's a painting depicting the brave Burgemeester van der Werff who, at the height of the siege, offered his own body as food to the faltering citizens. They refused but were fired by his courage to hold out even longer. (In the painting they look well-fed and a little embarrassed by the offer.)

Around the Stadhuis

Leiden's **Stadhuis** (city hall) was built in 1597, though the unattractive brick pile you see today dates back to the 1930s, rebuilt after the old Stadhuis had been razed. All that was left was the front façade (which you can still see, in Breestraat). At one corner of the Stadhuis stands a sturdy 17th-century **Waag** (weighing house), once the focus of an enormous marketplace: many of the street names in the area still end with 'markt', from Kaasmarkt (cheese) to Aalmarkt (eels) and Beestenmarkt (cattle), giving you an idea of just how large the market was. A walk through the elegant classicist buildings that once accommodated the fish market brings you to **De Burcht** (The Stronghold). The dumpy fortress was built around AD 1000 on a mound between two branches of the Rhine to protect a small settlement of fishermen and farmers from marauding Vikings, fractious local lords and the fickle water levels. You can still march around its sturdy battlements and look out over the whole city.

Rijksmuseum van Oudenheden

Rapenburg 28, t (071) 516 3163, w www.rmo.nl. Open Tues–Fri 10am–5pm, Sat and Sun noon–5pm; adm €6.

The country's leading archaeological museum houses the entire 1st-century AD **Temple of Taffeh** donated in 1960 by the Egyptian government to the Dutch in gratitude for their contribution to UNESCO excavations in Abyssinia. The squat stone building is in the museum foyer (it was a condition of the gift that no one should pay to see it) and overhead lighting simulates the passage of the sun (a second stipulation). The museum has a thrillingly gruesome collection of **mummies** (including one of a crocodile), and good stores of Greek and Roman antiquities. Star exhibits are the **tomb statues of Maya and Merit**. Maya was Director of the Treasury to Tutankhamun; his wife was a priestess. Although the statues arrived in Holland in 1832, their provenance was obscure, and it was only in 1986 that the tomb was rediscovered (a CD-ROM tells the story).

Hortus Botanicus

t (071) 527 7249, w www.hortusleiden.nl. Open April–Sept daily 10am–6pm; Oct–March Sun–Fri 10am–4pm; adm €4.

The part of the university most worth visiting is its botanical garden. Planted in 1594, it is one of the oldest botanical gardens in Europe. It is here that the botanist Clusius planted the first tulip bulbs in Holland. They had come from Turkey via an embassy garden in Switzerland, where Clusius had spotted them. Unfortunately, the professor never saw his plants bloom: they were stolen one night before spring came. Today, Clusius' garden has once again been laid out in its original form. When you have inhaled the perfume of scores of roses, visited the 350-year-old laburnum, and grown tired of the elegantly laid-out shrubberies, you can push your way through hothouses to the massive *Victoria Amazonia* lily, reputed to be able to support the weight of three men on its pads, and which flowers but one night a year.

Pieterskerk

t (071) 512 4319. Open daily 1.30–4pm.

The 15th-century Pieterskerk is in the heart of the student quarter. The church was originally called St Pieters, but was stripped of its saintly title, and any other papist ornamentation, during the Reformation. By far the most interesting thing to see in the plain, cavernous church is a **mummified body**. It was found, dried out by the draught, in a secret room under the pulpit and now lies in the church with its ankles neatly crossed and its head on a pillow. No one knows how it got there, or even how old it is. Some suspect murder, or a priest's secret lover; others mutter darkly about Nazis and the Occupation.

You can also see a chart tracing **George 'Dubya' Bush's family tree**, showing his descent from the Pilgrim Fathers. From 1609 to 1620 a group of Puritans, finding the religious atmosphere in Holland more congenial than in England, settled in Leiden with their preacher, John Robinson. **Jan Pesijnshofje** (Pieterskerkhof 21), a late 17th-century almshouse near the church, now marks the site where Robinson lived and preached. The congregation felt the need for an even freer climate, so in 1620 they boarded the Mayflower and set sail for the New World. Robinson stayed behind and is buried in the Pieterskerk.

Naturalis

Darwinweg 2, t (071) 568 7600, w www. naturalis.nl. Open Tues–Sun 10am–6pm, and Mon during school holidays 10am–6pm; adm €8.

Naturalis is the National Museum of Natural History, situated just behind Leiden station. The entrance building was originally put up in the 17th century as a *pesthuis* (hospital for sufferers from the plague). Nowadays a covered walkway transports you past a couple of life-size rhinos to a modern high-rise that's been hollowed out and filled with tiers of dinosaur skeletons, minerals, stuffed animals, preserved fish and thousands of plants and neatly ranged insects. No mangy bears and faded parrots here: everything is in tip-top better-than-real-life condition, and interestingly presented. There are intriguing displays on environment and the planet, and a wealth of multimedia facilities.

KEUKENHOF

t (0252) 465 555, w www.keukenhof.nl. Open late March–late May daily 8am–7.30pm; adm adults €12, under-12s €6.

In spring, the fields of North Holland blaze with the colours of millions of tulips and other bulbs, and attract nearly that number of tourists. Coachloads pour out of Amsterdam, to return traumatized by the sight of great cutting-machines churning through the bulb fields scrunching up the flowers. (Most plants are grown for the bulb rather than the bloom, and a swift blade to the stalk makes the bulb subdivide.)

The Keukenhof (literally 'kitchen garden') was, in the 15th century, the herb and vegetable patch of the Countess Jacoba van Beieren. Whatever she grew there enabled her to get through four husbands (including a duke of Gloucester and a dauphin of France) before her own death at the age of 35. In 1949 a group of Dutch bulb-growers

Getting There

The VVV tourist office and various agencies around Amsterdam's Centraal Station can help with organized tours to the Keukenhof area, but it's far better to go on your own by train or car. The town to head for is Lisse, and the garden to see is the Keukenhof. Centraal Station will usually have details of special discount offers on a combined rail/bus ticket to the Keukenhof. Alternatively, you could combine a visit to the gardens with a trip to Leiden or Haarlem – there's a bus connection from both to the Keukenhof in the season (details from VVV).

Eating Out

The cafés around the Keukenhof are crowded and fairly unexciting. You'd be well advised to pack yourself a picnic.

took over the land as a shop-window for the bulb industry. It turned out to have a much wider appeal.

Today there are some 74 acres (30ha) of nearly 7 million plants and a further 54,000sq ft (5,000sq m) of flowers under glass. The best time to go is from mid- to late April, when tulips, daffodils, narcissi and hyacinths are all flowering at once.

GOUDA

Gouda (pronounced with an aspirated guttural G, 'HGowda') is not all cheese and ersatz medieval markets. There's a thriving crafts industry, an imaginative historical museum and, in the longest church in the Netherlands, stained glass so beautiful that even the iconoclasts left it alone.

During the 15th century Gouda prospered on the beer trade, then diversified into making pipes and ceramics – by 1750 about half the population was employed in the pottery trade. It wasn't until the mid-19th century that candlemaking took over as the dominant local industry.

Getting There

Gouda is 18 miles (29km) southwest of Amsterdam. The easiest way to get there is by **train** from Centraal Station. The journey takes about 50mins and it's a 15min walk from Gouda Station to the market square. Trains average two an hour and a day return costs €15. The main tourist sights are clustered around the market square and are just a few minutes' walk apart.

Tourist Information

VVV, Markt 27, **t** 0900 468 32888, **w** www. gouda.nl (*open April–Oct Mon–Sat 9am–5pm, Nov–Mar Mon–Sat 10am–4pm, and Sun July and Aug noon–3pm*). The office can let you know about excursions and short bicycle rides to nearby dairy farms where you can follow the whole cheesemaking process from cow to bulging yellow cartwheel.

Festivals

In mid-December Gouda holds a **candle festival**. All electric lights in the market square are switched off. The Stadhuis windows and surrounding houses are decorated with candles, and an enormous Christmas tree is lit up. It's well worth a special trip.

Eating Out

Gouda **t** *0182–*

De Beursklok, *Hoge Gowe 10*, **t** *514 163*. **Moderate.** Cosy *eetcafe* with a waterside terrace beneath the colonnades of an old fish market – and, appropriately, the fish here is good, though there are steak-and-sauce meat dishes and vegetarian options, too.

De Goudsche Stal, *Achter de Waag 20*, **t** *686 689*. **Moderate**. Situated in the old city stables, and decorated appropriately with agricultural implements and the odd sheaf of wheat. Good-value three-course menus, with such dishes as fish lasagne in Nouilly Prat sauce.

Stadtscafé De Zalm, *Markt 34*, **t** *507 679*. **Moderate**. Popular city café in a former inn beside the Waag, with a terrace that spills out onto the town square. A good lunchtime stop for a salad or light meal.

Het Goudse Winkeltje, *Achter de Kerk 9a*, **t** *527 874*. **Inexpensive**. Busy café just behind the Grotekerk that sells delicious pancakes and sandwiches.

Van den Berg, *Lange Groenedaal 32*, **t** *529 975*. **Inexpensive**. The place to go to try the local speciality: sweet, sticky Gouda waffles.

Markt

Stadhuis

t *(0182) 588 758*. **Open** *Mon–Fri 9am–5pm, Sat 11am–3pm*; **adm** *€0.75*.

An exuberantly Gothic Stadhuis, built in 1450, is plonked right in the middle of the market square. With its pixie-capped spires, bright-red shutters and cheerful carillon, it can't be missed. It's one of the most popular places in the country for weddings (in Holland you can plight your troth in any town you like) and couples are churned through every few minutes. Nip in between ceremonies for a look at the carved fireplaces and 17th-century tapestries. Remember to walk up the left-hand side of the double staircase at the entrance – criminals used to descend the one on the right on their way to the gallows, and it's considered bad luck to use it.

Waag

t *(0182) 529 996*. **Cheese museum open** *April–Oct Tues, Wed and Fri–Sun 1–5pm, Thurs 9am–5pm*; **adm** *€2*.

Behind the Stadhuis is the solid, square Waag (public weighing house), built in 1668. An enormous gable stone shows cheeses being weighed. Nowadays the Waag is a cheese museum comprising mainly interactive computer installations that tell you all you ever wanted to know about cheese, and a lot more besides. Downstairs, on one of the original scales, an attendant weighs young visitors. Anyone weighing under 40 Dutch pounds gets in free.

Every Thursday morning throughout the summer, farmers and porters dress in traditional costume, and everyone goes through the rituals of an old market beside the Waag, mainly for the benefit of tourists. The real cheese-trading takes place a few hours earlier, at 9am, and has more of the appearance of a car-boot sale. A handful of farmers gather around the market square to sell their wares from the backs of cars, slapping hands with customers to seal the deal.

St Janskerk or Grotekerk

t (0182) 512 684, **w** *www.st-janskerkgouda.nl.* **Open** *Mar–Oct Mon–Sat 9am–5pm; Nov–Feb Mon–Sat 10am–4pm; **adm** €2.*

St John's Church, also known as the Great Church, just off the market square, is the pride of the town. Earlier churches on the site seem to have been singled out by divine wrath; after three successive buildings had been destroyed by fire or lightning, the present cruciform basilica was begun in 1552. Soft soil precluded any towering Gothic spire, so the building spread horizontally and became the longest church in the Netherlands (403ft/123m). The church is famous for its 70 16th-century stained-glass windows, the most detailed and richly coloured of which are by the brothers Dirck and Wouter Crabeth. Not only did the glass survive the scourges of the iconoclasts, but the Reformed Church added some of its own. Rather than scenes from the lives of the saints, these depicted moments of historic glory – like the Relief of Leiden with its celebrated portrait of William of Orange. During the Second World War the windows were taken out and safely stored, and so survive beautifully intact.

Het Catharina Gasthuis

Oosthaven 9, **t** *(0182) 258 8440.* **Municipal museum open** *Mon–Sat 10am–5pm, Sun noon–5pm; **adm** €3.60; ticket also valid for De Moriaan Museum.*

On the lane behind St Janskerk (helpfully called Achter de Kerk – 'Behind the Church') is the tall red-brick **Lazaruspoortje** (Lazarus Gate) with a relief showing poor, pustule-ridden Lazarus and the rich man who will never make it to the bosom of Abraham (Luke 16:19–31). This 17th-century entrance to a Lepers' Hospice was transferred here in the 1960s to serve as the back entrance to Het Catharina Gasthuis (St Catherine's Hospital), now a municipal museum, with an intriguing collection of 14th–17th-century buildings Renovations over the past few years have led to more space to show off the collection, while at the same time revealing more of the buildings themselves. There's a small, but alluring collection of 17th-century art that includes a characteristically riotous Jan Steen inn scene (ostensibly a painting of Anthony and Cleopatra) and an exquisite *Woman Spinning* by the much-neglected Michael Sweerts. You can see a reconstructed 19th-century apothecary's shop (very much in demand as a period film set) and a medieval surgeon's room. The museum also has a good collection of paintings from the French Barbizon school and the Hague School and a fine collection of medieval silver (especially the ornate 15th-century Chalice of Jacoba of Bavaria).

De Moriaan Museum

Westhaven 29, **t** *(0182) 588 444.* **Open** *Mon–Sat 10am–5pm, Sun noon–5pm; **adm** €3.60.*

Five minutes' walk down the canal from the Catharina Gasthuis, you'll find De Moriaan ('The Blackamoor'), a 17th-century merchant's house and tobacco shop named after the carving over the door. It now houses some of the finest pieces of the city's collection of Gouda faience, with exceptional pieces from the 1920s.

Arts and Crafts

Adrie Moerings

Peperstraat 76, **t** *(0182) 512 842.* **Open** *Mon–Fri 9am–5pm, Sat 11am–5pm; **adm** free.*

Watch the luxuriously moustachioed Adrie Moerings make clay pipes in the traditional way. Try to persuade him to make a *door-roker*. This pipe has a plain bowl, but as you use it, a pattern begins to emerge in the clay.

Delft Blue Pottery

Lange Groenendaal 73, t (0182) 514 702. **Open** *Tues–Sat 10am–5pm; adm free. De Drietand Stavorenweg 5, t (0182) 516 494.* **Open** *Mon–Sun 8.30am–4.30pm; adm €2.05.*

At these two locations you can watch award-winning designers paint the blue and white Delft patterns onto jugs and plates. Gouda also has its own ceramic style, which uses richer colours, is far more beautiful and considerably more expensive.

De Roode Leeuw

Vest 65, t (0182) 522 041. **Open** *Thurs 9am–2pm, Sat 9am–4pm; adm €1.25.*

At this windmill you'll meet Marcel Koop, a real rosy-cheeked, flour-covered miller. In the early 1980s he gave up his job as an engineer to renovate the 17th-century windmill. Now it's the only working mill in the Netherlands also lived in by the miller.

UTRECHT

Anyone who arrives in Utrecht by train might be forgiven for thinking that half the city is a shopping mall. One of the Netherlands' most unfortunate 1960s architectural aberrations, a gigantic shoppers' warren (59 acres/24ha in extent, with over 200 shops trailing along 3 miles/5km of passageways, if you really want to know), sprawls around the station. It can take a determined ten-minute walk to reach the outside world.

But the ordeal is worth it. 'Amsterdam,' say the locals, 'was built by man; Utrecht by God himself.' The old centre of Utrecht is one of the most alluring in the land: spruce and stately, yet at the same time low-key and romantic – graced with two long canals and a network of sidestreets, rows of chic and quirky shops, a handful of top museums, and an impressive Gothic spire to navigate by.

Along the Oudegracht

The Oudegracht – a sunken canal, unique in the Netherlands – has run through the heart of Utrecht for more than 700 years. As the water level dropped over the centuries, the resourceful burghers responded by building a second sidewalk below street level, and digging cellars in the former canal walls. Today, many of these cellars are restaurants or cafés. The shops here along the Oudegracht and in its surrounding squares and alleys sell designer clothes, antiques and knick-knacks, and curiosities from all over the world. Many of the streets are pedestrian-only, and – unlike in so many other Dutch cities – care has been taken not to destroy old gables with hideous new shopfronts.

Museum Voor Het Kruideniersbedrijf Betje Boerhave

Hoogt 6 t (030) 231 6628. **Open** *Tues–Sat 12.30–4.30pm; adm free.*

Just east of Oudegracht you can step into shopping nostalgia at the Grocer's Museum, a reconstructed 1873 grocer's store complete with old-fashioned scales, open barrels of beans, and rows of old tins and cartons.

National Museum van Speelklok tot Pierement

Buurkerkhof 10, t (030) 231 2789, w www.museumspeelklok.nl. **Open** *Tues–Sat 10am–5pm, Sun noon–5pm; guided tours in English, duration 1hr, on the hour, but frequency according to demand at busy times; adm €6, including tour.*

One of the delights of Utrecht is this National Music Box and Barrel Organ Museum, a vast collection of automated musical instruments from the 15th to the 20th centuries. You can wander about part of the museum alone, but are strongly advised to wait for a tour, showing you the full collection and letting you to hear some of the machines in action – from a furry bunny that wiggles its ears in time to the music, through pianolas to a machine that plays three violins simultaneously.

Getting There

Trains leave Amsterdam's Centraal Station for Utrecht four times an hour, and the journey takes just over 30mins (€10 return). If you arrive at the railway station, follow the unobtrusive 'Centrum' signs to escape the shopping mall. Utrecht is about half an hour's drive from Amsterdam on the A2. If you arrive by **car**, bear in mind that the inner part of the city is a pedestrianized zone. There is ample parking beneath the afore-mentioned shopping mall (follow signs to Hoog Catharijne or Vredenburg).

Getting Around

Utrecht's main sights are reachable on foot, but for the Nederland Spoorweg-museum and Rietveld Schröder House you will need some sort of mechanization; however, **buses** are plentiful, and your Amsterdam *strippenkaart* (see p.64) is valid here. You can hire **pedalos** from Canalbike, on the Oudegracht opposite the Stadhuis.

Tourist Information

VVV, Vredenburg 90 (follow the signs through the shopping mall), **t** 0900 128 8732, **w** www.utrecht-city.com (open Mon–Wed and Fri 9.30am–6.30pm, Thurs 9.30am–9pm, Sat 9.30am–5pm, Sun 10am–2pm).

Festivals

Utrecht's main festivals are cultural ones. There's a lively **Festival of Modern Dance** and a **Jazz Festival** in April, and an experimental **Arts Festival** in May. The city has a strong international reputation for Old Music – the **Festival Oude Muziek**, held in late August/early September, is world renowned. The **Nederlands Filmfestival**, held in late September, is beginning to rival the Rotterdam Film Festival in reputation.

Eating Out

Utrecht **t** *030–*

Sot-l'y-laisse, *Zadelstraat 20*, **t** *232 1573. Booking recommended.* **Expensive**. Tiny, 'you're at a dinner party really' restaurant, with excellent cuisine. There's no menu: you choose your wine and set a limit to the number of courses you want, then just sit back and enjoy what comes – very much in a rich Franco-Dutch culinary tradition.

Het Grachtenhuys, *Nieuwegracht 33*, **t** *231 7494.* **Moderate**. Popular restaurant in a gracious old canal house. Good ingredients and careful, unfussy preparation make for an excellent meal. Good vegetarian options.

De Soepterrine, *Zakkendragerssteeg 40*, **t** *231 7005.* **Inexpensive**. Busy soup-kitchen down an alley near the Vredenburg Music Centre. Mouthwatering home-made soups include not only Dutch favourites, but exotica from Mexico or Japan.

Winkel van Sinkel, *Oudegracht 158*, **t** *230 3030.* **Inexpensive**. Busy, trendy, cavernous café built as a department store in the 1830s. The gigantic, cast-iron caryatids propping up the front portico were made in England, and were so heavy that they caused the canal wall beneath them to collapse. Pastas, salads and dishes of the day.

The Dom

Cathedral open May–Sept Mon–Sat 10am–5pm, Sun 2–5pm; Oct–April Mon–Sat 11am–4pm, Sun 2–4pm; adm free. Tower open May–Aug Mon–Sat 10am–8pm, Sun noon–8pm, Oct–Apr Mon–Sat 10am–5pm, Sun noon–5pm; guided tours on the hour, last tour 7pm (summer), 4pm (winter); adm €6.80.

Bishop Hendrik van Vianen laid the first stone of Utrecht's Dom (cathedral) in 1254. An earlier cathedral had been razed to the ground, and its replacement was to be in the very latest French Gothic style – including a 367ft/112m-high **tower** that rises in three magnificent stages, and is topped by an octagonal filigreed cone. The tower was completed only in 1382, and building went on until 1517. But in 1674 a hurricane hit Utrecht, completely demolishing the nave. This was never rebuilt, so today only chancel and tower remain, separated by an open space. You can climb the tower for a view that reputedly includes Rotterdam and

Amsterdam on a clear day, or pop into the remaining building for an idea of how vast and glorious the cathedral must once have been. Behind the chancel is a 15th-century **cloister** with a formal herb garden (divided into squares for medicinal, kitchen and dyeing plants), which was replanted in the 1960s. Have a look at one of the Gothic arches in the southwestern corner of the cloister – a jokey stonemason has carved ropes around the Gothic tracery, apparently holding the delicate stonework together.

Museum Catharijneconvent

Nieuwegracht 63, t (030) 231 3835, w www. catharijneconvent.nl. Open Tues–Fri 10am–5pm, Sat and Sun 11am–5pm; adm €6.

A short walk south of the Dom brings you to the Museum Catharijneconvent, housed in a late medieval convent. The museum offers an overview of Dutch religious art, with beautiful medieval manuscripts, richly embroidered vestments, carved altarpieces, and 16th- and 17th-century paintings by the likes of Rembrandt, Frans Hals and Saenredam. You can see the sobering influence of the Reformation on art (though there's also a painting of a pope that turns upside down to become a portrait of the devil), and the museum is known for excellent temporary exhibitions.

The Centraal Museum

Agnietenstraat 1, t (030) 236 2362, w www. centraalmuseum.nl. Open Tues–Sun 11am–5pm; adm €8.

Substantially renovated and extended in 1999, the Centraal Museum occupies a number of buildings around a large garden (to which visitors have access). You walk through underpasses and up spiral stairways, travel in glass-box lifts to Gothic chapels and large halls, explore cellars and suddenly discover attics. The collection is vast and varied, the presentation modern and imagi-

native, and the layout mind-boggling – though it's a pleasure to get lost.

In the depths of one part of the building, accompanied by a whiff of something like creosote, is the skeleton of a **wooden boat**, dating from around 997. A long former stables building contains parallel exhibitions of **fashion, interior design and contemporary art**, arranged not chronologically but along a spectrum from sober to extravagant. In the main building you can see part of the museum's extraordinary collection of **Golden Age** art – including Jan van Bronkhorst's beautifully pensive *Young Woman* (1655), and famed artists of the Utrecht School such as Van Scorel, Bloemaert and Terbrugghen – as well as **modern and contemporary Dutch painting**. Across the way, an entire wing is devoted to De Stijl architect and designer **Gerrit Rietveld**.

Nederland Spoorwegmuseum

Maliebaan Station, t (030) 230 6206, w www. spoorwegmuseum.nl; bus 3 from Centraal Station. Open Tues–Fri 10am–5pm, Sat and Sun 11.30am–5pm; adm €6.80. Closed for renovations until mid-2005.

To the east of the centre, just beyond the former city wall, is the National Railway Museum. A converted 19th-century train station holds a shiny collection of over 60 old locomotives, trams and carriages, from the earliest days of steam and horse-drawn trams, to sleek electric trains.

Rietveld Schröder House

Erasmuslaan 9, t (030) 236 2310, w www. centraalmuseum.nl; bus 4 to De Hoogstraat. Open Wed–Sat 11am–4.30pm, guided tours only (six per day), booking recommended; adm €6.

A little farther east is the Rietveld Schröder House, a high point of De Stijl architecture, designed by Gerrit Rietveld in 1924 for Mrs

Truus Schröder, who lived there until her death in 1985. The house preserves original features, including bold yellow, red and blue colours, lamps and furniture designed by Rietveld, and an upper floor that is almost entirely subdivided by movable screens.

AROUND THE GREEN HEART

Hélène Müller loved art. Her husband, Anton Kröller, loved nature. She was heiress to a blast-furnace industry; he married the boss's daughter. Together they developed the family firm into a prosperous multinational and used their fortune to realize a dream. Between 1909 and 1914 Anton bought up tracts of wild land near Arnhem. Hélène built up a superb and inspired collection of late 19th- and early 20th-century art. They restocked the land with game, planted copses, built a lodge to live in and a museum for the paintings. Today the Kröller-Müller Museum, set in the vast and varied landscape of De Hoge Veluwe national park, is one of the most delightful places to visit in the Netherlands. The estate now covers 13,000 acres (5,500 hectares) of land, the art collection is still growing and there really is something for everyone. You can picnic in forests or lie about on dunes, gallop through the fens on horseback or cycle sedately along leafy lanes. You can birdwatch, look for wild boar or nestle in animal hides waiting for red deer. The airy, intimate museum is a pleasure to walk around, and the collection is one of the best in the country. The sculpture park could detain you for hours and the lodge is unstuffy and well-preserved. There are all the cafés, restaurants and children's playgrounds you could wish for, without the horrid ambience of a theme park or tourist trap. On the outskirts of the park is Paleis Het Loo, a royal residence for three centuries, now open to public view.

De Hoge Veluwe National Park

t (0318) 591 627, w www.hogeveluwe.nl. **Open** *daily, April 8am–8pm, May 8am–9pm, June and July 8am–10pm, Aug 8am–9pm, Sept 9am–8pm, Oct 9am–7pm, Nov–March 9am–5.30pm;* **adm** *adults €10, 6–12s €5, plus €5 per car (includes admission to museum and sculpture park).*

De Hoge Veluwe national park is a curious amalgam of drifting sand dunes, watery fens, thick cultivated forests and open heathland. Mrs Kröller-Müller loved autumn colours – so you'll find forests of oak, birch, beech and rowan trees as well as the older plantations of pine and junipers. In the summer there are gloriously coloured thickets of rhododendrons, and purple heather covers the heath in August and September. Anton Kröller filled the park with magnificently antlered red deer, moufflons (a curly-horned wild sheep from Sardinia), wild boar, roe deer and even kangaroos. All, except the poor roos, survive in multitudes and have such violent fun in the rutting season (September to October) that you're confined to your car in some parts of the park. There are marked walks throughout the area, though you don't have to keep to the paths. The visitors' centre can put you in touch with a local stables if you'd like to hire a horse, or you can pick up a bicycle (free, no deposit necessary) from the shelter in the central square.

Kröller-Müller Museum and Sculpture Park

t (0318) 591 241, e information@kmm.nl, w www.kmm.nl. **Museum open** *Tues–Sun 10am–5pm;* **sculpture park open** *Tues–Sun 10am–4.30pm.*

The Kröller-Müller Museum and Sculpture Park are now state-owned. A collection of exceptional quality is growing around the core of Hélène Kröller-Müller's bequest. It's a far more pleasant place to see **Van Goghs** than the crowded museum in Amsterdam – and Mrs Kröller-Müller had nearly 300 of the painter's works: a version of *The Potato*

Getting There and Around

The easiest way to get to and about De Hoge Veluwe and the surrounding villages is by **car.** You can drive about in the park, and abandon the car where you wish. Take the A1 to Apeldoorn or the A2 and A12 to Arnhem. There are gates to the park at the villages of Otterlo, Schaarsbergen and Hoenderloo. The journey takes about 1½hrs.

The nearest **train** stations are at Arnhem and Apeldoorn. The journey from Amsterdam to Arnhem takes just over an hour and costs €25.20 return. Trains leave twice an hour. Take bus 107 from Arnhem station for the park, changing at Otterlo to bus 110. There are about two trains an hour from Amsterdam to Apeldoorn. Journey time is one hour and tickets cost €20.40 return plus two strips on a *Strippenkaart* for the bus. Bus 110 takes you into the park, and bus 126 or 104 runs direct from Apeldoorn station to Paleis Het Loo. Trains also go from Centraal Station to Ede-Wageningen (€18.60 return), where you can change for bus 110 (seven strips on a *Strippenkaart*).

Once in De Hoge Veluwe Park you can get about on the (free) white **bicycles**.

Getting to surrounding villages by public transport is trickier. Buses 102 and 104 run from Appeldoorn to the stop 'De Echoput' near Hoog Soeren every half-hour, but then it's a half-hour's walk into the village. Bronkhorst is best reached by bus 82 from Zutphen, but again you'll have to be prepared for a 20min walk from the bus stop into the village.

Tourist Information

Visitors' Centre (Hoenderloo Gate), **t** (0318) 591627 (*open daily, Nov–March 9am–5.30pm, April 8am–8pm, May–Aug 8am–10pm*). Maps are for sale at the entrance gates.

Eating Out

De Hoge Veluwe is the perfect place for a picnic. You can pick up supplies in Apeldoorn or Arnhem.

Balzaal, *Paleis Het Loo*, **t** (055) 577 2400. **Inexpensive**. Salads, sandwiches and snacks in the grand setting of a former palace ballroom.

Café-Restaurant Hoog Soeren, *Hotel Hoog Soeren, Hoog Soeren 15, just off the N344 west of Apeldoorn (near Paleis Het Loo)*, **t** (055) 519 1231. **Open** *daily noon–10pm*. **Inexpensive**. Pleasant Old Dutch-style family restaurant complete with open hearth and hunting trophies, good for a game lunch.

The Kröller-Müller Museum Café, *Hoge Veluwe*, **t** (0318) 591 041. **Inexpensive**. Good salads and a large terrace.

Museum Café, *Paleis Het Loo*, **t** (0318) 591 657. **Open** *Tues–Sun 10am–4.30pm*. **Inexpensive**. Light snacks and cakes in the old orangerie, with a terrace that catches the sun.

Eaters, fine self-portraits and landscapes and some of his best drawings. You'll find good examples of **Braque**, **Picasso** and the rather neglected Cubist painter **Fernand Léger**, colourful stippled Pointillist paintings by **Seurat**, and a touching study of an ageing clown by **Renoir** – in fact most major movements and artists of the last 100 years are represented. Before you leave have a look for Dutch artist **Jan Toorop**'s eerie fairy-tale drawings and a dreamy pink and green screen by the French Symbolist painter **Odilon Redon**.

Out in the sculpture park you'll find pieces not only by old familiars like **Rodin**, **Henry** **Moore** and **Barbara Hepworth**, but also exciting work by contemporary artists. The park reflects Hélène Kröller-Müller's vision of the way art, nature and architecture can interrelate. The long, low, stone and glass museum blends perfectly into the surrounding landscape. In the pond outside, **Marta Pan**'s enormous, curvaceous, abstract Swan is gently blown about by the wind. In a little hollow, over a hill, rusty iron sheets seem to grow up from the soil. Boulders hang suspended in rope hammocks between the trees; giant, seed-shaped balls of clay, slate igloos and odd tent-like structures are scattered about open grass patches. A frail needle of aluminium pipes and steel wire towers 92ft (27m) into the sky, higher than most of the trees. Anyone under the age of 12 makes a beeline for **Jean Dubuffet**'s *Jardin d'Email* (1972/3). From the outside it's a tall white wall, but once you climb the narrow stairs you're in a big, bumpy white landscape cut up by irregular black lines. Bemused adults sit around the edges, while children tear about, trip over the mounds and bang their heads.

Jachthuis St Hubertus

Open *April–Oct;* **guided tours** *daily, every half-hour 10am–5pm, Jan Sat and Sun only.*

Before leaving De Hoge Veluwe, pay a quick visit to the Jachthuis St Hubertus (St Hubert's hunting lodge). The Kröller-Müllers' family home and its artificial lake were built in 1914 by H.P. Berlage, the father of modern Dutch architecture (*see* p.54). It's a compact brick building with an ugly, incongruous tower. Inside, however, the house has a cosy 'lived-in' atmosphere – and some superb Art Deco furniture. Coloured bricks and brightly glazed tiles abound, and the motifs on hunting, of the story of St Hubertus (the patron saint of hunters), and of the sun, run throughout the interior design.

Paleis Het Loo

t (055) 577 2400, *w www.paleishetloo.nl.* **Open** *Tues–Sun 10am–5pm;* **adm** *adults €9, under-18s €3.*

Adjoining the national park is the Koninklijke Domeinen (royal estate) and the magnificent Baroque Paleis Het Loo. Built in 1685 as a hunting lodge for Stadhouder William III (of 'William and Mary' fame), the palace was used as a royal residence until 1962. Nowadays it is open to the public. You wander through a succession of lavishly decorated state rooms and boudoirs. Each is done up using furniture that reflects the taste of one of the royal occupants, in sequence from the 17th century to the 1930s. But most splendid of all are the **gardens**, laid out again in the 1980s following the 17th-century plans by Daniel Marot, who also originally designed the palace interior. View the exquisite formal layout from the roof of the palace, then descend to stroll among rose bushes, brush against fragrant herbs and wander through the gazebo.

THE HAGUE

The wide boulevards and graceful architecture of The Hague (Den Haag) speak of quiet, established wealth, and Amsterdammers, in particular, tend to complain that The Hague is a stuffy domain of diplomats, civil servants and businessmen. (Though Amsterdam is the capital of the Netherlands, The Hague is the centre of government and the chosen seat of the present queen.) It may not be the place you would go to bop until dawn or throng singing through the streets, but the spotless architecture, acres of greenery and inimitable museums give it an atmosphere of tranquil refinement which is rather alluring. The Hague offers the bonus of the seaside resort of Scheveningen, on its north-western perimeter, and the town of Delft to the south.

History

Around the year 1230, Floris IV, Count of Holland, built himself a country cottage beside a pond in the North Sea dunes. His son William II, who was elected King of the Romans and Emperor of Germany in 1247, thinking that a grander hunting lodge better befitted his status, began to put up a small palace on the site. The settlement that grew up around it was known as 's-Gravenhage ('the Count's hedge'), and this is still The Hague's official name. Over the centuries, successive counts added to the original buildings and put up new palaces. They progressed from being mere counts to becoming *stadhouders* and eventually kings of Holland. The Hague became their official seat and, after 1578, the meeting place of the States General, the predecessor of the present-day Dutch parliament.

Getting There

Trains take 50mins, with about four an hour. The Hague has two railway stations: Den Haag HS (Hollands Spoor) and Den Haag CS (Centraal Station). There are frequent tram and rail links between the two, but the CS is the more convenient.

Getting Around

Most of the tourist sites are within very easy walking distance of each other, though you will probably prefer to hop onto **tram** 8 for the Panorama Mesdag and the Museon. Tram 9 takes you via Madurodam to Scheveningen. **Bicycle hire** is available beside Station Hollands Spoor, **t** (070) 389 0830.

Tourist Information

VVV, Koning Julianaplein 30, just outside Centraal Station, **t** (0900) 340 3505, **w** *www. denhaag.com* (*open Mon 10am–5.30pm, Tues–Fri 9am–5.30pm, Sat 10am–5pm, plus June–Sep Sun 11am–3pm*).

Festivals

The Hague knows how to let its hair down with some lively summer festivals. In June there's a 10-day long Indonesian market, the **Pasar Malam Besar**; the **International Kite Festival at Scheveningen**; and a two-day **International Horse Show** on the Lange Voorhout, a large green square in the middle of town. The **North Sea Jazz Festival**, held annually in mid-July, is one of the world's most important celebrations of jazz.

Eating Out

The Hague **t** *070–*

The Hague is renowned for the quality of its Indonesian restaurants.

Calla's, *Laan van Roos en Doorn 51A*, **t** *070 345 5866*. **Expensive**. Muted, restrained and coolly sedate, the epitome of how many people see The Hague: as a genteel counterpart to the wild capital Amsterdam. But the mood is by no means stuffy – there's a good streak of Hague chic among the clientele, and hints of the hipper end of the diplomatic world.

Le Restaurant, *Hotel Des Indes, Lange Voorhout 54–6*, **t** *361 2345*. **Expensive**. Service is impeccable and the cuisine a skilful combination of the best of Dutch and French traditions, with a touch of Indonesian exoticism.

Bogor, *Van Swietenstraat 2*, **t** *346 1628*. **Moderate**. Excellent Indonesian cooking in an elegant Jugendstil house.

The Raffles, *Noordeinde 196*, **t** *345 8587*. **Moderate**. An Indonesian restaurant that dares to be a little different.

't Achterommetje, *Achterom 71*, **t** *364 5876*. **Inexpensive**. Cosy, traditional Dutch lunch spot tucked behind a grand neoclassical shopping arcade, where you can get good soups and filling wraps and rolls, some with an Indonesian touch.

Make Your Own, *Plein 3*, **t** *360 4418*. **Inexpensive**. Hip hangout near the Mauritshuis, where you compile your own salads and sandwiches from fresh and imaginatively combined ingredients at food bars.

De Posthoorn, *Lange Voorhout 39A*, **t** *360 4906*. **Inexpensive**. Serves light snacks and sandwiches and has a pleasant terrace overlooking the tree-lined marketplace.

See You at Noon, *Korte Houtstraat 14*, **t** *345 8147*. **Inexpensive**. Smart modern lunch venue offering soups, salads and sandwiches.

Yet the counts and their successors contrived to keep The Hague detached from the strife of day-to-day politics. Great battles were fought at Leiden, Breda and Utrecht. Assemblies were held and treaties signed at Brussels and Bruges. Amsterdam swept to glory and heady riches on the back of the Dutch East India Company during the Golden Age. The Hague remained serenely apart from the fray, and was officially classed as a 'village' well into the 19th century. But all the time it was gaining importance as an administrative and judicial centre. In 1511 the highest court of Holland was established here, and by the 17th century The Hague had become such a vortex of intrigue among foreign diplomats that it was called 'the whispering gallery of Europe'.

In 1899 the Permanent Court of Arbitration (later to become the International Court of Justice) was established in The Hague, giving this long tradition a mark of respectability. But in the meantime, the 'village' had suffered a sharp blow to its pride. During the French occupation (1806–13), King Louis Napoleon had lingered in The Hague just a few months, before deciding to move his capital to Amsterdam. After the French had withdrawn from the Netherlands, Amsterdam retained this status – although the new Dutch king, William I, moved the seat of parliament back to The Hague. Rivalry between the two cities remains intense. As recently as 1953 there was a massive attempt to have The Hague reclassified as the Dutch capital, and the public wrangling was finally resolved only after an appeal to original documents signed by King William I. But each city still regards the other as in some way second-best.

Binnenhof

*Guided tours of the Binnenhof and Houses of Parliament Mon–Sat 10am–4pm (last tour 3.45pm), **t** (070) 364 6144 to book in advance; **adm** from €4.30. All tours start at the Ridderzaal, but after that the itinerary varies according to which house is in session: try to get on a tour that visits the old rather than the new chambers.*

The count's courtyard, the Binnenhof, remains the centre of town, though now it's an amalgam of architectural styles. On the third Tuesday in September, Queen Beatrix sweeps into the courtyard in a gold carriage to open parliament. The ceremony takes place under the high oak vaulting and delicate turrets of the **Ridderzaal** (the 'hall of knights') in the centre of the Binnenhof. The Ridderzaal, the oldest building in the complex, was built to host the early Counts of Holland's hunting parties. Later it served as a court. High up in the rafters of the barrel-vaulted roof are small carved heads. The judges encouraged miscreants and witnesses to tell the truth by warning them

that these 'eavesdroppers' listened to all they said and passed it on to God. By far the best view of the Binnenhof is from the outside – across the **Hofvijver** ('court pond'), a glassy expanse of water graced with a softly spraying fountain.

The **First Chamber** of the States General (the equivalent of the British House of Lords or the US Senate) still meets within the Binnenhof complex, in a grand Baroque ball-room. The **Second Chamber** (the effective governing body of the Netherlands) now meets in a modern building round the corner from the Ridderzaal. Completed in 1993, the new chambers are decorated in a way intended to portray the Dutch landscape. This is done with disarming honesty: one wall represents sheets of pouring rain, and the ceiling of the plenary hall is painted to symbolize a low blue-grey sky.

Mauritshuis

*Korte Vijverberg 8, **t** (070) 302 3435, **w** www. mauritshuis.nl. **Open** Tues–Sat 10am–5pm, Sun 11am–5pm; **adm** €7.*

Next to the parliament buildings, on a corner of the Hofvijver, the Mauritshuis, a grand 17th-century mansion built for a favoured general, is now home to the Royal Collection of paintings once owned by stad-houders William IV and William V. High points of three centuries of Dutch and Flemish art cover the walls, stacked one above the other (a fashionable way of displaying pictures in the 18th century). You can see a moving self-portrait by **Rembrandt**, as well as his first Amsterdam commission, *The Anatomy Lesson of Professor Tulp* (1632) – the corpse, like the painter, had just arrived in Amsterdam from Leiden, and the erudite surgeon was renowned for his advice that patients drink 50 cups of tea a day. There are three **Vermeers** (including the famous *Girl with a Pearl Earring*), **Frans Hals'** manic *Laughing Boy*, **Paulus Potter's** nightmarish, meticulously finished *Young Bull* (complete with frogs and flies) and works by **Rubens** and **Holbein**. There are also nine paintings by the 17th-century innkeeper **Jan Steen**, including his postcard-sized cheekily lascivious *Girl Eating Oysters*.

Palaces and Churches

The Counts of Holland were incorrigible palace-builders. On Noordeinde you can see the classicist pile of the **Paleis Noordeinde** (restored to the appearance it had in 1640). Paleis Noordeinde is where Queen Beatrix, very much a workaday monarch, clocks in to do her share of the country's administration, and it is not open to the public.

In the centre of town, on Lange Voorhout, is a vast tree-filled square. Part of this was at one time a medieval tournament field. Visitors can see the neat, modest 18th-century **Het Paleis** (*Lange Voorhout 74; open Tues–Sun 11am–5pm; adm €4.50*). Het Paleis was once the winter home of Queen Emma (Beatrix's great-grandmother) but now hosts temporary art exhibitions.

Just south of Paleis Noordeinde is the imposing, rather gloomy **Grote Kerk**, or Great Church (*t (070) 365 8665; open by request*). It dates back to 1539, though most of the structure you see today was built a century later, after a fire had destroyed the earlier church. Next door is the elaborately decorated 17th-century **Oude Stadhuis**, now a restaurant.

Vredespaleis

Carnegieplein 2, t (070) 302 4137, w www. vredespaleis.nl. Open May–Oct Mon–Fri 10am–5pm; Nov–April Mon–Fri 10am–4pm; guided tours only, 10, 11am, 2, 3 and 4pm; adm €3.50.

The 1899 Hague Peace Conference established the Permanent Court of Arbitration – a court with global jurisdiction, still widely respected and considered neutral – but gave it a rather dingy home. In 1903 the American millionaire Andrew Carnegie donated $1.5 million to build a more appropriate palace for the court. Countries from all over the world contributed ironwork, stained glass,

statuary and furniture to create a quirky hotchpotch of a building.

Panorama Mesdag

Zeestraat 65, t (070) 364 4544, w www. panoramamesdag.com; tram 8. Open Mon–Sat 10am–5pm, Sun noon–5pm; adm €4.

Hendrik Willem Mesdag (1831–1915) was a leading member of the Hague School of painters. He considered his *Panorama* – painted in the 1880s during a craze for such entertainments – to be his most important work, because it gave 'such an awesome impression of nature'. At the Panorama Mesdag you walk about under a canvas canopy and look out on all sides, across real sand dunes littered with clogs and empty gin bottles, at a huge, circular view of Scheveningen. The painting is done with such realism that contemporaries accused Mesdag of having projected new-fangled photographs on to the canvas and traced them. Though it was an artistic success, the Panorama was a commercial failure, helping drag the Belgian company that funded it into bankruptcy. Eventually it was bought by the artist himself, and is now jointly owned by 33 of his descendants.

A few minutes' walk away is the **Museum H.W. Mesdag** (*Laan van Meerdervoort 7F; open Tues–Sun noon–5pm*), where you can see the artist's own collection of Hague School paintings, as well as works of the related French Barbizon School and a reconstruction of Mesdag's living quarters and studio.

Gemeente Museum Complex

Gemeente Museum

Stadhouderslaan 41, t (070) 338 1111, w www. gemeentemuseum,nl. Open Tues–Sun 11am– 5pm; adm €7.

The superb Municipal Museum was designed in 1935 by the influential architect H.P. Berlage. The spacious tiled interior looks, at first glance, like a bank – or a very upmarket public lavatory. It houses a beautiful collection of **glass and silverware**, some important **19th-century paintings**, superbly reconstructed **period rooms** and one of the best **modern art** collections in the country. You'll find lots of familiar names from the first half of the 20th century – Monet, Picasso, Egon Schiele – as well as the pick of modern Dutch artists like Jan Toorop, Pyke Koch and the painters of the COBRA movement, Karel Appel and Constant. There are a number of early works by Mondriaan – realistic landscapes and bright Impressionistic studies – that hint only slightly at the abstract style for which he later became famous. Don't leave without visiting the **music department**, which displays instruments ranging from exquisitely crafted harpsichords and viols to an Indonesian gamelan.

Museon

Stadhouderslaan 41, t (070) 338 1338, w www. museon.nl. Open Tues–Fri 10am–5pm, Sat and Sun noon–5pm; adm €6.

Adjoining the Gemeente Museum is the Museon, which offers a romp through the world of popular science. Computers, CD-i players and imaginative displays bring to life everything from the Big Bang to contemporary electronics.

GEM and Fotomuseum Den Haag

Stadhouderslaan 43, t (070) 338 1133, w www. 2-gem-online.nl and www.fotomuseumden-haag.nl. Open Tues–Sun 2–10pm; café open noon to midnight; adm adults €5, under-18s free (ticket valid for both museums).

The latest addition to the Gemeente Museum complex is a hip new combined contemporary art and photography museum, with a waterside café attached. Both museums host international and local temporary exhibitions, but there is special emphasis on Dutch art and photography, so this is a good place to find out what's happening in Holland.

Omniversum

President Kennedylaan 5, t 0900 666 4837, w www.omniversum.nl. Programmes on the hour Mon noon–5pm, Tues and Wed 10am–5pm, Thurs–Sun and holidays 10am–9pm; phone or contact VVV for programme details; adm adults €8.80, under-12s €6.

Lasers and films are projected onto a dome-shaped screen, sounds explode all about you and special 'sub-woofers' produce bass notes so deep you can only feel them.

Madurodam

George Maduroplein 1, t (070) 416 2400, w www.madurodam.nl; tram 9 from Centraal Station; bus 22 from Centraal Station. Open daily Mar–June 9am–8pm, July–Aug 9am–10pm, Sept–Mar 9am–6pm (last entry 1hr before closing); adm adults €11, 4–11s €8.

You can see models of landmarks from all over the Netherlands, little residential canals, football grounds, an airport, railways and a harbour – all on a scale of 1:25. By far the most enjoyable sight, however, is from up on the coffee terrace where you can watch the visitors tramp, Gulliver-like, up and down the paths.

Scheveningen

Tram 9 from Den Haag Centraal Station.

At its northwestern end, The Hague merges with the fishing port and seaside resort of Scheveningen. (Don't worry if you can't pronounce it – only the locals can. During the Second World War, Dutch Resistance fighters made suspected German infiltrators say it as a test of their true nationality.) The long, white stretch of sand, lapped by the grey-brown waters of the North Sea, somehow seems in its element on blustery days when tiny figures, buttoned up and bent over, battle against the wind. The pink bodies that stretch out in deckchairs on sunny days look curiously out of place.

Badly bombed during the war and hastily rebuilt, Scheveningen is a tacky resort. But you will find the **Kurhaus**, a gracious *grande dame* of a hotel, built in 1885 and now a national monument. The kings and queens of Europe have stayed here; Dietrich, Piaf, Chevalier and even the Rolling Stones have played in the concert hall. A little further along the promenade in the only other old building of note in Scheveningen, a pavilion built for King William I in 1826, is **Museum Beelden aan Zee** (*Sculptures by the Sea; Harteveltsraat 1, t (070) 358 5857, w www.beeldenaanzee.nl; open Tues–Sun 11am–5pm; adm €5*). Set in a tranquil hollow in the dunes, it is devoted to sculptures of the human form. Have a look at Igor Mitoraj's mysterious, veiled marble reliefs, then don a sou'wester off the rack and step out onto the terraces to see Arthur Spronken's idiosyncratic portrayal of the Dutch royal family.

Nearby, the **Sealife Centre** (*Strandweg 13, t (070) 354 2100, w www.sealife.nl; open daily 10am–6pm, July and August 10am–8pm; adm adults €9.50, 4–11s €6*) is home to creatures of the deep, from shrimps to stingrays. Presentation is imaginative (at one point you walk through an underwater glass tunnel, with sharks swimming above your head), and the centre is a great hit with children.

DELFT

Though overrun by tourists in season, of all the towns on the Randstad Delft manages to preserve its age-old charm the best. Get there early before the crowds descend and you might suddenly glimpse a canal, bridge, alley, patch of skyline, or a stretch of façades, that could come right out of the *View of Delft* by the city's most famous son, the painter Johannes Vermeer (*c.* 1632–75).

Established early in the 11th century, Delft soon became a prosperous weaving and brewing town. In 1645, an exploding arsenal destroyed much of the medieval town, but a massive rebuilding programme soon restored its former glory. It was around this time that De Porceleyne Fles started making and exporting the blue and white earthenware that was to make the town famous.

The Markt

Facing each other proudly across the market square are the Stadhuis and the Nieuwe Kerk. In between come rows of cafés, restaurants, souvenir shops selling tacky ersatz Delftware, and – on Thursdays – a busy general market. Of the medieval **Stadhuis** only the 13th-century tower remains. The surrounding solid grey stone building, with its scarlet shutters and fussy cornice, was put up in 1618 by leading Renaissance architect Hendrick de Keyser, after a fire had destroyed the original city hall. The late-Gothic **Nieuwe Kerk** (*open April–Oct Mon–Sat 9am–6pm, Nov–March Mon–Fri 11am–4pm and Sat 11am–5pm; adm €2.50 including entrance to Oude Kerk*) took more than a century to build, between 1383 and 1510. Even then the stonemasons could not down chisels, because the church was badly damaged by the fire that swept Delft in 1536 and by the arsenal explosion a hundred years later. It wasn't until 1872 that the flamboyant architect P.J.H. Cuypers shot the tower up to its present 109m. Inside the church is the sumptuous black marble and alabaster tomb of William of Orange, together with a carving of the prince and, nearby, his small dog, which pined to death after William was assassinated. A stone slab in the floor marks the entrance to the royal mausoleum, where all but a few Dutch monarchs have been buried ever since.

Oude Delft

Oude Kerk

Open *April–Oct Mon 9am–6pm; holidays noon 9am–6pm; Nov–Mar Sun–Fri 11am–4pm and Sat 11am–5pm;* ***adm*** *€2.50 (with Niewekerk).*

A walk along the Oude Delft canal, lined with elegant patrician mansions, provides a charming impression of the old city. At one end, the tower of the Oude Kerk seems to tilt in four directions simultaneously – with a 6ft tilt to the east and 3ft to the north. The tower houses a 9-ton carillon that, understandably, is rung only on special occasions.

Getting There

Delft is 1hr by **train** from Amsterdam's Centraal Station. Delft is also part of The Hague's urban network: **tram** journeys take 20 and 15mins respectively. There are also train connections between The Hague CS and Delft.

Getting Around

Most sights are within walking distance, ranged around the Markt. To reach the Markt from Delft station, cross the Westsingelgracht and Oude Delft canals and turn left at Koornmarkt.

Tourist Information

VVV, Markt 85, **t** (015) 212 6100, **w** *www.vvvdelft.nl* (open April–Oct Mon–Fri 9am–6pm, Sat 9am–5pm, Sun 10am–3pm; Nov–March Mon–Fri 9am–5.30pm, Sat 9am–5pm).

Eating Out

Delft **t** *015–*

Explore the side streets between Koornmarkt, Oude Delft and Phoenixstraat for the cosiest cafés and best eats.

Le Vieux Jean, *Heilige Geestkerkhof 3*, **t** *213 0433*. **Moderate**. Long-time family-run favourite. Son Robert-Jan Polman is giving new verve to his parents' traditional good cooking by slipping the odd bit of curry in with the langoustines, or adding figs to the duck with red wine sauce.

De Kurk, *Kromstraat 20*, **t** *015 214 1474*. **Inexpensive/Moderate**. Old-fashioned place in an historic building, and somehow off the tourist circuit, though it's in the centre of town, Good, down-to-earth Dutch soul food.

Kleyweg's Stadskoffyhuis, *Oude Delft 133*, **t** *212 4625*. **Inexpensive**. Crispy pancakes, a relaxed neighbourhood-café atmosphere, and a view onto the prettiest canal in town.

The church was begun in the 13th century, though much of its austere interior dates from 200 years later. Inside you'll find the graves of Vermeer, and famous Dutch admirals Martin Tromp and Piet Hein.

Prinsenhof Museum

St Agathaplein 1, **t** *(015) 260 2358*, **w** *www.gemeentemusea-delft.nl*. **Open** *Tues–Sat 10am–5pm, Sun 1–5pm; **adm** €3.50*.

Across the way from the church, off a quiet courtyard, is the Prinsenhof Museum. The former cloister houses the Delft historical museum – stocked with pottery, silver, tapestries and royal portraits – but is more famous as the spot where William of Orange was assassinated by Catholic fanatic Balthasar Geraerts. You can still see the bullet holes the murderer left behind in the wall of the stairwell.

Across the courtyard is the **Nusantara Museum** (*t (015) 260 2358; open same hours, adm €2.50*), well worth a peek for its colourful and fascinating collection of costumes and artefacts from the Dutch East Indies – much of it being booty brought back

during the 17th century by members of the Dutch East India Company.

Museum Lambert van Meerten

Open *Tues–Sat 10am–5pm, Sun 1–5pm; **adm** €2.50*.

Further up the canal, just beyond the Prinsenhof, is the Museum Lambert van Meerten, which offers a fine opportunity to view a canal house from inside. As well as finely furnished rooms, you'll find a vast collection of Delft tiles and ceramics from around the world.

De Porceleyn Fles

Rotterdamseweg 196, **t** *(015) 251 2030*, **w** *www.royaldelft.com*. **Open** *April–Oct daily 9am–5pm; Nov–Mar Mon–Sat 9am–5pm; **adm** €2.50*.

If it's porcelain you're after, head to this famous Delftware factory, where you can see the blue and white ceramics being hand-painted, and buy the real thing rather than the repro tack sold in most souvenir shops.

ROTTERDAM

For over 25 years Rotterdam, on the delta of the River Maas, has topped the list of the world's largest ports. Unlike anywhere else in the Netherlands, Rotterdam has the skyline, pace and aggressive edge of a big city. Locals dub it 'Manhattan-on-the-Maas'.

Old Rotterdam was all but flattened by bombs early in the Second World War. The imagination and sense of adventure that the authorities brought to rebuilding their city has resulted in some bravura feats of modern architecture. As you step out of Rotterdam Centraal Station, you are confronted by the tallest office block in the Netherlands – a shard of black glass 500ft high, belonging to an insurance company. The shapes, angles and colours of the buildings beyond it grow increasingly weird. But Rotterdammers take to this innovation with gusto, even giving some of the odder buildings nicknames. 'Rotterdam,' they say, 'will never be finished.' But there is another side to the city. Recently, the few patches of historic dockland that survived the bombing have been restored and injected with new life, largely in the form of cafés and restaurants.

Boijmans-Van Beuningen Museum

Museumpark 18–20, t (010) 441 9400, w www. boijmans.nl. Open Tues–Sat 10am–5pm, Sun 11am–5pm; adm €7, under-18s free.

Amsterdam and The Hague both cornered royal art collections for the foundation of their showpiece museums. Not only did Rotterdam lack the advantages of royal patronage, it had to contend with a series of philistine city councillors, who turned down offers of at least two magnificent private collections. Yet today the Boijmans-Van Beuningen Museum can stand shoulder to shoulder with the Rijksmuseum and the Mauritshuis as one of the finest collections of art and design in the country, including *Child in a Landscape*, the only Titian in any

Dutch collection; and *Lane of Poplars near Nuenen*, the first Van Gogh ever to appear in a public collection.

In 2003 a long-lasting renovation and restructuring of the museum was finally completed, revealing spacious new exhibition rooms and some stylish new presentation. On the left, just past the ticket office, is a **Digital Depot** – a marvellous miscellany of what the museum has to offer. Sixteenth-century portraits hang alongside 1960s spherical TV sets; moving projections flicker over sculptures made of tennis balls. The other ground-floor wing contains a glass-walled café (complete with scores of different designer chairs), which overlooks a pond and **sculpture garden**, and a section devoted to **design**. Here cabinets are arranged thematically, such as 'Chamber Pots 1400 to Present Day' and tea services.

Upstairs, in the older part of the museum, you'll find a large hall devoted to **temporary exhibitions**, surrounded by smaller rooms of modern art and a gallery of **Surrealists**. The museum's Surrealist collection was once unparalleled. Unfortunately most of it was on 'permanent' loan from the English eccentric (and purported illegitimate son of King Edward VII) Edward James, who in the 1970s wrested it back from the museum as he needed money to fund a scheme to fill a Mexican jungle with Surrealist sculpture. The museum managed to buy back a few prime works, including pieces by **Dalí**, **Duchamp**, **Man Ray** and **Magritte**.

In the wing opposite you'll find the Old Masters, with a wealth of canvases by the likes of **Rubens**, **Frans Hals** and **Rembrandt** (including a touching portrait of his son Titus). Famous images, such as **Breughel**'s *Tower of Babel* and **Hieronymus Bosch**'s *The Vagabond*, hang alongside lesser-known but nonetheless exquisite pieces such as **Bartholomeus van der Helst**'s intimate, 17th-century *Portrait of Abraham del Court and Maria de Keerssegieter*.

A central wing contains paintings from 1700–1930, with work by the Amsterdam artist **George Breitner** (look out especially for

Getting There

Rotterdam is 45 miles (72km) south of Amsterdam along the A4 and A13, and 18 miles (28km) from The Hague. **Trains** from Amsterdam's Centraal Station (there are four to five an hour) take 60mins (return €20.20). Delft is 10mins by train, and The Hague is 15mins.

Getting Around

If you don't feel like legging it, the most convenient form of public transport is the **metro**. Lines going in a similar direction stop at the same stations for most of their length, only fanning out in the distant suburbs – so the metro is easy to negotiate. There's also an efficient network of **trams** and **buses**. *Strippenkaarten* (*see* p.64) are valid.

Should you want a close-up view of the world's largest port, you can go on a **harbour tour**. Spido Havenrondvaarten, Leuvehoofd on the Leuvehaven, **t** (010) 275 9988, offers a variety of boat tours starting from €7.50.

Bicycle hire is available at Rijwiel Shop, Stationsplein 1, **t** (010) 412 6220.

Tourist Information

VVV, Coolsingel 57, **t** 0900 403 4065, **w** www.vvv.rotterdam.nl (open Mon–Thurs 9.30am–6pm, Fri 9.30am–9pm, Sat 9.30am–5pm). Not only can staff supply maps and the usual information, but they can suggest walking routes for people interested in modern architecture.

Festivals

The **Rotterdam Film Festival**, held in late January and early February, screens the pick of the latest art movies as well as commercial hits. In August, the **Heineken Jazz Festival** fills cafés (and sometimes streets) with eager fans of popular jazz and improvised music. There is also a two-month-long **Summer Festival** in July and August, which involves a wide variety of outdoor events and street entertainment.

Eating Out

Rotterdam **t** 010–

Parkheuvel, *Heuvellaan 21*, **t** 436 0530. **Expensive**. Modern restaurant with a view over the Maas, a classic ambience and a reputation almost unrivalled by any in the land. Scallops with acorn bread and truffles; langoustines and sole with sun-dried tomatoes and grilled artichoke.

Hotel New York, *Koninginnenhoofd 1*, **t** 439 0500. **Moderate–expensive**. Popular café and restaurant in an historic hotel on the harbour. There's an impressive seafood platter, but perhaps better for a snack or drink than a full meal.

De Tijd Geest, *Oost Wijnstraat 14*, **t** 233 1311. **Moderate**. Popular spot overlooking the Oude Haven. Formal décor under the high ceilings of a 19th-century building – with the occasional startling flash of fake cheetah-skin upholstery. Dishes such as duck breast with lavender honey and shiitake mushrooms.

Eethuisje de Parel, *Voorhaven 54B*, **t** 476 5558. **Moderate**. A tiny restaurant beside the harbour at Delfshaven. Oddball décor – as if Dalí had been let loose in an aquarium, though the food is less bizarre. Try the smoked pork chops with mushrooms.

Foody's, *Nieuwe Binnenweg 151*, **t** 436 5163. **Moderate**. Hippest new restaurant in town, serving really excellent Franco-Dutch cuisine. Book well in advance.

Bazar, *Witte de Withstraat 16*, **t** 206 5151. **Inexpensive**. Lively all-day restaurant with an artsy clientele, and serving food with a Turkish and Moroccan touch. The 'Middle Eastern Breakfast' (comprising fresh cheese and jams) is a popular Sunday morning hang-out.

his beautifully poised *The Earring*), and **Kees van Dongen**'s pensive portrait of a woman with *Finger on the Cheek*. Foreigners get a good look in – an early, figurative **Picasso**, plus a number of **Impressionists** and **Degas**' sculpture of a little dancing girl.

The Boijmans is also renowned for the quality of its temporary exhibitions, and has a large museum shop, well stocked with art books and designer knick-knacks.

Nederlands Architectuurinstituut

Museumpark 25, t (010) 440 1200 w www. nai.nl. **Open** *Tues–Sat 10am–5pm, Sun 11am–5pm;* **adm** *€5.*

The Netherlands Architecture Institute was designed by local architect Jo Coenen in 1993. A glass box, apparently suspended from scaffolding and with an arcaded offshoot that lights up in different colours at night, this is a zany home for the nation's architectural archive. There is no permanent display, but the institute holds temporary exhibitions on architectural themes.

Het Schielandshuis

Korte Hoogstraat 31, t (010) 217 6767 w www. hmr.rotterdam.nl. **Open** *Tues–Fri 10am–5pm, Sat and Sun 11am–5pm;* **adm** *€2.70 (ticket also valid in De Dubbelde Palmboom).*

Built between 1662 and 1665 as government offices for the surrounding province of Schieland, the pristine white Schielandshuis is a beautiful example of the poise and proportion of restrained Dutch Classicism. Though the building burnt down in 1864, the façade survived, and the rest was carefully restored. Today it houses a historical museum, most noted for the **Atlas van Stolk**. In 1835, the timber merchant Abraham van Stolk began to compile a 'historical atlas' of prints that depicted events in Dutch history and portrayed his own life and times. Only a tiny fragment of the Atlas goes on show at any one time, on the ground floor, usually in the form of an exhibition arranged around a specific theme. Also on the ground floor is a series of exceptional **Baroque- and Rococo-style rooms**, taken from mansions around Rotterdam and reassembled here. Upstairs you'll find displays on the **history of Rotterdam** (including some intriguing old children's toys) and a collection of **costumes**.

The Eastern Docklands

Blaak

Metro *Blaak.*

Emerging from the space-age metro station at Blaak, you are confronted with two of Rotterdam's most photographed modern buildings, an apartment block nicknamed '**the Pencil**' (for reasons that are quite evident), and the **Blaakse Bos** ('Blaak Forest'). The 'forest' comprises a thicket of cube-shaped apartments, up-ended on one corner and perched on tall stalks. Designed by Piet Blom in 1984, these curious homes are all occupied except one, which you can visit: the **Kijk-Kubus**, or Show-Cube (*Overblaak 70, t (010) 414 2285, w www.kubuswoning.nl; open Jan–Feb Fri–Sun 11am–5pm, Mar–Dec daily 11am–5pm; adm €1.75*). It is surprisingly ordinary inside.

Oude Haven

Metro *Blaak.*

Stretching out on the other side of the Blaakse Bos is the Oude Haven (Old Harbour), the first of a series of docks that were the predecessors of today's busy port. Nowadays the Oude Haven is filled with boats of the **Openlucht Binnenvaart Museum** (*open access; adm free*), workaday vessels that have plied the inland waterways over the centuries. The old warehouses that once surrounded the docks have gone, but as you wander from Oude Haven to **Scheep-maker-shaven** ('shipbuilders' harbour') and **Wijnhaven** ('wine harbour') these colourful, much-used old boats stand in startling contrast against a backdrop of angular modern architecture. There is even a whiff of tar and diesel in the air.

Maritiem Museum Prins Hendrik

Leuvenhaven 1, t (010) 413 2680, w www. maritiemmuseum.nl. **Open** *Tues–Sat 10am–5pm, Sun 11am–5pm, July–Aug and school holidays also Mon 10am–5pm;* **adm** *€3.50.*

Models and paintings of ships abound in the Maritime Museum. Unless your interest is passionate, you could skim through the first two floors stopping off only at the **Schatkamer** (treasury). After that, displays become more varied and interesting, with lots of hands-on exhibits for children. But by far the most riveting part of the museum is moored in the harbour outside: the 19th-century warship **Buffel**. The ship has been perfectly restored, from the rows of enamel basins in the crew's washroom to the polished mahogany and leather of the captain's cabin. You can see the shining, pumping engines and drop in on the ship's jail, situated in the bow just behind the battering ram.

The Western Docklands

The Erasmusbrug

The spectacular white Erasmusbrug is a 1,250ft/410m-long suspension bridge hanging from a single 424ft/139m-high pylon. It is nicknamed 'the swan' by those who like it. Those who don't refer to it rather unkindly as the 'washing-up brush'. The Erasmusbrug opened in 1996 but was forced to close again a few weeks later because the cables flapped alarmingly in the first strong wind. Across the water behind it you can see the twin towers of the former headquarters of the Holland-Amerika Lijn, the company that ferried so many people across the Atlantic to a new life in the USA. Nowadays the building is a hotel.

Euromast

Parkhaven 20, **t** *(010) 436 4811* **w** *www. euromast.com.* **Open** *April–June and Sept daily 10am–7pm; Oct–March daily 10am– 5pm; July and Aug Tues–Sat 10am–10.30pm, Sun and Mon 10am–7pm;* **adm** *€7.75.*

In a small park is Rotterdam's post-office tower, the Euromast. A lift takes you up 280ft (92m) to the viewing platform, then you have to hold onto your hat as – amidst much roaring and dry-ice smoke – the Space Adventure capsule will shoot you up to the top of the tower, all of 564ft (185m) above the ground, for a huge view that extends to the North Sea.

Delfshaven

The most appealing of all Rotterdam's historic harbours is Delfshaven (*w www. delfshaven.info*), which managed to get through the Second World War relatively unscathed. Delfshaven was once a separate town, made rich by jenever distilleries and as the main port serving the textile factories and potteries at Delft. The narrow harbour (it's more like a canal) runs past an old wind-mill, once used to grind grain for the distilleries, and is edged with dainty gabled buildings, mostly dating from the 17th century. Nowadays they house art galleries, antiques shops and a string of cafés and restaurants, giving Delfshaven a sedate, leisurely air that makes it seem quite detached from the rest of Rotterdam.

De Dubbelde Palmboom

Voorhaven 12, **t** *(010) 476 1533,* **w** *www. hmr.rotterdam.nl;* **metro** *Delfshaven.* **Open** *Tues–Fri 10am–5pm, Sat and Sun 11am–5pm;* **adm** *€2.70.*

In this converted 19th-century warehouse you can see a number of exhibits on working life in the area. These range from an Iron Age farmstead to a faithful reconstruction of the interior of a worker's cottage built early in the 20th century.

Oude Kerk

Open *Sat noon–5pm;* **adm** *free.*

A few minutes' walk further up the harbour is the Oude Kerk. This is the church where, on 21 July 1620, the Pilgrim Fathers spent their last night on Dutch soil, praying for safe conduct and sleeping on the pews. The next morning they embarked on the *Speedwell* for Plymouth, where they changed ships for the *Mayflower*.

Where to Stay

It's a summer Friday afternoon, the Amsterdam Tourist Board information office opposite Centraal Station is brimming with hopeful weekenders looking for accommodation. But by 4 o'clock Amsterdam is full. Frustrated visitors are being dispatched to surrounding towns like Leiden or Haarlem – pretty towns, and commuting is swift and cheap, yet this is always going to be second best.

The truth is, to really relish Amsterdam you need to stay right in the centre, preferably on a canal, and to do that you should make sure you book a hotel room well in advance – two to three weeks at least, more in the summer or over holiday weekends. There is, of course, always the chance of catching a cancellation, and some hotels do keep back a room or two until the last minute. If you cannot book in advance, try calling the hotel direct just before noon – the witching hour between check-out and check-in – and try your luck.

All sorts of canal houses – poky, grand and resonantly historic – have been given new life as hotels. Many of these are privately owned and have been lovingly turned into little havens of *gezelligheid* (cosiness) or storehouses of antiques. These are the best places of all to stay – but most have built up a dedicated clientele and require booking some time in advance. Rooms in the same house will vary enormously in size, and *en suite* bathrooms tend to have showers only. If you hear of a particularly desirable room, try to book it specifically by number.

Reservations

Reservations can be made, once you're in the country, through the Tourist Office (*see* 'Tourist Offices' in the 'Practical A–Z' chapter, p.77). They charge a €13 booking fee. The Netherlands Board of Tourism in your home country can give you a list of hotels, but unfortunately can't make bookings. Also try **Amsterdam Reservation Centre**, **t** 0900 400 4040, **e** *reservations@ amsterdamtourist.nl*, **w** *www. visitamsterdam.nl* (**open** Mon–Fri 9am–4pm).

Because accommodation is at such a premium, you'll find that most hotels will ask for a deposit or the security of a credit card number. Some simply won't accept weekend reservations unless you book, or at least pay for, Friday, Saturday and Sunday.

Accommodation Categories

Standards of cleanliness and service are high, and unless you're scraping along at the very bottom of the price range, you're unlikely to find yourself sharing your room with local fauna, thumping faulty electrical equipment or speculating about the origins of the hairs on the sheets. Facilities can be quite spartan, however, and a lot of the smaller hotels offer rooms of the bed-bedsidetable-wardrobe-only variety. Yet even these are usually tastefully done up and almost invariably impeccably clean.

Hotels are graded by the Benelux star system (one to five stars), though this isn't a particularly useful guide as it is based on an inventory of facilities and tells you nothing about location, service or ambience. Around the top end of the moderate range (€120+) you should be assured of at least a TV and telephone in your room. Beyond that lies the world of minibars, *en suite* Jacuzzis and telephones in the loo.

The hotels below are listed by neighbourhood and price range. Nearly all of them are within easy walking distance of the main tourist sites and museums, and have been chosen because of their pleasant atmosphere, location or historical significance.

The hotels in the 'expensive' range tend to be business hotels.

Here you're paying for facilities like fax machines and meeting rooms. Such places are briskly efficient, but are often soulless and used to expense-account customers. You can be just as comfortable, and will probably be far happier, in one of the more idiosyncratic hotels from the top of the 'moderate' range.

Price Categories

The following prices are for a double room and include services and taxes and (unless otherwise stated) Dutch breakfast. For prices of single rooms deduct 15–20%.

luxury	€250 and over
expensive	€150–250
moderate	€100–150
inexpensive	€75–100
cheap	under €75

The Centre: Old Side

Luxury

(30) The Grand Amsterdam H6
Oudezijds Voorburgwal 197, 1001 EX, **t** 555 3111, **f** 555 3222, **e** *hotel@ thegrand.nl*, **w** *www.thegrand.nl*; *tram 4, 9, 16, 24, 25*.
Built as an inn in 1578, then used as Admiralty Headquarters, and finally serving as Amsterdam's city hall (from 1808 to 1988). Many fine 1920s interior fittings remain (including the Wedding Room in which Queen Beatrix plighted her troth), but some people are put off by the proximity of the Red Light District. Five-star facilities, with TVs, swimming pool, business facilities, gym and parking.

(35) Hotel de l'Europe H7
Nieuwe Doelenstraat 2–8, 1012 CP, **t** 531 1777, **f** 531 1778, **e** *hotel@ leurope.nl*, **w** *www.leurope.nl*; *tram 4, 9, 16, 24, 25*.
An elegant 19th-century hotel in the grand old style. Knocks spots off the Doelen down the road. Has all the five-star facilities – swimming pool, gym, parking, air-con and TVs.

Expensive

(32) Nes I7
Kloveniersburgwal 137, t 624 4773, f 620 9842, e mail@hotelnes.com, w www.hotelnes.nl; tram 4, 9, 16, 24, 25.
A well-run and quiet hotel with 39 rooms set in an attractive gabled canal house in a quiet corner of the old centre. Family suites are available and children under 12 are accommodated for free. Breakfast is included; TVs in rooms.

(34) NH Doelen H7
Nieuwe Doelenstraat 24, 1012 CP, t 554 0600, f 622 1084, w www. nhhotels.com; tram 4, 9, 16, 24, 25.
One of Amsterdam's oldest hotels, though fading in grandeur. Rembrandt painted *The Night Watch* here in 1642. 24-hour parking nearby; TVs and business facilities.

Moderate

(11) France I5
Oudezijdskolk 11, 1012 AL, t 422 3311, f 535 3925, e info@francehotel.nl, w www.francehotel.nl; metro Centraal Station; wheelchair accessible.
On a tranquil canal near St Nicolaaskerk, and just a few hundred yards from the station. Rooms are a little nondescript, but all have bathroom, TV and phone.

(20) De Gerstekorrel H6
Damstraat 22, 1012 JM, t 624 1367, f 623 2640, e gersteko@euronet.nl, w www.gerstekorrel.com; tram 4, 9 16, 24 25.
A small hotel with a lift leading to airy rooms (with TV) on a busy street in the heart of Amsterdam. Staff are friendly and helpful, though rooms can be a little noisy.

(21) Rho H6
Nes 5, 1012 KE, t 620 7371, f 620 7826, e reception@rhohotel.com, w www.rhohotel.com; tram 4, 9, 16, 24, 25; wheelchair accessible.
A large place just off the Dam with a good range of facilities, friendly staff and cavernous

reception hall. All rooms are *en suite*, with TV, minibar, telephone and safe. Private parking €20.

Inexpensive

(12) Amstel Botel J5
Oosterdokskade 24, 1011 AE, t 626 4247, f 639 1952, e info@amstel botel.nl, w www.amstelbotel.nl; tram 1, 2, 5, 9, 13, 17, 24, 25.
A floating three-star hotel with four storeys. Rooms are small but well maintained and with facilities such as TV, video and small bathroom. An unusual hotel experience, but cramped. Be sure to pick a room overlooking the Oosterdok.

(33) Amsterdam House I7
's Gravenlandseveer 7, 1011 KN, t 626 2577, f 626 2987, e amshouse @euronet.nl, w www.amsterdam house.com; tram 4, 9, 16, 24, 25; metro Waterlooplein.
Well positioned in a relatively quiet spot on the southern edge of the old centre, near Waterlooplein. The main attractions are not the rather plain hotel rooms, but the fully equipped canalboat apartments, which are available for short-term rentals. TVs and children's facilities.

(13) Vijaya I5
Oudezijds Voorburgwal 44, t 626 9406, f 620 5277, e hotelvijaya@ hetnet.nl, w www.hotelvijaya.com; tram 4, 9, 14, 16, 24, 25.
Situated in a bell-gabled 18th-century canal house in the Red Light District. The basic, functional rooms all have bathroom and TV, and are good value considering the central location. Babysitting and private parking available. If you take a room on the top floor, bear in mind that there's no lift. Doubles from €55.

(16) Winston H5
Warmoesstraat 129, 1012 JA, t 623 1380, f 639 2308, e winston@ winston.nl, w www.winston.nl; tram 4, 9, 14, 16, 24, 25; wheelchair accessible.
A playful, kitsch budget hotel, with modern art everywhere and themed rooms, including one

sponsored by Durex and another by the Absolute Danny fetish shop. Downstairs is a funky bar. Has up to six-person rooms. One room is fully adapted for disabled access. 24-hour room service. TVs.

The Centre: New Side

Luxury

(17) NH Grand Hotel Krasnapolsky H6
Dam 9, 1012 JS, t 554 9111, f 626 1570, e info@nhkrasnapolsky.nh -hotels.nl, w www.krasnapolsky. nh-hotels.nl; tram 1, 2, 4, 5, 9, 13, 14, 16, 17, 24, 25; wheelchair accessible.
Excellent position, right in the centre of town. Very grand from the outside, and inside a mix of period charm and all mod cons – including TVs, air-con, pool, gym, business and babysitting facilities. Stunning 'winter garden' with glass roof where guests eat breakfast. Breakfast €22.50.

(4) Victoria I5
Damrak 1–5, 1012 LG, t 623 4255, f 625 2997, e vicres@parkplaza hotels.nl, w www.parkplaza europe.com; metro Centraal Station; wheelchair accessible.
A plush business-oriented hotel opposite the station with every comfort and impeccable service. There are a restaurant, bar, breakfast terrace, swimming pool, business facilities, air-con, gym and Turkish bath. Babysitting is available and some of the rooms have been adapted for use by disabled visitors.

Expensive

(28) Estherea G6
Singel 303–9, t 624 5146, f 623 9001, e estherea@xs4all.nl; w www.estherea.nl; tram 1, 2, 5, 13, 17; partly wheelchair accessible.
An elegant hotel in a 17th-century canal house on the Singel. Rooms are plush, with bathroom, phone, TV, minibar and safe. Babysitting facilities and bar.

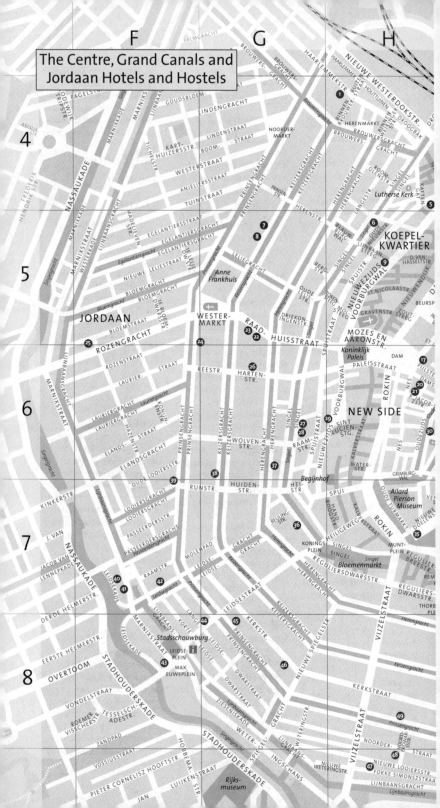

The Centre, Grand Canals and
Jordaan Hotels and Hostels

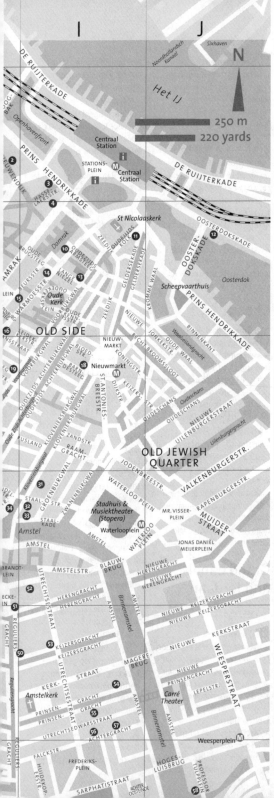

(52) NH Schiller I7
Rembrandtplein 26–36, 1017 CV,
t 554 0777, f 624 0098,
e reservations@nhschiller.nh
-hotels.nl, w www.nh-hotels.com;
tram 4, 9, 14.
Decorated with paintings of its
19th-century owner, the downstairs café was once the meeting
place of actors and artists. The
hotel itself is smart, comfortable
and overlooks a lively square. With
a gym, children's facilities, TVs and
babysitting service. Breakfast €16.

Moderate

(36) Agora G7
Singel 462, 1017 AW, t 627 2200,
f 627 2202, e info@hotelagora.nl,
w www.hotelagora.nl; tram 1, 2, 5.
The owner is interested in fine
furniture – and it shows. Rooms
overlooking the canal or back
garden are the best. Cheaper
rooms are without *en-suite*. TVs.

(29) Nova H6
Nieuwezijds Voorburgwal 276, 1012
RS, t 623 0066, f 627 2026, e nova
hotel@wxs.nl, w www.bookings.
nl/hotels/nova; tram 1, 2, 5.
A family-run hotel just off a
pleasant square. All rooms are *en*
suite, with TV, telephone and
refrigerator. Family rooms available.

(3) Prins Hendrik I4
Prins Hendrikkade 53, 1012 AC,
e hotel-prins-hendrik@xs4all.nl,
w www.hotel-prinshendrik.nl, t 623
7969, f 627 4391; metro Centraal
Station.
A simple hotel decorated in ruddy
Dutch style and situated directly
opposite Centraal Station. All
rooms are *en suite*, with phone
and TV, and there's a bar.

Inexpensive

(6) Brouwer H5
Singel 83, 1012 VE, t 624 6358, f 520
6264, e akita@hotelbrouwer.nl,
w www.hotelbrouwer.nl; tram 1, 2,
5, 13, 17.
A gem. Canal house with rooms
tastefully done up with lovely old
furniture. Most have a good view.

(27) Hoksbergen G6
Singel 301, 1012 WH, t 626 6043,
f 638 3479, e info@hotelhoks
bergen.nl, w www.hotel
hoksbergen.nl; tram 1, 2, 5.
No-nonsense knotty pine, some
canal views, clean rooms and
friendly management. TVs.

(5) St Nicolaas H4
Spuistraat 1A, 1012 SP, t 626 1384,
f 623 0979, e info@hotelnicolaas.
nl, w www.hotelnicolaas.nl; tram 1,
2, 5, 13, 17.
A well-placed hotel with comfortable *en suite* rooms and a
wood-styled bar downstairs.
Roads run along either side of the
building, so it can be noisy. All
rooms have TV and phone.

Cheap

(2) Groenendael H4
Nieuwendijk 15, t 624 4822,
w www.hotelgroenendael.com;
tram 4, 9, 16, 24, 25.
Offers 16 tiny rooms in a central
location. There's a lounge where
guests can relax and breakfast is
included in the price. Doubles €50.

(15) Travel H5
Beursstraat 23, t 626 6532, f 627
1250, e info@travelhotel.nl,
w www.travelhotel.nl; tram 4, 9,
16, 24, 25.
Tucked away behind the Beurs van
Berlage building, this small and
straightforward hotel offers
rooms for one to five people –
some *en suite* – and a 24-hour bar.

Grand Canals and Jordaan

Luxury

(43) American F8
Leidsekade 97, 1017 PN, t 556 3000,
f 556 3001, e american@ichotels
group.com, w www.amsterdam
-american.crowneplaza.nl; tram 1,
2, 5, 6, 7, 10; wheelchair accessible
(only one room with full wheel-
chair facilities).
An Art Deco extravaganza of a
hotel overlooking the thronging
Leidseplein. The café downstairs
was once the meeting place for

Amsterdam's literati. With a gym
and babysitting service. From
€355. Breakfast €15.50. TVs, air-con.

**(58) Amstel
Intercontinental** J9
Professor Tulpplein 1, 1018 GX, t 622
6060, f 622 5808, e amstel@
interconti.com, w www.interconti.
com; tram 6, 7, 10.
Amsterdam's most luxurious (and
expensive) hotel, with everything
from a health club to a canalboat
service and stiffly dressed staff.
The dramatic lobby is ringed by
sumptuous banqueting halls
(used for business meetings and
functions), while the spacious
rooms upstairs are decorated with
Delftware motifs. The Michelin-
starred restaurant in the
basement (La Rive) means you can
dine in similar opulence without
leaving the building. Pay that little
bit more for one of the riverside
rooms. From €490 (€2,890 if you
fancy a night in the Royal Suite).
Parking, air-con, swimming pool.

(38) Blakes G6
Keizersgracht 384, 1016 GB, t 530
2010, f 530 2030, e hotel@blakes.nl,
w www.blakesamsterdam.nl; tram
1, 2, 5.
British designer Anouska Hempel
has cast a minimalist spell over
this 17th-century canal house on
the Keizersgracht. Rooms are
individually styled with monochromatic elegance and a hint of
the Orient, while the acclaimed
restaurant set in the old bakery
downstairs serves up a fusion of
Mediterranean, Thai and Japanese
cuisine. At €18 the Blakes breakfast is worth every cent. A unique
and exclusive experience, though
homey it is not. Standard double
room €370.

(24) Pulitzer G5
Prinsengracht 315–31, 1016 GZ,
*t 523 5235, f 627 6753, e res100_*
amsterdam@starwoodhotels.com,
w www.luxurycollection.com/
pulitzer; tram 13, 14, 17.
Twenty-four canal houses linked
up to form a warren of oak-
beamed rooms. The hotel has a
peaceful garden and a magnifi-

cent 18th-century restaurant. With a babysitting service, TVs, gym and bar. From €430; breakfast €25.

(45) Seven One Seven G8
Prinsengracht 717, 1017 JW, t 427 0717, f 423 0717, e info@717hotel.nl, w www.717hotel.nl; tram 1, 2, 5.
Superb, antique-filled suites on one of the smartest canals in town. The owners have aimed at creating a relaxed, cosy atmosphere – which is extremely chic and well-appointed. From €375. Price includes breakfast, afternoon coffee and drinks from the bar in the evening. There's also a babysitting service. Air-con in one room; TV.

Expensive

(37) Ambassade G6
Herengracht 335–53, 1016 AZ, t 555 0222, f 555 0277, e info@ambassade-hotel.nl, w www.ambassade-hotel.nl; tram 1, 2, 5.
Eight converted houses, dotted about with antiques and with a magnificent breakfast room overlooking the canal. Breakfast €16.

(44) Dikker & Thijs Fenice G8
Prinsengracht 444, 1017 KE, t 626 7721, f 625 8986, e info@dtfh.nl, w www.dtfh.nl; tram 1, 2, 5; wheelchair accessible (partial, in five rooms).
Plum in the middle of it all, in a hectic and lively area of town. Modern furnishings in a 100-year-old shell. From €245. TVs in rooms.

Moderate

(48) Arthur Frommer H9
Noorderstraat 46, 1017 TV, t 622 0328, f 620 3208, e H1032@accor-hotels.com, w www.mercure.nl; tram 16, 24, 25.
Although it's part of an international chain, this hotel is far from faceless. Situated in a private courtyard, in a quiet corner of town, yet just minutes from city hot-spots, it incorporates several atmospheric old houses. Rooms not overlarge, but well-equipped. TV, air-con, limited parking.

(8) Het Canal House G5
Keizersgracht 148, 1015 CX, t 622 5182, f 624 1317, e info@canalhouse.nl, w www.canalhouse.nl; tram 13, 14, 17.
Stunning converted canal house, filled to the brim with the owner's carefully chosen antiques. The breakfast room has a piano and a drippingly beautiful crystal chandelier. The hotel has the feel of a tastefully (if grandly) decorated private home, and it even has a lift (quite a rarity in these historic houses). No children under 12.

(50) Seven Bridges I8
Reguliersgracht 31, 1017 LK, t 623 1329, f 624 7652; tram 4, 16, 24, 25.
The most charming small hotel in Amsterdam. Beautifully decorated rooms – and breakfast served in bed. TVs in rooms.

(7) Toren G5
Keizersgracht 164, 1015 CZ, t 622 6352, f 626 9705, e hotel.toren@tip.nl, w www.toren.nl; tram 13, 14, 17; bus 21.
Seventeenth-century canal house with high moulded ceilings, and antiques scattered among the modern furniture. With air-con, minibar, TV and safe in all rooms. Breakfast €12.

Inexpensive

(57) De Munck I8
Achtergracht 3, 1017 WL, t 623 6283, f 620 6647, w www.hoteldemunck.com; tram 4.
Charming hotel with really friendly management, in an 18th-century former sea-captain's house, near a quiet canal. Rooms are simple and tasteful, all have TV and most have bathroom *en suite*. There's an attractive garden out the back, and a delightfully 1960s retro breakfast room.

(54) Orlando I8
Prinsengracht 1,099, 1017 JH, t 638 6915, f 625 2123; tram 4.
Canalside house with just five rooms, individually decorated in a modern style. You'll need to book well in advance.

(41) Quentin F7
Leidsekade 89, 1017 PN, t 626 2187,

f 622 0121, w www.quentinhotels.com; tram 1, 2, 5.
Popular with musicians playing at Melkweg round the corner, and with gay travellers. Posters of past (now famous) residents adorn the walls. Spotless, tastefully decorated and with good views over the canal. From €75 excluding breakfast. TVs in rooms.

(39) Wiechmann F7
Prinsengracht 328–30, 1016 HX, t 626 3321, f 626 8962, e info@hotelwiechmann.nl, w www.hotelwiechmann.nl; tram 13, 14, 17; bus 21.
Carefully converted canal houses with an air of old-world charm, and a noble breakfast room.

Cheap

(51) De Admiraal H8
Herengracht 563, 1017 CD, t 626 2150, f 623 4625; tram 4, 9, 14.
Friendly owner, plus views over two canals and a good breakfast (€5). From €70–115; some rooms with shower.

(49) Amsterdam Prinsengracht H8
Prinsengracht 1015, 1017 KN, t 623 7779, f 623 8926, e prinsengracht.hotel@worldonline.nl, w www.prinsengrachthotel.nl; tram 16, 24, 25.
Friendly staff, all mod cons and canal views, though the décor is a little bland. TVs in rooms.

(23) Aspen G5
Raadhuisstraat 31, t 626 6714, f 620 0866, e info@hotelaspen.nl, w www.hotelaspen.nl; tram 13, 17.
Well priced considering its location near the Dam and the Anne Frankhuis. Fair-size rooms, but only eight of them, so book well in advance. Doubles without bath from €46; with bathroom €66.

(26) Belga G6
Hartenstraat 8, 1016 CB, t 624 9080, f 623 6862, e hotelbelga@zonnet.nl, w www.hotelbelga.nl; tram 13, 14, 17.
Unpretentious, family-run hotel in a quaint shopping alley. Without bathroom €75, €110 with.

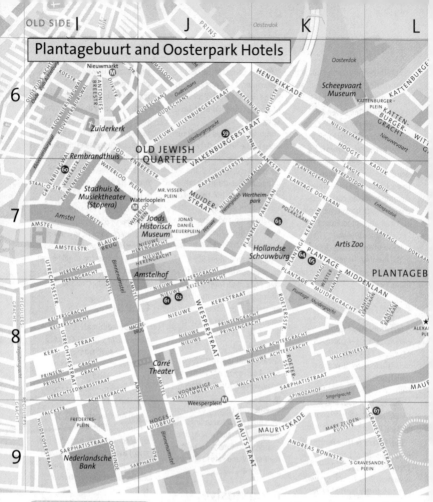

Plantagebuurt and Oosterpark Hotels

Map Key

(47) Euphemia H9
*Fokke Simonszstraat 1–9, 1017 TD,
t 622 9045, f 638 9673, e info@
euphemiahotel.com, w www.
euphemiahotel.com; tram 16, 24,
25; wheelchair accessible (ground
floor only).*
Comfortable rooms at reasonable
prices. Situated just north of the
Heineken Experience and the
mile-long Albert Cuypmarkt.
Popular with a diverse crowd.
There is a PC with Internet access
for use by guests. From €35.

(53) Get Lucky Guesthouse I8
*Keizersgracht 705, t 420 6466, f 622
9617, e getlucky@xs4all.nl, e agnes
getlucky@hotmail.com, w www.
getluckyamsterdam.com; tram 4.*
Only four rooms (one with
shower) and perennially popular.
All rooms have PCs and canal
views, and there's a welcoming
lounge full of Eastern collectables.
The owners admit to being eccentric and are always happy to spout
forth on the city. If the guesthouse
is full, they will point you in the
direction of several local families
who extend the hospitality of
their homes. The Get Lucky houseboat (moored on the IJ, a few
kilometres from the centre) is also
available to groups of four, with
cooking facilities and bicycles.
Doubles €50–85.

(56) Hemp I8
*Frederiksplein 15, t 625 4425,
e mila@hemp-hotel.com,
w www.hemp-hotel.com; tram 4.
Amex not accepted.*
This environmentally minded
hotel makes good use of the by-
products of Amsterdam's liberal
drugs policies: you'll find hemp
mattresses and furnishings in all
of the rooms, many of which take
on Asian or Caribbean themes. In
the bar downstairs you can try out
hemp beer, or hemp ice cream. A
vegetarian breakfast is included in
the price. Doubles from €65 (no
bath), or €70 with shower.

M

KATTENBURG

WITTENBURG

Kromhout
Museum

HOOGTE

KADIJK

ENTREPOTDOK

UURT

Muiderpoort

MAURITSKADE

Tropenmuseum

N

Oosterpark

250 m
220 yards

Oosterpark

(40) Impala F7
*Leidsekade 77, 1017 PM, t 623 4706,
f 624 2578, e info@hotel-impala.nl,
w www.hotel-impala.nl; tram 1,
2, 5.*
Clean, laid-back hotel with a
young crowd. At weekends the
rates go up to put the hotel in the
moderate price category.

(55) Prinsenhof I8
*Prinsengracht 810, 1017 JL, t 623
1772, f 638 3368, e info@
hotelprinsenhof.com, w www.
hotelprinsenhof.com; tram 4.*
Quiet, thoughtfully decorated
hotel with friendly management.
From €60–80 without bathroom.

(22) De Westertoren G5
*Raadhuisstraat 35B, 1016 DC,
t/f 624 4639, e info@hotel
westertoren.nl, w www.hotel*

---

*westertoren.nl; tram 13, 14, 17;
bus 21.*
Well kept, if a little noisy.

Waterlooplein and the Plantagebuurt

Expensive

(59) Ibis Amsterdam Stopera J6
*Valkenburgerstraat 68, 1011 LZ, t 531
9135, f 531 9145, e h3044@
accor-hotels.com, w www.ibis.com;
metro Waterlooplein; tram 4, 9, 14.
Two rooms wheelchair accessible.*
On a main road just northeast of
Waterlooplein and west of leafy
Plantage, this is a safe bet among
Amsterdam's chain hotels. There's
an *estaminet* and all rooms
are *en suite*, with TV, phone
and safe.

Moderate

(64) Lancaster K7
*Plantage Middenlaan 48, 1018 DH,
t 535 6888, f 535 6889, e res.
lancaster@edenhotelgroup.com,
w www.edenhotelgroup.com; tram
9, 14; partly wheechair accessible.*
A functional and largely non-
descript hotel, with three-star
facilities. Situated among the
broad avenues of the 19th-century
Plantagebuurt, just east of the
Hortus Botanicus. Family rooms
are available and the rooms
have TV.

Inexpensive

(62) Adolesce J8
*Nieuwe Keizersgracht 26, 1018 DS,
t 626 3959, f 627 4249, e adolesce@
xs4all.nl, w www.adolesce.nl; tram
9, 14.*
Cheerful, simple hotel with a
sunny breakfast room. A good one
to opt for if you have children, as it
is one of the few establishments
that genuinely welcomes them.
Some rooms are without bathroom. There's a restaurant and bar,
and rooms have TV.

---

(61) Fantasia J8
*Nieuwe Keizersgracht 16, t 623
8259, f 622 3913, e info@fantasia
-hotel.com, w www.fantasia
-hotel.com; tram 9, 14. Closed Jan.*
Situated on a quiet stretch of
canal east of the Amstel and
conveniently placed within
walking distance of the old centre,
this is a clean and well run hotel. A
full Dutch breakfast is included in
the price, and rooms all come with
a shower, phone and safe. Doubles
start from €80.

(63) Rembrandt K7
*Plantage Middenlaan 17, 1018 DA,
t 627 2714, f 638 0293, e info@
hotelrembrandt.nl, w www.
hotelrembrandt.nl; tram 9, 14.*
Another option among the green
stretches of the Plantagebuurt,
this characterful little hotel has 16
rooms (each equipped with bathroom, phone, TV and kettle). The
16th-century breakfast room is
veritably stuffed with antiques.
Doubles are very well priced and
start from €75.

(60) Rembrandtplein I7
*Groenburgwal 27, 1011 HR, t 428
4244, f 428 4248, e info@
rembrandtpleinhotel.nl,
w www.rembrandtpleinhotel.nl;
metro Waterlooplein; tram 4, 9, 14.*
On a quiet tree-lined canal across
the Amstel from Rembrandtplein,
this is notably well positioned for
all the sights. Rooms are fairly
straightforward, but have good
facilities (bath/shower, TV,
minibar, phone, safe). There's a bar
downstairs.

Cheap

(65) Kitty K7
*Plantage Middenlaan 40, t 622
6819; tram 9, 14.*
A tranquil 10-room hotel near the
zoo and the Hortus Botanicus, run
by a kind lady in her 80s (she's
proud of her age!). Doubles are on
offer for €60, while there is just
one single room for €45. Breakfast
is not available.

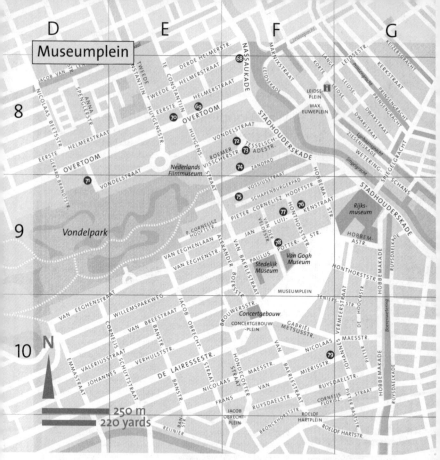

Map Key

- (68) Crystal
- (69) Princess
- (70) Abba
- (71) De Filosoof
- (72) Engeland
- (73) Owl
- (74) Vondelpark Stay Okay Hotel
- (75) The Flying Pig Palace
- (76) Acro
- (77) Jan Luyken
- (78) Acca International
- (79) Washington

Museumplein

Expensive

(77) Jan Luyken F9
Jan Luykenstraat 58, 1071 CS, t 573 0730, f 676 3841, e jan-luyken@ bilderberg.nl, w www.janluyken.nl; tram 2, 5.
A smart, efficient business hotel in a quiet area near Museumplein.

TVs, spa, air-con and businesss facilities.

Moderate

(78) Acca International F9
Van de Veldestraat 3A, 1071 CW, t 662 5262, f 679 9361; tram 2, 5.
Modern, functional hotel near the museums. Breakfast €7. TVs.

(71) De Filosoof D9
Anna Vondelstraat 6, 1054 GZ, t 683 3013, f 685 3750, e reservations@hotelfilosoof.nl, w www.hotelfilosoof.nl; tram 2, 5.
Rooms (with TV) are named after well-known thinkers, and decorated accordingly; some are done in national architectural themes. The hotel can arrange consultations with one of Holland's practising philosophers, many of whom frequent the bar.

(73) Owl F8
Roemer Visscherstraat 1, 1054 EV, t 618 9484, f 618 9441, e info@ owl-hotel.nl, w www.owl-hotel.nl; tram 1, 3, 6, 12; wheelchair accessible (through garden).
Smart family hotel with a large garden. In the museum neighbourhood. With a bar and babysitting service. TVs.

Inexpensive

(76) Acro F9
Jan Luykenstraat 44, 1071 CR, t 662 0526, f 675 0811, e info@acro. hotel.nl, w www.acro.hotel.nl; tram 2, 5.
Sparkling, simple, if a little soulless. Set in the quiet museum district. There's a bar and garden. TVs in rooms.

(68) Crystal F8
Tweede Helmersstraat 6, t 618 0521, f 618 0561; tram 1.
A good-value option alongside Vondelpark. It's situated on a quiet street across the Singelgracht from Leidseplein and offers more

facilities than its marginally cheaper sister hotel the Princess (*see* below). Basic doubles without shower €65; *en suite* doubles with TV €102.

(72) Engeland F8
Roemer Visscherstraat 30, 1054 EZ, t 689 2323, f 685 3148, w www. quentinhotels.com; tram 1, 3, 6, 12; partly wheelchair accessible.
Set in a quaint row of six 19th-century houses built to show different national architectural styles, this 50-room hotel is just across the street from the Vondelpark. Breakfast is extra. TVs.

(79) Washington F10
Frans van Mierisstraat 10, 1071 RS, t 679 6754, f 673 4435, w www. hotelwashington.nl; tram 3, 5, 12, 16.
Set in a large 19th-century house on a peaceful avenue near the Concertgebouw. Furnishings are simple but tasteful, but the rooms do include TVs, and there's a small back garden. With a friendly, homey atmosphere much appreciated by visiting concert musicians.

Cheap

(70) Abba E8
Overtoom 122, t 618 3058, f 685 3477, e info@abbabudgethotel. com, w www.abbabudgethotel. com; tram 1.
A well-priced hotel near to the museums and Vondelpark, with friendly management and pleasing, modern rooms (not all have showers *en suite*). Bear in mind that Overtoom is a busy road. A filling buffet breakfast is included in the price. Doubles are from around €45–80.

(69) Princess E8
Overtoom 80, t 612 2947, f 616 0409; tram 1.
Close to (and under the same management as) Crystal, across the water from Leidseplein. The simple rooms are perfectly adequate (but none are *en suite*), with TVs, and a hearty breakfast is included in the price. Doubles start from €70.

De Pijp

Okura H12
Ferdinand Bolstraat 333, 1072 LH, t 678 7111, f 671 2344, e sales@ okura.nl, w www.okura.nl; tram 12, 25; wheelchair accessible (one room specifically adapted). Luxury.
At over 250ft tall, this five-star hotel is a modern landmark in De Pijp district. As well as all the expected facilities (TVs and air-con, business facilities, gym and parking), there are four restaurants serving French and Japanese cuisine, and there's Internet access in every room. If you can't afford to stay, take the lift up to the Ciel Bleu restaurant for a glass of wine and some of the best views over the city. Doubles from €375.

Van Ostade H11
Van Ostadestraat 123, t 679 3452, f 671 5213, e info@bicyclehotel.com, w www.bicyclehotel.com; tram 24, 25. Inexpensive.
This place near the Albert Cuypmarkt in De Pijp district labels itself as a 'bicycle hotel' – bikes are rented out to guests for a nominal fee and space is provided indoors for chaining them up at the end of the day. The rooms are basic, though all have TV. Doubles without bathroom from €65; *en suite* €105.

New South

Luxury

Bilderberg Garden E11
Dijsselhofplantsoen 7, 1077 BJ, t 570 5600, f 570 5654, e garden. reservations@bilderberg.nl, w www.gardenhotel.nl; tram 5, 24.
A modern five-star hotel in the New South district – 10mins' walk south of Vondelpark and Museumplein. Though its position near the RAI congress centre betrays its focus as a business hotel, it stands as a true luxury hotel in its own right – all of the 100 rooms have Jacuzzis, air-con and TVs, while the restaurant

(Mangerie de Kersentuin) is rated by many as one of the best in Amsterdam. The hotel offers the full range of facilities such as a gym.

Expensive

Amsterdam Hilton E11
Apollolaan 138–40, 1077 BG, t 710 6000, f 710 9000, e sales_ amsterdam@hiltonint.com, w www.hilton.com; tram 5, 24; wheelchair accessible.
Modern building with five-star services including babysitting, gym, parking, business facilities, air-con, beauty salon and sauna. Scene, in 1969, of John Lennon's and Yoko Ono's week-long 'bed-in' for world peace. The suite they occupied has been renovated in an appropriate style and can be specially requested

Apollofirst E11
Apollolaan 123, 1077 AP, t 577 3800, f 675 0348, e info@apollofirst.nl, w www.apollofirst.nl; tram 5, 24.
A smallish family-owned hotel with a classical interior, 24-hour room service, bar and conference facilities, and TVs. Ten minutes from Museumplein on foot.

Moderate

Beethoven E12
Beethovenstraat 43, 1077 HN, t 683 1811, f 616 0320, e reserveringen@ ams.nl, w www.ams.nl; tram 5, 24; partly wheelchair accessible.
A functional four-star hotel with an attractive brasserie that spills out beneath a covered terrace onto Beethovenstraat. All rooms are *en suite*, with telephone, TV and minibar. A 20min tram ride from the centre.

Oosterpark

(67) Arena L9
's Gravesandestraat 51, 1092 AA, t 850 2400, f 850 2425, e info@ hotelarena.nl, w www. hotelarena.nl; tram 3, 6, 9, 10, 14; wheelchair accessible. Moderate.
Erstwhile seedy hippy sleep-in, which has now been considerably

smartened up in minimalist style. On the edge of Oosterpark. With a restaurant, garden and attached nightclub. From €100. There are TVs in the rooms.

(66) NH Tropen M8
Linnaeusstraat 2C, 1092 CK, **t** *692 5111,* **f** *663 0979,* **e** *reservations@ nhtropen.nh-hotels.nl,* **w** *www.nh -hotels.com;* **tram** *9, 14;* **wheelchair accessible. Moderate.**
One of the few hotels in the Oosterpark region, beside the Tropenmuseum. There is a lot of greenery out here, and the hotel occupies a multi-storey building, so there are good views over the parkland and city centre. All 80 rooms are *en suite* with TV and phone. Half-board available. Free parking.

Western Islands and Scheepvaartbuurt

Expensive

Tulip Inn Amsterdam Art E1
Spaarndammerdijk 302, 1013 ZX, **t** *410 9670,* **f** *681 0802,* **e** *art@ westcordhotels.nl.nl,* **w** *www. westcordhotels.nl;* **bus** *22, 35;* **wheelchair accessible.**
Located at the northern end of the quiet Westerpark district, with views over the IJ. This is a new hotel with reasonable prices for what are effectively four-star facilities (restaurant, bar, free parking, and in all rooms a minibar, TV, air-con, radio, phone and safe). Work by local artists is displayed throughout the hotel. Doubles cost €160.

Inexpensive

(1) Arrivé H4
Haarlemmerstraat 65, **t** *622 1439,* **f** *622 1983;* **bus** *18, 22.*
A very plain and basic hotel with one dorm (or family room) in a newly trendy part of town.

De Bloeiende Ramenas G3
Haarlemmerdijk 61, **t** *624 6030,* **f** *420 2261,* **e** *ramenas730@*
hotmail.com, **w** *www.amsterdam hotels.com;* **bus** *18, 22;* **metro** *Centraal Station then 10min walk.*
A peaceful well-priced hotel to the west of Centraal Station – just out of the action but well placed for the northern section of the canal belt and the cafés and markets of Jordaan. Doubles for €80 with shared bathroom, or €100 for *en suite*. TV.

Far South

Hilton International Schiphol Off maps
Herbergierstraat, 1118 ZK, **t** *710 4000,* **f** *710 4080,* **w** *www.res_apt -schipolhilton.com;* **train** *Schiphol; wheelchair accessible (four rooms adapted). Luxury.*
Part of the Schiphol complex (15mins from the centre by train) around the airport. Shuttle bus from the airport. TVs, air-con, business facilities and sauna.

Youth Hostels

(9) Bob's Youth Palace H5
Nieuwezijds Voorburgwal 92, 1012 SG, **t** *623 0063,* **f** *675 6446;* **tram** *1, 2, 5, 13, 17. Cash only.*
A popular stopping-off point on the world travellers' route. Dorms are mixed (though there's a girls-only dorm if you prefer) and there's no age limit. A very relaxed youthful place. Dorm bed and breakfast for €18.

(19) The Bulldog H6
Oudezijds Voorburgwal 220, **t** *620 3822,* **f** *627 1612,* **e** *hotel@bulldog. nl,* **w** *www.bulldog.nl/hotel;* **tram** *4, 9, 14, 16, 24, 25.*
Part of the Bulldog chain of coffeeshops, this large hostel right in the centre of it all offers a wide range of rooms and dorms, many with TV. Dorm bed and breakfast from €32; double rooms from €82.

(75) The Flying Pig Palace F9
Vossiusstraat 46, 1071 AJ, **t** *(head office) 421 0583,* **f** *421 0802,* **w** *www.flyingpig.nl;* **tram** *2, 5.*
Hostel with a friendly crowd, clean dorms, free lockers and a cosy café beside the Vondelpark. Dorm beds from €20 per person; double rooms from €63. The Vondel Park branch is quieter and more attractively situated than the city branch.

(46) Hans Brinker Budget G8
Kerkstraat 136–8, 1017 GR, **t** *622 0687,* **f** *638 2060,* **w** *www.hans -brinker.com;* **tram** *1, 2, 5, 16, 24, 25.*
Amsterdam's largest hostel, with plenty of single and double rooms as well as dorms. It's loud, brash and good fun, with a sociable bar and restaurant. Doubles from €70; dorm beds €21.

(42) International Budget Hotel F7
Leidsegracht 76, 1016 CR, **t** *624 2784,* **f** *772 4825;* **tram** *1, 2, 5.*
Set on a canal near Leidseplein and popular with a young crowd. Doubles and dorms are available and all bathrooms are shared. Doubles from €70; dorm beds from €27.

(31) IYMF City Hostel Stadsdoelen I7
Kloveniersburgwal 97, 1011 KB, **t** *624 6832,* **f** *639 1035;* **tram** *4, 9, 16, 24, 25.*
Members €19.25 per person (including breakfast, sheets and locker); non-members €21.75. Curfew 2am.

(14) Meeting Point I5
Warmoesstraat 14, 1012 JD, **t** *627 7499,* **f** *330 4774,* **w** *www.hostel meetingpoint.nl;* **tram** *4, 9, 16, 24, 25. Cash only; no pre-booking.*
A basic hostel with dorm accommodation only (from 4 to 18 beds per room). It's situated right in the Red Light District and there's a 24-hour bar for guests. Dorm beds from €18; four-person room from €70.

(18) Shelter City I6
Barndesteeg 21, **t** *625 3230,* **f** *623 2282,* **e** *city@shelter.nl,* **w** *www. shelter.nl;* **metro** *Nieuwmarkt. Cash only.*
A non-smoking Christian youth hostel on one of the tiny streets off Nieuwmarkt. You'll find the cheapest beds in town here, though there's more than a hint

of evangelical intention in some of the staff. Dorms are for 4–8 people, and men and women are segregated. A decent breakfast is included in the price. Curfew is midnight during the week and 1am at weekends. 16–35s only. Dorm bed and breakfast for €16.50.

(25) Shelter Jordan F5
Bloemstraat 179, 1016 LA, t 624 4717, f 627 6137, e jordan@shelter.nl, w www.shelter.nl; tram 13, 14, 17. Cash only.
The sister hostel (also non-smoking) to Shelter City, in the quieter milieu of trendy Jordaan. This one's a little larger and better equipped and, again, you won't find a cheaper bed in town. Dorms are for 4, 8, 12 or 20 people, and men and women are segregated. Curfew 2am. 15–35s only. Dorm bed and breakfast for €16.50.

(74) Vondelpark Stay Okay Hotel F8
Zandpad 5, 1054 GA, t 589 8996, f 589 8955, w www.stayokay.com/vondelpark; tram 1, 2, 5, 6, 7, 10.
One of the two official International Youth Hostel Federation hostels, with 500 beds. From €22 (dorm) and €76 (double).

(10) Youth Budget Hotel Kabul I5
Warmoesstraat 38–42, 1012 JE, t 623 7158, f 620 0869; tram 4, 9, 14, 16, 24, 25.
A good central option if you're travelling in a group and on a budget. Plain, friendly and very large, just off the Dam. There's a bar downstairs and no curfew. Doubles from €75; dorm beds from €19.

Bed and Breakfast

Despite their easy assimilation of things British, Amsterdammers do not seem much taken by B&B. When you do find private accommodation, it probably won't be all that much cheaper than (or very different from) a room in a small hotel. For information contact:

Bed and Breakfast Holland
Theophile de Bockstraat 3, 1058 TV, t 615 7527, f 669 1573.
An agency with a number of B&Bs on its books. Prices range from €55 per night for a minimum 2-night stay and there is a €10 booking fee per reservation. Advance bookings only.

Mark's B&B F3
Van Beuningenstraat 80A, t 776 0056, f 682 7372, w www.geocities.com/CollegePark/plaza/3686/theplace.html; tram 10.
A hip little hotel in a former working-class district just west of the centre. The rooms, decorated in rich colours with a heavy hint of camp, are lots of fun. There's also a leafy garden terrace.

Camping

Amsterdamse Bos Off maps
Kleine Noorddijk 1, 1187 NZ Amstelveen, t 641 6868, f 640 2378, e camping@dab.amsterdam.nl, w www.campingamsterdambos.nl; bus 171 from Centraal Station, 169 from Schipol. Open April–Oct. Cash only.
A campsite half an hour south of the centre in the beautiful woodland of Amsterdamse Bos. If you don't have a tent with you, there are wooden cabins for hire with cooking facilities. On site you'll find a shop, bar, restaurant and pay phones. Adults for €5, 4–12s for €2.50, under-4s free, cars €3, caravans €3.50, €3 per night electricity charge for camper vans and caravans. Cabins from €21.50.

Gaasper Camping Off maps
Loosdrechtdreef 7, 1108 AZ t 696 7326; metro Gaasperplas; bus 59, 60, 158. Open mid-March–end Dec. Cash only.
A good campsite for kids, in the Gaasperplas park with shop, bar, restaurant and launderette. There's also a lake for watersports and swimming. Adults €4.25, under-12s €2, cars €3.75.

Vliegenbos Off maps
Meeuwenlaan 138, 1022 AM, t 636 8855; w www.vliegenbos.com; bus 32 (10mins from Centraal Station); wheelchair accessible. Open April–Sept.
'Youth Campsite' – all ages welcome but be prepared for late-night high spirits. €8.90 per person including tent and hot showers; wood cabins (holding 4 people) €53. With a restaurant and shop.

Apartments

Amsterdam Apartments
Kromme Waal 32, 1011 BV, t 626 5930, f 626 9544.
Privately owned flats around town; mostly flats let by Amsterdammers away on holiday – from €500 per week.

GIS Apartments
Keizersgracht 33, 1015 CD, t 625 0071, f 638 0475, w www.gis-apartments.nl.
From the simple to the luxurious. From €1,000 per month, minimum three months, though most are for at least 6 months. The agency charges the equivalent of one month's rent.

Eating Out

Erasmus, the great 16th-century Dutch humanist and man of letters, was pleased to note that his fellow countrymen were not given to much wild or ferocious behaviour, treachery or deceit, indeed were 'not prone to any serious vices except, that is, a little given to pleasure, especially to feasting'. Two centuries later the national ability to tuck in and drink up was still impressive enough to shock the British – themselves no mean feasters. In 1703 the seven or so deacons of the Arnhem guild of surgeons dispatched, at one sitting, 14lb of beef, 8lb of veal, six fowl, stuffed cabbages, apples, pears, bread, pretzels, assorted nuts, 20 bottles of red wine, 12 bottles of white wine and some jugs of coffee. Today, eating is still a supreme Dutch enthusiasm, and one in which any visitor can happily join.

Specialities

Paradoxically, native Dutch cuisine is not all that inspiring. The Dutch culinary clichés are *hutspot* ('hotchpotch'), a well-boiled stew that was much appreciated by starving citizens after the siege of Leiden, and its enjoyment still requires a similar state of ravenousness; and *erwtensoep*, a porridgy pea soup which comes (vegetarians beware) with bits of sausage floating in it and a side dish of bread and raw bacon. The quality of *erwtensoep* is judged by testing whether or not your spoon will stand up on its own in the middle of the bowl. These are the staples of many a 'tourist menu', but (like the English) the Dutch have recently begun to explore more exciting avenues in their local cuisine – with game and fish especially. Other palatable traditional foods include *pannenkoeken* (pancakes) with sweet or savoury fillings, and *haring* (herring) eaten raw by tossing your head back and dropping a whole fillet down your throat. If you can stomach it, this is a marvellous cure for a hang-over. *Belegde broodjes* are crusty rolls filled with a delicious variety of fillings – travellers' tales of sliced beef layered on buttered bread predated anecdotes about Lord Sandwich's invention by about a century. Waffles, dripping with syrup or smothered with fruit and cream, are sold on the streets and are treacherously gooey and unmanageable, but quite irresistible. Cones of *frites* (potato chips), usually with a large dollop of mayonnaise, are ubiquitous. They're normally cooked with good-quality potatoes in clean oil.

In the absence of a stimulating local tradition, Dutch chefs have looked further afield. French cuisine first came into fashion during the Napoleonic occupation, and remains the cornerstone of many of the best kitchens. Nowadays most menus are alluringly eclectic, showing influences from Japan, Indonesia, Surinam and Turkey. This makes for some curious – but usually delicious – combinations. Don't be surprised to find peanut sauce, saffron pasta and oysters on the same menu. The Dutch were enjoying 'fusion cuisine' years before trendy London and New York chefs could distinguish lemon grass from lime leaves. Ingredients are usually market-fresh and microwave cookers are pleasingly thin on the ground. Food is cooked to order in most restaurants, so expect an unhurried meal.

Specialist ethnic restaurants abound. Reasonable Indian and Italian food is to be had all over town, with Thai and Japanese restaurants an increasingly popular alternative. It's the culinary heritage of Holland's imperial past, however, that makes for the best binge. Treat yourself to an Indonesian *rijsttafel* – a personal banquet of rice or noodles with myriad spicy side dishes. (See 'Language', pp.273–4, for a selection of Dutch and Indonesian food terms.)

Eating Out

The Dutch eat early in the evening – between 7 and 9pm – and many kitchens are closed by 10 or 11pm.

Budget eating is easy, and needn't be boring. Many restaurants offer a three-course 'Tourist Menu' for under €30, but you're generally better off looking out for signs advertising a *dagschotel* (dish of the day). You usually end up with an oversized white plate with some well-prepared meat and a constellation of pickles and salads. Many cafés serve food – menus change daily and often offer the best value of all (see 'Cafés', below). Best bet budget restaurants are Axum (see p.225),

Vegetarian Restaurants

Vegetarians will have a difficult time. The Dutch are great carnivores, and if you enquire about vegetarian dishes you're often offered *kabeljauw* (cod). However, in the 1970s the tastes of the hippies spawned a few vegetarian restaurants and more have opened recently.

Chefs in better kitchens are beginning to be more imaginative with their vegetarian options, and the chances are that a restaurant will have at least one vegetarian meal on the menu.

Try one of the following vegetarian restaurants:

Bolhoed (Grand Canals and Jordaan; see p.225), **Golden Temple** (Grand Canals and Jordaan; see p.225), **Green Planet** (New Side; see p.221), **De Waaghals** (De Pijp; see p.231).

Restaurants that put special effort and imagination into the vegetarian options on the menu are:

Griet Manshande (Western Islands and Scheepvaartbuurt; see p.232), **De Luwte** (Grand Canals and Jordaan; see p.224), **Woeste Walmen** (The Centre: New Side; see p.222).

Kingfisher (see p.239), Moeders Pot (see p.232) and La Place (see p.221).

Takeaway foodstalls punctuate markets and shopping streets all over town. As well as *frites*, *haring* and waffles, you can sample all sorts of foreign delights: Turkish kebabs, Israeli falafel, Japanese sushi and spicy nibbles from Surinam and Indonesia. Under signs flashing 'Automatiek' you can select a deep-fried croquette from a row of tiny windows displaying this and similar wares: drop in your €1.50, pull a lever and collect your reward. 'Snack' was originally a Dutch word. Snack bars are the Amsterdam equivalent of street food. At worst they sell pre-prepared mushy croquettes, but at best they are tiny family-run establishments that hover in the middle ground between restaurant and takeaway. Often run by immigrants, they have simple décor, a scattering of tables and some of the best foreign food in town. Try Bird (Thai; Zeedijk 77), Kismet (Turkish; Albert Cuypstraat 64), Maoz (Israeli falafel; Reguliersbreestraat 45) or Riaz (Surinam; Bilderdijkstraat 193).

Amsterdam is very much a cash city. Many smaller restaurants don't accept **credit cards**, and there's an air of reluctance about those that do. Even some of the larger establishments don't like plastic – so it's always a good idea to check in advance. Feasting Amsterdammers and hungry tourists fill up most good restaurants pretty quickly, so it's wise to **reserve** a table by telephone.

The list of restaurants below is a personal selection from the hundreds of good restaurants Amsterdam has to offer. A wander around the Jordaan, through the alleys that crisscross the canals (from Reestraat to Huidenstraat), along Utrechtsestraat, or in the area around Ferdinand Bolstraat and Albert Cuypstraat will reveal even more.

Cafés are at the centre of an Amsterdammer's social life. Those

listed below are notable for their food: some of them are *eetcafés* (literally, 'eating cafés'); others are simply good places to put your feet up and have an afternoon snack. Along with the 'smoking coffeeshops', those cafés that are predominantly drinking establishments are listed in the 'Nightlife' chapter, pp.235–9. **Times** given are the opening times of the kitchen (cafés often stay open much longer than this). **Numbers in brackets** before restaurant names refer to map locations.

Price Categories

The restaurants below are all graded according to the approximate price of a three-course meal, without wine or beer. You'll find eating out cheaper than in most large cities. The bill will include tax and may also include a 15% service charge – though if you feel you've been well looked after you can leave a little extra. It's usual to leave behind any small change. It's worth checking out expensive restaurants, even if they seem above your budget, as many offer special three- or four-course meals for between €20 and €35.

expensive	over €55
moderate	€20–55
inexpensive	under €20

The Centre: Old Side

Restaurants

Expensive

(80) Excelsior H7
*Hotel l'Europe, Nieuwe Doelenstraat 2–8, t 531 1705; **tram** 4, 9, 16, 24, 25; wheelchair accessible. **Open** daily 8am–11pm.*
Grand without being pompous. Waiters in tails bring you *haute cuisine* classics or the very best in new Dutch cooking, and there's a superb view over the Amstel. €65. Jacket and tie required.

(28) Restaurant Vermeer I5
*Golden Tulip Barbizon Palace, Prins Hendrikkade 59–72, t 556 4885; **bus**

Couples' City

For a special evening out, when money is less of an object (or you'd like to pretend that it is), try one of the following restaurants, picked for their intimate atmosphere or stylish food and décor: **Het Begijntje** (The Centre: New Side; see p.220), **Blakes** (Grand Canals and Jordaan; see p.222), **Breitner** (Grand Canals and Jordaan; see p.223), **Club Inez** (The Centre: New Side; see p.220), **De Compagnon** (The Centre: Old Side; see p.217), **Excelsior** (The Centre: Old Side; see p.216), **l'Indochine** (Grand Canals and Jordaan; see p.223), **De Luwte** (Grand Canals and Jordaan; see p.224), **Pier 10** (The Centre: New Side; see p.221), **Shibli** (The Centre: New Side; see p.220), **La Storia Della Vita** (Grand Canals and Jordaan; see p.224), **Supper Club** (The Centre: New Side; see p.220), **Zuidlande** (Grand Canals and Jordaan; see p.224).

22, 32, 33, 34, 35, 39; **metro** Centraal Station. **Open** Mon–Fri noon–3pm and 6–10pm, Sat 6–10pm.
Young chef Pascal Jalhaij made Benelux history by picking up a Michelin star in his first year at Restaurant Vermeer, then topping it with a second star the following year. The décor is a muted mixture of Grand Hotel and Old Dutch, and comes with genteel attentiveness. The cuisine, likewise, is one of subtle touches, fine ingredients and quiet surprises, such as grilled turbot with baby artichokes, served on a grainy polenta and given extra verve by a gamey poultry sauce.

Moderate

(38) Blauw aan de Wal I6
*Oudezijds Achterburgwal 99, t 330 2257; **tram** 4, 9, 16, 24, 25. **Open** daily 6–11.30pm. Diners Club not accepted.*
A haven in the hurly-burly of the Red Light District. Down a quiet side alley you'll find a spacious restaurant in cool minimalist style; suave clientele, and excellent modern Dutch cuisine.

(31) Centra I5
*Lange Niezel 29, t 622 3050; tram 4,
9, 14, 16, 24, 25; metro Centraal
Station. Open daily 1–11pm. Cash
only.*
Busy, garish, cafeteria-like atmos-
phere, and some of the best
Spanish food in town.

(29) De Compagnon I5
*Guldehandsteeg 17, t 620 4225;
tram 4, 9, 14, 16, 24, 25; metro
Centraal Station. Open Mon–Fri
noon–2pm and 6–10pm, Sat
6–10pm.*
Down an alley in the Red Light
District, through a green door, a
series of tiny rooms, perched on
top of each other, filled with
antique bric-a-brac, and with
views across the little harbour on
the Damrak. An unexpected find,
romantic and intimate, and with
excellent Franco-Dutch cuisine.

Inexpensive

(32) Bird I5
*Zeedijk 77, t 420 6289; tram 1, 2, 4,
5, 9, 13, 14, 16, 17, 24, 25; metro
Nieuwmarkt or Centraal Station.
Open daily 3–10pm. Cash only.*
A tiny Thai snack bar with a
kitchen one end, a trendy crowd
and enticing Thai cuisine. For
some reason, the food here is
better than in the restaurant
run by the same people across
the road.

(33) Nam Kee I5
*Zeedijk 111, t 624 3470; tram 1, 2, 4,
5, 9, 13, 14, 16, 17, 24, 25; metro
Nieuwmarkt or Centraal Station.
Open daily noon–11pm. Cash only.*
A long-established top-notch
Chinese restaurant. Inside there's
a marketplace atmosphere, with
gesticulating waiters rushing
about to serve the crowds. Prices
are unbelievably low and the
steamed oysters are divine.
Takeaway available. Another
branch nearby (open same hours)
at Geldersekade 117, t 639 2848.

(39) Oriental City I6
*Oudezijds Voorburgwal 177, t 626
8352; tram 4, 9, 16, 24, 25. Open
daily 11.30am–10.30pm.*
A three-storey establishment
which fills to the brim every

Sunday when *dim sum* is on offer.
Chinese families feast on traditional steamed dumplings and
more exotic offerings, such as
boiled ducks' feet.

(36) Song Kwae I6
*Kloveniersburgwal 14, t 624 2568;
tram 4, 9, 14, 16, 24, 25; metro
Nieuwmarkt. Open daily
1–10.30pm.*
The place to go for Thai food when
you've been unable to squeeze
into Bird (*see* above). Lots more
space, and good food, too.

**(66) Upstairs
Pannekoekhuis** H6
*Grimburgwal 2, t 626 5603; tram 4,
9, 16, 24, 25. Open Mon–Fri
noon–6pm, Sat and Sun
noon–5pm. Cash only.*
Home-made pancakes up an
almost vertical stairway, in a tiny
room overhanging the street with
space for about 10 customers. The
owner's collection of teapots
outnumbers clients 10–1. Pancakes
from around €5.

Cafés

(35) Eetcafé Van Beeren I6
*Koningsstraat 54, t 622 2329; tram
4, 9, 14, 16, 24, 25; metro
Nieuwmarkt. Open daily
5.30–10.30pm. Cash only.*
Quiet neighbourhood café with
an imaginative chef and a courtyard garden.

(65) Engelbewaarder I7
*Kloveniersburgwal 59, t 625 3772;
tram 4, 9, 16, 24, 25. Open Mon–Sat
noon–1am, Sun 2pm–1am; kitchen
open 5.30–10pm.*
Writers gulp down pasta and
scribble away on wooden tables.
Heated discussions about art and
life abound.

(81) De Jaren H7
*Nieuwe Doelenstraat 20, t 625 5771;
tram 4, 9, 16, 24, 25. Kitchen open
daily 5.30–10.30pm.*
Amsterdam's most spacious grand
café, right on the Amstel.
Comfortable chairs, high ceilings,
newspapers in all languages, and
anyone who's anyone in
Amsterdam arts. Sandwiches and

light meals for €5–15.

(64) Kaptein Zeppos H6
*Gebed Zonder End 5; tram 4, 9, 16,
24, 25. Kitchen open daily
11am–4pm, 5.30–11pm.*
The street name means 'prayer
without end' – the narrow alley
used to wind through 10 different
cloisters and was always
crammed with muttering clerics.
The restaurant serves simple,
well-prepared food in an airy,
relaxed environment. On some
afternoons you'll find a Romany
violinist or jazz band.

(30) Het Karbeel I5
*Warmoesstraat 58, t 627 4995;
tram 4, 9, 16, 24, 25. Kitchen open
daily 10am–11pm.*
An upmarket café on the edge of
the Red Light District. It started
life in 1534 as an inn and is still
connected to the Damrak by a
secret smugglers' passage. Good
sandwiches, snacks and fondues.

(40) Ricky's Koffiehuis I6
*Oudezijds Voorburgwal 206, t 623
1589; tram 4, 9, 16, 24, 25. Open
Mon–Thurs 7am–3pm, Fri
7am–1pm, closed Sat and Sun.*
Starts early as a workers' café and
changes clientele as the day
progresses. Accordions hang from
the walls, sugar is served from
zinc buckets and there's a large,
cheery communal table in a nook
at the back.

(37) Tofani I6
*Kloveniersburgwal 16, t 624 3073;
tram 4, 9, 16, 24, 25. Open April–Oct
noon–midnight.*
Genuine Italian ice-cream parlour
that also has great espresso and
warm rolls stuffed with tomato,
fresh basil and meltingly soft
mozzarella cheese.

(34) De Waag Café I6
*Nieuwmarkt, t 422 7772; tram 4, 9,
14, 16, 24, 25; metro Nieuwmarkt.
Kitchen open daily 10am–5pm and
6–10.30pm.*
The medieval city gate and weigh-
house is now a café with long
communal tables, plenty of
reading material and a terrace on
the Nieuwmarkt.

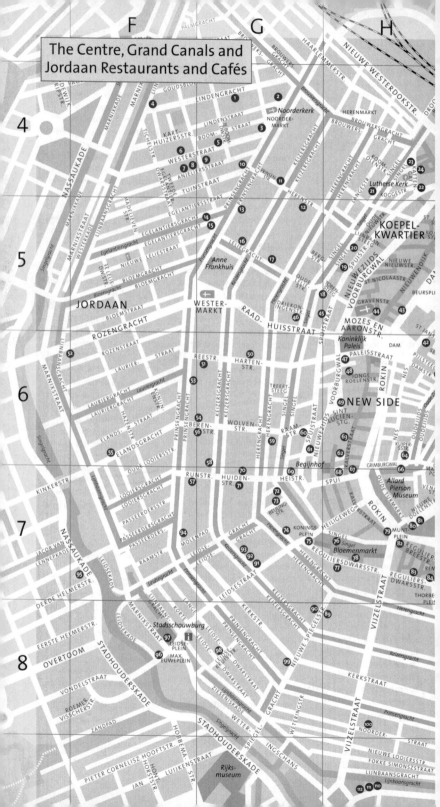

The Centre, Grand Canals and Jordaan Restaurants and Cafés

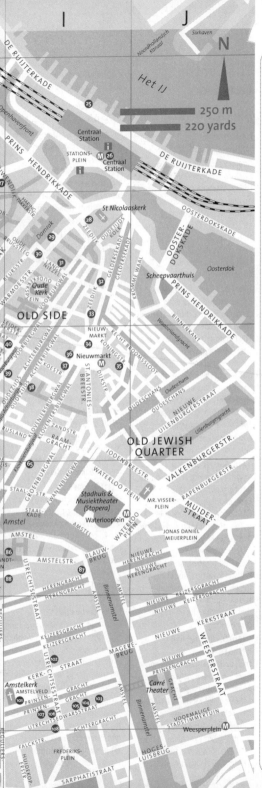

Map Key

(1) Ristorante Toscanini
(2) Bordewijk
(3) Winkel Lunchcafé
(4) Caramba
(5) De Eetkamer van de Jordaan
(6) Local
(7) De Curtis
(8) Stoop
(9) Jean Jean
(10) Bolhoed
(11) Vennington
(12) Chez Georges and Betsie
(13) The Pancake Bakery
(14) Varend Restaurant
(15) De Prins
(16) Christophe
(17) De Luwte
(18) Villa Zeezicht
(19) Krua Thai
(20) Greenwoods
(21) Woeste Walmen
(22) De Silveren Spiegel
(23) Village Bagels
(24) Koepelcafé
(25) Pier 10
(26) Grand Café Restaurant 1e (Eerste) Klas
(27) Dorrius
(28) Restaurant Vermeer
(29) De Compagnon
(30) Het Karbeel
(31) Centra
(32) Bird
(33) Nam Kee
(34) De Waag Café
(35) Eetcafé Van Beeren
(36) Song Kwae
(37) Tofani
(38) Blauw aan de Wal
(39) Oriental City
(40) Ricky's Koffiehuis
(41) Shibli
(42) NH Grand Hotel Krasnapolsky Winter Garden
(43) De Roode Leeuw
(44) 't Nieuwe Kafé Restaurant
(45) Green Planet
(46) d'Theeboom
(47) Schuim
(48) Supper Club
(49) Dolores
(50) Van Harte
(51) Dining Eleven
(52) Pielanen
(53) Van Puffelen
(54) Hein
(55) Balthazar's Keuken

Map Key Continued

The Centre: New Side

Restaurants

Expensive

(41) Shibli H6
Dam 9, t 330 8082; tram 4, 9, 16, 24, 25. Open Wed–Sat from 7pm.
For an interesting array in a unique setting, track down this underground Bedouin tent attached to the famous NH Grand Hotel Krasnapolsky. The theme is taken to its very limits, with veiled staff and a masque-like atmosphere.

(22) De Silveren Spiegel H4
Kattengat 4–6, t 624 6589; tram 1, 2, 5, 13, 17; metro Centraal Station. Open Mon–Sat 6–10.30pm.
The building, all Delft tiles and cosy corners, dates from 1614. The visionary chef comes up with such dishes as guinea fowl with rose-petal sauce, and uses prime local ingredients, such as lamb from the North Sea island of Texel (where the creatures frolic freely and eat wild herbs). Service is personal and friendly.

(48) Supper Club H6
Jonge Roelensteeg 21, t 244 6400; tram 4, 9, 16, 24, 25. Open daily 8pm–midnight.
Considering how much they charge, the international cuisine here isn't likely to win your heart (or your stomach), but people still flock here for the huge beds and fluffy pillows (in place of chairs), the performers and masseurs, the surreal vibe and floaty clientele that make this place a one-off experience.

(60) D'Vijff Vlieghen (The Five Flies) G6
Spuistraat 294–302, t 530 4060; tram 1, 2, 5. Open daily 5.30–10pm.
An intriguing conglomeration of antique-filled rooms in a wonky 17th-century inn. It gets its unfortunate name from the original owner, Jan Vijff Vlieghen. In the 1950s and 60s it was frequented by the likes of Orson Welles, Benjamin Britten, Jean Cocteau and Walt Disney. An instituion, but also something of a tourist trap.

Moderate

(62) Het Begijntje H6
Begijnensteeg 6, t 624 0528; tram 1, 2, 4, 5, 16, 24, 25. Open Mon–Sat noon–2.30pm and 6–10pm.
Excellent ingredients, carefully prepared with a classic French touch. A cosy, quiet and romantic place. Dishes include lobster baked with orange caramel, or duck breast with port sauce.

(72) Casa di David G7
Singel 426, t 624 5093; tram 1, 2, 5. Open daily 5–11pm.
Pizzeria with wooden beams and canalside charm. The food is good as well – pasta made on the premises, excellent antipasti, and fragrant, crusty pizzas cooked in a wood-burning oven. It's child-friendly, too.

(82) Club Inez H7
Amstel 2, t 639 2899; tram 4, 9, 14. Open daily 7–10pm. No Amex or Diners Club.
An artsy crowd gather in a restaurant hidden upstairs near the Munttoren. Great views and adventurous cuisine – such as chicken baked in straw.

(27) Dorrius H4
Nieuwezijds Voorburgwal 5, t 420 2224; tram 1, 2, 5, 13, 17. Open daily 6–11pm; wheelchair accessible.
The Dutch meals here are as comforting and authentic as the décor, with its traditional wood panelling and Delft tiles. No-smoking area and private room available.

(61) Haesje Claes G6
Spuistraat 273–5, t 624 9998; tram 1, 2, 5. Open daily noon–midnight.
Touristy, but unhurried. Folksy Old Dutch interior, solid tasty Dutch food, and lots of salad and vegetables. Tourist menu for €19.

(19) Krua Thai H5
Spuistraat 90A, t 620 0623; tram 1, 2, 5. Open daily 5–10.30pm. Amex and Diners Club not accepted.
After much audible campery in the kitchen, spectacular dishes are

Outdoor City

For the rare occasions when it's warm in Amsterdam, try one of these cafés and restaurants, where you can eat outside:

Café Vertigo (Museumplein and Vondelpark; *see* p.229), **Coffeeshop Le Monde** (The Centre: New Side; *see* p.222), **Hortus Botanicus Orangery** (Waterlooplein and the Plantagebuurt; *see* p.228), **Het Land van Walem** (Grand Canals and Jordaan; *see* p.226), **Mas Tapas** (De Pijp, *see* p.230), **Moko** (Grand Canals and Jordaan; *see* p.224), **'t Nieuwe Café Restaurant** (The Centre: New Side; *see* p.222), **De Prins** (Grand Canals and Jordaan; *see* p.227), **La Rive** (Oosterpark and The East; *see* p.231), **Van Puffelen** (Grand Canals and Jordaan; *see* p.227), **Villa Zeezicht** (The Centre: New Side; *see* p.222), **Village Bagels** (The Centre, New Side; *see* p.222), **De Waag Café** (The Centre: Old Side; *see* p.217), **Wilhelminadok** (Across the IJ; *see* p.232).

brought out. The hot-and-spicy beef salad is unbeatable, and the stuffed chicken wings divine.

(25) Pier 10 I4
De Ruyterkade Steiger 10 (behind Centraal Station), t 624 8276; metro Centraal Station. Open daily 5–11.30pm.
A little wooden hut, once a shipping line office, right on the end of a pier in the IJ. Watch the boats chug past as you devour scrumptious Dutch or French food.

(43) De Roode Leeuw H5
Damrak 93–4, t 555 0666; tram 4, 9, 16, 24, 25; wheelchair accessible. Open daily 7–10am and noon–10pm.
If you're trying to track down a true Dutch meal, many people will point you in the direction of this long-established restaurant. The warm and cluttered décor, the no-nonsense menu (Dutch pea soup, sausage and mash) instantly confirm the authenticity of the place. The waiters are polite, sincere and particularly welcoming to children.

(77) Rose's Cantina H7
Reguliersdwarsstraat 38, t 625 9797; tram 4, 9, 14, 16, 24, 25. Open daily 5–11pm.
Crowds of Bright Young Things, tasty Tex-Mex food and lethal margaritas.

(75) Saturnino G7
Reguliersdwarsstraat 5H, t 639 0102; tram 4, 9, 14, 16, 24, 25. Open daily noon–midnight. Amex and Diners Club not accepted.
Trendy Italian restaurant on Amsterdam's main gay street. The atmosphere is glitzy, but the food has a wholesome home-made touch.

(78) Sichuan Food H7
Reguliersdwarsstraat 35, t 625 8775; tram 4, 9, 14, 16, 24, 25. Open daily 5.30–11pm.
Proud possessor of the first Michelin star awarded to a Chinese restaurant in the Netherlands. Aperitifs made from flowers, sautéed oysters with tangy sauces; local Western restaurants are beginning to imitate the seafood dishes.

(46) d'Theeboom G5
Singel 210, t 623 8420; tram 13, 14, 17. Open Mon–Fri noon–2.30pm and 6–10pm, Sat and Sun 6–10pm.
Georges Thubert scorns rip-off prices and culinary pretension. He runs his restaurant, in a converted canalside warehouse, in classic French style, and offers excellent value and fine cooking.

(68) Vasso H7
Rozenboomsteeg 10–14, t 626 0158; tram 4, 9, 14, 16, 24, 25. Open daily 6–10.30pm. Diners Club not accepted.
Fresh pasta and fine Italian food in a restaurant that has the lively atmosphere of the kitchens of a faded palazzo.

Inexpensive

(69) Convivio G7
Singel 371, t 638 8839; tram 1, 2, 5. Open daily 6–11pm.
A designer interior where you can mull over a bottle of wine and nibble on a variety of dishes in a lively, tapas-bar atmosphere.

(49) Dolores H6
Nieuwezijds Voorburgwal opposite 289, t 620 3302; tram 1, 2, 5. Open Mon–Sat 11am–6pm, Thurs 11am–9pm, Sun noon–6pm. Cash only.
A former street-side wooden police hut sees new life as a lunch and snack venue, whose stylish, low-key design has made the pages of style magazines. Sandwiches, croquettes and other Dutch fare here taste a little better, as ingredients are organic.

(45) Green Planet H5
Spuistraat 122, t 625 8280; tram 1, 2, 5, 13, 14, 17. Open Mon–Sat 11am–10pm. Cash only.
Cheery service and a cook whose style isn't cramped by not using meat make this a hot tip for carnivores and vegetarians alike. Dishes such as sweet-potato dumplings, filled with spinach, ricotta and cashew nuts, with a red-wine vegetable ragout, come beautifully presented.

(67) Helder H7
Taksteeg 7, t 320 4132; tram 4, 9, 14, 16, 24, 25. Open Mon–Sat 11am–6pm. Cash only.
Teensy lunch venue convenient for shoppers, which offers imaginative daily-changing menus of pastas, salads and filled rolls.

(79) La Place H7
Rokin 162, t 620 2364; tram 4, 9, 16, 24, 25; wheelchair accessible. Open Tues–Sat 10am–8pm, Sun noon–8pm, Mon 11am–8pm.
Serve yourself at various counters – a great salad bar, fresh pastas and grilled meats cooked while you wait. Most of the ingredients are organic, you sit in one of a honeycomb of rooms in an atmospheric 17th-century building – and it's inexpensive and child-friendly.

(85) Surinam Express H7
Halvemaansteeg 18, t no tel; tram 4, 9, 14. Open Sun–Thurs 5pm–3am, Fri and Sat 5pm–6am. Cash only.
Tiny sandwich shop off Rembrandtplein with searingly authentic Surinamese food – spicy vegetable and tangy curry fillings. Eat fuller meals, too, at a counter along the wall.

(23) Village Bagels, H4
Stromarkt 2, t 528 9152; tram 1, 2, 5, 13, 17. **Open** *Mon–Sat 7.30am–7pm, Sun 9am–6pm. Cash only.*
Busy bagel joint, with a great terrace, and (rare for Amsterdam) open for an early breakfast.

(21) Woeste Walmen H4
Singel 46, t 638 0765; metro Centraal Station. **Open** *Sat evening (phone to reserve). Cash only.*
Decorated with quirky flair and run by squatters who come up with food that they have obviously enjoyed cooking. Usually one meat and one non-meat option for the main course.

Cafés

(86) Café l'Opera I7
Rembrandtplein 19, t 620 4754; tram 4, 9, 14. **Kitchen open** *daily 11am–10pm; wheelchair accessible.*
Catches the last patch of afternoon sun.

(88) Café Schiller I7
Rembrandtplein 26, t 624 9846; tram 4, 9, 14. **Open** *Daily 6–9.30pm.*
A front-runner for the best café food in town, produced in a kitchen not much larger than the average double bed. There are always imaginative vegetarian options and big salads, as well as full meals such as duck with organic local sausage and a fruity gravy. And the genuine Art Deco café makes an attractive backdrop.

(84) Coffeeshop Le Monde H7
Rembrandtplein 6, t 626 9922; tram 4, 9, 14. **Open** *8am–midnight; kitchen open daily 8am–10.30pm.*
The friendliest of the otherwise indistinguishable pavement cafés.

(63) David and Goliath H6
Kalverstraat 92 (at the entrance to the Amsterdams Historisch Museum), t 623 6736; tram 1, 2, 4, 5, 9, 16, 24, 25. **Open** *Mon–Fri 10am–5pm.*
After visiting the museum, the best place to relax and ponder the delights within is at the feet of a life-sized wooden David and an

Amsterdammers' City

If you'd like to taste traditional Dutch food, try:
De Blonde Hollander (Grand Canals and Jordaan; *see p.225*), **Dorrius** (The Centre: New Side; *see p.220*), **Haesje Claes** (The Centre: New Side; *see p.220*), **Piet de Leeuw** (Grand Canals and Jordaan; *see p.224*), **De Roode Leeuw** (The Centre: New Side; *see p.221*), **Rosereijn** (Western Islands and Scheepvaartbuurt; *see p.233*), **Le Soleil** (Grand Canals and Jordaan; *see p.227*).

enormous Goliath, rescued from a 17th-century pleasure garden.

(76) Divertimento G7
Singel 480 (in the flower market), t 622 9690; tram 1, 2, 4, 5, 9, 16, 24, 25. **Open** *Mon–Fri 8.30am–5.30pm, Sat 8.30am–6pm, Sun 10am–5.30pm.*
A fragrant café that serves enormous ice creams as well as inexpensive sandwiches and snacks. It's kid-friendly, too.

(26) Grand Café Restaurant 1e (Eerste) Klas I4
Platform 2B, Centraal Station, t 625 0131. **Open** *daily 9.30am–10pm.*
Recently restored First Class dining room, now open to all. It's timeless railway camp. You wouldn't bat an eyelid if you saw women in cloche hats whispering in the corner or an Edwardian touring party march through the door. Coffee, snacks and also much grander meals (from around €20 for a main course).

(20) Greenwoods H5
Singel 103, t 623 7071; tram 1, 2, 5, 13, 17. **Open** *daily 9.30am–7pm.*
Real home-made English afternoon tea for €6.50.

(24) Koepelcafé H4
Kattengat 1, Koepelkwartier, t 551 2043; tram 1, 2, 5, 13, 17; metro Centraal Station. **Open** *daily 10am–11pm.*
Part of the Renaissance Hotel. A rather bland café, but open on a Sunday morning.

(42) NH Grand Hotel Krasnapolsky Winter Garden H6
Dam 9, t 554 9111; tram 4, 9, 16, 24, 25.
Careful redecoration in the early 1990s gave the Krasnapolsky back some of the old elegance that an insensitive 1970s job had destroyed. In the Winter Garden you can sit surrounded by palms and flattering mirrors and enjoy a genteel lunch. Breakfast (6.30am–10.30am) €21, buffet lunch (noon–2pm) €30. Call to reserve and mention 'Wintertuin', or you'll end up in the brasserie.

(44) 't Nieuwe Kafé Restaurant H5
Eggertstraat 8 (next door to the Nieuwe Kerk), t 627 2830; tram 4, 9, 16, 24, 25; wheelchair accessible. **Open** *daily 10am–6pm.*
A noisy terrace but quieter interior. Set breakfasts, snacks and fuller meals, plus a children's menu.

(47) Schuim H6
Spuistraat 189, t 638 9357; tram 1, 2, 5. **Kitchen open** *daily noon–8pm.*
Shop-window café full of students during the day, and artsy types at night who admire their friends' paintings.

(18) Villa Zeezicht H5
Torensteeg 7, t 626 7433; tram 1, 2, 5, 13, 17. **Kitchen open** *daily 8am–8pm.*
Lively sandwich bar where you can get tasty snacks and cakes. The canalside terrace is a great place to sun yourself in good weather.

Grand Canals and Jordaan

Restaurants

Expensive

(58) Blakes G6
Keizersgracht 384, t 530 2010; tram 1, 2, 5, 7, 13, 14, 17 then 5min walk. **Open** *daily noon–2pm, 6.30–10.30pm (no lunch Sat).*
Black and white chic work wonderfully well in the bakery of

a former almshouse (the ovens are still in place), and the fusion food is just as unusual and visually appealing. One of the city's top dining spots, if you're willing to splash out around €70.

(95) Blue Pepper F7
*Nassaukade 366, t 489 7039; **tram** 1, 3, 6, 7, 12, 17. **Open** daily 6–10pm, closed on Mon in summer.*
Indonesian cooking taken to *haute cuisine* levels. Subtle fish dishes, spicy meat and new, imaginative variations on traditional themes. The restaurant is tiny and popular, so book well in advance.

(2) Bordewijk G4
*Noordermarkt 7, t 624 3899; **bus** 18, 22. **Open** Tues–Sun 6.30–10.30pm.*
Smartly dressed Jordaan locals enjoy the understated décor and cunning culinary combinations served here, such as scallops with a confit of tomato and sweet sherry, with grated truffles on top.

(87) Breitner I7
*Amstel 212, t 627 7879; **tram** 1, 2, 4, 5, 9, 14; **metro** Waterlooplein. **Open** Mon–Sat 6–10.30pm.*
A sublime view, with a highly imaginative menu. The relaxed, chic atmosphere and excellent cuisine are a great attraction to artistes from the Opera House.

(12) Chez Georges and Betsie G5
*Herenstraat 3, t 626 3332; **tram** 1, 2, 5, 13, 17, then 5min walk across canals. **Open** Mon, Tues and Thurs–Sat 6–10pm.*
A good old-fashioned Belgian restaurant with floral wallpaper, slightly kitsch artwork and superb cuisine. Subtle sauces, truffles, fish with saffron paella or Irish beef are some of the options. Car park available.

(16) Christophe G5
*Leliegracht 46, t 625 0807; **tram** 13, 14, 17. **Open** Tues–Sat 6.30–10.30pm.*
A little stuffy, but Algerian-born Jean-Christophe Royer comes up with superb French cuisine enlivened by zesty north-African flavours.

(73) l'Indochine G7
*Beulingstraat 9, t 627 5755; **tram** 1, 2, 5. **Open** Tues–Sun 5.30–10.30pm.*
Beautifully presented Vietnamese fare from a bustling kitchen served in calm surroundings. Everything is wonderfully fresh and flavourful, while the great variety of this country's cuisine is reflected in the menu. A good romantic spot.

(9) Jean Jean G4
*1e Anjeliersdwarsstraat 14, t 627 7153; **tram** 3, 10. **Open** Tues–Sun 6–10pm. Amex and Diners Club not accepted.*
Stark modern design, and elaborate modern cuisine. Highly fashionable spot where the chef blends Eastern, French and Italian influences in virtuoso creations – snails in sage butter, alongside light vegetable soup with fried shallot wontons.

(108) Segugio I8
*Utrechtsestraat 96A, t 330 1503; **tram** 4. **Open** Mon–Sat 6–11pm. Diners Club not accepted.*
Hip new Italian restaurant that departs a little from traditional norms – though the starters are more exciting than the mains, and you might consider making a meal of antipasti entirely.

(57) Takens F7
*Runstraat 17D, t 627 0618; **tram** 1, 2, 5. **Open** daily 6–11pm.*
An upmarket but unpretentious establishment where you can expect imaginative but unfussy cuisine served by friendly staff. Try warm potato salad with North Sea shrimps as a starter, then poussin with aubergine fritters.

(104) De Utrechtsedwarstafel I8
*Utrechtsedwarsstraat 107, t 625 4189; **tram** 4. **Open** Tues–Sat 7pm–midnight. Diners Club, MasterCard and Visa not accepted.*
Igor, a culinary whizz, works single-handedly in the kitchen; Hans, an expert on wines, is front-of-house. There's no menu, just a grid offering three, four or five courses, at a simple, medium or gourmet level. Wine is included in

the price. You pick your level, tell them if there is anything you prefer not to eat, and wait to be surprised. Igor comes out to tell you about the meal; Hans chats about the wine, tailor-making choices as you go along.

(14) Varend Restaurant G5
*Egelantiersgracht 12, t 419 4141; **tram** 13, 14, 17. **Open** Wed from 7pm. Amex, Diners Club not accepted.*
Spend an evening cruising the canals in a dinner-boat, with a meal provided by a top chef (rather than the dull food so often supplied on such jaunts). Board at Egelantiersgracht 12 (Café 't Smalle).

(109) Yoichi I9
*Weteringschans 128, t 622 6829; **tram** 6, 7, 10. **Open** Thurs–Tues 6–10.30pm. Diners Club not accepted.*
Amsterdam's oldest Japanese restaurant, and still one of the best. Traditional food; high prices.

Moderate

(4) Caramba F4
*Lindengracht 342, t 627 1188; **bus** 18. **Open** daily 5.30–10.30pm.*
Lively South American restaurant where an arty crowd consumes tortilla and vicious margaritas.

(7) De Curtis F4
*2e Anjeliersdwarsstraat 6, t 420 0767; **tram** 3, 10. **Open** Mon–Sat 6–10.30pm. Cash only.*
Lively Italian restaurant run by two young guys who generally cope single-handed. The evening's fare is chalked up on a blackboard (pasta mostly), and the atmosphere is relaxed and casual.

(51) Dining Eleven G6
*Reestraat 11, t 620 7968; **tram** 1, 2, 5, 13, 14, 17. **Open** daily 6–10pm.*
A family-run concern that proves you can maintain old-fashioned standards of service, yet still be cool and trendy. The food is rich, but supremely well done, and beautifully presented in a designer setting. Wines are affordable and chosen with considerable insight and care.

(5) De Eetkamer van de Jordaan G4

Westerstraat 78, t 625 0746; bus 18, 22. Open Mon–Fri 5.30–10pm.
A traditional down-to-earth Jordaan eatery with an upmarket edge. A lively professional clientele enjoy steak and chips alongside *ren en spring* (run and jump), a duo of emu and kangaroo meats. Takeaway available.

(110) Felicità H9

Weteringschans 187C, t 422 1088; tram 6, 7, 10, 16, 24, 25. Open noon–midnight. Cash only.
Great Italian food – there's no menu, you take pot luck. The chef clatters away in the kitchen and comes up with fine meals that (in true Italian style) rely on simple combinations of good ingredients.

(17) De Luwte G5

Leliegracht 26, t 625 8548; tram 13, 14, 17. Open daily 6–10pm. Amex and Diners Club not accepted.
Romantic candlelit restaurant, with trompe l'oeil on the walls, by a small canal. Delicious meals with fresh (often organic) ingredients.

(101) Moko I8

Amstelveld 12, t 626 1199; tram 4. Open daily noon–11pm.
Situated in part of a 17th-century church, and boasting one of the best terraces in town – under tall trees, overlooking a canal, and without traffic thundering past. A good place for a lunchtime salad or light meal.

(90) Pasta e Basta G8

Nieuwe Spiegelstraat 8, t 422 2229; tram 1, 2, 5, 16, 24, 25. Open Tues–Sun 6–11pm.
You might expect 'pasta and plenty' from a romantic Italian, but enduring the staff regaling you with live opera while you eat is another matter altogether.

(52) Pielanen F6

Rozengracht 89, t 639 3292; tram 13, 14, 17; wheelchair accessible. Open Mon–Sat 6–10pm.
Low-key, cosy brasserie without fuss or pretensions – but where you could possibly have the best *confit de canard* you've ever tasted. Good organic wines.

(100) Piet de Leeuw H8

Noorderstraat 11, t 623 7181; Tram 16, 24, 25. Open Mon–Fri noon–11pm, Sat and Sun 5–11pm. Diners Club not accepted.
The sort of place you might take a Dutch person who had been living abroad for 20 years, longing for home. Behind the lace-curtained windows you are lost in a time-warp of wood-panelled walls, background accordion music, and good solid meals of steak and onions, smoked eel on toast, or liver and bacon.

(89) Pygma-Lion H8

Nieuwe Spiegelstraat 5A, t 420 7022; tram 1, 2, 5, 16, 24, 25. Open Tues–Sun 11am–11pm.
South African restaurant that's great for a hearty salad, an ostrich *sosatie* (curried kebab) and other African fare – or simply for a coffee and *melktert* (a sort of custard pie).

(1) Ristorante Toscanini G4

Lindengracht 75, t 623 2813; bus 18; wheelchair accessible. Open Mon–Sat 6–10.30pm.
Cavernous, rowdy and very Italian. A gastric and sensual delight, but service is exceedingly slow. Child-friendly.

(8) Stoop F4

1e Anjeliersdwarsstraat 4, t 639 2480; tram 10, 13, 14, 17; wheelchair accessible. Open daily 6.30–11pm.
Small, busy restaurant: pastrami salad with ginger and yoghurt dressing, and fried guinea fowl wrapped in Serrano ham with pumpkin and an apple-calvados gravy. Child-friendly.

(112) La Storia Della Vita H9

Weteringschans 171, t 623 4251; tram 6, 7, 10. Open Mon–Sat 6–11pm.
A spacious, candlelit restaurant where the table is yours for the whole evening, so you can truly relax and enjoy the waves of Italian treats that get sent your way. There's no choice, but for your money you get a veritable feast of snacks, bread, soup, pasta, meat, fish and pudding.

(83) Tomo Sushi H7

Reguliersdwarsstraat 131, t 528 5208; tram 4, 9, 14. Open daily 5.30–11.30pm.
Simple, but really good sushi bar with prime fresh ingredients and surprisingly affordable prices.

(102) Tujuh Maret I8

Utrechtsestraat 73, t 427 9865; tram 4. Open Tues–Sat 12.30–10pm, Sun 4–10pm. Cash only.
Treat yourself to a flavoursome feast of Indonesian *rijsttafel*. The *soto ayam* (chicken broth) has a fine bouillon base, and the different chicken and meat dishes are just that – different. Beef in a mild sauce of soya and nutmeg, or a zippier version cooked with red peppers and tamarind; chicken as a tangy curry, or with a gentle coconut sauce.

(50) Van Harte G6

Hartenstraat 24, t 625 8500; tram 13, 14, 17. Open Wed–Mon 11am–10pm.
Modest, yet excellent kitchen. Berries and wild mushrooms in the sauces, tender meats and charming service.

(111) Van Vlaanderen H9

Weteringschans 175, t 622 8292; tram 6, 7, 10. Open Tues–Sat 6.30–10.30pm.
Backing onto a canal, this calm, cool retreat is decorated with old oil paintings, offsetting pristine linen and plain white walls. The menu is a mixture of Dutch comfort food, like croquettes, and more exclusive dishes such as free-range chicken stuffed with truffles and goose liver.

(103) Zuidlande I8

Utrechtsedwarsstraat 141, t 620 7393; tram 4; wheelchair accessible. Open Tues–Sat 7–10.30pm.
Strong flavours and generous portions abound at this romantic spot, softly lit by oil lamps and candelabra. There's delicious French-influenced cuisine such as terrine made from confit of duck breast, blood sausage and marinated duck's liver, along with an excellent and reasonably priced wine list.

(74) Zuid Zeeland G7
Herengracht 413, t 624 3154; tram 1, 2, 5. Open Mon–Fri noon–3pm and 6–11pm.
Specializes in fish dishes from Belgium and the south of Holland, but the menu also includes meat dishes that have a French and Japanese influence.

Inexpensive

(105) Axum I8
Utrechtsedwarsstraat 85–7, t 622 8389; tram 4. Open Tues–Thurs and Sun 5–11pm, Fri and Sat 5pm–12.30am. Cash only.
Authentic Ethiopian cuisine – a giant communal pancake and a few sizzling pots of stews and curries. Toss on some salad and yoghurt sauce, add a spoon of stew, and roll up mouth-sized bites with your fingers. Appropriate décor and utterly charming service.

(55) Balthazar's Keuken F6
Elandsgracht 108, t 420 2114; tram 13, 14, 17, then walk. Open Wed–Fri 6–11pm.
The kitchen takes up a third of the room, and diners crowd around a few small wooden tables. Starters are usually *meze*-style: cockles with ginger and parsley or red-pepper salad with anise pepperoni. There's a fish-or-flesh choice for the main course: try buttery pink salmon in a crackly coat of nori, scattered with crisp-fried green asparagus, served with sepia risotto and a perky anchovy sauce.

(98) De Blonde Hollander G8
Leidsekruisstraat 28, t 626 5291; tram 1, 2, 5. Open Mon–Thurs 6–10.30pm, Fri and Sat 6–11.30pm, Sun 6–10pm. Cash only.
A new generation has taken over the family restaurant and redecorated it in hip lounge-bar style. The menu still comprises Dutch nursery-food favourites, such as *erwtensoep* and *bal gehakt* (a huge meatball), but here done with top-rate, often organic, ingredients, which make a world of difference.

(10) Bolhoed G4
Prinsengracht 60, t 626 1803; tram 13, 14, 17. Open daily noon–10pm.
A veggie restaurant with exotic Thai statues, quirky lamps, bright colours and soft lighting. The cuisine has a Mexican touch, and is imaginative and tasty. There are vegan dishes available, and fish too, and the daily three-course menu is excellent value.

(106) Golden Temple I8
Utrechtsestraat 126, t 626 8560; tram 4. Open daily 5–9.30pm. Cash only.
Simple décor, but tasty vegetarian food with strong Indian flavours. Vegan options.

(71) Goodies G7
Huidenstraat 9, t 625 6122; tram 1, 2, 5. Open Tues–Sat 9.30am–10.30pm, Sun 11am–10.30pm, Mon noon–5.30pm.
Arty hangout that sells good sandwiches and salads by day, and pasta by night. Child-friendly.

(6) Local F4
Westerstraat 136, t 423 4039; tram 3, 10. Open Mon–Sat 6–11pm. Cash only.
Headily hip bar-style eaterie, where you sit on stools at long communal tables to eat a variety of kebabs – from curried ostrich to blackened turkey.

(11) Vennington G4
Prinsenstraat 2, t 625 9398; tram 1, 2, 5, 13, 17. Open daily 8am–4pm.
Friendly, unpretentious little sandwich and snack bar, convenient if you're shopping on the 'Negen Straatjes'. They do a great club sandwich.

Cafés

(107) Backstage Boutique (a.k.a 'The Twins') I8
Utrechtsedwarsstraat 65–7, t 622 3638; tram 4. Open Mon–Sat 10am–5.30pm.
Teas, coffee and home-made cakes in a coffeeshop that doubles as a boutique for fluorescent knitwear, tarot-reading parlour and local gossip shop. Sit among the gaudy

---

Architectural City

The following restaurants are remarkable either for the buildings they're in or for their décor:
De Belhamel (Western Islands and Scheepvaartbuurt; *see p.232*), **Café Américain** (Grand Canals and Jordaan; *see p.226*), **Café Schiller** (The Centre: New Side; *see p.222*), **Café De Sluyswacht** (Waterlooplein and the Plantagebuurt; *see p.228*), **Convivio** (The Centre: New Side; *see p.221*), **Dorrius** (The Centre: New Side; *see p.220*), **De Gouden Reael** (Western Islands and Scheepvaartbuurt; *see p.232*), **Grand Café Restaurant 1e (Eerste) Klas** (The Centre: New Side; *see p.222*), **De Groene Lanteerne** (Western Islands and Scheepvaartbuurt; *see p.232*), **Hollandsche Manege Café** (Museumplein and Vondelpark; *see p.229*), **Het Karbeel** (The Centre: Old Side; *see p.217*) **De Kas** (Oosterpark and the East; *see p.231*), **Metz Café** (Grand Canals and Jordaan; *see p.227*), **La Place** (The Centre: New Side; *see p.221*), **Plancius** (Waterlooplein and the Plantagebuurt; *see p.227*), **Pompadour** (Grand Canals and Jordaan; *see p.227*), **De Silveren Spiegel** (The Centre: New Side; *see p.220*), **D'Vijff Vlieghen** (The Centre: New Side; *see p.220*), **De Waag Café** (The Centre: Old Side; *see p.217*).

---

jerseys and tea-cosy hats and enjoy your tea with the transvestites, busy mums, pretty young men and local lads who come in for the owner's infectious humour and good food.

(59) 't Buffet van Odette en Yvette G6
Herengracht 309, t 423 6034; tram 1, 2, 5. Open Mon–Fri 8.30am–5.30pm, Sat 10am–5.30pm. Cash only.
From brownies to BLTs, with a few Dutch favourites in between – and with a view out onto the Herengracht. A pleasant breakfast and lunch café.

Plantagebuurt, Oosterpark and Eastern Islands Restaurants and Cafés

Map Key

(113) Scheepvaart Museum Café
(114) Kilimanjaro
(115) Raap en Peper
(116) Rosario
(117) Café De Sluyswacht
(118) Puccini
(119) Frenzi

(120) Soup en Zo
(121) King Solomon
(122) Anda Nugraha
(123) Hortus Botanicus Orangery
(124) Plancius
(125) De Groene Olifant
(126) ToDine
(127) La Rive
(128) De IJsbreker

---

(96) Café Américain F8
American Hotel, Leidseplein, t 556 3232; tram 1, 2, 5. Open Sun–Tues noon–3pm and 6–10.30pm, Wed–Sat noon–3pm and 6–11.30pm.
Art Nouveau grand café. Once the hangout of Amsterdam's literati, it's now visited mainly by tourists, but is just the right environment for a pot of fresh coffee and an extravagantly gooey cake. It also serves snacks and fuller meals. Child-friendly.

(97) Café Cox F8
Marnixstraat 429 (beneath the Stadsschouwburg), t 620 7222; tram 1, 2, 5, 6, 7, 10. Open Sun–Wed 12.30–3.30pm, 5.30–10.30pm, Thurs–Sat 12.30–3.30pm, 5.30–11pm.
Named after the theatre's erstwhile director Cox Habbema. It serves scrumptious salads and light meals.

(54) Hein G6
Berenstraat 20, t 623 1048; tram 1, 2, 5, 13, 14, 17. Open daily 9.30am–3pm.
One of the new wave of lunch venues that have opened in opposition to the ubiquitous *broodjeszaken* (sandwich shops) with their boring fare of cheese, ham, and plasticky mayonnaise-drenched salads. Half the room is taken up by the kitchen, and lunches (and great Sunday breakfasts) have a home-made touch, from salads to fry-ups.

(92) Het Land van Walem G7
Keizersgracht 449, t 625 3544; tram 1, 2, 5. Open daily 10am–4.30pm and 6–10.30pm.

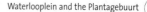

jazz band into one corner. A smoky, dreamy place to while away a Sunday afternoon.

(93) Morlang G7
Keizersgracht 451, **t** *625 2681;* **tram** *1, 2, 5.* **Open** *daily 10.30am–11pm.*
Brittle, trendier-than-thou atmosphere, but good food.

(56) Nielsen G6
Berenstraat 19, **t** *330 6006;* **tram** *1, 2, 5, 13, 14, 17.* **Open** *Tues–Fri 8am–4pm, Sat 8am–5pm, Sun 9am–4pm. Amex and Diners Club not accepted.*
Behind a large picture window, with something of the atmosphere of a disordered domestic dining room, Nielsen is homey, relaxed, with an edge of hip, and some extraordinarily good apple pie. Tasty sandwiches and lighter meals include a range of vegetarian options. Another local Sunday breakfast favourite.

(13) The Pancake Bakery G5
Prinsengracht 191, **t** *625 1333;* **tram** *13, 14, 17.* **Open** *daily noon–9.30pm.*
A low-beamed cellar that boasts the best pancakes in town. They could well be right. Sweet and savoury pancakes from €5. It's kid-friendly, too.

(70) Pompadour G7
Huidenstraat 5, **t** *623 9554;* **tram** *1, 2, 5.* **Open** *Tues–Sat 9am–6pm.*
A *chocolaterie* and patisserie. The interior – hardly bigger than an average kitchen – somehow incorporates carved oak panels, a staircase and a balustrade from an 18th-century town hall near Liège. Sit in this matchbox splendour and choose from a selection of nearly 50 different hand-made choccies, or (and?) have a pastry with your coffee.

(15) De Prins G5
Prinsengracht 124, **t** *624 9382;* **tram** *13, 14, 17.* **Kitchen open** *daily 10am–10pm, Fri and Sat 10am–2am.*
Trendy café with a sunny canalside terrace. Serves good sandwiches and snacks.

(99) Le Soleil G8
Nieuwe Spiegelstraat 50, **t** *622 7147;* **tram** *1, 2, 5, 16, 24, 25.* **Open** *daily 10am–6pm. Cash only.*

Traditional Dutch pancakes (sweet and savoury) served at communal tables. The chairs are painted in the pastel pink and green enamels you usually find in seaside tearooms, and the walls are cluttered with Art Deco knick-knacks.

(53) Van Puffelen F6
Prinsengracht 377, **t** *624 6270;* **tram** *13, 14, 17.* **Kitchen open** *Mon–Fri 6–11pm, Sat noon–4pm, 6–11pm, Sun noon–4pm, 5.30–10pm.*
Sawdust on the floor, and cherubs on the ceiling. A good restaurant at the back, a terrace on a barge on the canal in front, and a smart clientele. Child-friendly.

(3) Winkel Lunchcafé G4
Noordermarkt 43, **t** *623 0223;* **bus** *18;* **metro** *Centraal Station then walk.* **Open** *Mon–Sat 7am–5.30pm. Cash only.*
Good salads. Gets its produce (much of it organic) fresh from the farm, though the standard of service often spoils the lunch.

Waterlooplein and the Plantagebuurt

Restaurants

Moderate

(119) Frenzi I7
Zwanenburgwal 232, **t** *423 5112;* **metro** *Waterlooplein.* **Open** *daily 11am–11pm.*
Bright waterside restaurant serving food from around the Mediterranean. They do a mouthwatering, multi-tiered plate of tapas/antipasti/mezes that makes a great lunch.

(124) Plancius K7
Plantage Kerklaan 61A, **t** *330 9469;* **tram** *9, 14.* **Open** *daily 10am–4.30pm and 6–10pm. Amex not accepted.*
An ultra-trendy converted garage that appeals to arty types of all ages. Inside it's all bold colours and bright lights with lots of metal and geometry. The mood is laid-back, with cheerful staff and an excellent international menu.

Friendlier than the Morlang next door (*see below*), with a bigger terrace and a garden at the back.

(91) The Metz Café G7
455 Keizersgracht, **t** *520 7020;* **tram** *1, 2, 5.* **Open** *daily 10am–5pm.*
Amsterdam from high up is a rare sight. The glass cupola on top of one of its poshest department stores is a good place to sip a coffee and change your perspective of the city – but not for a meal. It dishes up dull railway-station fare. Service is rather indifferent until you try to take a photograph.

(94) Het Molenpad F7
Prinsengracht 653, **t** *625 9680;* **tram** *1, 2, 5.* **Open** *daily noon–10.30pm.*
A brown café that serves good food and sometimes crams a live

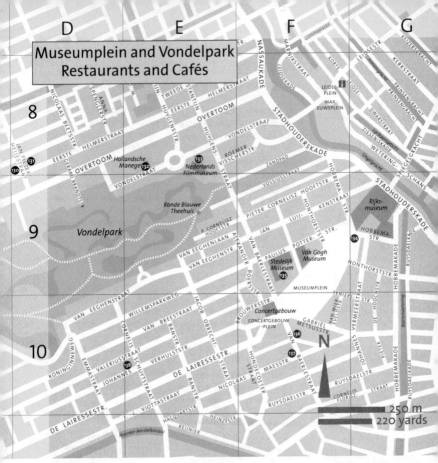

Map Key

(129) Riaz
(130) Waroeng Asje
(131) Paloma Blanca
(132) Hollandsche Manege Café
(133) Café Vertigo
(134) Cobra Café
(135) Stedelijk Museum Café
(136) Zabars
(137) De Knijp
(138) Hondertien

Inexpensive

(122) Anda Nugraha I7
Waterlooplein 369, t 626 6064;
tram 9, 14; metro Waterlooplein.
Tasty home-cooked Indonesian
food. Rijsttafel €27 for two people.

(121) King Solomon J7
Waterlooplein 239, t 625 5860;
tram 9, 14; metro Waterlooplein.
Open Sun–Thurs noon–11pm, Fri
noon–6pm (summer), 11am–3pm
(winter), Sat open after shabbat.
Cash only.

Lively, simple, family-filled kosher
restaurant in the Old Jewish
Quarter serving kebabs, Yemeni
specialities and old favourites
from chicken soup to gefilte fish.

(120) Soup en Zo I7
Jodenbreestraat 94A, t 422 2243;
tram 9, 14; metro Waterlooplein.
Open Mon–Sat 11am–8pm, Sun
1–7pm. Cash only.
A wide selection of down-to-earth
soups (and some less conventional combinations) made on the
whole with organic ingredients.
All soups are served with chunky
bread and can be taken away if
you prefer to eat on the move.

Cafés

(117) Café De Sluyswacht I6
Jodenbreestraat 1, t 625 7611; tram
9, 14; metro Waterlooplein. Open
Mon–Thurs 11.30am–1am, Fri and
Sat 11.30am–3am, Sun 11.30am–
7pm (no food in evenings).

Quaint café in a 17th-century lock-
keeper's house, which these days
rivals the tower at Pisa for tilt. A
good place for a light lunch (bread
rolls) with a tranquil terrace above
waters of Oude Schans.

(123) Hortus Botanicus
Orangery J7
Hortus Botanicus, t 625 9021; tram
9, 14. Open Mon–Fri 9am–5pm, Sat
and Sun 11am–5pm. Closes 1hr
earlier Oct–Mar.
Cakes and coffee under the trees
or behind hothouse glass –
though you'll need a ticket to the
gardens to get in.

(118) Puccini I7
Staalstraat 21, t 620 8458; tram 9,
14; metro Waterlooplein. Open
8.30am–6pm. Cash only.
Classy modern café with delicious
cakes. The air is enticingly filled
with the aroma of chocolate
steaming in the vats of the
adjoining 'Dessert Shop'.

Museumplein and Vondelpark

Restaurants

Moderate

Aujourd'hui Off maps
*Cornelis Krusemanstraat 15, **t** 679 0877; **tram** 2, 6, 16. **Open** Mon–Fri noon–2.30pm and 6–10pm, Sat 6–10pm.*
A little out of the way (just south of Vondelpark), this place is extremely popular with business lunchers, who sit around the open kitchen and enjoy the excellent service and delectable French cuisine – all at reasonable prices.

(138) Honderdtien E10
*Johannes Verhulststraat 110, **t** 771 8660; **tram** 2, 16. **Open** Mon–Sat 11am–11pm.*
A neighbourhood eaterie – but then this is a very chic neighbourhood, so expect designer décor, high-fashion from nearby boutiques, and cuisine that caters to demanding palates. The menu changes as the day progresses, and has an Italian lilt, with good vegetarian options, such as broccoli pasta with roast paprika, or aubergine, caper, olive and lime salad.

(137) De Knijp F10
*Van Baerlestraat 134, **t** 671 4248; **tram** 3, 12. **Open** Mon–Fri noon–3pm and 5.30pm–12.30am, Sat and Sun 5.30pm–12.30am.*
Fresh oysters are a speciality. Straight-laced place with an older clientele.

(131) Paloma Blanca D8
*Jan Pieter Heijestraat 145, **t** 771 4606; **tram** 1, 6, 7, 17. **Open** Mon–Wed 6–11pm, Fri–Sun 6–11.30pm. Cash only. No alcohol.*
Friendly, family-run Moroccan restaurant, which serves lip-smacking tagines and couscous dishes. The home-made lamb sausages are a must – though it's just mum slaving away in the kitchen and service can be frustratingly slow.

(136) Zabars F10
*Van Baerlestraat 49, **t** 679 8888; **tram** 3, 12. **Open** Tues–Fri 11am–11pm, Sat–Mon 5.30–11pm.*
It doesn't look much from the outside, but inside you'll find a cheery crowd enjoying wonderfully flavourful Mediterranean food: Moroccan lamb casserole or crunchy Greek halva.

Inexpensive

(129) Riaz E7
*Bilderdijkstraat 193, **t** 683 6453; **tram** 3, 12. **Open** Mon–Fri 11.30am–9pm, Sun 2–9pm.*
Great Surinamese curries, eaten with rice or *roti* – a pancake in which you roll up your food and eat it with your fingers. You'll find it north of Vondelpark.

(130) Waroeng Asje D8
*Jan Pieter Heijestraat 180, **t** 616 6589; **tram** 1, 6. **Open** Sun–Fri 12.30–9.30pm, Sat 3–9.30pm.*
Surinamese/Indonesian takeaway with a few tables near the Vondelpark. The *soto soep* (spicy meat-and-veg soup with a bowl of rice; €4) is a meal in itself.

Cafés

(133) Café Vertigo E8
*Nederlands Filmmuseum, Vondelpark 3, **t** 612 3021; **tram** 1, 3, 6, 12. **Open** 11am–1am.*
In the cellar of the Filmmuseum and spills out into the park in good weather. The cuisine surpasses that of any museum restaurant in town; it even has appropriate themed menus during film festivals.

(134) Cobra Café G9
*Hobbemastraat 18 (behind Rijksmuseum), **t** 470 0111; **tram** 2, 5. **Open** daily 10am–9pm. Diners Club not accepted.*
This bright airy café has a large terrace on the Museumplein. A handy stopover at any time of day when you're museumed out – whether it's for lunchtime salad, afternoon coffee and apple pie, or a plate of sushi and a glass of wine in the evening.

(132) Hollandsche Manege Café E8
*Vondelstraat 140, **t** 618 0942; **tram** 1, 3, 6, 12. **Open** Mon–Fri 10am–midnight, Sat 10am–5pm, Sun 10am–4pm.*
Overlooks the arena of the elegant 19th-century riding school. A quiet place to sip coffee and watch the horses, though there are occasional invasions of groups of 11-year-olds in jodhpurs.

(135) Stedelijk Museum Café F9
*Paulus Potterstraat 13, **t** 573 2911; **tram** 2, 3, 5, 12, 16. **Open** daily 11am–5pm. Museum may close for refurbishment (see p.136).*
The best café on the museum circuit. You can lounge about in basket chairs reading art magazines, or sit in the sun and look out at the sculptures.

De Pijp

Restaurants

Expensive

Ciel Bleu H11
*Okura Hotel, Ferdinand Bolstraat 333, **t** 678 7450; **tram** 12, 25; wheelchair accessible. **Open** daily 6.30–11pm.*
On the 23rd floor with wonderful views. The cuisine is appropriately *haut*. Jacket and tie required. €55.

VisaandeSchelde G13
*Scheldeplein 4, **t** 675 1583; **tram** 4, 12, 25. **Open** Tues–Fri noon–2pm and 5.30–11pm, Sat 5.30–11pm, Sun 3–9pm.*
Minimalist décor. Fish comes perfectly cooked: marinated salmon with asparagus steeped in vanilla and orange, tuna with just a tinge of pink, meltingly soft monkfish, excellent bouillabaisse, tuna in a red-wine and flageolet-bean sauce.

Yamazato H12
*Okura Hotel, Ferdinand Bolstraat 333, **t** 678 8351; **tram** 12, 25; wheelchair accessible. **Open** daily 7.30–9.30am, noon–2pm and 6–9.30pm.*
Superb Japanese cuisine, quite exquisitely presented.

Late-night Food

Bojo, *Lange Leidsedwarsstraat 51;* ***tram** 7, 6, 10.* ***Open** Mon–Fri until 2am, Fri and Sat until 5.30am.* An Indonesian restaurant.

Gary's Late-Nite Bagel Shop, *Reguliersdwarsstraat 53;* ***tram** 4, 9.* ***Open** daily until 3am.* Sells genuine New York bagels, cheese-cake and muffins until the wee hours.

Maoz, *Reguliersbreestraat, near the Tuschinski Cinema;* ***tram** 4, 9.* ***Open** 24 hours.* Serves scrumptious falafel and salads all through the night.

Moderate

District V H11

Van der Helstplein 17, ***t** 770 0884;* ***tram** 12, 25.* ***Open** daily 6–10.30pm.* This trendy restaurant on the Parisian-style square Van der Helstplein makes the most of the readily available fresh produce on its doorstep (the Albert Cuypmarkt is just up the road). The extraordinary toilets and stylish crockery reflect the fact that it's run by artists.

Mamouche H10

Quellijnstraat 104, ***t** 673 6361;* ***tram** 16, 24, 25.* ***Open** Tues–Sun 6.30–10pm.* Stratospherically hip Moroccan restaurant, all rose petals and silver samovars, where the 'world-famous in Holland' customers all seem to know each other, but where the cuisine is supreme.

De Ondeugd H10

Ferdinand Bolstraat 15, ***t** 672 0651;* ***tram** 12, 25.* ***Open** daily 6–11pm.* Just minutes from the Albert Cuypmarkt: the fish and vegetables are alarmingly fresh. Goose liver on apple *compôte*, Thai soup or grilled swordfish with tomato *beurre blanc*. Main dishes come with delicious *frites* and home-made mayonnaise. Child-friendly.

De Pijp H10

Ferdinand Bolstraat 17–19, ***t** 670 4161;* ***tram** 16, 24, 25.* ***Open** daily noon–1opm.* *Cash only*

Most trustworthy newcomer in an area that is rapidly becoming one of the most popular dining-out quarters in town. In a spacious, grand café atmosphere you're offered good basic dishes, but also some imaginative new-Dutch combinations.

Puyck H10

Ceintuurbaan 147, ***t** 676 7677;* ***tram** 3, 12, 25.* ***Open** Tues–Sat 5.30–10.30pm.* Amex and Diners Club not accepted.
Perhaps unfortunately named for an English-speaking clientele, but well worth a visit. Paintings by local artists line the walls; the minimalist design is softened by warm lighting, and the menu has a distinct Eastern touch – think soft-shell crab with marinated ginger; or monkfish with rice noodles, morels and lemon-grass sauce. East–West fusion reaches startling levels when it comes to pudding: sticky Greek pastries with tomato marmalade, saffron, orange and olive-oil sorbet, and pistachio custard.

White Elephant I10

Van Woustraat 3, ***t** 679 5556;* ***tram** 4.* ***Open** daily 3–11pm.* Top-class Thai cuisine that makes few allowances for wimpy Western palates, served in a setting of tasteful traditional décor.

De Witte Uyl G9

Frans Halsstraat 26, ***t** 670 0458;* ***tram** 16, 24, 25.* ***Open** Tues–Sat 5.30–11pm.* Big tables, comfortable chairs, a carefully chosen wine list, and a menu of imaginative medium-sized dishes.

Inexpensive

l'Angoletto I10

Hemonystraat 18, ***t** 676 4182;* ***tram** 4, 6, 7, 10.* ***Open** Sun–Fri 6–11.30pm.* Amex, Diners Club and MasterCard not accepted.
More likely than not, when you step through the door of this tiny Italian restaurant you'll be asked to wait outside. Ten minutes later, with a grim look on his face, the

owner will wave you towards a table. As soon as you're in, his face will break into a friendly smile, then he'll serve you thick coils of *bucatini*, or a series of delicious *antipasto vegetariano*. Whatever you choose, you'll understand why many rate this as the best Italian in town for your money.

Balti House G10

Albert Cuypstraat 41, ***t** 470 8917;* ***tram** 16, 24, 25.* ***Open** daily 4–11pm.* Diners Club not accepted.
Tasty basic Indian cuisine of the sort that will be familiar to British visitors, but which is hard to find done well in Amsterdam.

Cambodja City G10

Albert Cuypstraat 58–60, ***t** 671 4930;* ***tram** 16, 24, 25.* ***Open** Tues–Sun 2–1opm.* Amex and Diners Club not accepted.
Headily kitsch décor, but healthy, delicately prepared Cambodian, Vietnamese and Thai cuisine, at very affordable prices.

Mambo Pasta H10

Eerste Van der Helststraat 66, ***t** 679 1295;* ***tram** 16,24,25.* ***Open** Mon–Sat 9am–8pm.* *Cash only.*
Pleasant stop-off beside the Albert Cuyp Market, where you can get focaccia and ciabatta with tasty Italian fillings, pasta, and a variety of thin, crusty pizzas.

Mas Tapas G10

Saenredamstraat 37, ***t** 664 0066;* ***tram** 16, 24, 25.* ***Open** daily 5–10.30pm.* *Cash only.*
Lively, authentic tapas bar that has a row of tables out on a tree-lined street in good weather. Tuck into tortilla, crispy-fried sardines, kidneys cooked in sherry and other traditional delights.

Orontes G10

Albert Cuypstraat 40, ***t** 679 6225;* ***tram** 16, 24, 25.* ***Open** Tues–Sun 5–11pm.* *Cash only.*
Lovingly prepared eastern Mediterranean food – salads with walnut and pomegranate, char-grilled marinated fish – served in a simple setting. Go for a three-course meal, or order up a selection of starters and salads.

De Waaghals G9

Frans Halsstraat 29, t 679 9609;
tram 16, 24, 25. Open Tues–Sun
5–9.30pm.
Vegetarian cuisine with organic
ingredients and international
influences: Tunisian bean casserole, or coconut and aubergine
soup. Flavours are sometimes
rather bland.

Zen G10

Frans Halsstraat 38, t 627 0607;
tram 16, 24, 25. Open Tues–Sun
noon–8pm. Cash only.
Plain tables, minimal décor and an
excellent range of sushi, sashimi
and warmer Japanese snacks. A
healthy lunch break if you're
visiting the Albert Cuyp Market.

Cafés

De Duvel H10

Eerste Van der Helststraat 59–61,
*t 675 7517; **tram 3, 16, 24, 25. Kitchen***
open Tues–Sat 12.30–4.30pm and
6–11pm, Sun and Mon 6–11pm.
Busy café with a large terrace near
the Albert Cuypmarkt.

De Engel H10

Albert Cuypstraat 182, t 675 0544;
tram 16, 24, 25. Open daily
9am–11pm.
Vast café decorated with religious
paraphernalia, and a great place
to take a break from the busy
Albert Cuyp Market. There's a
restaurant on the mezzanine
layer, though the food isn't much
to get ecstatic about.

De Taart van m'n Tante H9

Ferdinand Bolstraat 10, t 776 4600;
tram 16, 24, 25. Open Tues–Sat
10am–5.30pm, Sun noon–6pm.
Cash only.
A long-famous (if not notorious)
cake shop now brings its
Tellytubbyland-meets-erotic-
camp style to a sit-down tea
room. Gloriously tacky décor, great
cakes and a few savouries.

New South

Djago G13

*Scheldeplein 18, t 664 2013; **bus 15;***
tram 4, 12, 25. Open Sun–Fri
5–9.30pm. Moderate.

It's worth the short tram ride
south to savour excellent
Indonesian cuisine, in a traditionally decorated restaurant that is
popular with the local Indonesian
and Surinamese community.

Kong Kha J12

*Rijnstraat 87, t 661 2578; **tram 4.***
Open Tues–Sun 4–10pm.
Inexpensive.
Small, bustling restaurant and
takeaway, with authentic Thai
home-cooking. Well worth the
short tram ride. The fishcakes are
delicious, and the chicken and
coconut soup sweet and soothing.

Meidi-Ya F11

Beethovenstraat 19–20, t 673 7410;
tram 5. Kitchen open Mon–Sat
10.30am–6pm.
Japanese delicatessen. Sushi to
take down to the canal, or more
elaborate dishes to eat there.

Delcavi E12

Beethovenstraat 40, t 662 2904;
tram 5. Open Mon–Fri 7am–8pm,
Sat and Sun 8am–8pm.
A café that's a haunt of the well-
heeled locals. Sandwiches and
home-cooked meals.

Villa Maas H13

*Maasstraat 74, t 676 2051; **tram 4,***
25. Open 10am–6pm. Cash only.
Big sofas and low coffee tables
give this café a lounge-like
atmosphere, and in fine weather
there are a few tables on the
square outside. A relaxing place
for a lunch after looking at
Amsterdam School architecture in
the neighbourhood, or for their
speciality – full English High Tea.

Oosterpark and the East

De Kas N11

Kammerlingh Onneslaan 3, t 462
*4562; **tram 9; bus 59, 120, 126. Open***
Mon–Fri noon–2pm, 6.30–10pm,
Sat 6.30–10pm. Expensive.
Situated in a the greenhouse of a
former city nursery, with its own
vegetable patch outside – now a
smart designer restaurant where
the chef makes up a different set
menu daily, depending on what's

ready in the garden. You'll need to
book well in advance, or pitch up
at the very last moment hoping
for a cancellation.

(127) La Rive J9

*Prof. Tulpplein, t 520 3273; **tram 6, 7,***
*10; **wheelchair accessible. Open***
Mon–Fri noon–2pm and 6.30–
10.30pm, Sat 6.30–10.30pm.
Expensive.
La Rive is something of an institution. Situated in a grand hotel,
there's a terrace for warmer
weather, but don't presume you
can sit there: at the slightest puff
of wind the chef will usher his
guests indoors. Jacket and tie
required. Around €85.

Vandemarkt K11

Schollenbrugstraat 8, t 468 6958;
tram 12; wheelchair accessible.
Open Mon–Sat 6–10pm. Expensive.
With a trendy minimalist design
with bright striped walls, this is a
relaxed place with easy, efficient
service. Dishes include wild duck
in a sage sauce served with endive
stamppot – a gourmet version of
traditional Dutch mash.

(128) De IJsbreker J9

*Weesperzijde 23, t 468 1808; **tram***
*3, 6, 7, 10; **metro Weesperplein.***
Kitchen open 5.30–9.30pm.
A café attached to the contemporary music venue. Tranquil
riverside terrace.

(126) ToDine L9

's Gravesandestraat 51, t 850 2400;
tram 3, 7, 10. Open Sun–Thurs
6.30pm–1am, Fri and Sat
6.30pm–2am. Moderate.
Foodie part, with ToDrink (bar) and
ToNight (club), of the hip triumvi-
rate at the Arena hotel, offering
large salads, nifty starters and
main courses such as red mullet
baked with thyme and lemon, to a
young crowd of nightlifers.

Across the IJ

Wilhelminadok K4

*Noordwal 1, t 632 3701; **ferry free***
from landing stage 7, behind
Centraal Station, then 5min walk.
Open daily noon–10pm (Mon film
and dinner). Moderate.

If you venture across the IJ (use the free ferry), track down this restaurant with views across the river and a dreamy terrace. With country-kitchen décor and super-friendly staff. The cooking is simple and tasty – fish soup or lamb cutlets with grilled paprika and couscous.

Café Ot en Sien J3
Buiksloterweg 27, across the water from Centraal Station, t 636 8233; ferry free from landing stage 7. Open Sun–Fri noon–9pm.
A friendly, family-run café in a lane of country gardens and old wooden houses.

Western Islands and Scheepvaartbuurt

Restaurants

Expensive

De Gouden Reael H2
Zandhoek 14, t 623 3883; bus 35. Open Tues–Sun 6–10pm; sandwiches etc. from 9am–5pm.
A 17th-century house on a quayside in the Western Islands. Renowned for its French provincial cuisine – a different area every three months. Child-friendly.

De Groene Lanteerne H4
Haarlemmerstraat 43, t 624 1952; bus 18, 22. Open Mon–Sat 6.30–11pm.
The narrowest restaurant in the world, run by a couple who are renowned for their hearty French fare. With its own car park.

Marius G2
Barentszstraat 243, t 422 7880; tram 3. Open Tues–Sat, two sittings 6pm and 8pm. Cash only.
Tiny two-hander (one person cooks, the other serves) with a communal table and a country-kitchen atmosphere. At the early sitting (€17.50 with wine) you join the owners for their evening meal – a simple pasta or risotto perhaps, with salad, but made with prime ingredients. The second sitting (€41.50 per person,

four courses including wine) takes you into heady realms of inventive, Franco-Dutch cuisine, though you still take pot luck.

Moderate

De Belhamel H4
Brouwersgracht 60, t 622 1095; bus 18, 22; metro Centraal Station. Open daily noon–2.30pm and 6–10pm.
Art Nouveau restaurant on Amsterdam's most photographed canal. A relaxed, arty crowd eat snacks or meals with imaginative sauces (like saffron tagliatelle with oysters, cream, blue cheese, wine and sunflower seeds); or 'boeuf Belhamel' – beef with Chinese, spinach, oyster mushrooms and taragon sauce.

La Brasa G3
Haarlemmerdijk 16, t 625 4438; bus 18, 22.
One of the more intimate of the Argentinian grills, this one has cow-hide seats and serves juicy beef on a wood grill.

Griet Manshande G3
Keerpunt 10, t 622 8194; bus 18, 22; wheelchair accessible. Open Wed–Sun 6–10pm.
Relaxed neighbourhood restaurant hidden in a corner of a modern housing estate on Bickerseiland. The daily selection includes anything from coq au vin to roast skate with beurre noir. Friendly service and skilled cooking. Child-friendly.

Lof H4
Haarlemmerstraat 62, t 620 2997; bus 18, 22. Open Tues–Sun 6.30–11pm. Cash only.
A long-standing favourite among fashionable Amsterdammers, managing to remain high on the hip-list because of consistently good food, rather than through a preciously trendy atmosphere. A limited menu changes daily, with such dishes as home-made duck-liver terrine, or lamb with Banyul sauce. Bare wooden tables, dish-cloths as napkins, and chatty staff all do their bit towards creating an easy-going ambience.

The Movies Wild Kitchen G3
Haarlemmerdijk 159, t 626 7069; bus 18, 22. Open. 5.30–10pm.
Crowded restaurant attached to an old Art Deco cinema, offering challenging concoctions such as halibut poached in coconut bouillon, served with Basmati rice and spinach.

Inexpensive

Moeders Pot (Mother's Cooking) G3
Vinkenstraat 119, t 623 7643; bus 18, 22. Open Mon–Sat 5–10pm.
A one-person affair run by a huge hairy man who simply must have 'mother' tatooed somewhere under his white T-shirt. Meat and ten veg for under €12.

Small World G3
Binnen Oranjestraat 14, t 420 2774; bus 18, 22. Open Wed–Sat, 10.30am–8pm, Sun noon–8pm.
Aussie Sean shows the Dutch how to do it. This is one of the first places to depart from the dull local ham-and-cheese lunchtime fare, with prime ingredients, inspired roll fillings, and unequalled cakes and tarts. A popular expat Sunday brunch spot – though there are only a few bar stools to sit at. Takeaways available.

Stout! H4
Haarlemmerstraat 73, t 616 3664; bus 18, 22. Open Mon–Sat 10am–10pm, Sun 11am–10pm.
Trendy glass-box lunch venue (the intriguingly strange name actually means 'naughty' in Dutch), offering soups, salads and sandwiches, often with a Japanese touch, while you people-watch passers-by on the hip Haarlemmerstraat.

Cafés

Jordino G3
Haarlemmerdijk 25, t 420 3225; bus 18, 22. Open. Tues–Sat 10am–8pm, Sun and Mon 1–8pm.
When the heart begins to flutter and the knees begin to fail, ice cream and mega-chocolates from

heaven will set you on your way again. Home-made and way over the top.

Rosereijn G3
Haarlemmerdijk 52, near Haarlemmerplein, t 626 8027; bus 18, 22. Kitchen open noon–4.30pm and 6–10.30pm.
Brown café with a neighbourhood atmosphere, huge plates of wholesome Dutch home-cooking and an 'English Lunch' that involves fried eggs and baked beans.

Eastern Islands and Around

Restaurants

Moderate

(114) Kilimanjaro K6
Rapenburgerplein 6, t 622 3485; bus 22, 32, 33, 34, 35, 39. Open Tues–Sun 5–10pm.
Fish soup from Guinea, crocodile from Senegal, Tanzanian red snapper curry and Castle lager from South Africa, plus home-made ginger beer or hibiscus and baobab cocktail.

(115) Raap en Peper J6
Peperstraat 23, t 330 1716; bus 22, 32, 33, 34, 35, 36, 39. Open Tues–Sun 6–11pm.
A cosy restaurant with dark wainscotting, old tiles and painted wooden furniture. The food is simple but wonderfully prepared – creamy garlic soup, followed by tournedos with chips and mayonnaise.

(116) Rosario J6
Peperstraat 10, t 627 0280; bus 22, 32, 33, 34, 35, 36, 39. Open Mon–Sat 6–11pm. Amex and Diners Club not accepted.
A small, busy restaurant in a romantic corner of town. Rosario uses his Italian granny's recipes, but adds his own inspired touches to produce creamy risotto, delicate fish dishes and tasty meats and pastas.

Cafés

(125) De Groene Olifant (The Green Elephant) M7
Sarphatistraat 510, t 620 4904; tram 7, 9, 10, 14. Open 11am–4.30pm and 6–10pm.
Cosy bar flooded with light. The folk are friendly and the food delicious.

(113) Scheepvaart Museum Café K6
Kattenburgerplein 1, t 523 2222; bus 22, 32. Open Tues–Sun 10am–5pm.
A good place to sip coffee and look out over the harbour.

Nightlife

Café-Bars and Coffeeshops

Amsterdam's nightlife centres on cafés. They offer everything from a quiet evening over the backgammon board to jolly sing-songs in just about any language you choose. There are even some cafés where you can dance, though a handful of good night-clubs serve those who really like to bounce and sweat (see 'Clubs', below).

The term 'café' covers a wide range of establishments. At one end of the spectrum are the poky bars, where you go to knock back a few beers (with the odd jenever chaser); at the other end you'll find enormous, airy **grand cafés** and places that offer such sumptuous fare that they're really indistinguishable from small restaurants (see the cafés listed in the 'Eating Out' chapter). Wooden floors and furniture, and walls stained by years of cigarette smoke, have inspired the name '**brown café**'. Here you can drink seriously or just snack and sip coffee. But most of all you sit and talk, or while away the time leafing through the day's papers or glossy magazines. There's seldom any grating background music – though in friendly neighbourhood bars the clientele may burst into song. Some rather startling newcomers made an appearance during the 1980s: the **designer bars** are the complete antithesis of the brown café – hard metal furniture, bright light and colours, and loud music – but are now very much part of the Amsterdam scene.

Whether it's in a tiny café supported by a handful of locals, or a stylish new bar with an arty crowd, you'll find that Amsterdammers create an atmosphere where they can relax and feel both *uit* and *thuis* ('out' and 'at home').

Most Amsterdammers drink **beer**. Ordering *een Pils* at the bar will get you a small glass of lager topped with a finger or two of froth. If you really want to show off your local knowledge, ask either for a *vaasje* ('fars-ye' – a 'vase', about the same as half a pint); or a *fluitje* ('flow-ee-che' – a 'whistle', similar in quantity to a champagne flute).

Or you might prefer a **jenever** (Dutch gin – oilier and weaker than its British counterpart, with a whiff of juniper berries). In this case ask for a *borrel*. You can have either *oud* (old – more mellow) or *jong* (young – sharper). Jenever may also be flavoured: *citroenjen-ever* (lemon) or *besenjenever* (blackberry) are popular. Ask for a *kamelenrug* (camel's back) and your glass will be filled to the rim. Traditionally, you knock back all of your jenever with a single gulp. Should you require both beer and gin simultaneously, request a *kopstoot* (literally, 'knock on the head'). On freezing winter days a quick visit to a **proeflokaal** will warm your blood. These were once free tasting-houses attached to spirit-merchants and taphouses. These days you have to pay, but the procedure is much the same: walk in, drink up, walk out.

Coffeeshops never serve alcohol. Since the 1970s, though, a number of them (the so-called **smoking coffeeshops**) have openly sold marijuana. These are easily distinguishable at first glance/sniff. They are painted psychedelic colours, often have leaf designs on the windows and emit loud music and fazed customers.

Most cafés close at 1 or 2am at weekends. They begin opening their doors around 11am, though some don't get it together until 3 or 4pm.

The Centre: Old Side

In 't Aepjen I5
Zeedijk 1, **t** *626 8401;* ***tram*** *4, 9, 16, 24, 25.* **Open** *daily 3pm–1am.*
Fills the tiny ground floor of a 15th-century seamen's lodging house. It's a '*rariteitencafé*' crammed with antiques, leather armchairs and barrels. The painted wall panels were rescued from a 1920s travelling dance hall.

De Buurvrouw H6
St Pieterpoortsteeg 29, **t** *625 9654;* ***tram*** *4, 9, 14, 16, 24, 25.* **Open** *Sun–Thurs 8pm–2am, Fri and Sat 8pm–3am.*
A cosy and sometimes raucous bar on one of the tiny side streets off the bottom end of Oudezijds Voorburgwal. There's sawdust on the floor, strange art on the walls, and an alternative bunch of drinkers swanning round a pool table. Open-mike nights, poetry recitals and live bands are frequent.

Café Cuba I6
Nieuwmarkt 3, **t** *627 4919;* ***tram*** *4, 9, 14, 16, 24, 25;* ***metro*** *Nieuwmarkt.* **Open** *daily noon–1am.*
Escape the red-hued claustrophobia of the Old Centre by stepping out onto the Nieuwmarkt square and sipping Cuban cocktails at this attractive café. There's a pool table and a smoking area tucked away at the back.

Café 't Loosje I6
Nieuwmarkt 32–4, **t** *627 2635;* ***tram*** *4, 9, 14, 16, 24, 25;* ***metro*** *Nieuwmarkt.* **Open** *Sun–Thurs 9.30am–1am, Fri and Sat 9.30am–3am.*
A popular brown café with old wooden furnishings and a terrace stretching out onto the Nieuwmarkt square. Good selection of beers.

Crea Café H6
Grimburgwal, **t** *525 1423;* ***tram*** *4, 9, 16, 24, 25.* **Open** *daily 9am–1am.*
Spacious student café with tatty pool tables, earnest groups arguing in corners and tired-eyed academics.

Greenhouse Effect I5
Warmoesstraat 55, **t** *623 7462;* ***tram*** *4, 9, 16, 24, 25.* **Open** *Sun–Thurs 9am–1am, Fri and Sat 9am–3am.*
A well-known little coffeeshop right in the glow of the Red Light District. The clientele is a mixed bag of tourists and hip locals.

Outdoor City

The following bars and cafés have outside terraces or balconies, for outdoor drinking when the weather's good:

Café Ebeling (Museumplein and Vondelpark; *see* p.238), **Café Hoppe** (The Centre: New Side; *see* p.236), **Café 't Loosje** (The Centre: Old Side; *see* p.235), **Café Vertigo** (Museumplein and Vondelpark; *see* p.238), **De Duvel** (De Pijp; *see* p.239), **De Jaren** (The Centre: Old Side; *see* p.236), **Twee Prinsen** (Grand Canals and Jordaan; *see* p.238), **Wildschut** (De Pijp; *see* p.239).

De Jaren H7

Nieuwe Doelenstraat 20, t 625 5771; tram 4, 9, 14, 16, 24, 25. Open Mon–Thurs 11.30am–1am, Fri and Sat 11.30am–3am, Sun 11.30am–7pm.

Amsterdam's most spacious grand café, right on the Amstel. Comfortable chairs, high ceilings, newspapers in all languages, and anyone who's anyone in Amsterdam arts.

Het Karbeel I5

Warmoesstraat 58, t 627 4995; tram 4, 9, 16, 24, 25. Open Mon–Fri 9.30am–midnight, Sat and Sun 9.30am–2am.

An upmarket café on the edge of the Red Light District. It started life in 1534 as an inn and is still connected to the Damrak by a secret smugglers' passage.

Rusland I6

Rusland 16, t 627 9468; tram 4, 9, 16, 24, 25. Open Sun–Thurs 10am–midnight, Fri and Sat 10am–1am.

Privately owned, intimate and relaxedly scruffy coffeeshop.

VOC Café I5

Prins Hendrikkade 94, t 428 8291; tram 4, 9, 14, 16, 24, 25; metro Centraal Station. Open Mon–Thurs 10am–1am, Fri and Sat 10am–3am, Sun noon–8pm.

Set in the Schreierstoren, the battlement tower (built in 1480) that once formed part of the medieval city walls. They serve a fair few beers, liquors and jenevers.

The Centre: New Side

ARC H7

Reguliersdwarsstraat 44, t 689 7070; tram 16, 24, 25. Open Sun–Thurs noon–2am, Fri and Sat noon–3am.

Frantically popular designer bar with a mixed gay/straight clientele, a restaurant and dancing till the early hours.

Café Esprit H7

Spui 10, t 622 1967; tram 1, 2, 5. Open Fri–Wed 10am–6pm, Thurs 10am–10pm.

Trendy aluminium-box café on the Spui.

Café Hoppe G7

Spui 18–20, t 420 4420; tram 1, 2, 5. Open Sun–Thurs 8am–1am, Fri and Sat 8am–2am.

Dates from 1670 and popular with local office workers. On summer evenings there's standing room only on the terrace, and it looks a bit like a cocktail party.

Café Karpershoek I4

Martelaarsgracht 2, t 624 7886; metro Centraal Station. Open daily 10am–1am.

Claims to be Amsterdam's oldest bar (dating from 1629 – but *see* Café Chris, p.237). Once right on the waterfront, it was a popular seamen's tavern. It still has sand on the floor, as in the 17th century.

Café Luxembourg G7

Spui 22–4, t 620 6264; tram 1, 2, 5. Open Sun–Thurs 9am–1am, Fri and Sat 9am–2am.

Grand café that becomes crammed with young professionals on the way home from work, and with local writers and journalists on Sunday mornings.

Café Schiller I7

Rembrandtplein 26, t 624 9846; tram 4, 9, 14. Open Sun–Thurs 4pm–1am, Fri and Sat 4pm–2am.

A perfectly preserved Art Deco interior and a haven from the tourist throngs.

Café van Zuylen H5

Torensteeg 8, t 639 1055; tram 1, 2, 5, 13, 17. Open Sun–Thurs 11am–1am, Fri and Sat 11am–3am.

A mellow, convivial café-bar popular with students. Candlelit tables and low-volume music make it a good place to relax later in the evening.

De Drie Fleschjes H5

Gravenstraat 18, t 624 8443; tram 1, 2, 5, 13, 17. Open Sun–Thurs noon–midnight, Fri and Sat noon–1am.

Proeflokaal behind the Nieuwe Kerk that dates from 1650.

De Kroon Royal Café I7

Rembrandtplein 17 (upstairs), t 625 2011; tram 4, 9, 14. Open Sun–Thurs 10am–1am, Fri and Sat 10am–2am.

All air and light with Louis XV chairs, modern paintings and chandeliers hanging from distant ceilings. Tango evenings on Mondays.

Wijnand Fockink H6

Pijlsteeg 31, t 639 2695; tram 4, 9, 16, 24, 25. Open daily 3–9pm.

Delightfully cramped and crooked old proeflokaal with a range of flavoured jenevers and sticky liqueurs.

Waterlooplein and the Plantagebuurt

Bluebird I6

St Antoniesbreestraat 71, t 622 5232; tram 9, 14; metro Waterlooplein or Nieuwmarkt. Open daily 9.30am–1am.

An old coffeeshop famous for the breadth of its menu. Step in to acquaint yourself with the different varieties of weed and hash available in Amsterdam. If you don't like the smoky atmosphere, you can walk straight out with your purchase to continue your evening elsewhere.

Café Dantzig I7

Zwanenburgwal 15, t 620 9039; tram 9, 14; metro Waterlooplein. Open Mon–Fri 9am–1am, Sat 9am–2am, Sun 9am–midnight.

Part of the Stopera (Muziektheater) complex. Deeply trendy, postmodern café.

Café De Sluyswacht I6
Jodenbreestraat 1, t 625 7611; **tram** *9, 14;* **metro** *Waterlooplein.* **Open** *Mon–Thurs 11.30am–1am, Fri and Sat 11.30am–3am, Sun 11.30am–7pm.*

A landmark building, built in 1695 and leaning precariously. It's a tranquil place to spend the evening overlooking the waters of Oude Schans.

De Eik en Linde K7
Plantage Middenlaan 22, next to the Hollandse Schouwburg, **t** *622 5716;* **tram** *9, 14.* **Open** *Mon–Sat 11am–1am.*

Brown café with a diverse local crowd. It was once connected by an upstairs corridor to the theatre next door.

Greenhouse Namaste J7
Waterlooplein 345, t 622 5499; **tram** *9, 14;* **metro** *Waterlooplein.* **Open** *Sun–Thurs 9am–1am, Fri and Sat 9am–2am.*

One of the few good-quality coffeeshops in the Old Jewish Quarter. Smoky, candlelit and (naturally) relaxed.

De IJsbreker J9
Weesperzijde 23, t 668 1805, **w** *www.ysbreker.nl;* **tram** *3, 6, 7, 10;* **metro** *Weesperplein.* **Open** *Sun–Thurs 10am–1am, Fri and Sat 10am–2am.*

A tranquil and sophisticated bar and music venue on the quiet eastern bank of the Amstel. Jazz and contemporary classical concerts are performed round the year. A good selection of wines.

Tisfris I6
St Antoniesbreestraat 142, t 622 0472; **tram** *9, 14;* **metro** *Waterlooplein or Nieuwmarkt.* **Open** *Tues–Sat 9am–8pm, Sun and Mon 9am–6pm.*

A good place to start the evening and watch the to-ings and fro-ings of Amsterdammers in this part of town. They serve excellent snack food, plus the usual drinks, and if you're lucky you might catch a set from a local DJ.

Grand Canals and Jordaan

De Admiraal G6
Herengracht 319, t 625 4334; **tram** *1, 2, 5.* **Open** *Mon–Sat 4.30pm–midnight.*

Proeflokaal for Amsterdam's last remaining independent distillery, De Ooiyevaar. Here you will find soft sofas, and also potent liqueurs like 'Hempje ligt op' and 'Pruimpje prik in' (the names translate obscenely).

t'Arendsnest G5
Herengracht 90, t 421 2057; **tram** *16, 24, 25.* **Open** *Sun–Thurs 11am–1am, Fri and Sat 11am–2am.*

Reproduction Art Deco lamps, snooker tables and numerous varieties of Belgian beer.

De Blaffende Vis (The Barking Fish) F4
Westerstraat 118, t 625 1721; **bus** *18, 22.* **Open** *Sun–Thurs 9am–1am, Fri and Sat 9am–2am.*

A busy Jordaan café frequented by traditional Jordaaners and the new generation of young artists.

The Bulldog F8
Leidseplein 15, t 627 1908; **tram** *1, 2, 5, 6, 7, 10.* **Open** *Sun–Thurs 10am–1am, Fri and Sat 10am–3am.*

A 1970s institution, it was one of the first places allowed to sell marijuana on the premises. It's now a slick commercial enterprise with alcohol upstairs, dope downstairs and even a souvenir shop.

Café Aas van Bokalen G6
Keizersgracht 335, t 623 0917; **tram** *1, 2, 5.* **Open** *daily 5pm–1am.*

Good brown café with an arty crowd and a restaurant-sized menu.

Café Chris F5
Bloemstraat 42, t 624 5942; **tram** *13, 14, 17.* **Open** *Sun–Thurs noon–1am, Fri and Sat noon–2am.*

Across the canal from the Westerkerk. A taphouse since 1624, it predates the bar that calls itself 'Amsterdam's oldest' by five years. The workers who built the Westerkerk received (and spent) their wages here. It's so small

there's no room for a cistern in the men's loo; you flush it from a handle on the wall once you're back in the bar.

Café 't Papeneiland G4
Prinsengracht 2, just up from the Noorderkerk, t 624 1989; **bus** *18, 22;* **metro** *Centraal Station.* **Open** *Mon–Thurs 10am–1am, Fri and Sat 10am–2am, Sun noon–1am.*

Full of pink-faced old men. A 17th-century café with a shady past. It was originally a funeral parlour that sold beer on the side. There's an unexplained secret passage running from the cellar to the house over the canal.

Café 't Smalle G5
Egelantiersgracht 12, t 344 4560; **tram** *13, 14, 17.* **Open** *Sun–Thurs 10am–1am, Fri and Sat 10am–2am.*

Restored *proeflokaal* of Pieter Hoppe's 18th-century liqueur distillery. Now sells a wider range of drinks and snacks.

Eland F6
Prinsengracht 296, t 623 7654; **tram** *1, 2, 5.* **Open** *Mon–Fri noon–1am, Sat noon–2am, Sun noon–1am.*

Traditional brown café.

De Gijs F4
Lindengracht 249, t 638 0740; **bus** *18;* **tram** *3.* **Open** *Sun–Thurs 11am–midnight, Fri and Sat 11am–1am.*

Tiny eccentric two-tier bar.

Het Hok G8
Lange Leidsedwarsstraat 134, t 624 3133; **tram** *1, 2, 5, 7, 6, 10.* **Open** *Mon–Thurs 9am–1am, Sat 11am–2am, Sun noon–1am.*

A refuge from the hordes, filled with quiet people playing chess.

De Kat in de Wijngaert G4
Lindengracht 160, t 622 4554; **tram** *1, 2, 5, 13, 17.* **Open** *Sun–Thurs 10am–1am, Fri and Sat 10am–3am.*

Quiet and friendly.

De Magere Brug J8
Amstel 81, t 622 6502; **tram** *4.* **Open** *Mon–Thurs noon–1am, Fri and Sat noon–2am, Sun 4pm–1am.*

A brown café on the banks of the Amstel near the 'Skinny Bridge', hence the name.

Architectural City

If you fancy drinking in a bar with an unexplained secret passage, a medieval tower or an Art Deco interior, try one of the following:

In 't Aepjen (The Centre: Old Side; *see* p.235), **Café Chris** (Grand Canals and Jordaan; *see* p.237), **Café Karpershoek** (The Centre: New Side; *see* p.236), **Café 't Papeneiland** (Grand Canals and Jordaan; *see* p.237), **Café Schiller** (The Centre: New Side; *see* p.236), **Café De Sluyswacht** (Waterlooplein and the Plantagebuurt; *see* p.237), **De Druif** (Eastern Islands and Around; *see* p.239), **Het Karbeel** (The Centre: Old Side; *see* p.236), **DuLac** (Scheepvaartbuurt and the West; *see* p.239), **'t Ronde Blauwe Theehuis** (Museumplein and Vondelpark; *see* p.238), **VOC Café** (The Centre: Old Side; *see* p.236).

Het Molenpad F7
Prinsengracht 653, t 625 9680; tram 7, 10. Open Sun–Thurs noon–1am, Fri and Sat noon–2am.
A brown café that sometimes crams a live jazz band into one corner. A smoky, dreamy place to while away a Sunday afternoon.

Nol G4
Westerstraat 109, t 624 5380; bus 18, 22. Open Mon–Thurs 9am–3am, Sat and Sun 9am–4am.
Outrageously kitsch bar. Locals, gangsters and visitors get swept into singsongs.

Rooie Nelis F6
Laurierstraat 101, t 624 4167; tram 13, 14, 17. Open Sun–Thurs 9am–1am, Fri and Sat 9am–3am.
A Jordaan institution. Bursting with locals and visitors having a good time.

De Tuin G4
2e Tuindwarsstraat 13, t 624 4559; tram 3, 10, 13, 17. Open Mon–Thurs 10am–1am, Fri and Sat 11am–2am, Sun 11am–1am.
Dim light, board games and a twinge of eccentricity. A classic brown café.

Twee Prinsen G4
Prinsenstraat 27, t 624 9722; tram 3, 10. Open Sun–Thurs 10am–1am, Fri and Sat 10am–3am.
Heated terrace and a friendly, alternative crowd who profess great rivalry with the 'yuppies' at the Vergulde Gaper on the opposite corner.

Twee Zwaantjes G5
Prinsengracht 114, t 625 2729; tram 13, 14, 17. Open Sun–Thurs noon–1am, Fri and Sat noon–2am.
Electric organ music, accordions and unforgettable big ladies with big voices from the Jordaan.

De Wetering G8
Weteringstraat 37, t 622 9676; tram 16, 24, 25. Open Sun–Thurs 10am–1am, Fri and Sat 10am–2am.
A real log fire in winter and an ancient television for crucial football matches.

Museumplein and Vondelpark

Café Ebeling E8
Overtoom 52, t 689 4858; tram 1, 3, 6, 12. Open Mon–Thurs 11am–1am, Fri and Sat 11am–3am, Sun noon–1am.
A large in-vogue bar housed in an old bank, with a terrace and cable TV. A sociable hangout with the younger crowd.

Café Vertigo E8
Vondelpark 3, t 612 3021, w www.vertigo.nl; tram 1, 2, 3, 5, 6, 12. Open 11am–1am.
This smart and popular bar is attached to the Filmmuseum, which overlooks Vondelpark. It has a sprawling outside terrace, as well as an enormous balcony terrace, which makes it an ideal spot to drink away a summer evening.

Café Welling F10
J.W. Brouwersstraat 32, behind the Concertgebouw, t 662 0155; tram 2, 3, 5, 12, 16. Open Sun–Thurs 4pm–1am, Fri and Sat 3pm–2am.
A traditional brown café. The main door is always locked – the entrance is round the side.

CaffePC F9
P.C. Hooftstraat 87, t 673 4752; tram 2, 5. Open Fri–Wed 9am–7.30pm, Thurs 9am–9.30pm.
Hyper-hip café in the heart of the fashion district. Pile up those designer-labelled shopping bags, take the weight off those Prada shoes and sip an espresso.

't Ronde Blauwe Theehuis E9
Vondelpark, t 662 0254; tram 1, 2, 3, 5, 6, 12. Open Sun–Thurs 9am–1am, Fri and Sat 9am–3am.
'The Round Blue Teahouse' is an odd piece of 1930s New Functionalist architecture in the middle of the Vondelpark. After years of mediocrity as a café, it has taken on a new life as a trendy watering hole.

De Ruimte E7
Eerste Constantijn Huygenstraat 20, t 489 3619, w www.smart projectspace.net; tram 3, 12. Open Tues–Sun noon–2am.
This trendy bar and restaurant is part of a project to promote contemporary art, for which its exhibition space is designed. Jazz plays in the background as smart arty types mingle.

Tweedy E8
Vondelstraat 104, t 618 0344; tram 1, 6. Open daily 10am–midnight.
Train compartments form part of the unusual furnishings at this coffeeshop on the edge of Vondelpark. Stalk round a pool table or reach up to the overhead racks for a backgammon board.

De Pijp

De Badcuyp H10
Eerste Sweelinckstraat 10, t 675 9669, w www.badcuyp.demon.nl; tram 4, 16, 24, 25. Open Tues–Thurs 5pm–1am, Fri and Sat 5pm–3am, Sun 5pm–1am.
Right in the thick of the Albert Cuypmarkt, with reading material scattered about and lots of space (the building once served as a bath-house). There are regular dance nights upstairs later in the evening.

De Duvel H10

1e Van der Helststraat 59–61, t 675 7517; tram 3, 6, 12, 24, 25. Open Sun–Thurs 11am–1am, Fri and Sat 11am–2am.

Busy café with a large terrace near the Albert Cuypmarkt.

Gambrinus H11

Ferdinand Bolstraat 180, t 671 7389; tram 3,12,16, 24, 25. Open Sun–Thurs 11am–1am, Fri and Sat 11am–2am.

A traditional brown café worth tracking down in the De Pijp district. It appears to be increasingly popular with a younger professional crowd, and there's an upbeat feel to the place.

Granny H10

1e van der Helststraat 45, t 679 4465; tram 3, 12, 16, 24, 25. Open Sun–Thurs 3pm–midnight, Fri and Sat 4pm–1am.

Some of the best *appelgebak* in town.

Greenhouse J11

Tolstraat 91, t 673 7430; tram 4. Open Sun–Thurs 10am–1am, Fri and Sat 10am–2am.

A coffeeshop highly recommended by locals. The quality of its ware is unprecedented – it wins the *High Times* Cannabis Cup most years – while the pouffes and couches provide the necessary comfort.

Kingfisher H10

Ferdinand Bolstraat 24, t 671 2395; tram 16, 24, 25. Open Mon–Thurs 1pm–1am, Fri and Sat 11am–3am.

A local brown café with bags of atmosphere and a good, cheap 'dagschotel'. Near the top end of Ferdinand Bolstraat, and so accessible from the Canal Belt.

Krull H10

Corner of 1e van der Helststraat and 1e Jan Steenstraat, t 662 0214; tram 3, 16, 24, 25.

A friendly café with a busy terrace.

Wildschut F11

Roelof Hartplein 1–3, t 676 8820; tram 3, 5, 12, 24, 25. Open Sun–Thurs 11am–1am, Fri 11am–2am, Sat 11am–3am.

Art Deco interior, though noisy and smoky. The terrace is crammed in the afternoon and early evening.

Scheepvaartbuurt and the West

Barney's H4

Haarlemmerstraat 102, t 625 9761; bus 18, 22; metro Centraal Station then walk. Open daily 8am–8pm.

Somewhere to start the evening gently – or else to have breakfast over a smoke after a night out on the town.

DuLac H4

Haarlemmerstraat 118, t 624 4265; bus 18, 22; metro Centraal Station. Open Sun–Thurs 4pm–1am, Fri and Sat 4pm–2am.

Peter Barent, the owner, is inspired by Gaudí and the French illustrator Edmund Dulac. He's transformed a 1920s bank into a grown-up's fairy grotto. Gothic spires stick out horizontally from pillars; it's lit by huge brass chandeliers (salvaged from a nearby church); stuffed fish hang from the ceiling; wooden figures, strange paintings and more brass adorn the green-blue walls.

Reibach G3

Brouwersgracht 139, t 626 7708; bus 18, 22; metro Centraal Station. Open Sun–Thurs 11am–midnight, Fri and Sat 11am–1am.

German specialities, such as wickedly alcoholic fruit from the Rumtopf jar, and a view over a beautiful canal.

Siberië H4

Brouwersgracht 11, t 623 5909; bus 18, 22; metro Centraal Station. Open Sun–Thurs 11am–11pm, Fri and Sat 11am–midnight.

One of the most welcoming coffeeshops in the city, located on beautiful Brouwersgracht. There's always something going on here – an exhibition, a gig, or else a heated chess competition.

Tramlijn Begeerte Off maps

Van Limburg Stirumplein 4, t 686 5027; tram 10. Open Mon–Fri 9am–1am, Sat 11am–1am, Sun noon–1am.

An attractive brown café (translates as 'Streetcar Called Desire') in the suburban Westerpark district. It's a bit of a way out, so you'll be among locals in their element.

Eastern Islands and Around

Azart Ship of Fools O5

Docked behind Laan 13, KNSM-eiland, w www.azart.org; bus 32, 59, 79. Open Fri 10pm–late.

If you're looking for an alternative experience on a Friday night, then head out to KNSM-eiland and find this moored ship full of wacky artists, who will entertain you throughout the night with live skits and music. It's worth checking their website first, as they often weigh anchor and sail off towards the edges of the world.

De Druif K6

Rupenburgerplein 83, at the gate to the Entrepotdok, t 624 4530; tram 9, 14; bus 22. Open daily 11am–1am.

Opened in 1631. A brown café with barrels to the ceiling and a rare antique jenever pump on the counter. Locals maintain that naval hero Piet Heyn was a regular visitor. His entrance would have caused a stir, as Heyn died in 1629.

Kanis & Meiland O5

Levantkade 127, t 418 2439; bus 28, 32, 59. Open Sun–Thurs 10am–1am, Fri and Sat 10am–3am.

If you venture out to the recently developed (and newly gentrified) KNSM-eiland, stop in for refreshment at this airy café.

Clubs

Amsterdam nightclubbers don't suffer the fashion neuroses of their London or New York counterparts. You can dress up, down, wild or straight: there's seldom any need to shock or impress the doorman before you're let in. Entrance prices are low enough – and the city small enough – for you to wander from one club to the next. The mood is carefree and unpretentious – late-night clubbing seems just an extension of early-evening café life.

There is a new club-culture scene that holds all-night warehouse parties in deserted areas of town, yet even here you'll find playful Dutch touches. Club nights on the beach at Zandvoort are the current focus of the summer dance scene. The *Queer Fish* booklet is a good source of information about one-nighters or parties. The commercial discos (chart music, plastic palm trees, expensive drinks and posses of drunken men) cluster around Leidseplein. Below is a list of places for those with rather different tastes. Most venues close at 4am (5am at weekends). Tip the doorman as you leave (about €3), and avoid using cabs cruising outside, but get a legal cab from a rank or ask the club to phone for you.

Bloemendaal Beach Off maps
Bloemendaal aan Zee; train from Centraal Station to Zandvoort, then half-hour walk up the beach, or train to Haarlem then bus to Bloemendaal aan Zee. Open May–Sept Sun from noon.
A half-hour train ride west of the centre is a string of beach pavilions hosting Sunday parties. On a warm summer afternoon, with white sand under your toes and a Mexican beer in your hand, it's hard to imagine you're in Holland.

Dansen bij Jansen H7
Handboogstraat 11, t 620 1779, w www.dansenbijjansen.nl; tram 1, 2, 5. Open Sun–Thurs 11pm–4am, Fri and Sat 11pm–5am.
A bit like a Students' Union bop. You usually need to prove membership of a college or university to get in. Frequent theme and fancy-dress nights.

Escape H7
Rembrandtplein 11, t 622 1111, w www.escape.nl; tram 4, 9, 14. Open Thurs and Sun 11pm–4am, Fri and Sat 11pm–5am.
A cavern of a place that's a hyper-trendy club, complete with shops and even a hairdresser.

Korsakoff F6
Lijnbaansgracht 161, t 625 7854, w www.korsakoff.nl; tram 10, 13, 14, 17. Open Sun–Thurs 11pm–3am, Fri and Sat 11pm–4am.
An alternative rock venue, heavily grungy and popular with a young crowd. Live bands on Wednesdays.

Mazzo F5
Rozengracht 114, t 626 7500, w www.mazzo.nl; tram 13, 14, 17. Open Wed, Thurs and Sun 11pm–4am, Fri and Sat 11pm–5am.
Comfortable club with a good atmosphere and an excellent range of music, often with live local bands.

De Melkweg F8
Lijnbaansgracht 234A, t 531 8181, w www.melkweg.nl; tram 1, 2, 5, 6, 7, 10. Open various dates 7.30pm–5am.
A long-standing venue with a huge variety of live acts and themed club nights. It's worth checking the listings to see what's on here.

Ministry G7
Reguliersdwarsstraat 12, t 623 3981, w www.ministry.nl; tram 16, 24, 25. Open Thurs and Sun 10pm–4am, Fri and Sat 11pm–5pm.
A relatively new club near Rembrandtplein, quite smart and featuring a wide variety of nights, from jazz to speed garage.

Odeon H7
Singel 460, t 624 9711; tram 1, 2, 5. Open Sun–Thurs 10pm–4am, Fri and Sat 10pm–5am.
Multi-roomed venue in a converted canal house. Often packed with adolescent tourists.

Paradiso F8
Weteringschans 6–8, t 626 4521, w www.paradiso.nl; tram 1, 2, 5, 6, 7, 10. Open various dates 8pm–5am.
This 19th-century church, which has exchanged choral music for dance beats, is seen by many as the best club venue in Amsterdam. The capacity is big and various nights offer the full range of mainstream music.

Sinners in Heaven I7
Wagenstraat 3, t 620 1375, w www.sinners.nl; tram 4, 9, 14. Open Thurs and Sun 11pm–4am, Fri and Sat 11pm–5am.
Weird and wonderful décor; world-famous-in-Holland clientele.

Time H6
Nieuwezijds Voorburgwal 163–5, t 06 2906 0665; tram 1, 2, 5, 13, 17. Open Thurs and Sun 11pm–4am, Fri and Sat 11pm–5am.
Attractive open-plan club with reggae, house and drum 'n' bass. Slightly older crowd.

ToNight L9
's Gravesandestraat 51, t 694 7444; tram 3, 6, 7, 10. Open Thurs 11pm–4am, Fri and Sat 10.30pm–4am.
This place used to be a non-descript dancefloor attached to the Arena hostel. The hostel has smartened up its act to become a hotel, and the club has gained in independence and popularity.

Trance Buddha I6
Oudezijds Voorburgwal 216, t 524 4000; tram 4, 9, 14, 16, 24, 25. Open Sun–Thurs 11pm–4am, Fri and Sat 11pm–5am.
Young New Age crowd with appropriate soundtrack.

Winston Kingdom I5
Warmoesstraat 123–9, t 623 1380, w www.winston.nl; tram 4, 9, 16, 24, 25. Open Sun 9pm–3am and occasionally Sat.
Local DJs play at this trendy Sunday club night for those who just can't stop. Attached to the Winston Hotel.

Entertainment

Entertainment in Amsterdam is particularly accessible to foreigners. Films are usually shown in their original language, with Dutch subtitles; there's a strong tradition of visual theatre, and many performances in English; and the Muziektheater provides a venue for touring opera and dance companies. Amsterdam has high international status in the various music worlds. Up-and-coming British rock bands test the water here before facing jaded audiences at home; there are some good jazz festivals, and recent immigration has upped the quality of salsa and Latin American music. The acoustically superb Concertgebouw attracts leading classical artists and conductors, and there's a healthy contemporary music scene.

Information

The tourist office publishes a monthly *Day by Day* (€1.20; available from the Amsterdam Tourist Board and around town). The free monthly *Uitkrant* (from the Tourist Board, AUB, libraries, museums and theatres) is more comprehensive and, although it's in Dutch, fairly easy to follow. An even better bet (also in Dutch) is the 'PS Weekend' supplement to *Het Parool*. *Queer Fish* (free from larger newsagents) is a twice-monthly guide to trendy Amsterdam, focusing mainly on clubs and with a strong gay slant. *Oor* (from newsagents) is the Dutch equivalent of *NME*, the British rock-music newspaper. Both the Amsterdam Tourist Board and the AUB booking office can reserve tickets. The AUB also has an up-to-the-minute What's On noticeboard (good for pop music) and masses of leaflets. The Web site *www.aub.nl* has up-to-the-minute information on shows and exhibitions, and a bookings service, too. Also *see* the 'Festivals' chapter, p.269.

AUB, *Leidseplein 26, t 0900 0191, w www.uitlijn.nl; tram 1, 2, 5, 6, 7, 10 (F8). Open daily 10am–6pm.*

Music

Classical and Opera

After a lull during the 1980s, Dutch music has undergone a renaissance. Baroque and period instrument orchestras are reaching particularly high standards (try to catch the Amsterdam Baroque Orchestra or the Orchestra of the 18th Century). The Nederlandse Opera repeatedly comes up with sharp, adventurous productions, often of 20th-century works, and the contemporary-music scene is very lively (look out for pieces by Louis Andriessen and performances by the refreshingly unorthodox Ricciotti Ensemble). The famed Royal Concertgebouw Orchestra first established its reputation before the Second World War under the baton of Willem Mengelberg. He built up a close working relationship with Mahler and Richard Strauss and devoted 50 years to establishing his orchestra as one of the greatest in the world, only to be sacked after the war for pro-German sympathies. In the 1960s the orchestra was propelled to even greater heights by Bernard Haitink. Now, conductor Riccardo Chailly is giving it new life.

Tickets will seem cheap if you're used to London or New York prices, but they sell out quickly. You can try for returns half an hour before a performance, but there are no last-minute discounts, and systems of selling return tickets (especially at the Muziektheater) can be disorganized. Churches are favourite venues for concerts and recitals: the Oude Kerk, the Nieuwe Kerk, the Engelse Kerk and the Waalse Kerk. Other venues include:

Beurs van Berlage H5
Damrak 213, t 521 7575, w www.beursvanberlage.nl; tram 4, 9, 14, 16, 24, 25.

Home to the Netherlands Chamber Orchestra and the Netherlands Philharmonic respectively. Set in beautifully converted concert halls in the old Beurs van Berlage (*see* p.96).

Concertgebouw F10
Concertgebouwplein 2–6, t 671 8345, w www.concertgebouw.nl; tram 2, 3, 5, 12, 16.
The Grote Zaal (Large Hall) has perfect acoustics and is used for orchestral concerts and visiting pop stars and jazz bands. Nervous students from the Sweelinck Conservatorium across the road make their professional debuts in the Kleine Zaal (Small Hall). There are free lunchtime concerts on Wednesdays (*see* p.141).

De IJsbreker J9
Weesperzijde 23, t 693 9093, w www.ysbreker.nl; tram 3, 6, 7, 10; metro Weesperplein.
A deservedly famous centre for contemporary music which offers a stimulating programme of local and international composers and improvisers.

Koninklijk Theater Carré J8
Amstel 115–25, t 0900 252 5255, w www.theatercarre.nl; tram 4, 6, 7, 10.
A major music venue for opera, musicals and cabaret performances.

Muziektheater (Stopera) I7
Waterlooplein 22, t 625 5455, w www.muziektheater.nl; tram 9, 14; metro Waterlooplein. Backstage tours Wed and Sat 4pm; €4, book in advance on t 551 8103 for English guide.
Home to the national ballet and opera companies, but subject of one of the biggest architectural and property-development controversies of the 20th century, and of angry complaints by musicians and audience alike about the bad acoustics (*see* 'Opera and Stopera', p.106). It does, however, have an attractive, cosy auditorium – rare for a modern theatre.

De Rode Hoed G4
Keizersgracht 102, t 638 5606,
w www.rodehoed.nl; tram 1, 2, 5,
13, 17.
Varied programmes in a converted
church.

Stadsschouwburg F8
Leidseplein 26, t 624 23 11, w www.
stadsschouwburgamsterdam.nl;
tram 1, 2, 5, 6, 7, 10.
The municipal theatre on busy
Leidseplein, which also hosts
performances of opera.

Rock and Pop

Chart-busters and stadium-
packers like Madonna and Prince
used to give Amsterdam a miss
and head for the larger venues of
Rotterdam. But in 1996
Amsterdam gained a state-of-the-
art sports and entertainment
stadium. The Amsterdam ArenA
looks like a giant spaceship,
hovering on the southeast
outskirts of the city. It opened
with concerts by Tina Turner and
Michael Jackson, and has been
packing in the audiences ever
since. Keep an eye out also for
Dutch stars who have made it
internationally – such as Mathilde
Santing, Eton Crop and the not-so-
gently-ageing Golden Earring –
who have a loyalty to the old town
and come back for a gig or two at
venues in the centre.

Young British bands (who see an
Amsterdam tour as the penulti-
mate rung on the ladder to fame
and glory) are often the best bet if
you're looking for good rock. Many
of these head for Paradiso or De
Melkweg, though they often also
strain the sound systems of
smaller venues around town such
as a new dance and concert hall
called (confusingly) Arena. Many
bands who have since made it big
have a soft spot for Paradiso and
De Melkweg. In 1995 The Rolling
Stones popped in for an unsched-
uled 'unplugged' concert in
Paradiso before a first-come-first-
served audience of just 500.

In the summer everyone heads
for the Vondelpark, where good

musicians give free concerts and
the park swings with a party
atmosphere.

The listings magazines are your
best guide to what's on (*see*
'Information', above). Prices range
from free entrance to around €10,
and starting times are usually
between 9 and 11pm.

Akhnaton H5
Nieuwezijds Kolk 25, t 624 3396,
w www.akhnaton.nl; tram 1, 2, 5,
13, 17. Open Fri and Sat 11pm–4am;
adm around €8. Cash only.
Recording studios, rehearsal facilities and a forum for much of the
liveliest new music, hip-hop, Latin
and World music.

AMP Studios O5
KNSM-laan 13, t 418 1111,
w www.ampstudios.nl; bus 28.
Open daily 1pm–1am. Cash only.
Out east on newly hip KNSM-
eiland, this rehearsal space and
bar is a good place to catch live
music, particularly at the
weekend.

Amsterdam ArenA Off maps
Arenaboulevard 1, t 311 1333,
w www.amsterdamarena.nl;
metro Bijlmer. Adm €20–30.
Cash only.
Sports stadium that is the venue
for visiting megastars.

Cruise Inn P7
Zuidergeeuwerf 29, t 850 2400,
w www.cruiseinn.com; tram 6, 10.
Open Fri and Sat 10pm–3am. Cash
only.
Flotsam from the 1950s shake,
rattle and roll in an old wooden
clubhouse.

De Koe F7
Marnixstraat 381, t 625 4482;
tram 7, 10.
Regular pop and rock gigs are held
here. They also provide information on the general music scene in
Amsterdam.

Korsakoff F6
Lijnbaansgracht 161, t 625 7854,
w www.korsakoff.nl; tram 10, 13,
14, 17.
A venue for headbanging post-
punks, which nods towards heavy
metal and Gothic teeny-boppers.

The Last Waterhole I5
Oudezijds Armsteeg 12, t 624 4814,
w www.lastwaterhole.nl; tram 4,
9, 16, 24, 25; metro Centraal
Station. Open Sun–Thurs noon–
2am, Fri and Sat noon–4am; adm
free. Cash only.
An old bar hidden away in the Red
Light District. Local bands play
rock and blues.

De Melkweg F8
Lijnbaansgracht 234A, t 531 8181,
w www.melkweg.nl; tram 1, 2, 5, 6,
7, 10. Open usually daily
7.30pm–5am; adm membership
€2.50 per month plus for live
music. Cash only.
A long-standing venue with a
huge variety of live acts and
themed club nights. It's worth
checking the listings to see what's
on here.

Paradiso F8
Weteringschans 6–8, t 626 4521,
w www.paradiso.nl; tram 1, 2, 5, 6,
7, 10. Opens some time after 8pm
when there's live music; adm
membership €2.50 for 1 month plus
for live music. Cash only.
An institution. A gloomy-looking
church that has been converted
into a bright and buzzing venue
for good music – anything from
big rock names to jazz, African,
Latin and even contemporary
classical.

ToNight L9
's Gravesandestraat 51, t 694 7444;
tram 3, 6, 7, 10, 14; metro Weesper-
plein. Open Thurs–Sat 11pm–4am;
adm €5–10. Cash only.
The old hippy Sleep-In has undergone a transformation into one of
the trendiest music and dance
venues in town.

Jazz, Latin and Folk

The mellow tones of jazz seem
to suit the atmosphere of the
brown cafés, and many have a live
band on a Saturday night or
Sunday afternoon. There are often
special gigs around the same time
as the Holland Festival in June (*see*
'Festivals', p.269).

Amsterdam's large Indonesian and Surinamese populations swell many a bar with pulsating rhythms. The Latin and South American music scene is especially lively. Bars and cafés with live music often don't charge entrance, but have more expensive drinks.

De Badcuyp H10

Eerste Sweelinckstraat 10, t 675 9669, w www.badcuyp.demon.nl; tram 4, 16, 24, 25. Open Tues–Thurs 5pm–1am, Fri and Sat 5pm–3am, Sun 5pm–1am; adm free.
Neighbourhood café-cum-artscentre in a converted bath-house. A lively venue for jazz and salsa.

Bimhuis J6

Oudeschans 73, t 623 1361, w www.bimhuis.nl; tram 9, 14; metro Waterlooplein. Open usually Mon and Wed–Sat from 8pm; adm €10–20. Cash only.
Major jazz venue. Visiting artists and the best locals; free sessions on Monday and Wednesday.

Bourbon Street G8

Leidsekruisstraat 6–8, t 623 3440; tram 1, 2, 5, 6, 7, 10. Open daily 10pm–4am; adm €1–2.50. Cash only.
Soulful jazz sessions are held at this bar most nights.

Brasil Music Bar G8

Lange Leidsedwarsstraat 70, t 06 5065 2950; tram 1, 2, 5.
Live samba and a gyrating throng of Latin expatriates.

Casablanca I5

Zeedijk 26, t 625 5685, w www.casablanca-amsterdam.nl; tram 4, 9, 16, 24, 25. Open Sun–Thurs 9pm–2am, Fri and Sat 10pm–4am; adm free. Cash only.
Café hosting mainstream and standard bands, with the occasional jam session. Next door is a small cabaret theatre with a restaurant attached, where you can intersperse courses with *chanson*. Look out especially for shows by Fifi l'Amour.

Jazzcafé Alto G8

Korte Leidsedwarsstraat 115, t 626 3249, w www.alto-jazz-cafe.nl;
tram 1, 2, 5, 6, 7, 10. Open daily 9pm–3am. Cash only.
Live jazz in a cosy brown café in a brash touristy street.

Jazz Cruise G9

Starts at Rijksmuseum, t 623 9886; tram 1, 2, 5, 6, 7, 10. Held April–Nov Sat 8pm and 10pm.
An hour and a half of jazz on a canal boat, with beer, wine and cheese thrown in for €39.

Maloe Melo F6

Lijnbaansgracht 163, t 420 4592; tram 13, 14, 17. Open daily 9pm–3am; adm free. Cash only.
Enduring, rather poky, blues café.

Meander H7

Voetboogstraat 3, t 625 8430, w www.cafemeander.nl; tram 1, 2, 5. Open daily 8.30pm–3am; adm €2.50–5. Cash only.
Lively café where student types swing to salsa, bop to funk and chill out to jazz.

Mulligan's I7

Amstel 100, t 622 1330, w www.mulligans.nl; tram 4, 9, 14. Open daily.
Rousing Irish singalongs.

Nol G4

Westerstraat 109, t 624 5380; bus 18, 22. Open Mon–Thurs 9am–3am, Sat and Sun 9am–4am.
An outrageously kitsch bar. Locals, gangsters and visitors get swept into singsongs accompanied by accordion.

Odeon Jazz Kelder G7

Singel 460, t 624 9711; tram 1, 2, 4, 5, 9, 14, 16, 10, 24, 25. Open daily from 11pm.
Traditional jazz in an intimate atmosphere.

Rembrandt Bar H7

Rembrandtplein 3, t 623 0688; tram 4, 9, 14.
Dutch folk music.

Soeterijn M8

Linnaeusstraat 2, t 568 8500, w www.kit.nl/tropentheater; tram 9, 14.
The top venue for music from Africa, Indonesia, Eastern Europe and the Middle East.

Twee Zwaantjes G4

Prinsengracht 114, t 625 2729; tram 13, 14, 17. Open Sun–Thurs noon–1am, Fri and Sat noon–2am.
Electric organ music, accordions and unforgettable big ladies with big voices from the Jordaan.

Film

The Dutch tend to be avid movie-goers. Most cafés and some restaurants have a list of the week's films pinned up on the wall. Home-grown products haven't, however, made much of an impact internationally – though director Paul Verhoeven is known for *Robocop* and *Total Recall*, and a Dutch film, *Antonia*, picked up the 1996 Oscar for Best Foreign Film. The British director Peter Greenaway has for many years collaborated with Dutch film-makers.

You'll find most of the multi-screen commercial cinemas in the area around Leidseplein, where they offer pretty standard fare. The Tuschinski must be a hot contender for the most beautiful cinema in the world and is worth a visit no matter what's showing (or you can join a guided tour; *see* p.100). Cinema prices range from €5 to €10 and there are often discounts on week nights.

In the rare cases where an English film has been dubbed over, you'll see 'Nederlands gesproken' on the publicity.

Mainstream

Cinerama F8

Marnixstraat 400–402, t 623 7814; tram 1, 2, 5, 6, 7, 10.
Two connected cinemas, near Leidseplein, which show mainstream films and premieres.

Pathé de Munt H7

Vijzelstraat 15, t 0900 1458, w www.pathe.nl/demunt; tram 4, 9, 14, 16, 24, 25.
A modern movie complex situated to the west of Rembrandtplein. offering screenings of mainstream international films.

Tuschinski Cinema H7
*Reguliersbreestraat 26–8, t 0900
1458, w www.pathe.nl/tuchinski;
tram 4, 9, 14, 16, 24, 25.*
A beautiful Art Deco movie
theatre which opened in 1921 and
is certainly Amsterdam's most
exclusive cinema. Six screens, with
an interesting mix of screenings.
There are silent movies with live
organ music every now and then.

Art Houses

Amsterdam offers nothing to
rival the internationally important
Rotterdam Film Festival (held
Jan/Feb; information from the
ATB), but art movies get a good
showing in some rather romantic
old cinemas.

Cinecenter F8
*Lijnbaansgracht 236, t 623 6615,
w www.cinecenter.nl; tram 1, 2, 5, 6,
7, 10.*
International programme of films
in an attractive little complex of
screens. Check for subtitles.

Het Ketelhuis Off maps
*Haarlemmerweg 8–10, t 684 0090,
w www.ketelhuis.nl;* Located in
the Westergasfabriek
complex (renovated industrial
architecture) to the west of the
centre. Screens exclusively Dutch
films, some with subtitles.

Kriterion K8
*Roeterstraat 170, t 623 1708,
w www.kriterion.nl; tram 6, 7, 10.*
Cult American movies and erotic
French late-nights.

The Movies G3
*Haarlemmerdijk 161, t 638 6016,
w www.themovies.nl; tram 3.*
Some of the programming verges
on the mainstream, but the 1920s
interior is a delight and there's a
vibrant café-restaurant.

Nederlands Filmmuseum E8
*Vondelpark 3, t 589 1400, w www.
filmmuseum.nl; tram 1, 2, 3, 5, 6, 12.*
Frequent changes of programme,
usually with something from the
museum's extensive archive –
such as tinted silent movies.

Rialto H10
Ceintuurbaan 338, t 676 8700,

*w www.rialtofilm.nl; tram 3, 12,
24, 25.*
Good retrospectives, sci-fi, animation and children's films.

Tropeninstituut Theater L8
*Linneausstraat 2, t 568 8500,
w www.kit.nl/tropenmuseum;
tram 9, 10, 14; bus 22.*
Occasionally screens series of
related films from around the
world. Attached to the
Tropenmuseum on the edge of
Oosterpark.

De Uitkijk G8
*Prinsengracht 452, t 623 7460,
w www.uitkijk.nl; tram 1, 2, 5, 6,
7, 10.*
Amsterdam's oldest cinema
(dating from 1913), squashed into
an even older canal house. It
features a white grand piano
that has long since tinkled its
last notes but is too big to be
removed.

Theatre

Like England, the Netherlands
experienced a 17th-century
Golden Age of the theatre.
Playwrights of that era, such as
Vondel, Hooft and Bredero, wrote
plays that are still performed in
Holland. The 18th and 19th
centuries saw the growth of
extravagant stage spectacles. By
the end of the 19th century,
theatre had ossified from a
popular into an élitist form. The
'Tomato Action' of 1968 put an
end to that. A disgruntled new
generation of actors began
throwing tomatoes at their older
colleagues during performances
and sparked off a theatrical revolution. In the decade that
followed, Amsterdam theatres like
the Mickery and the Shaffy earned
a worldwide reputation for high
quality avant-garde work.
Government cuts and changing
tastes have curtailed the mud-
wading and body-painting, but
there is still a strong tradition of
excellent, highly visual theatre
(look for work by Orkater Theatre
Company and spectacular outdoor
romps by the Dogtroep).

There is no national theatre
company; the chief mainstream
company is the rather stolid
Toneelgroep Amsterdam, resident
at the Stadtsschouwburg (*see*
p.246). Two local English-speaking
companies compete with foreign
touring productions for the
Amsterdam audience. The In
Theatre presents small-scale
productions, usually upstairs in a
converted prop room at the
Stadsschouwburg, and Boom
Chicago offers improvised comedy
in their own supper theatre next
door. The Nes (off Damstraat) and
the banks of the Amstel are traditionally theatreland, but these
days no old warehouse, factory or
stable is safe from troupes of
eager actors.

The best thing to do is check the
listings magazines for touring
companies, or **w** *www.theater.nl* –
and here's a short list of venues
where you're likely to find good
work in English.

**Amsterdamse Bos
Theatre** Off maps
*Amsterdamse Bos, t 670 0250; bus
170, 171, 172.*
An open-air theatre set in
Amsterdam's largest green space.
Shakespeare plays are performed
during the summer months.

Boom Chicago F8
*Leidseplein 12, t 423 0101, e office@
boomchicago.nl, w www.boom
chicago.nl; tram 1, 2, 5, 6, 7, 10.*
Stand-up comedy sketches and
improvisations performed year
round in English. Look out for
Boom!, their free quarterly guide
to Amsterdam.

Cosmic Theatre H6
*Nes 75, t 626 6866 tram 4, 9, 14, 16,
24, 25.*
A theatre and dance company
addressing issues surrounding
modern multicultural society.
Originated in the Caribbean.

Felix Meritis G6
*Felix Meritis Building, Keizersgracht
324, t 626 2321, w www.felix.
meritis.nl; tram 1, 2, 5, 13, 17.*
A descendant of the Shaffy, which
was at the forefront of the avant-

garde during the 1970s and 80s, and housed in a building with a rich cultural past. Still a place to catch exciting new work.

't Fijnhout Trajectum Theater D8
Jacob van Lennepkade 334, **t** *685 3755;* **tram** *1, 7, 17.*
A popular theatre with English-language touring companies.

Koninklijk Theater Carré J8
Amstel 115–25, **t** *0900 252 5255,* **w** *www.theatercarre.nl;* **tram** *4, 6, 7, 10;* **metro** *Weesperplein.*
Built for a circus – a function it still performs over the Christmas period. The home of most big Amsterdam musicals, but more off-the-wall performances slip into gaps in the programme.

De Melkweg F8
Lijnbaansgracht 234A, **t** *531 8181,* **w** *www.melkweg.nl;* **tram** *1, 2, 5, 6, 7, 10.*
One of Amsterdam's major cultural centres, which attracts touring international theatre productions, as well as home-grown theatre.

Stadsschouwburg F8
Leidseplein 26, **t** *624 2311,* **w** *www. stadsschouwburgamsterdam.nl;* **tram** *1, 2, 5, 6, 7, 10.*
Amsterdam's municipal theatre. A wide range of national productions and visiting international companies. There's a good theatre bookshop near the main entrance.

Vondelpark Theater E9
Vondelpark, **t** *673 1499;* **tram** *1, 2, 3, 5, 6, 12.*
An open-air theatre in the middle of Amsterdam's favourite park, with varied performances through the summer months.

Dance

Until recently, Dutch dance was sagging sadly, propped up by a rather unvivacious Nationale Ballet and the practically moribund Scapino Ballet. Only the Nederlands Danstheater had the verve and energy to prevent complete artistic prolapse. But the tide has turned, inspired perhaps

by the big stage at the relatively new Muziektheater, an influx of foreign dancers and traditional rhythms from the former colonies.

The Nationale Ballet has imported Canadian Wayne Eagling to be its artistic director, has expanded its repertoire, and is benefiting from the visits of touring companies who now have a suitable venue, the Muziektheater. The Scapino is dusting off the cobwebs and has appointed Ed Wubbe as their daring new choreographer; the Nederlands Danstheater keeps up a salvo of fine ballet and modern dance. Look out also for work by Djazzex (jazz dance) and Dansgroep Krisztina de Chatel (vivid theatrical style).

Once again, the listings magazines (*see* 'Information', above) will tell you what's on, but the following venues are worth checking out.

Bellevue F8
Leidsekade 90, **t** *530 5301,* **w** *www. theaterbellevue.nl;* **tram** *1, 2, 5, 6, 7, 10.*
With modern-dance touring companies.

Frascati H6
Nes 63, **t** *626 6866,* **w** *www.nes theaters.nl;* **tram** *4, 9, 14, 16, 24, 25.*
Established modern dance companies.

Het Internationale Danstheater I6
Kloveniersburgwal 87–9, **t** *623 9112;* **metro** *Nieuwmarkt.*
A dance venue with internationally influenced performances.

International Theaterschool I6
Jodenbreestraat 3, **t** *527 7640,* **w** *www.ahk.nl/the;* **tram** *9, 14;* **metro** *Waterlooplein.*
Regular dance (and drama) performances from students and teachers at this renowned school.

Lucent Danstheater Off maps
Spuiplein 152, The Hague, **t** *(070) 880 0333,* **w** *www.intdanstheater. nl;* **train** *from Centraal Station to Den Haag (40mins).*
Home to the famous Nederlands Danstheater and the best dance

and music venue in the Netherlands. Worth the journey.

Muziektheater (Stopera) I7
Waterlooplein 22, **t** *625 5455,* **w** *www.muziektheater.nl;* **tram** *9, 14;* **metro** *Waterlooplein.*
If you want to see something in this relatively new opera house, ballet may be the best choice as the acoustics are a little iffy.

Arts Centres

Amsterdam RAI G13–14
Europaplein 12, **t** *549 1212,* **w** *www. rai.nl;* **tram** *4.*
A business congress centre which houses large concerts and touring musicals. Venue for Kunst RAI, an annual contemporary art fair (*see* 'Festivals', p.269).

De Brakke Grond H6
Nes 45, **t** *626 6866,* **w** *www. brakkegrond.nl;* **tram** *4, 9, 14, 16, 24, 25.*
Attractive venue for Flemish art and performance. Excellent dance programmes.

De Meervaart Centrum Off maps
Meer en Vaart 1, **t** *410 7777,* **w** *www.meervaart.nl;* **tram** *1, 17.*
A good variety of film, theatre, dance and music (classical and jazz).

De Melkweg (Milky Way) F8
Lijnbaansgracht 234a, **t** *531 8181,* **w** *www.melkweg.nl;* **tram** *1, 2, 5, 6, 7, 10.* **Open** *usually daily 7.30pm–5am;* **adm** *membership €2.50 per month. Cash only.*
A vibrant centre for the arts converted in the 1960s from an old dairy. The theatre hosts companies from around the world (often in English) with extraordinarily imaginative plays. The small cinema shows films from mainstream to cult. The concert hall stages excellent African and South American bands, and acts as a try-out venue for up-and-coming rock groups. At weekends an alternative disco takes over. The coffeeshop was one of the first where the sale of marijuana was tolerated by the authorities.

Shopping

What is there that's not found here
Of corn; French or Spanish wine
Any Indies goods that are sought
In Amsterdam may all be bought
Here's no famine – the land is fat.

Constantijn Huygens,
17th-century Dutch poet
Amsterdam's prosperity in the Golden Age turned it into an exotic emporium mundi. The little shops below the decorative *uithangborden* (painted signs) were crammed with Nuremberg ceramics, Lyons silk, Spanish wines, mysterious Egyptian potions and an abundance of local pastries, cheeses, linen and boots. When Marie de Medicis made her grandiose entry into Amsterdam in 1638, the first thing she did when she had a moment's spare time (amidst the lavish ceremonies celebrating her arrival) was to swoop down on the Amsterdam shops, where, apparently, she haggled with the adept confidence of someone reared in a marketplace.

Amsterdam's markets, boutiques and eccentric speciality shops are still one of the city's greatest allures. The range of goods and oddity of the shops can keep you browsing for hours. The only barriers against your absolute financial ruin are the inconvenient opening hours. Calvinism wins over tourism – despite the recent relaxation of laws governing shop hours, you'll find very few places at all open on a Sunday. Amsterdammers enjoy their weekends, and the fun tends to overflow into Monday: many shops also stay closed on Monday mornings, if not for the whole day. However, most stay open late on Thursday nights. (Thursday, the night before the weekenders descend on the city, has a wild feeling of local festivity that dissipates under the influx of outsiders.) Weekday opening hours are generally 9am–6pm. On Saturday, shops close around 5pm. Some shops in the city centre now

open from noon to 6pm on Sundays. Many of the smaller shops can be quite idiosyncratic about when they open, but all have a little black and yellow timetable of opening hours posted on an outside window.

Dutch sales tax (BTW – 19% on most goods) is included in the marked price, though many stores offer tax-free shopping to non-EU tourists. See 'Money, Banks and Taxes', p.74.

After-hours Shopping

Some larger stores in the city centre (such as Hema and De Bijenkorf) are now also open on Sunday afternoons. To locate a late-night pharmacy contact **t** 592 3315. Most neighbourhoods have one or two shops that open around 5pm and stay open until between 11pm and 1am. Here you can buy, at a suitably inflated price, emergency groceries. Look out for signs reading 'Avondverkoop' or 'Nightshop'.

Albert Heijn Supermarket G7
Koningsplein; tram 1, 2, 5. Open Mon–Sat 10am–10pm, Sun noon–6pm.
A conventional supermarket with normal prices.

Big Bananas G7
Leidsestraat 76; tram 1, 2, 5. Open Mon–Fri and Sun noon–1am, Sat 11am–2am.
Big price tags on the food. Rude assistants.

Heuft's First Class Nightshop J12
Rijnstraat 62; tram 4, 25. Open Mon–Sat 5pm–1am, Sun 3pm–1am.
Late-night oysters and champagne. They deliver, too.

Antiques

Rokin (the street running from the Dam to Muntplein) was once the traditional stretch for antique-dealers. Now there are only a few crusty die-hards here – the sort of shop where you have to ring a bell

before they let you in. These days the most stylish, outlandish and enticingly chaotic treasure-troves are to be found in the Spiegelkwartier (*see* p.125) and around the Looiersgracht (*see* p.126).

Fifties-Sixties G7
Huidenstraat 13, t 623 2653; tram 1, 2, 5.
Piled high with lamps and electrical equipment from the 1950s and 60s.

De Jong's Droomfabriek G8
Nieuwe Spiegelstraat 9B, t 620 0760; tram 1, 2, 54, 16, 24, 25.
'Dr Jong's Dream Factory', south of Oosterpark, is crammed full of fans, antique dolls, porcelain, chandeliers and much more.

Nic Nic G6
Gasthuismolensteeg 5, t 622 8523; tram 1, 2, 5.
Delightfully cluttered with eccentric gifts, Art Deco kitsch and lots more.

Bicycles

Macbike J7
Mr Visserplein 2, t 620 0985; tram 4, 9, 14; metro Waterlooplein.
Second-hand bikes. Parts, repairs and sympathy.

't Mannetje G9
Frans Halsstraat 35 2, t 771 8648; repairs around the corner at 1e Jacob van Canpenste 27 t 779 1060; tram 6, 7, 10, 16, 24, 25.
Tandems, three-wheelers and other curious designs.

Books

Good antiquarian bookshops pop up all over the city, but especially around the university at the southern end of the Red Light District. New books in English are usually quite expensive in Amsterdam.

American Book Center H6
Kalverstraat 185 2, t 625 5537; tram 4, 9, 16, 24, 25.
After Waterstone's, the best stock in town of English fiction and non-fiction, magazines and children's books.

Architectura & Natura G5
Leliegracht 44 2, t 623 6186; tram 13, 14, 17.
Just what it says, with an impressive collection of books on Amsterdam.

Athenaeum G7
Spui 14–16 2, t 622 6248; tram 1, 2, 5.
Stamping ground of the city's intelligentsia. Good selection of magazines and English non-fiction.

Book Exchange I6
Kloveniersburgwal 58 2, t 626 6266; metro Nieuwmarkt.
Essential in this town of outrageous prices.

A la Carte I8
Utrechtsestraat 110–12 2, t 626 0679; tram 4.
Maps, streetplans and guidebooks.

English Bookshop F6
Lauriergracht 71 2, t 626 4230; tram 13, 14, 17.
Carefully selected range, some second-hand.

Intertaal F9
Van Baerlestraat 76 2, t 575 6756; tram 3, 5, 12.
Everything you need to learn Dutch or teach English.

De Kinderboekwinkel G6, F5
Nieuwezijds Voorburgwal 344, t 622 7741; tram 1, 2, 5, 13, 17.
Rozengracht 34, t 622 4761, tram 13, 14, 17.
Children's bookshop with a good selection of books in English.

Kok Antiquariaat I6
Oude Hoogstraat 14, t 623 1191; metro Nieuwmarkt.
Has a good range of second-hand books, maps and engravings.

Lambiek G8
Kerkstraat 78, t 626 7543; tram 1, 2, 5.
Cheery comic shop. Collectors' pieces and cartoon gallery.

Lankamp & Brinkman G8
Spiegelgracht 19, t 623 4656; tram 1, 2, 5, 6, 7, 10.
Children's books in English.

Robert Premsela F9
Van Baerlestraat 78, t 662 4260; tram 3, 5, 12.

Art books a cut above the museum shops.

De Slegte H6
Kalverstraat 48, t 622 5933; tram 1, 2, 4, 5, 16, 24, 25.
A grand bookshop with a large remaindered art-book section and a good selection of material on Amsterdam.

Waterstone's H7
Kalverstraat 152, t 638 3821; tram 1, 2, 4, 5, 9, 16, 24, 25.
Large well-stocked branch of the British chain.

Clothes

Until recently, Dutch designers hadn't made much impact on the world of fashion. That was until zany avant-garde duo Viktor & Rolf took Paris by storm in the new millennium. There are fine examples of less extreme (and perhaps more wearable) design, too, as well as tasteful, well-cut clothes in fine fabrics at much lower prices than in other capitals. P.C. Hooftstraat and Van Baerlestraat (*see p.142*) are the corridors of high fashion and the top designers – here you'll find international labels and Dutch designers.

Clubwear House G6
Herengracht 265, t 622 8766; tram 1, 2, 5.
Clubwear for the brave and the beautiful.

Cora Kemperman G7
Leidsestraat 72, t 625 1284; tram 1, 2, 5.
Slightly off the wall yet supremely stylish.

D&A Fashion G8
Lijnbaansgracht 299, t 620 6119; tram 1, 2, 5, 16, 24, 25.
A selection of sleek numbers for women by top designers, including Vivienne Westwood.

Edgar Vos F9
P.C. Hooftstraat 136, t 671 2748; tram 2, 3, 5, 12.
Nifty suits for high-powered businesswomen.

Emporio Armani F9
P.C. Hooftstraat 39–41, t 471 1121; tram 2, 3, 5, 12.
Famous fashion store on Amsterdam's highbrow shopping street.

Eva Damave F6
Tweede Laurierdwarsstraat 51C, t 920 9318; tram 13, 14, 17.
Colourful designer knitwear.

Heren F9
P.C. Hooftstraat 104, t 671 7730; tram 2, 3, 5, 12.
Small designer boutique with top-quality clothing for men.

Housewives on Fire H5
Spuistraat 102, t 422 1067; tram 1, 2, 5, 13, 17.
Funky clubwear and sleek after-hours outfits for women. They also operate a hip hairdresser's.

Laundry Industry H7
Spui 1, t 420 2554; tram 1, 2, 4, 5, 9, 16, 24, 25.
Some of the best of Dutch design in simple wintery colours.

The Madhatter H11
Van der Helstplein 4, t 664 7748; tram 12, 25.
Zany winter headgear in fake fur and feathers.

Mart Visser E12
Beethovenstraat 107, t 670 1779; tram 5.
More subdued designer items in the classic mode. In the New South district.

Mateloos E7
Kinkerstraat 77, t 689 4720; tram 7, 17.
Hip and happening fashions in larger sizes.

De Nieuwe Kleren van de Keizer F7
Runstraat 29, t 422 6895; tram 1, 2, 5.
'The Emperor's New Clothes' sells stylish items from the world over.

Razzmatazz G6
Wolvenstraat 19, t 420 0483; tram 1, 2, 5.
Designer fashion hot off the catwalks.

Robin & Rik G7
Runstraat 30; tram 1, 2, 5.
Leatherwear from functional to fetish.

Sissy Boy F9
Van Baerlestraat 15, t 671 5174; *tram 2, 3, 5, 12.*
Middle-of-the-road elegance at fast-lane prices.

Van Ravenstein G7
Keizersgracht 359, t 639 0067; *tram 1, 2, 5.*
Zany designs by Dutch designers.

Wolff & Kiewiet de Jonge G7
Keizersgracht 494, t 627 6090; *tram 1, 2, 5.*
Stylish suits and glittering ball gowns.

Lingerie

Tothem H5
Nieuwezijds Voorburgwal 149, t 623 0641; *tram 1, 2, 5.*
Swimsuits and sexy underwear for men.

Second-hand

The second-hand clothes shops attract stall-grubbers from around the globe. Clusters of shops rub elbow patches with each other in the zigzag of lanes from Huidenstraat to Haartenstraat (*see p.120*). You could also try:

Hans en Grietje D9
Overtoom 255, t 685 0787; *tram 1, 6.*
Ethnic and colonial bits and bobs.

Petticoat G4
Lindengracht 99, t 623 3065; *tram 3.*
Fifties retro, hats, shawls, cufflinks and zooty underwear.

Puck I6
Nieuwe Hoogstraat 1A, t 625 4201; *metro Nieuwmarkt.*
Upmarket second-hand clothes store, offering silk kimonos, antique lace and 1930s cocktail dresses.

Shoes and Accessories

If you're into something demure, head for P.C. Hoofstraat again. Or try one of the following places:

Antonia by Yvette G6
Gasthuismolensteeg 12–16, t 627 2433; *tram 1, 2, 5, 13, 14, 17.*
Shoes from the stylish to the extreme, with boots and high heels a speciality.

Betsy Palmer H6
Rokin 9–15, t 422 1040; *tram 4, 9, 16, 24, 25.*
Hip seasonal footwear.

Big Shoe G5
Leliegracht 12, t 622 6645; *tram 3, 14, 17.*
Unisex for big feet.

Fred de la Bretoniere H6
St Luciensteeg 19, t 623 4152; *tram 1, 2, 5, 13.*
Classic fine shoes and bags, with a men's section too.

Seventy Five I6
Nieuwe Hoogstraat 24, t 626 4611; *metro Nieuwmarkt.*
Stylish shoes for nights out.

Shoebaloo G7
Koningsplein 7–9, t 626 7993; *tram 1, 2, 5.*
Glitz, ruffs and teetering heels for the oddly shod (unisex).

Children's

Bam Bam H5
Magna Plaza, Nieuwezijds Voorburgwal 182, t 624 5215; *tram 1, 2, 5, 13, 17.*
Clothes and diminutive furniture pieces for trendy toddlers.

Oilily F9
P.C. Hooftstraat 133, t 672 3361; *tram 2, 3, 5, 12.*
Clothes for tiny tots whose mums and dads have big pockets.

Storm H5
Magna Plaza, Nieuwezijds Voorburgwal 182, t 624 1074; *tram 1, 2, 5, 13, 17.*
Designer clothes for 2–14-year-olds, including Paul Smith and DKNY, and a selection of fun gifts for kids.

Commercial Galleries

There are over 140 commercial art galleries in Amsterdam.

They're scattered all over town, though you'll find a number of the more established ones along the Keizersgracht (*see p.120*) and in the Spiegelkwartier (*see p.125*).

The listings magazine *What's On in Amsterdam* (€1.60 from the Amsterdam Tourist Board, newsagents and hotels) will guide you to mainstream exhibitions. For a fuller picture, pick up a copy of *Alert* (€2.50 from most galleries), the monthly Amsterdam gallery diary. Although this is in Dutch, the pages of photographs, clear symbolic coding and detailed maps give you a good idea of what's showing around town and where to find it.

Look out also for 'Open Atelier' posters – artists working in one neighbourhood will open their studios for a day, and you can wander in for a chat, a look and possibly (they hope) a happy purchase. 'Open Ateliers' are also listed on the gallery pages ('Beeldende Kunst') of the *Uitkrant* (a 'what's-on' freebie available at cafés and from the Uit Buro).

Animation Art H5
Nieuwendijk 91–93, t 622 2203; *tram 1, 2, 4, 5, 9, 13, 16, 24, 25.* **Open** Tues–Fri 11am–6pm, Sat 10am–5pm.
Original drawings of everyone from Popeye to Betty Boop.

De Appel G8
Nieuwe Spiegelstraat 10, t 625 5651; *tram 16, 24, 25.* **Open** Tues–Sun noon–5pm.
Innovative gallery that shows anything from artsy chairs to videos, from a spectrum that runs from lesser-known artists to famous names.

Carla Koch G8
Prinsengracht 510, t 639 0198; *tram 1, 2, 5.* **Open** Wed–Sat noon–6pm.
Top of the list for arty glass and ceramics.

The Frozen Fountain F7
Prinsengracht 629, t 622 9375; *tram 1, 2, 5.* **Open** Mon 1–6pm, Tues, Wed and Fri 10am–6pm, Thurs 10am–9pm, Sat 11am–5pm.

Household items from waste-paper baskets to sofas elevated to high art.

Galerie Atelier Amsterdam G9
Weteringschans 221, t 627 8083; tram 6, 7, 10. **Open** *Mon–Sat 10am–5pm.*
Bright and imaginative art from a group of people with learning difficulties, who also have their studio on the premises.

Mokum H6
Oudezijds Voorburgwal 334, t 624 3958; tram 4, 9, 14, 16, 24, 25. **Open** *Wed–Sat 11am–6pm.*
Dutch realistic art – a good place to find work by Magic Realists (*see* p.51).

Rob Jurka H4
Singel 28, t 627 6343; tram 1, 2, 5, 13, 17. **Open** *Wed–Sat 1–6pm.*
One-time establishment-rattler Rob Jurka has linked up with go-getting digger-out of new talent Barbara Farber to make one of the most respected galleries on the Amsterdam scene.

SBK Kunstuitleen J7
Nieuwe Herengracht 23, t 623 9215; tram 4, 9; metro Waterlooplein. **Open** *Tues and Thurs 1–8pm, Fri 1–5pm, Sat 9am–5pm.*
Art library that hires out original work by Amsterdam artists from €12 per month – and you get the option to buy.

Stedelijk Museum Bureau Amsterdam F6
Rozenstraat 59, t 422 0471; tram 2, 3, 5, 12, 16. **Open** *Tues–Sun 11am–5pm.*
An offshoot of the museum that exhibits and sells work by challenging up-and-coming artists on the international scene.

Torch F6
Lauriergracht 94, t 626 0284; tram 7, 10. **Open** *Thurs–Sat 2–6pm.*
Specializes in video and photography, but is currently a leading light in other media, too.

W 139 I5
Warmoesstraat 139, t 622 9434; tram 4, 9, 14, 16, 24, 25. **Open** *Wed–Sun 1–6pm.*
Cavernous space used by fledgling artists. Sometimes the work is dire, sometimes plain curious – but occasionally you'll find a gem, and will seldom be bored.

Delftware and Clogs

De Klompenboer I6
St Antoniesbreestraat 51, t 623 0632; metro Nieuwmarkt.
Upstairs there's a zany toy shop, with curious cuddly animals and weird mobiles. In the cellar downstairs the owner carves clogs – not just for the tourist market, but for people to wear (the Dutch still do, mainly for gardening, though you sometimes see farmers and road workers shod in wood).

Rinascimento Galleria d'Arte F5
Prinsengracht 170, t 622 7509; tram 13, 14, 17.
Old and new Delftware (the real thing, not souvenir-shop tat). Watch the designs being painted.

Department Stores and Malls

De Bijenkorf H5–6
Dam 1, t 621 8080; tram 4, 9, 16, 24, 25.
'The Beehive' – aptly named. Bustling shop with a wide range of good-quality merchandise, and no pretensions to being Harrods.

Hema H6
Kalvertoren, Kalverstraat (and all around town), t 422 8988; tram 1, 2, 4, 5, 9, 16, 24, 25.
The Dutch Woolworth's or five-and-dime – but all in good taste. An excellent one-stop shop to stock up on essentials.

Magna Plaza H5
Nieuwezijds Voorburgwal 182, t 626 9199; tram 1, 2, 5, 13, 14, 17.
A 19th-century shopping mall which was once the city's main post office. Many of the original features remain. Inside is a range of chic shops across the board.

Maison de Bonneterie H7
Rokin 140, t 531 3400; tram 4, 9, 16, 24, 25.
An old and elegant department store decorated with chandeliers and classic good taste. Top-quality household goods and clothes by mainstream designers.

Metz & Co. G7
Keizersgracht 455, t 520 7020; tram 1, 2, 5.
Liberty prints, stylish kitchenware and design-museum furniture. Superb view from the glass-walled café on the top floor.

Vroom & Dreesman H7
Kalverstraat 201, t 622 0171; tram 4, 9, 14, 16, 24, 25.
Popular department store a notch less upmarket than De Bijenkorf.

Food

Look out for two kinds of bakery. A *warme bakker* sells breads and biscuits and a *banketbakker* sells pastries and wonderful creamy things. Many also sell handmade chocolates. In the better cheese shops you'll be given a sliver to taste before buying. Choose from *mild jong* (young), or the more tangy *belegen* (matured) or *extra belegen*.

Albert Heijn
Koningsplein (also Waterlooplein, Nieuwezijds Voorburgwal and Vijzelstraat); tram 1, 2, 4, 5, 9, 13, 14, 16, 17, 24, 25.
The most popular supermarket chain. The largest branch is the one behind the Koninklijk Paleis. They are all open on Sundays.

Arkwrights F5
Rozengracht 13, t 320 3879; tram 13, 14, 17.
British and other expat provisions for the homesick.

Arxhoek H6
Damstraat 19, t 622 9118; tram 4, 9, 16, 24, 25.
Farm cheeses.

Beune's H3
Haarlemmerstraat 156, t 624 8356; bus 18, 22.
If you take this confectioner's your photograph, they'll reproduce it in icing on the cake of your choice. The result is a white slab with a

sombre sepia image, rather like a Portuguese tombstone.

De Bierkoning H6
Paleisstraat 125, t 625 2336; tram 1, 4, 5, 13, 14, 17.
Cosy shop behind the palace. Glasses of all shapes and around 750 brands of bottled beer.

Geels & Co. I5
Warmoesstraat 67, t 624 0683; tram 4, 9, 16, 24, 25.
Amsterdam's best tea and coffee specialists.

Hendrikse B9
Overtoom 472, t 618 0472; tram 1, 6.
Tarts and cream cakes fit for Queen Beatrix.

Holtkamp's Patisserie H8
Vijzelgracht 15, t 624 8757; tram 16, 24, 25.
Mouth-watering goodies close to the town centre.

Natuurwinkel G9
Weteringschans 133 (and all around town), t 638 4083; tram 6, 7, 10.
Everything from organic vegetables to vitamins and tofu-burgers.

Pompadour G7
Huidenstraat 12, t 623 9554; tram 1, 2, 5.
Delicious handmade chocolates and sweets.

Puccini Bomboni G5
Singel 184, t 427 8341; tram 13, 14, 17.
Tempting handmade sweets and Baroque-style chocolates.

Runneboom H10
1e van der Helstraat 49, t 673 5941; tram 13, 14, 17.
Delicious ryebread, Greek village loaves, healthy wholemeals and crispy white rolls.

Household Goods and Design

Christodoulou & Lamé F5
Rozengracht 42, t 320 2269; tram 13, 14, 17.
An Aladdin's cave of silks and sequins, with beautiful Indian embroidery and luxurious cushions.

The Frozen Fountain F7
Prinsengracht 629, t 622 9375; tram 1, 2, 5. Open Mon 1–6pm, Tues, Wed and Fri 10am–6pm, Thurs 10am–9pm, Sat 11am–5pm.
Everything from a candle-holder to a sitting-room suite by young interior designers.

Trunk G6
Rosmarijnsteeg 12, t 638 7095; tram 1, 2, 5.
Cushions, crockery, fabrics and knick-knacks of mainly oriental origin keep up with the latest trends.

World of Wonders O5
KNSM-laan 293, t 418 4067; bus 28, 32, 59.
One of the most alluring design shops in the trendy eastern docklands, selling furniture as well as smaller furnishings and kitchenware.

Jewellery

BLGK G6
Hartenstraat 28, t 624 8154; tram 13, 14, 17.
Stylish contemporary jewellery from Amsterdam gold- and silversmiths.

Diva I6
Nieuwe Hoogstraat 12, t 625 5423; metro Nieuwmarkt.
Showy jewellery with showers of crystal and dangly coloured-glass earrings.

Hans Appenzeller H6
Grimburgwal 1, t 626 8218; tram 4, 9, 16, 24, 25.
Simple elegant jewellery in gold, silver, aluminium or steel.

Jorge Cohen G7
Singel 414, t 623 8646; tram 1, 2, 5.
Supremely tasteful old and new designs, from Art Deco brooches to state-of-the-art studs.

Diamonds

Where you buy depends on your personal taste, but do shop around and stick to established dealers. You can watch diamonds being cut in a number of shops.

Coster Diamonds F9
Paulus Potterstraat 2–6, t 305 5555; tram 2, 3, 5.
See p.142.

Rokin Diamonds H6
Rokin 12, t 624 8572; tram 4, 9, 16, 24, 25.

Van Moppes G10
Albert Cuypstraat 2–6, t 676 1242; tram 4, 16, 24, 25.

Markets

Albert Cuypmarkt H10
Albert Cuypstraat; tram 4, 16, 24, 25. Held Mon–Sat 9am–4.30pm.
Foodstuffs, clothes and hardware (see p.146).

Bloemenmarkt (Flower Market) H7
Singel, between Muntplein and Koningsplein; tram 1, 2, 5, 24, 25. Held daily 9am–6pm.
Amsterdam's floating flower market (see p.102).

Boerenmarkt G4
Noordermarkt; metro Centraal Station. Held Sat 10am–3pm.
Organic produce and ethnic crafts.

Lapjesmarkt F–G4
Westerstraat; bus 18, 22. Held Mon 7.30am–1pm.
Bargain clothes and spectacular fabrics.

Lindengracht F–G4
Metro Centraal Station. Held Sat 9am–4pm.
Small general market, but the best.

De Looier Indoor Antiques Market F7
Elandsgracht; tram 10, 13, 14, 17. Held Sat–Thurs 11am–5pm.
Mid-price antique market with a wide variety of stalls, from jewellery to 1950s furniture.

Noordermarkt G4
Bus 18, 22. Held Mon 7.30am–1.30pm.
Pile upon pile of junk. Get there early for a treasure hunt.

Oudemanhuis Book Market H6
Oudemanhuispoort; tram 4, 9, 16, 24, 25. Held Mon–Sat 10am–4pm.
A dim alley smelling of musty binding and yellowing paper.

Stamp Market H6

Near Nova Hotel, Nieuwzijds Voorburgwal 276; **tram** *1, 2, 5, 13, 17.* **Held** Wed and Sat 11am–4pm.
Grizzled collectors swap stamps, currency, medals and esoteric jokes.

Waterlooplein fleamarket I–J7
Tram 9, 14; **metro** *Waterlooplein.* **Held** Mon–Sat 10am–4pm.
The city's famous fleamarket (see p.108).

Specialist Shops and Gifts

Amsterdam abounds in idiosyn-cratic speciality shops: old family businesses and outlets for the fantasies of quixotic visionaries. Here are but a few:

**De Beestenwinkel
(The Animal Shop)** I7
Staalstraat 11, **t** *623 1805;* **tram** *9, 14;* **metro** *Waterlooplein.*
Stuffed bunnies, tiger puppets and teddy bears to put your pyjamas in.

Brillenwinkel G6
Gasthuismolensteeg 7, **t** *421 2414;* **tram** *1, 2, 5, 13, 14, 17.*
Classic spectacle frames, from Mahatma Gandhi to Dame Edna.

Condomerie Het Gulden Vlies H5
Warmoesstraat 141, **t** *627 4174;* **tram** *4, 9, 16, 24, 25.*
Condom as consumer item.

Cortina Paper G6
Reestraat 22, **t** *623 6676;* **tram** *13, 14, 17.*
Handmade paper, beautifully bound notebooks, designer pencils and more.

Details F6
Berenstraat 22, **t** *421 1690;* **tram** *1, 2, 5.*
For original gifts from erotic paint-ings to kitsch candelabra.

Emaille Keizer I10
Eerste Sweelinckstraat 15, **t** *664 1847;* **tram** *4.*
Brightly enamelled metal utensils from around the world.

Hangmatten Maranón H7
Singel 488–90, **t** *622 5938;* **tram** *4, 9, 14, 16, 24, 25.*
Bright and breezy hammocks from around the world.

The Head Shop I6
Kloveniersburgwal 39, **t** *624 9061;* **metro** *Nieuwmarkt.*
Accessories for dope devotees.

Imported I8
Utrechtsestraat 68, **t** *626 9333;* **tram** *4.*
Piles of hand-crafted Indonesian gifts and collectables, both antique and modern.

Jacob Hooy & Co. I6
Nieuwmarkt 12, **t** *624 3041;* **metro** *Nieuwmarkt.*
A herbalist selling ecologically sound products, with barrels and boxes of herbs stacked to the ceiling.

Joe's Vliegerwinkel I6
Nieuwe Hoogstraat 19, **t** *625 0139;* **metro** *Nieuwmarkt.*
Kites weird and wonderful.

Kitsch Kitchen F5
Rozengracht 8, **t** *428 4969;* **tram** *13, 14, 17.*
Gaudy plastic goodies, brightly patterned enamel bowls and curious implements.

Klamboe Unlimited F6
Prinsengracht 232, **t** *622 9492;* **tram** *13, 14, 17.*
Mosquito nets – the best way to ward off the pests.

Kramer F6
Reestraat 20, **t** *626 5274;* **tram** *13, 14, 17.*
Candles and candlesticks – ethnic to high altar.

Olivaria F6
Hazenstraat 2A, **t** *638 3552;* **tram** *13, 14, 17.*
Entirely devoted to olive oil; there's even a tasting bar.

P.G.C. Hajenius H6
Rokin 92–6, **t** *623 7494;* **tram** *4, 9, 14, 16, 24, 25.*
Tobacconist with famed house-brand cigars.

Poppendokter F6
Reestraat 20, **t** *626 5274;* **tram** *13, 14, 17.*
Dolls and parts of dolls.

La Savonnerie F6
Prinsengracht 294, **t** *428 1139;* **tram** *13, 14, 17.*
Dozens of different colours and flavours of handmade soaps.

Vlieger H7
Amstel 34, **t** *623 5834;* **tram** *4, 9, 14, 16, 24, 25.*
Pencils, pigments and piles of inspiring paper.

Waterwinkel F11
Roelof Hartstraat 10, **t** *675 5932;* **tram** *3, 12, 24.*
Over 100 types of mineral water from around the world, and mud from the Dead Sea.

De Witte Tanden Winkel G7
Runstraat 5, **t** *623 3443;* **tram** *1, 2, 5.*
Champagne-flavoured tooth-paste, and toothbrushes, toothbrushes, toothbrushes.

Toys

Keystone Novelty Store G7
Huidenstraat 28, **t** *625 2660;* **tram** *1, 2, 5.*
A charming shop full of old toys, board games and Disney stuff.

Knuffels I6
Nieuwe Hoogstraat 11, **t** *427 3862;* **metro** *Nieuwmarkt.*
An exciting melange of soft toys, puppets, puzzles and mobiles.

Mechanisch Speelgoed G4
Westerstraat 67, **t** *638 1680;* **tram** *3, 10;* **bus** *18.*
A tiny shop full of good, old-fashioned, low-tech toys. Crammed with skipping ropes, pretty paper cut-outs and sorts of little things that will keep parents and kids digging about for ages.

Pinokkio H5
Magna Plaza, Nieuwezijds Voorburgwal 182, **t** *622 8914;* **tram** *1, 2, 5, 13, 17.*
Traditional wooden, tin, mechan-ical and cuddly toys; musical instruments; puppets and dolls' houses. A huge treasure trove of children's goodies.

TinkerBell G8
Spiegelgracht 10, **t** *625 8830;* **tram** *1, 2, 5, 6, 7, 10.*
Good range of toys for children of all ages.

Sports and
Green Spaces

Amsterdam is not a very hearty, sporting city. Most people seem to get the exercise they need from all the walking and cycling they do. However, if you're wandering in Amsterdam South, you might be astonished to see brightly dressed figures, swathed in ropes, scaling the walls of the old firemen's barracks. This is the Netherlands Mountaineering Club acting out of desperation. They are not alone. Every year, from May to October, squads of eager '**horizontal mountain-climbers**' don shorts and sneakers and slop knee deep through sucking quagmires of black mud off the Frisian coast. This they do for two to four hours at a time, before returning home.

Another odd national pastime is **pole-sitting**. Every year, around the beginning of August, men sit on poles in the North Sea (at Noorderwijkerhout just north of The Hague) until they fall off. The last one to do so is the winner.

Korfball is an indigenous hybrid of netball and volleyball played between teams comprising equal numbers of men and women. It's a rule-bound battle of the sexes in which players have to toss a ball around at great speed and try to shoot it into a hoop 11ft (3.5m) off the ground. The nation does, however, also participate in less esoteric sports.

Spectator Sports

Basketball and American Football

The local basketball team, Canadians Amsterdam, is one of the best in the country. They play at the **Apollohal**, Stadionweg 3–5, **t** 671 3910 (**bus** 15; **tram** 5, 24; G12). Fans of American football might be lucky enough to catch an Amsterdam Admirals, **t** 465 0550, game at the **Amsterdam ArenA** (see 'Football', below) or the recently renovated **Olympisch Stadion**, Stadionplein 2 (**tram** 24; **bus** 15, 63; off maps).

Football (soccer)

The most popular national sport is football. The Dutch team have not had many resounding international successes, but the local Amsterdam team, Ajax, has a vociferous and enthusiastic following. Ajax won European Cups three times in the 1970s, and managed again in 1995. If you want to see the team for yourself, head for their flashy home:

Amsterdam ArenA and Ajax Museum Off maps *Arena Boulevard 3, t 311 1333, w www.amsterdamarena.nl; metro Strandvliet; wheelchair accessible.* **Museum open** *daily 9am–6pm; closed match days; adm for museum adults €3.50, under-13s €2.50; with tour adults €8.20, under-13s €7.20.* If you can't catch a match, take a tour of the huge new stadium and then visit the Ajax Museum. With a capacity of 51,000, the stadium looks like an enormous flying saucer. The tour includes the dugouts and the pitch itself, the top of the stands and the press room. The museum has many of Ajax's trophies, and videos of the club's greatest moments.

Hockey

Hockey (field hockey) is a sport in which both the men's and the women's national teams have been world champions. Many national home matches and some good club games are played on the grounds off Nieuwe Kalfjeslaan, on the edge of the Amsterdamse Bos (**bus** 142, 147, 170, 171, 172, 199, 222; off maps), **t** 640 1141.

Ice Hockey

If your taste inclines towards the faster and more furious, a good ice hockey team (S IJ S Amsterdam 89) plays at the **Jaap Edenhal** rink, Radioweg 64 (off maps), **t** 694 9652, from October to February.

Activities

Gyms and Saunas

Among the numerous well-equipped gyms and fitness centres around town are:

A Bigger Splash F7 *Looiersgracht 26–30, t 624 8404; tram 7, 10, 17.* **Open** *daily 7am–midnight; adm €16 per day, €40 per week, €68 for two weeks.* Weights, machines, sauna, steam, massage and aerobics.

Garden Gym J7 *Jodenbreestraat 158, t 626 8772; tram 9, 14; metro Waterlooplein.* **Open** *Mon, Wed, Fri 9am–11pm, Tues and Thurs noon–11pm, Sat 11am–6pm and Sun 11am–7pm; adm day pass €8.50, with sauna/shower €11.50, sauna only €9.50.* Mainly, though not exclusively, for women. Weights, dance, sauna (women only), solarium, massage, self-defence.

Sauna Deco H4 *Herengracht 115, t 623 8215; tram 1, 2, 5, 13, 17.* **Open** *Mon–Sat noon–11pm, Sun 10am–6pm; adm €11.50 noon–3pm, €14.50 per day.* An exhilarating experience. You sweat away those extra inches in a stylish Art Deco interior rescued from a famous 1920s Parisian department store.

Skating

In the winter, walking gives way to skating. If you're lucky you may be in Amsterdam in a year when the canals freeze over, and everyone whizzes around the city on skates. (Be careful, though: the ice can be thin and sometimes doesn't freeze under bridges.) If you don't have your own skates, head for **Jaap Edenhal**, Radioweg 64 (off maps), **t** 694 9894, **w** *www.jaapeden.nl* (**tram** 9; **open** Oct–March Mon–Sat 2–4pm, Sun 10am–4pm), a large rink complex where you can hire skates for €4.55 (you'll need your passport or a €45.50 deposit).

If the weather is really cold you'll hear talk of nothing else but the *elfstedentocht* ('11-city marathon'), which takes place on the canals and waterways between 11 towns in Friesland. It is only rarely that the freeze is good enough – if you hear it's happening, then it's certainly worth a trip north.

Snooker and Billiards

As gentler form of relaxation, you might try a little billiards, snooker or *biljart* (the pocketless Dutch variation).

Snookercentrum de Keizer G6
Keizersgracht 256, t 623 1586; tram 13, 14, 17. Open Mon–Thurs and Sun noon–1am, Sat noon–2am; adm €5 per hour before 7pm, then €6 for pool and €8 for snooker.
In a 17th-century canal house. The tables are in private rooms and you can phone down to the bar for drinks.

Snooker/Pool Centre Amsterdam Zuid H11
Van Ostadestraat 97, t 676 4059; tram 3, 12, 24, 25. Open Sun–Thurs 1pm–1am, Fri and Sat 1pm–2am; adm snooker €7.80 per hour, pool €7.30.
For billiards, snooker or *biljart*.

Squash and Tennis

If bats, rackets and balls are your forte:

Amstelpark Off maps
Koenenkade 8, t 301 0700; bus 170, 171, 172. Open daily 8am–11pm; adm indoor and outdoor courts €20 per hour.
There are 42 tennis courts, most of them outdoor.

Frans Otten Stadion Off maps
Stadionstraat 10, t 662 8767. Open Mon–Fri 9am–midnight, Sat 9am–8pm, Sun 9am–8pm; adm tennis €12.50 per hour before 5pm, then €15; squash €14 per hour

before 5pm then €19; racket hire €2.50.
Here you'll find squash and indoor tennis courts.

Squash City G3
Ketelmakerstraat 6, t 626 7883; bus 18, 22. Open Mon–Fri 8.30am–11pm, Sat and Sun 8.30am–8pm; adm €6.80 before 4.45pm, then €9, racket hire €2.50.
Also has a weights room and sauna for players to use.

Swimming

Swimming pools in Amsterdam are clean, well maintained and supervised. They often have small bars or coffeeshops at the water's edge so you can top up the calories after an energetic swim. Opening times are complicated, with periods set aside for club and naked swimming, so it's a good idea to phone first.

Mirandabad Off maps
De Mirandalaan 9, t 546 4444; tram 25. Open call for opening times; adm €3.15.
Has tropical temperatures, a pebble beach and a wave machine. There's an outdoor pool for good weather and a slide and whirlpool.

Zuiderbad G9
Hobbemastraat 26, t 678 1390; tram 2, 5. Open Hours vary as pool is sometimes given over to lessons for special groups, so phone first; adm €2.70.
Small but beautiful pool that dates back to the beginning of last century. Recently renovated, and still with many original features.

Walking and Cycling

Walking and cycling are the two great national pastimes, and the attractive canals and well-laid-out cycle paths make both a joy. If you want to be more serious about things, or fancy an uninhibited jog, head for the Vondelpark (see p.143) or the Amsterdamse Bos

(see 'Day Trips', p.174). The Amsterdam Tourist Board (see p.77) can offer suggestions for cycling or walking tours (for bicycle hire, see p.65). They will also be able to give you information on the Grachtenloop ('canal run'), Amsterdam's equivalent of the London Marathon. One Sunday early in June thousands of people come together to spend the best part of the day jogging set distances up and down the main canals.

Green Spaces

Amstelpark Off maps
Europaboulevard; t no phone; tram 4; bus 8, 48, 49, 60, 158. Open daily until dusk.
A fresh and lively park with ponies, farm animals, cafés, a rose garden and a labyrinth. A steam train tootles round the park every half-hour on weekends and Wednesday afternoons.

Amsterdamse Bos Off maps
Bus 170, 171, 172.
The city's largest expanse of greenery, to the southwest of the centre. The 'wood' (created in the 1930s as a means of providing jobs for the unemployed) covers more than 2,000 acres (800 hectares), and so serves as a popular escape for city dwellers – though the proximity of Schiphol Airport breaks the tranquillity somewhat. There are boating lakes, playgrounds, animal enclosures and untended meadows to explore. See also p.174.

Hortus Botanicus J7
Plantage Middenlaan, t 625 8411, w www.dehortus.nl; tram 9, 14; metro Waterlooplein. Open April–Sept Mon–Fri 9am–5pm, Sat and Sun 11am–5pm; Oct–March Mon–Fri 9am–4pm, Sat and Sun 11am–4pm; closed 1 Jan, 25 Dec; adm €6.
A botanical garden founded in 1682, and populated with tropical plants pillaged by the Dutch East India Company. It now holds more than 6,000 species, including

the giant water lily *Victoria Amazonica* and a range of carnivores (with roots). A peaceful spot, with a beautiful café terrace in the orangery.

Oosterpark L8–M9
Tram 3, 6, 9, 10, 14.
A quieter equivalent to Vondelpark in the less appealing eastern suburbs of town. The park was landscaped during the 19th century in the English style, with serpentine ponds and arcing pathways. The haunt of fishermen and overfed ducks.

Sarphatipark H–I10
Tram 3.
A pretty and unexpected patch of parkland just south of the Albert Cuypmarkt. It's a good spot for a picnic, once you've stocked up on fresh market produce. Has a reputation for being dangerous after dusk. *See* also p.147.

Vondelpark B10–E9
Tram 1, 2, 3, 5, 6, 12.
Vondelpark is more than your run-of-the-mill city park. On sunny weekends thousands converge on its elegantly landscaped ponds, gardens and carpets of grass to watch performance artists, meet friends, lounge under a tree with a

book, or feed the fowl. It is a surprisingly large park (about the same size as the entire old centre of the city) and contains cafés, animal enclosures and an open-air theatre. *See* also p.143.

Wertheimpark J–K7
Off Muiderstraat by the Nieuwe Herengracht canal; tram 9, 14.
This remaining patch of the old Plantage gardens is a popular place to lie back beside the Nieuwe Herengracht canal on a summer afternoon. In one corner of the park is the Auschwitz Monument, a series of smashed mirrors and an urn containing the ashes of some of those who died.

Children's and Teenagers' Amsterdam

Children

Amsterdam is a diminutive city, perfectly tailored to a small person's needs. Parents don't have to go to extraordinary expense or exercise great feats of imagination to give children a good time. Cycle lanes make bicycling quite safe, a pedalo on the canal can while away hours, even a ride on a clanging tram can be an event (there are reductions for children on public transport). In this chapter we list those attractions, activities and museums that are particularly suitable or tailored to kids. For children's clothes, book and toy shops, *see* the 'Shopping' chapter, p.247.

Babysitting

Oppascentrale Kriterion
t 624 5848. Open Thurs–Sun 4.30–8.30pm, Mon–Wed 9–11am and 4.30–8.30pm.

If you've had enough of the little darlings, you can get hold of vetted and reliable babysitters from here. Prices start at €5 an hour, plus €3 for administration and there's a €3.50 surcharge on Friday and Saturday. You're expected to provide drinks, food for long sessions and the cost of transport home after midnight.

Outdoor Attractions

Amstelpark Off maps
Europaboulevard, t no phone, tram 4; bus 8, 48, 49, 60, 158. Open daily dawn–dusk; adm free.
A fresh and lively place to bring children, with animals to pet, ponies to ride, ice-cream vans, cafés and snack carts galore. There's an enormous play area with an electric-car track and a pond for electric motorboats. There's also a crazy golf course. A steam train tootles round the park every half-hour at weekends and on Wednesday afternoons.

Artis Express **(Rederij Lovers)** I4
Centraal Station, t 530 1090. Open daily 9.30am–5pm; cruises depart every half-hour (duration 30mins out, 45mins back); adm (including entrance to Artis) adults €19, 4–11s €16.75.
Combine a trip to the Artis Zoo (*see* below) with a boat trip on the *Artis Express*. The boat from Centraal Station goes straight to Artis, but on the way back does a 45-minute guided tour of the canals, before returning to the station.

Artis Zoo K7–L8
Plantage Kerklaan 40, t 523 3400, w www.artis.nl; tram 6, 9, 14. Open daily summer 9am–6pm, winter 9am–5pm; adm adults €14, under-12s €10.50.
Artis is a zoo, a children's farm, a huge aquarium complex, a planetarium and a park with excellent play areas, all rolled into one – you could easily while away an entire day here. The zoo itself contains all the usual favourites, including lions, elephants and giraffes. At its northeast end is the African Savannah, a landscaped grassy area with zebras, wildebeest and meerkats.
In the middle of the savannah, the space-aged Twee Cheetahs restaurant is a good place to stop for lunch, with a video area where little ones who've had enough of the real animals can sit and watch their animated counterparts in Disney films. The state-of-the-art Jungle by Night building gives visitors an inkling of what goes on in a South American rainforest after dark.
In the aquarium there are two spectacular coral-reef tanks and a seawater section with sharks, stingrays and stonefish, while four entire ecosystems have been established in freshwater tanks. The children's farm contains endangered domesticated species, which children can pet and feed, and the planetarium offers performances specifically designed for children as young as three or four.

De Efteling Off maps
Europalaan 1, Kaatsheuvel, Noord Brabant, 70 miles (110km) from Amsterdam, t (0416) 288 111, e informatie@mail.efteling.nl, w www.efteling.nl. Open Apr–Oct daily 10am–6pm, July and Aug daily 10am–9pm; phone for winter opening times; adm (adults or children) €21 (€23 in July and Aug); train to s'-Hertogenbosch (1hr from Amsterdam Centraal) then bus to De Efteling.
By far the most exciting of the theme parks out of town, this is a surreal fantasy-land with an enormous Enchanted Forest, flying carpets, mysterious boat journeys, a Sleeping Beauty whose breasts heave, and all the usual (and some very unusual) rides.

Elektrische Museumtramlijn (Electric Tramline Museum) Off maps
Haarlemmermeerstation, Amstelveenseweg 264, t 673 7538, w www.trammuseum.demon.nl; tram 6, 16. Open Easter–Oct Sun and holidays 11am–5pm, plus Wed in July and Aug; adm adults €3 return, 4–11s €1.50 return.
A museum on the move. If trams prove to be a hit, try one of the antique trolleys that go to Amsterdamse Bos, a woody parkland where children can ride horses, eat pancakes, swim and run about to their heart's content (*see* p.174).

De Uylenburg Off maps
Staalmeesterlaan 420, t 618 5235; tram 13; bus 18. Open Sun–Wed 10am–5pm; adm free.
A city farm to be found in the Rembrandtpark, with free horse rides and a playground.

Activities

See also the 'Sports and Green Spaces' chapter, p.254.

Canal Bike G9
Rijksmuseum mooring, t 626 5574, w www.canal.nl; tram 1, 2, 5, 6, 7, 10. Open daily 10am–6.30pm, summer 10am–10pm; costs €8 per

person per hour (€7 if 2 people or more) plus €50 deposit.

Canal bikes are ultra-stable pedal boats which you can navigate around the canals of Amsterdam. Since they're self-driven, you can decide which of the tiny waterways you fancy exploring or head straight to the busiest water thoroughfares and follow a tour boat. If it rains you can pull up a waterproof rainshield to keep dry. Sinkings, capsizings and even wet feet are unheard of. There are other moorings at the Anne Frankhuis, Keizersgracht (at Leidsestraat) and Leidseplein. You can rent and drop off the canal bikes at any of the locations.

Jaap Edenhal Ice Rink Off maps *Radioweg 64, t 694 9894; tram 9. Open Oct–March Mon–Sat 2–4pm, Sun 10am–4pm; adm adults €3.50, children €2.25, skate hire €4 plus ID or €45.50 deposit.* A complex with both indoor and outdoor rinks, as well as a restaurant that you can skate right into. There's also a climbing wall for those who bore of the ice.

Mirandabad Off maps *De Mirandalaan 9, t 546 4444; tram 25. Open call for opening times; adm €3.15, under-3s free.* Amsterdam's best swimming complex, with three slides, a wave pool, a shallow paddling pool, a whirlpool and a powered water current. Adjoining the complex are two squash courts, a solarium and a restaurant.

Cycling

Amsterdam is made for cycling. The distances between attractions are small, the ground is flat, there is little traffic and there are cycle paths almost everywhere, making bikes a very safe proposition, even for younger children. There are even dedicated bicycle traffic lights. Cycling can also be extremely convenient for parents with young children, because carrying a young child on the front (or back) of a bike is much easier than trying to get a pushchair onto a bus or tram. You

will be hard pressed to find a cycling helmet anywhere in Amsterdam, so you'll have to bring your own.

Guided bike tours allow you to see Amsterdam without having to stop and look at a map every few minutes and, because you can speed through the streets on a bike much faster than you can walk, you can see a great deal in just a few hours. The tours take in most of the places of interest in the city and the guides are generally witty and well informed. The tour companies listed below have children's bikes and seats for smaller kids. Because the tours are fairly long (about three hours) they may prove to be too strenuous for children under 10 riding their own bikes.

Mike's Bike Tours G9 *Kerkstraat 134, t 622 7970, w www. mikesbiketours.com; tram 2, 5, 6, 7, 10, 16, 24, 25. Tours in English (allow 2½–3½hrs) depart from outside Rijksmuseum, Mar and April daily 12.30pm, May–Aug daily 11.30am and 4pm, Sep–Nov daily 12.30pm; costs €22, cash only.* Guides are native English-speakers. The tours stay on cycle paths and include historic sites as well as a stop out of town at a cheese farm and clog factory, which may be the highlight for children jaded by too many old buildings.

Yellow Bike Guided Tours H5 *Nieuwezijds Kolk 29, t 620 6940, w www.yellowbike.nl; tram 1, 2, 5, 13, 17. Tours (allow 3hrs) depart April–Oct Sun–Fri at 9.30am and 1pm, Sat 9.30am and 2pm; costs €17, children in child seat for free.* The best-known of such companies in Amsterdam; if you've spent any time in the city you'll probably have seen processions of yellow-caped riders rolling around the canals.

The tour takes in many of the well-known sights, including the Anne Frankhuis, Vondelpark, the Magere Brug and the Red Light District.

Indoor Attractions

Amstelkring Museum I5 *Oudezijds Voorburgwal 40, t 624 6604, w www.museum. amstelkring.nl; tram 4, 9, 14, 16, 24, 25; metro Nieuwmarkt. Open Mon–Sat 10am–5pm, Sun and hols 1–5pm; closed 1 Jan, 30 April; adm adults €6, under-18s €1.* Children are fascinated by the idea of a secret place. The Amstelkring Museum's secret is Our Lord in the Attic, a surprisingly spacious clandestine church hidden under the roof of an unassuming little house. For more information, *see* p.85.

Anne Frankhuis G5 *Prinsengracht 263, t 556 7100, w www.annefrank.nl; tram 13, 14, 17. Open April–Aug daily 9am–9pm, Sept–March daily 9am–7pm; closed 1 Jan, Yom Kippur, 25 Dec noon–7pm; adm adults €7.50, 10–18s €3.50.* Very popular with children over the age of about 10, but some of the exhibits may be upsetting for small children. For more information, *see* p.123.

Electric Ladyland F5 *Tweede Leliedwarsstraat 5, t 420 3776, w www.electric-lady -land.com; tram 13, 14, 17. Open Tues–Sat 1–6pm; adm €5.* A specialist gallery and museum dealing with fluorescent art and named after Jimi Hendrix's masterpiece. The museum introduces visitors to the fascinating world of fluorescent minerals and crystals that burst into colours when seen under different wavelengths of light. There are plenty of buttons for kids to press to operate lights and music.

Holland Experience I7 *Waterlooplein 17, t 422 2233, w www.holland-experience.nl; tram 9, 14; metro Waterlooplein. Open daily 10am–6pm (last show 5.30pm); duration 30mins; adm adults €8.50, 4–12s €7.25.*

A multi-sense, multimedia show of three-dimensional film, theatre, chair movement and synchronised smells. It is extremely tacky and the humour is slapstick, but many children, especially young ones, will love it.

Kattenkabinet H7

Herengracht 497, t 626 5378, e info@kattenkabinet.nl, w www.kattenkabinet.nl; tram 4, 9, 14, 16, 24, 25. Open Mon–Fri 9am–2pm, Sat and Sun 1–5pm; adm adults €4.55, children €2.30, under-5s free.

At this museum dedicated solely to cat-related works of art and objects you can enjoy drawings on feline themes by Rembrandt and Picasso, while the children make friends with the museum's cats.

Kindermuseum (Children's Museum) L–M8

At the Tropenmuseum, Linnaeusstraat 2, t 568 8542, w www. tropenmuseumjunior.nl; tram 9, 10, 14; bus 22. Open (programmes in Dutch only). Family programmes Sat, Sun, hols 11am–noon, Junior programmes (adults join children at beginning and end of programme; for 6–12s) Sat, Sun, hols 12.30–2pm and 3–4.30pm, special workshops (6–12s) Wed 2.30–4.30pm; adm (including Tropenmuseum) adults €9.50 (family programmes), €7.50 (other programmes), 6–12s €5.75.

The staff, who have all had experience of a developing-world country, create a village-like environment where children can learn first-hand about aspects of another culture – such as drumming, rice-making or dancing.

Madame Tussaud's H6

Dam 20, t 522 1010, e madame. tussauds@scenerama.com, w www.madame-tussauds.com; tram 1, 2, 4, 5, 13, 16, 17, 25. Open mid-July–Aug daily 9.30am– 8.30pm, Sept–mid-July daily 10am–6.30pm (last tickets sold 1hr before closing); adm adults €17.50, under-15s €10, under-4s free.

Most kids love waxworks. On a rainy day with restless kids,

Madame Tussaud's is hard to beat. Amsterdam's version of the famous waxworks museum attempts to make a visit educational as well as fun by devoting space to the city's Golden Age, alongside the usual line-up of rock stars and public figures.

Nationaal Brilmuseum G6

Gasthuismolensteeg 7, t 421 2414; tram 1, 2, 5. Open Wed–Fri 11.30am–5.30pm, Sat 11.30am–5pm; adm €4.50.

Offers the visitor a chance to catch up on the 700-year history of the art and culture of spectacles. Fascinating and fun, particularly if you wear glasses.

Nederlands Theater Instituut G5

Herengracht 168, t 551 3300, e info@tin.nl, w www.tin.nl; tram 13, 14, 17. Open Mon–Fri 11am–5pm, Sat and Sun 1–5pm; adm adults €4.50, under-17s €2.25, under-7s free.

Always has good exhibitions, usually of the sort where you push buttons or pull levers and make things happen. If there are three of you, you can raise a storm with the wind, thunder and lightning machines on the ground floor.

Nemo K5

Oosterdok 2, t 531 3233, w www. e-nemo.nl; bus 22. Open Tues-Sun, 10am–5pm; closed 1 Jan, 30 April, 25 Dec; adm €10.

With great views over the city from an upper deck that doubles as a beach in summer, this is a spectacular building (see p.156) crammed with exciting and often noisy exhibits which introduce children to the world of science and technology. Some of these are educational; others are just fun.

Tropenmuseum L–M8

Linnaeusstraat 2, t 568 8215, e tm@kit.nl, w www.kit.nl/tropen museum; tram 9, 10, 14; bus 22; wheelchair accessible. Open daily 10am–5pm; closed 1 Jan, 30 April, 5 May, 25 Dec; adm €7.50, under-17s €3.75.

Visiting the Tropenmuseum is like taking a journey on a magic carpet

around the most exotic countries of the world. As soon as you walk through the door you are immersed in the sights and sounds of Africa, Asia, Latin America and Oceania.

Eating Out

In the 'Eating Out' chapter we state in the text when we have found a restaurant particularly child-friendly, but here are some inexpensive favourites:

Casa di David G7

Singel 426, t 624 5093; tram 1, 2, 5. Open Tues–Sun 5–11pm.

Pizzeria with wooden beams and canalside charm. The food is good too – pasta made on the premises, and fragrant crusty pizzas cooked in a wood-burning oven.

Divertimento G7

Singel 480 (in the flower market), t 622 9690; tram 1, 2, 4, 5, 9, 16, 24, 25. Open Mon–Fri 8.30am– 5.30pm, Sat 8.30am–6pm, Sun 10am–5.30pm.

There are always plenty of children and mothers in this cheerful snack bar. The stuffed baguettes are simply enormous.

The Pancake Bakery G5

Prinsengracht 191, t 625 1333; tram 13, 14, 17. Open daily noon–9.30pm.

This low-beamed cellar near the Anne Frankhuis claims to sell the best pancakes in town.

Entertainment

Children's theatre is usually in Dutch, but you might be lucky enough to catch the odd mime or puppet show. Check the listings magazines under the following venues: Kindertheater Elleboog, De Krakeling, Poppentheater Diridas and Mirakel Poppentheater. If you're around at Christmas, try:

Koninklijk Theater Carré J8

Amstel 115–25, t 0900 252 5255, w www.theatrecarre.nl; tram 4, 6, 7, 10.

Built for a circus – a very popular function it still performs over the Christmas period.

Teenagers

Young teenagers might enjoy the exhibits at the **Stedelijk Museum** (*see* p.136), **Van Gogh Museum** (*see* p.138) and the **Nederlands Filmmuseum** (*see* p.143). The **Anne Frankhuis** is an obvious choice (*see* p.123). Teenagers may also enjoy browsing the **Waterlooplein flea-market** (*see* p.108) or along **Kalverstraat** (*see* p.98), Amsterdam's mainstream shopping street. Or try one of the following:

Amsterdam ArenA and Ajax Museum Off maps *Arena Boulevard 3, t 311 1333, w www.amsterdamarena.nl; metro Strandvliet; wheelchair accessible. Open daily 9am–6pm; closed match days; adm for museum adults €3.50, under-13s €2.50; with tour adults €8.20, under-13s €7.20.*

You don't have to be a fan of Ajax football team to enjoy a tour of the huge stadium and a visit to the Ajax Museum. With a capacity of 51,000, the stadium looks like an enormous flying saucer. The tour includes the dugouts and the pitch itself, the top of the stands and the press room. In the museum are many of Ajax's trophies, and videos of some of the club's greatest moments.

Six Flags Holland Off maps *Spijkweg 30, Biddinghuizen, t (0321) 329 991, w www.sixflags europe.com; 45 miles (72km) from Amsterdam via the A1 and A6. Open Easter–Aug daily from 10am (various closing times); Sept and Oct Fri–Sun from 10am (various closing times); adm adults €23, 3–11s €18.50; train from Amsterdam Centraal to Lelystad (40mins), then bus.*

The Netherlands' largest adventure park, with a number of spine-chilling rollercoasters and some tamer rides for the younger ones.

Gay and Lesbian Amsterdam

In the heady social upheaval of the 1960s and 70s, when pixie-hatted members of the Gnome Party held protest meetings on the Dam and troupes of hippies camped out in the Vondelpark, Amsterdam's lesbians and gays joined in the frolic. Homosexuality had been decriminalized in 1811, but the gay community wanted a city free of the petty prejudices and subtle discrimination they ran up against in day-to-day life. In many ways they succeeded.

Today Amsterdam is known as the Gay Capital of Europe. Gay bars and cafés, though often in clusters, aren't in ghettos. Nobody bats an eyelid if two men kiss or hold hands in public. The city was quick off the mark in coping constructively with AIDS; the council housing department gives gay couples the same status as married heterosexuals; and in 1987 the world's first memorial to persecuted lesbians and gays, the Homomonument, was unveiled (the three triangles of pink granite between the Westerkerk and the Keizersgracht are the focal point of many a party, protest or commemoration service).

There are gay bars, clubs, hotels, bookshops and restaurants all over town. You'll find most of the heavier leather bars lurking up the north end of Warmoesstraat; ribbons of coffeeshops, restaurants and bars along Kerkstraat and Reguliersdwars-straat; a jolly throb of clubs and pubs along the Amstel off Rembrandtplein; and scores of local neighbourhood cafés. Despite accusations that the Amsterdam gay scene is stagnating, gay tourists flock to the city. Over weekends, the hunk at the end of the bar is more likely to be a computer programmer from South London than a local lad. Many Amsterdammers respond to this invasion by staying at home, venturing out on Thursdays and Sundays when the occupying forces are thinner on the ground.

The atmosphere, though, is friendly and welcoming. Most gay venues distribute free maps of gay Amsterdam, leaflets and free magazines (such as *Rainbow*) giving you an idea of what's on about town; but as people are so open and chatty, word-of-mouth is often the best way to find out what the evening might have in store.

Here is an idiosyncratic selection of places to go; some are well known but others are quirky, local establishments, out of the tourist maelstrom.

Information

COC F5
Rozenstraat 14, office t 626 3087, info t 623 4079; tram 13, 14, 17. ***Open*** *Mon–Thurs 9am–5pm; for disco and coffeeshop hours, see 'Clubs' and 'Lesbian Amsterdam', below.*
Amsterdam's lesbian and gay social centre.

Gay and Lesbian Switchboard
*t 623 6565. **Open** 2–10pm.*
Gives information and advice in English.

Gay News Amsterdam
PO Box 76609, 1070 HE Amsterdam, editorial t 412 05 57, e info@gaynews.nl, w www.gay news.nl.
The Netherlands' biggest-selling gay publication. Bilingual and monthly. They also publish the *Amsterdam Gay Map*, which is widely available for free.

Homodok/Lesbisch Archief Off maps
Nieuwpoortkade 2A, Westerpark, t 606 0712, f 606 0713, w www. homodok-laa.nl; tram 10, 12, 15; bus 18, 21. Open Mon–Fri 10am–4pm.
Library and information centre.

Pink Point of Presence G5
Westermarkt Homomonument, t 412 4463, w www.pinkpoint.org; tram 13, 14, 17. Open daily noon–6pm.

A gay information stand at the Homo. For details contact the VVV at Centraal Station or Leidseplein.

Bookshops

The American Book Center H7
Kalverstraat 185, t 625 5537; tram 1, 2, 4, 5, 9, 14, 16, 24, 25.
Has a good gay section.

Boekhandel Vrolijk H6
Paleisstraat 135, t 623 5142; tram 1, 2, 5, 13, 14, 17.
Has a wide selection of literature, biographies and non-fiction of interest to lesbians and gay men.

Intermale G6
Spuistraat 251, t 625 0009; tram 1, 2, 5, 13, 14, 17.
Mostly for men.

Accommodation

Hotels are forbidden by law to discriminate against gay couples; many of Amsterdam's best 'straight' hotels are sympathetic places to stay, and many are gay-owned. See especially the Quentin Hotel (which has a large lesbian clientele; *see* p.207), Hotel Seven Bridges (*see* p.207) and Hotel Engeland (*see* p.211) in the 'Where to Stay' chapter. But here's a selection of specifically gay places to stay. The prices are for a double room with shower in season, with breakfast included.

Amsterdam House I7
's Gravenlandseveer 7, 1011 KN, t 626 2577, f 626 2987, e amshouse@euronet.nl, w www. amsterdamhouse.com; tram 4, 9, 14, 16, 24, 25; metro Waterlooplein.
Well positioned in a relatively quiet spot on the southern edge of the old centre, near Waterlooplein. The main attractions are not the rather plain hotel rooms, but the fully equipped canalboat apartments, which are available for short-term rentals. TVs in rooms. Just minutes from gay hotspots. Doubles from €80.

Black Tulip I5
Geldersekade 16, 1012 BH, **t** *427 0933,* **f** *624 4281,* **w** *www.black tulip.nl;* **tram** *1, 2, 4, 5, 9, 13, 16, 17;* **metro** *Centraal Station.*
All rooms are *en suite*, with adult channels and bondage equipment – hence the hotel's popularity with the S&M crowd. Ask what features are available when booking. From €110.

The Golden Bear G7
Kerkstraat 37, 1017 GB, **t** *624 4785,* **f** *627 0164,* **w** *www.goldenbear.nl;* **tram** *1, 2, 5, 16, 24, 25.*
In the 1940s this hotel first pro-claimed itself as exclusively for gay men and women. It's still going strong today, though there are only 11 rooms, most of which are booked up year round. Some rooms have shared facilities. From €70 without bath, €112 with bath.

Greenwich Village G7
Kerkstraat 25, 1017 GA, **t** *626 9746,* **f** *625 4081,* **w** *www.greenwich village.nl;* **tram** *1, 2, 5, 16, 24, 25.*
A lively hotel in the canal belt with old-world furnishings and a mainly gay clientele. From €50. TV.

International Travel Club/ITC I8
Prinsengracht 1051, 1017 JE, **t** *623 0230,* **f** *624 5846,* **e** *office@itc -hotel.com,* **w** *itc-hotel.com;* **tram** *4, 6, 7, 10.*
Quiet hotel overlooking one of Amsterdam's finest canals, popular with an older crowd. From €75; breakfast €7.50.

Orfeo G8
Leidsekruisstraat 14, 1017 RH, **t** *623 1347,* **f** *620 2348,* **w** *www.hotel orfeo.com;* **tram** *1, 2, 5, 6, 7, 10.*
This is an exclusively gay hotel, with owners who will point you in exactly the right direction for your explorations of gay Amsterdam. There are only 22 rooms, and it's a very popular hotel, so book well in advance. From €75 with shared facilities; €115 *en suite*.

Restaurants

Getto I5
Warmoesstraat 51, **t** *421 5151;* **tram** *4, 9, 16, 24, 25.* **Kitchen open** *Tues–Sun 6–11pm.* **Moderate.**
A young, friendly crowd and good food make this one of the most popular recent additions to the gay scene.

Hemelse Modder J5
Oude Waal 9, **t** *624 3203;* **metro** *Nieuwmarkt.* **Open** *Tues–Sun 6–10pm. Arrive early or book.* **Moderate.**
Adventurous, beautifully presented international cuisine in a bright and elegant space on the Oude Waal canal. The gay man-agement are endlessly courteous, while the cooking is some of the best you'll find in Amsterdam.

't Sluisje H5
Torensteeg 1, **t** *624 0813;* **tram** *1, 2, 5, 13, 17.* **Open** *Wed–Sun 6pm–1am.* **Moderate.**
A lively and eccentric restaurant where Dutch dishes are served up by a staff in semi-drag.

Le Monde H7
Rembrandtplein 6, **t** *626 9922;* **tram** *4, 9, 14.* **Open** *daily 8am–midnight.* **Inexpensive.**
Tiny, cheery snack café with a terrace on Rembrandtplein. The sister restaurant along the square does good Dutch food.

Café Nielsen F6
Berenstraat 19, **t** *330 6006;* **tram** *1, 2, 5.* **Open** *Tues–Fri 8am–6pm, Sat 8am–5pm, Sun 9am–5pm.* **Inexpensive.**
A great place to stop for lunch: pick up one of the English news-papers or magazines that are strewn about and choose from soups, bagels and pastries.

Cafés

Backstage Boutique (a.k.a. 'The Twins') I8
Utrechtsedwarsstraat 75, **t** *622 3638;* **tram** *4, 6, 7, 10.* **Open** *Mon–Sat 10am–6pm.*
Not exclusively gay, but with an atmosphere of stratospheric camp that shouldn't be missed.

COC F5
Rozenstraat 14, **t** *623 4079;* **tram** *13, 14, 17.* **Coffeeshop open** *Mon–Sat 8pm–midnight, Sun 3–7pm; Fri and Sat* **club** *until 4am.*
Spartan but amiable haven in Amsterdam's lesbian and gay 'culture centre'.

Downtown H7
Reguliersdwarsstraat 31, **t** *622 9958;* **tram** *1, 2, 4, 5, 9, 14, 16, 24, 25.* **Open** *daily 10am–8pm.*
A friendly daytime coffeeshop, popular with tourists and locals, in one of Amsterdam's gay streets. It serves food and has a sprawl of pavement tables on sunny days.

Reibach G4
Brouwersgracht 139, **t** *626 7708;* **bus** *18, 22;* **metro** *Centraal Station.* **Open** *daily, April–Sept 10am–8pm, Oct–Mar 10am–6pm.*
Trendy café with a Germanic edge, great cakes and a pleasant, small terrace on one of Amsterdam's most tranquil canals.

La Strada H5
Nieuwezijds Voorburgwal 93, **t** *625 0276;* **tram** *1, 2, 5, 13, 17.* **Open** *daily noon–1am (kitchen open Mon–Thurs 4–10.30pm, Fri–Sun noon–10.30pm).*
Brown café with good food and friendly staff, popular with local lesbians.

Bars

Amstel Taveerne H7
Amstel 54, **t** *623 4254;* **tram** *4, 9, 14, 16, 24, 25.* **Open** *Sun–Thurs 3pm–1am, Fri and Sat 3pm–2am.*
Beer mugs and bric-a-brac hang everywhere. Dutch reproductions on the walls. Dutch originals around the bar. A provincial pub in the middle of the city with sing-alongs and good cheer (all Dutch).

April H7
Reguliersdwarsstraat 37, **t** *625 9572;* **tram** *1, 2, 5, 9, 14, 16, 24, 25.* **Open** *daily 2pm–1am.*

More than double its previous size (and more attractively designed) following its renovation a few years back. Popular with young Amsterdammers during the week. Over the weekend, tourists swell numbers until the bar bursts into a street party.

Argos I5
Warmoesstraat 95, **t** *622 6595;* **tram** *4, 9, 16, 24, 25.* **Open** *Mon–Thurs 9pm–3am, Fri–Sun 9pm–4pm.*
Amsterdam's oldest leather bar sweats with bikers' jackets, cowboy chaps and denim. As you wander into the dimmer recesses, what the gay guides coyly term 'action' becomes quite lively.

Casa Maria I5
Warmoesstraat 60, **t** *627 6848;* **tram** *4, 9, 16, 24, 25.* **Open** *Sun–Thurs noon–1am, Fri and Sat noon–2am.*
In the heart of the Red Light District. A jukebox full of uproarious kitsch, a gregarious Spanish owner, and a picture window that offers the best people-watching possibilities in town.

Lellebel I7
Utrechtsestraat 4, **t** *427 5139;* **tram** *4, 9, 14.* **Open** *Mon–Thurs and Sun 9pm–3am, Fri and Sat 9pm–4am.*
A flamboyant transvestite bar with live entertainment over the weekend.

Mix Café H7
Amstel 50, **t** *420 3388;* **tram** *4, 9, 14.* **Open** *Sun–Thurs 8pm–3am, Fri and Sat 8pm–4am.*
This bar lives up to its name, with a mixed crowd of fun-lovers.

Montmartre H7
Halvemaansteeg 17, **t** *620 7622;* **tram** *4, 9, 14, 16, 24, 25.* **Open** *Sun–Thurs 4pm–1am, Fri and Sat 4pm–4am.*
Dancing barmen, original 1920s décor, loud music and a tight squeeze.

Queen's Head I5
Zeedijk 20, **t** *420 2474,* **w** *www. queenshead.nl;* **tram** *4, 9, 16, 24, 25.* **Open** *Mon–Thurs 5pm–1am, Fri 5pm–3am, Sat 4pm–3am, Sun 4pm–1am.*

A traditional bar overlooking the Geldersekade canal.

Le Shako I7
's Gravelandseveer 2, **t** *624 0209;* **tram** *4, 9, 14, 16, 24, 25.* **Open** *Sun–Thurs 9pm–2am, Fri and Sat 9pm–3am.*
A minuscule bar that attracts students, writers, academics and a good load of local scruffs. Cheap beer on Tuesdays and free snacks on Thursdays.

Soho H7
Reguliersdwarsstraat 36, **t** *616 1213;* **tram** *1, 2, 4, 5, 14, 16, 24, 25.* **Open** *Mon–Thurs 8pm–3am, Fri and Sat 8pm–4am, Sun 4pm–3am.*
A very trendy pub-style bar on the Reguliersdwarsstraat stretch.

The Web H5
Sint Jacobsstraat 6, **t** *623 6758;* **tram** *1, 2, 3, 5.* **Open** *Mon–Thurs and Sun 2pm–1am, Fri and Sat 2pm–2am.*
A wild leather bar with pool table, porn TV and 'Europe's largest darkroom'.

Clubs

COC F5
Rozenstraat 14, **t** *623 4079;* **tram** *13, 14, 17.* **Open** *Fri 8pm–4am (men's club night), Sat 8pm–4am (women's club night).*
Amsterdam's Gay Centre runs a disco which attracts a local crowd and ingénues from the provinces.

C'ring (or Cockring) I5
Warmoesstraat 96, **t** *623 9604;* **tram** *4, 9, 16, 24, 25.* **Open** *Sun–Thurs 11pm–4am, Fri and Sat 11pm–5am.*
Steamy, sweaty, swarming venue for emergency sex.

Exit H7
Reguliersdwarsstraat 42, **t** *625 8788;* **tram** *1, 2, 4, 5, 9, 14, 16, 24, 25.* April's (see 'Bars', above) busy disco-sister. **Open** *Sun–Thurs 11pm–4am, Fri and Sat 11pm–5am.*

iT I7
Amstelstraat 24, **t** *618 6040,* **w** *www.it.nl;* **tram** *4, 9, 14.* **Open** *Sun–Thurs 11pm–4am, Fri and Sat 11pm–5am.*

Amsterdam's largest and most well-known gay club, with a number of high-profile nights.

De Trut E7
Bilderdijkstraat 165, **t** *no phone;* **tram** *3, 7, 12, 17.* **Open** *Sun 11pm–4am.*
A trendy, but relaxed and pose-free club with a wide range of music, a (mainly) young crowd and a mix of lesbians and gay men. De Trut is in the cellar of what was once one of Amsterdam's biggest squats. The entrance is unmarked, but if you turn up between 11pm and midnight, you'll see where to go. Often the club gets so full you have to wait for someone to leave before you're allowed in.

Other Attractions

Thermos Day F7
Raamstraat 35, **t** *623 9158,* **w** *www.thermos.nl;* **tram** *1, 2, 5, 7, 10.* **Open** *Mon–Sat noon–11pm, Sun 11am–10pm;* **adm** *€14.*
Notorious sauna.

Thermos Night G8
Kerkstraat 60, **t** *623 4936;* **tram** *1, 2, 5.* **Open** *Sun–Fri 11pm–7am, Sat 11pm–10am;* **adm** *€14.*
The night-time version of the notorious sauna.

Zandvoort Off maps
Train from Centraal Station (about 30mins, frequent trains right through the day), then once you get to the beach, walk south along the promenade and then on past the 'Naakt Strand' (nudist beach) for about 5km.
If the sun's shining, the place to be is Zandvoort, on Amsterdam's gay beach. Zandvoort is not the forgotten patch in the dunes that such places usually are, although it's a bit of a trek to reach it. There are a couple of gay bars (Eldorado and Sans Tout; *both open daily 8am–midnight*) on the beach. *See* also p.174.

Lesbian Amsterdam

Lesbians are not as well catered for as gay men in Amsterdam, but there's a lively, friendly scene in places such as:

Café Saarein I7
Elandsstraat 119, t 623 4901; tram 7, 10. Open Mon 8pm–1am, Tues–Thurs and Sun 3pm–1am, Fri and Sat 3pm–2am.
A cosy local café, currently the citadel of Amsterdam's lesbian life.

Café Vive-la-Vie I7
Amstelstraat 5, t 624 0114; tram 4, 9, 14. Open Sun–Thurs noon–1am, Fri and Sat noon–2am.
Sociable crowd in a vaguely Art Deco bar with music that increases in volume as the night wears on.

COC F5
Rozenstraat 14; tram 13, 14, 17. Open Sat 8pm–4am.
Holds a house-oriented women-only disco on Saturdays.

You II I7
Amstel 178, t 421 0900; tram 4, 9, 14. Open Fri and Sat 11pm–5am, Sun and Thurs 10pm–1am.
More of a disco than Vive-la-Vie, and less heavily house than COC. Much-needed hip, yet pretty relaxed lesbian/mixed gay meeting place.

Festivals

Perhaps because of Amsterdam's Puritan heritage, you'll find little civic or royal pomp. Instead, the city lets its hair down at a number of fairs, arts festivals and street parties – the best celebration of all being Koninginnedag on 30 April. More details of all of the following events are available from the Amsterdam Tourist Office (see p.77). Here are some dates to aim for:

February

Carnival

Though it's more a southern, Roman Catholic tradition, Amsterdammers (always in the market for a party) have also taken to the traditional dressing up and last-minute boozing before Lent.

Commemoration of the February Strike

25 Feb

A solemn gathering at the *Dokwerker* statue on J.D. Meijerplein (see p.111).

March

Blues Festival

At the Meervaart Theatre.

Boat Show

A boat show featuring the latest pleasure craft at the RAI Congress Centre (on Europaplein).

Stille Omgang (Silent Procession)

Sunday night closest to 15 March

Roman Catholics from all over the world walk in silence along the Heiligeweg and up to St Nicolaaskerk to celebrate 'Amsterdam's Miracle' (see 'History', p.29).

April

GRAP Day

At De Melkweg (see p.243). Amsterdam's best new bands blast away well into the night.

National Museum Weekend

Usually the third weekend

All museums allow free entry and get very crowded. Unless you're exceptionally hard up, this is a date to avoid.

Koninginnedag (Queen's Day)

30 April

A national holiday to celebrate the Queen's birthday. Amsterdam declares a 'free market'. Anyone can sell anything anywhere and all bar and restaurant takings are tax-free. The whole city turns into a cross between London's Notting Hill Carnival and a fleamarket. Holland converges on the town to eat, drink, dance and be exceptionally merry, but with the usual charming Dutch relaxed tolerance. Up to 3 million people throng the streets (Amsterdam's population is only 700,000), yet you hardly see a policeman, there are no barricades, no rules and no problems – seldom more than 10 arrests over the whole day, and those are usually for pick-pocketing. The best time to join in is after midnight on the 29th, when everyone is setting up stalls and people are as fresh and excited as children on Christmas Eve.

World Press Photo Exhibition

Mid-April–mid-May

Displays the pick of newspaper and magazine photography from the preceding year (in the Oude Kerk).

May

Herdenkingsdag and Bevrijdingsdag

4–5 May

Remembrance Day and Liberation Day are not the pompous, jingoistic affairs such occasions often become. Queen Beatrix lays a wreath at the National Monument at 8pm on Remembrance Day and the whole city observes a two-minute silence. The next day erupts in street parties, live music and another free market. Vondelpark and Leidseplein are the best places to be. (Nowadays, Bevrijdingsdag is officially celebrated only every five years.)

June

Holland Festival

All month

This is Amsterdam's answer to the Edinburgh Festival, with an impressive constellation of international performers booked into opera, dance and theatre venues around the city. The festival forms part of the Amsterdam Arts Adventure, which keeps everyone from opera-lovers to movie-buffs entertained well into the summer.

Kunst RAI

Beginning of June/end May

The RAI Congress Centre plays host to an international contemporary art fair.

Grachtenloop

2nd Sunday

5,000 people go for a jog around the canals.

World Roots Festival

Mid–late June

Nine days of music, dance and theatre from non-Western cultures at De Melkweg.

July

Summer Festival

If the Holland Festival sounds too staid for your tastes, try the Summer Festival – a bonanza of the avant-garde that goes on all over town (sometimes in the strangest places).

August

De Parade

Most of the month

The Martin Luther King Park, beside the Amstel on the southern outskirts of town, is the scene of De Parade, a 'theatre funfair'. Various theatre groups and performers arrange bright show booths, some of them dating back to the first half of the 20th century, in a vast circle, and offer everything from cabaret to performance art. The Masters (and Mistresses) of Ceremonies present the players on stages outside the booths, then everyone troops in for the show. There's lots to eat and drink, too.

The Uitmarkt (Entertainment Market)
Last week

Groups from all over the Netherlands offer tantalizing snippets of what the coming cultural season has to offer. It's free, and takes place in theatres or in the open air – in fact, anywhere a company can find a suitable space.

Grachtenfestival (Canal Festival)
Last week

Open-air music is played during the three-day-long 'Canal Festival' – from boats opposite the Pulitzer Hotel (Prinsengracht 315–31).

September

Bloemen Corso (Flower Parade)
First Saturday

A parade of floats from Aalsmeer ('the flower capital') to Amsterdam on the first Saturday of the month. Check with the Amsterdam Tourist Board (*see* 'Tourist Offices', p.77) for details of the route and arrival times. Vijzelstraat and the Dam are the best places to watch from.

Jordaan Festival

The liveliest of a series of neighbourhood street parties. All over the Jordaan, the residents come out into the streets to booze, barbecue and try their luck in the often unabashedly dire local talent contests.

Monumentendag (Monument Day)
One weekend in Sept

'Monument Day' is when notable buildings that are not usually open to the public allow in streams of curious visitors.

November

Sinterklaas (Santa Claus)
Mid-Nov

Santa Claus arrives by steamboat at Centraal Station (supposedly from his home in Spain). He parades through the city on a white horse with his slave Black Pete (an oddly persistent tradition in modern, racially aware Amsterdam) and is given the keys of the city by the *burgemeester* on the Dam. Relax with a coffee on Rembrandtplein and watch the early part of the procession in relative comfort.

December

Pakjesavond (Parcel Evening)
5 Dec

The traditional Dutch time to give presents – rather than Christmas Day. It's usual to make up a short rhyme which caricatures the recipient. It's very much a family occasion, and unless you have Dutch friends you'll find the city awfully quiet.

Oudejaarsavond (New Year's Eve)
31 Dec

The perfect excuse for wild partying. People take to the streets with bottles of champagne, some bars stay open all night and there are fireworks everywhere.

Language

The language spoken in the Netherlands is Nederlands. In the Middle Ages it was known as Dietse or Duutsc (hence the English 'Dutch'), an equivalent of the German Deutsch meaning 'the language of the people' (as opposed to Latin – the language of scholars and the Church). You can hear variations spoken in Belgium (Flemish or Vlaams) and South Africa (Afrikaans).

The standard form of the language goes by the rather grand title of Algemeen Beschaafd Nederlands ('General Cultured Netherlandic' or ABN), though there are a multitude of regional dialects. Most of the Dutch you'll hear in Amsterdam will be ABN. But relax in a neighbourhood bar, or wander through one of the markets, and you'll hear the noisy rasping vowels of what detective-story writer Nicolas Freeling called the rooks' caw of the Amsterdam dialect.

Historically, Dutch is the same language as German, a descendant of the language spoken by West Germanic tribes and the Salic Franks. Even today there are many similarities of sentence structure and vocabulary between the two languages. But Dutch doesn't have the gloss and edge of German. It's a softer, cosier, muddy language that seems to have grown out of the bogs and polders. Dutch is not an easy tongue to grapple with. However, to a short-term visitor to Amsterdam this need present no problem, as nearly everyone you meet will speak such good English that you could almost consider it to be the city's second language. The list of words and phrases below will help the polite and adventurous who wish to master everyday courtesies, interpret the menu, or disentangle themselves from sticky situations.

Pronunciation

Pronunciation is a question of tackling some rather difficult vowel sounds. Happily, spelling is phonetic, so once you've learnt the sounds you'll be able to make a pretty accurate stab at pronouncing anything you read. The stress in Dutch, as in English, generally falls on the first syllable of a word.

Consonants

Most consonants are pronounced the same as they would be in English. However, *ps*, *ts* and *ks* aren't aspirated (i.e. they're pronounced without the accompanying puff of air). Say *ch* and *g* as in the Scottish 'loch' (*g* is more strongly voiced in northern parts of the country). Good luck in getting your tongue around the combined *s* and *ch* sounds in words like *schip* (ship), *school* (school) or *schrifter* (writer). You have a choice for *r* – you can roll it at the back of your mouth or trill it behind your teeth, but you must *always* pronounce it. Say *w* halfway between the English 'w' and 'v', except before *r*, when you pronounce it 'v'. The Dutch *v* is closer to English 'f'. Say *j* as English 'y', *sj* as English 'sh' and *tj* as English 'ch'.

Vowels

Pronounce the basic *a, e, i, o, u* sounds the same as you would in English, but *much shorter* (*a* as in 'hard', but shorter). Say *ie* as in 'neat', *oo* as in 'boat' and *oe* as in 'pool', but make all the sounds shorter. *Aa* is like the 'a' in 'cat', but longer, and *ee* is similar to the vowel sound in 'hail'. Say *eu* to rhyme with 'err', but round your lips tightly, and say *uu* as English *oo* in 'hoot'. The combination *ij* is a distinct letter in the Dutch alphabet, and is pronounced 'ay', whether it begins a word like *ijs* (ice/ice cream), or comes in the middle, as in *wijn* (wine). The stretch of water north of Centraal Station is Het Ij, 'het ay'. The diphthong *ui* is a killer. In getting their tongues around the streetname Spui, Americans usually come up with 'Spew-ee' and the Brits manage 'Spow'. The Dutch sound is closer to the way a French person would say *œil*. If that leaves you none the wiser, try running together 'er-ee', but with no hint of an 'r' sound.

Here are some practice sentences:

Dag! Ik wil graag een fles wijn
darHg! ik vil HgrahHg ayn fles veyn
(Hello, I'd like a bottle of wine, please)

Waar is de wc?
Vahr iss de vay say?
(Where is the loo?)

Echt? Wat leuk!
EHgt? Vut lerk!
(Really? How nice!)

Useful Words and Phrases

Do you speak English? *Spreekt u Engels?*
I don't understand *Ik begrijp het niet*
Could you speak more slowly? *Kunt u wat langzamer spreken?*
hello/goodbye *dag*
hi *hoi* (grating to some ears)
bye *doei* (grating)
goodbye *tot ziens*
see you later *tot straks*
good morning *goede morgen*
afternoon/night *middag/nacht*
good evening *goedenavond*
yes/no/maybe *ja/nee/misschien*
please *alstublieft*
thank you/thanks *dank u wel/bedankt*
don't mention it *niets te danken*
There is/there are... *er is/er zijn...*
There isn't/aren't... *er is/zijn geen...*
I have... *ik heb...*
I don't have any... *ik heb geen...*
I'd like... *ik wil graag...*
We'd like... *Wij willen graag...*
I like it *Ik vind het leuk*
I don't like it *Ik vind het niet leuk*
I like it (food) *Ik vind het lekker*
I don't like it (food) *Ik vind het niet lekker*
where *waar*
what *wat*
when *waneer*
which *welk*
who *wie*
why *waarom*

Where is the lavatory? *Waar is het toilet?*
May I...? *Mag ik...?*
Can you...? *Kunt u...?*
How much is...? *Hoeveel kost...?*
this/that? *dit/dat?*
expensive *duur*
cheap *goedkoop*
Can you help me? *Kunt u mij helpen?*
I'm in a hurry *Ik heb haast*
I'm lost *Ik ben verdwaald*
Call a doctor quickly *Roep vlug een dokter*
Call the police/ *Roep de politie/*
an ambulance *een ambulance*
entrance/exit *ingang/uitgang*
push/pull *duwen/trekken*
open/closed *open/gesloten (dicht)*

Meeting People

How are you? (formal) *Hoe maakt u het?*
How are you? (informal) *Hoe gaat het?*
Very well, thank you *Uitstekend, dank u*
Fine, thanks *Heel goed, dank je*
And you? (formal) *En u?* (familiar) *En jij?*
My name is... *Mijn naam is ...*
What are you having? (informal) *Wat neem je?*
What would you like? (polite) *Wat neemt u?*
May I get you a drink? *Mag ik u iets te drinken aanbieden?*
Do you have a light? *Hebt u/Heb je een vuurtje?*
Really? *Echt?*

Hotel

single room *eenpersoonskamer*
double room *tweepersoonskamer*
with private bath/shower/toilet *met privé bad/douche/toilet*
May I see the room? *Mag ik de kamer zien?*
Did anyone telephone for me? *Heeft er iemand voor mij gebeld?*
May I see the manager, please? *Mag ik de directeur spreken, alstublieft?*

Transport

airport *luchthaven/vliegveld*
customs *douane*
railway station *trein station*

platform *perron*
platform five *spoor vijf*
car *auto*
bicycle *fiets/rijwiel*
ticket *kaartje*
occupied/reserved *bezet/ gereserveerd*
Where can I get a taxi *Waar kan ik een taxi krijgen?*
What's the fare to...? *Wat kost het naar...?*
I want to go to... *Ik wil naar...*
How can I get to...? *Hoe kom ik bij...?*
Where is...? *Waar is...?*
the ticket office *het loket*
I'd like a ticket to... *Ik wil graag een kaartje naar...*
single/return *enkeltje/retourtje*
change (trains) *overstappen*
When does the next/ *Wanneer vertrek de volgende/*
first/last train leave? *eerste/ laatste trein?*
How long does it take? *Hoe lang duurt het?*
left/right/ *links/rechts/*
straight ahead *vooruit*

Driving

car hire *auto verhuur*
petrol/diesel *benzine/diesel*
leaded/unleaded *lood/loodvrij*
filling station *benzinestation*
garage (for repairs) *garage*
parking place *parkeerplaats*
parking garage *parkeer garage*
no parking *verboden te park eren/niet parkeren*
speed limit *snelheidslimiet*

Numbers

zero *nul*
one/two/three *een/twee/drie*
four/five/six *vier/vijf/zes*
seven/eight/nine *zeven/acht/negen*
ten/eleven/twelve *tien/elf/twaalf*
thirteen, fourteen etc. *dertien/veertien etc.*
twenty *twintig*
twenty-one *eenentwintig*
twenty-two *tweeëntwintig (etc.)*
thirty *dertig*
forty *veertig*
fifty *vijftig*
sixty *zestig*
seventy *zeventig*
eighty *tachtig*

ninety *negentig*
hundred *honderd*
two hundred and twenty *twee-honderd-twintig*
thousand *duizend*
million *een miljoen*
first/1st *eerste/1e*
second/2nd *tweede/2e*
third/3rd *derde/3e*
fourth/4th *vierde/4e*
eighth/8th *achtste/8e*

Time

What time is it? *Hoe laat is het?*
one o'clock *een uur*
a quarter past one *kwart over één*
half past one *half twee [sic]*
a quarter to two *kwart voor twee*
ten to/past three *tien voor/over drie*
twenty past five *tien voor half zes*
twenty-five to eight *vijf over half acht*
I'll come at 2 o'clock *Ik kom om twee uur*
today *vandaag*
yesterday *gisteren*
tomorrow *morgen*
morning/afternoon *morgen/ middag*
evening/night *avond/nacht*
Monday *maandag*
Tuesday *dinsdag*
Wednesday *woensdag*
Thursday *donderdag*
Friday *vrijdag*
Saturday *zaterdag*
Sunday *zondag*
day/week/month *dag/week/maand*
year *jaar*

Menu Guide

May I see the menu/wine list? *Mag ik de menukaart/wijnkaart zien?*
Bon appétit *Eet smakelijk*
It tastes good/bad *Het smaakt lekker/niet lekker*
May I have the bill, please? *Mag ik de rekening, alstublieft?*
service *bediening*
starter *voorgerecht*
soup *soep*
main course *hoofdgerecht*
dish of the day *dagschotel*
dessert *nagerecht*

Drinks

A beer, please *Een pils, alstublieft*
a bottle of wine *een fles wijn*
red/white *rode/witte*
sweet/dry *zoete/droge*
fresh orange juice *jus d'orange*
tomato juice *tomatensap*
fizzy mineral water *spa rood* (brand)
still mineral water *spa blauw*
coffee (with milk) *koffie (verkeerd)*
tea *thee*
(with milk/lemon) *(met melk/citroen)*

Fish

bass *zeebaars*
cod *kabeljauw*
eel *paling*
halibut *heilbot*
herring *haring*
salmon *zalm*
sole *tong*
trout *forel*

Meat, Poultry and Game

beef *rundvlees*
chicken *kip*
duck *eend*
lamb *lamsvlees*
pork *varkensvlees*
rabbit *konijn*
turkey *kalkoen*
veal *kalfsvlees*
venison *wild*

Vegetables

asparagus *asperge*
carrots *worteltjes*
garlic *knoflook*
mushrooms *champignons*
potato chips *patat frites*
potatoes *aardappelen*
salad *sla*
spinach *spinazie*

Desserts

fruit *vrucht*
ice cream *ijs*
ice cream and chocolate sauce *dame blanche*
whipped cream *slagroom*

Preparation

boiled *gekookt*
braised *gestoofd*
fried *gebakken*
grilled *geroosterd*
medium *half doorbakken*
poached *gepocheerd*
rare *rood*
roast *gebraden*
stuffed *gevuld*
well done *gaar*

Dutch Specialities

amandelbroodje sweet roll with almond-paste filling
appelgebak world-famous apple pie
appelmoes apple sauce (with everything)
belegd broodje bread roll with a variety of fillings
bitterbal ball of meat purée covered in breadcrumbs and deep fried
blinde vink slice of veal rolled around stuffing
boerenomelet omelette with vegetables and bacon
drie-in-de-pan fluffy pancake with currants
erwtensoep thick pea soup with sausages in it
frikandel sausage-shaped meatballs
hete bliksem potatoes, bacon and apples cooked in butter, salt and sugar
Hollandse nieuwe freshly caught filleted herring, cured
hutspot hotchpotch (beef and vegetable stew)
kroket croquette (with any filling imaginable)

pannenkoek pancake
poffertjes mini doughnut-like pancakes
rolpens fried slices of beef and tripe with apple
speculaas spiced almond biscuit
uitsmijter bread, ham and fried eggs (and variations)
vla custard, served with everything that doesn't have *appelmoes* (q.v.)
Vlaamse karbonade braised beef and onions – usually with beer
wentelteefje bread fried in egg batter, then sprinkled with cinnamon and sugar

Indonesian Dishes and Terms

ayam chicken
babi pangang roast suckling pig with sweet and sour sauce
bami goreng casserole of noodles, vegetables, pork and shrimps
daging beef
gado gado vegetables with peanut sauce
goreng fried
ikan fish
kroepoek fluffy deep-fried prawn crackers
loempia enormous spring roll
nasi rice
nasi goreng fried rice (with meat and vegetables)
nasi rames mini *rijsttafel* on a single plate
pedis spicy (tongue-searing)
pisang banana
rendang beef stewed in a dry, fiery sauce
rijsttafel plain rice, and up to 30 side dishes of spicy meats, vegetables, sauces and fruit
sambal hot chilli paste
saté skewered meat with peanut sauce
seroendeng spicy, fried coconut
tauge bean sprouts

Index

Numbers in **bold** indicate main references. Numbers in *italic* indicate maps.
Names beginning with 'de', 'het' and 'van' will usually be found under the main part of the name.

Also available from Cadogan Guides...

Italy

Italy
Bay of Naples & Southern Italy
Bologna & Emilia-Romagna
Central Italy
Italian Riviera & Piemonte
Lombardy & the Italian Lakes
Northeast Italy
Rome, Venice, Florence
Sardinia
Sicily
Tuscany, Umbria & the Marches
Tuscany
Umbria

France

France
Brittany
Corsica
Côte d'Azur
Dordogne & the Lot
Gascony & the Pyrenees
Loire
Normandy
Provence
South of France
Short Breaks in Northern France
Take the Kids: Paris & Disneyland®
    Resort Paris
Take the Kids: South of France

Spain

Spain
Andalucía
Bilbao & the Basque Lands
Northern Spain
Granada, Seville, Cordoba

Greece

Greece
Athens& Southern Greece
Greek Islands
Crete

The UK and Ireland

England
London–Paris

London Markets
Take the Kids: England
Take the Kids: London
Scotland
Scotland's Highlands & Islands
Ireland
Southwest Ireland
Take the Kids: Ireland

Other Europe

The Algarve
Madeira & Porto Santo
Malta, Gozo & Comino
Portugal

City Guides

Amsterdam
Barcelona
Bruges
Brussels
Edinburgh
Florence
London
Madrid
Milan
Paris
Prague
Rome
Venice

Flying Visits

Flying Visits: France
Flying Visits Germany
Flying Visits: Italy
Flying Visits Scandinavia
Flying Visits: Spain
Flying Visits Switzerland

Buying a Property

Buying a Property: Abroad
Buying a Property: Cyprus
Buying a Property: France
Buying a Property: Greece
Buying a Property: Ireland
Buying a Property: Italy
Buying a Property: Portugal
Buying a Property: Retiring abroad
Buying a Property: Spain

Cadogan Guides are available from good bookshops, or via **Littlehampton Book Services Ltd**, Faraday Close, Durrington, Worthing, West Sussex, BN13 3RB, **t** (01903) 828 503, **f** (01903) 828 802, *mailorder@ lbsltd.co.uk*; and **The Globe Pequot Press**, 246 Goose Lane, PO Box 480, Guilford, Connecticut 06437–0480, **t** (800) 458 4500/**f** (203) 458 4500, **t** (203) 458 4603. *www.cadoganguides.com*

Amsterdam
Street Maps

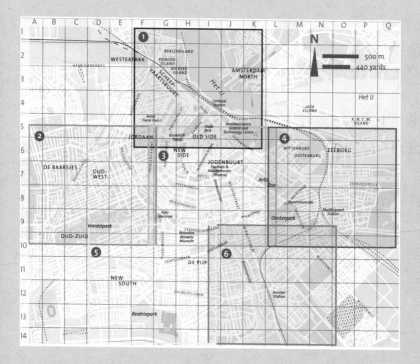

500 m
440 yards

1
REALENEILAND
WESTERPARK
PRINSEN-EILAND
SCHEEP VAARTSBUURT
BICKERS EILAND
HAARLEMMERWEG
AMSTERDAM NORTH
Het IJ
Central Station
Het IJ
JAVA EILAND
Anne Frank Huis
NewMetropolis Science and Technology Centre
2
JORDAAN
Koninklijk Paleis
Oude Kerk
OLD SIDE
K. N. S. M. EILAND
4
WITTENBURG
OOSTENBURG
ZEEBURG
NEW SIDE
3
DE BAARSJES
OUD-WEST
JODENBUURT
Stadhuis & Muziektheater (Stopera)
Artis Zoo
ZEEBURGERDIJK
Tropenmuseum
Muiderpoort Station
Rijks-museum
Oosterpark
Vondelpark
OUD-ZUID
Heineken Brewery Museum
STADHOUDERSKADE
5
CEINTUURBAAN
DE PIJP
6
NEW SOUTH
CHURCHILLLAAN
Amstel-Station
Beatrixpark

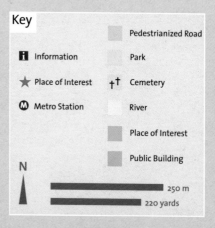

Key

i Information

★ Place of Interest

Ⓜ Metro Station

Pedestrianized Road

Park

†† Cemetery

River

Place of Interest

Public Building

N

250 m
220 yards

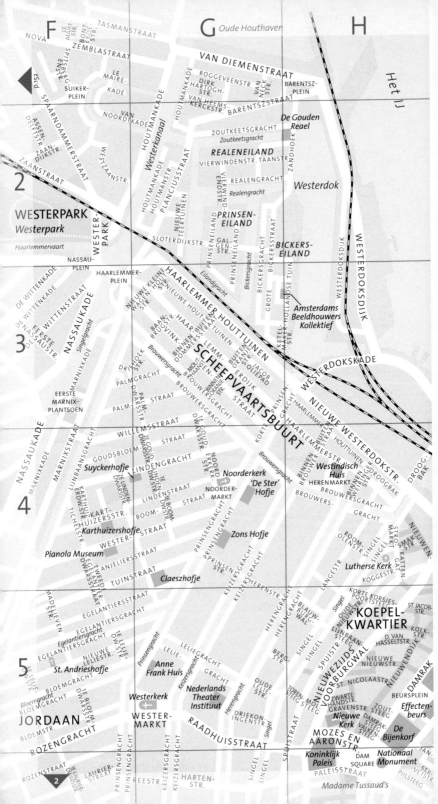

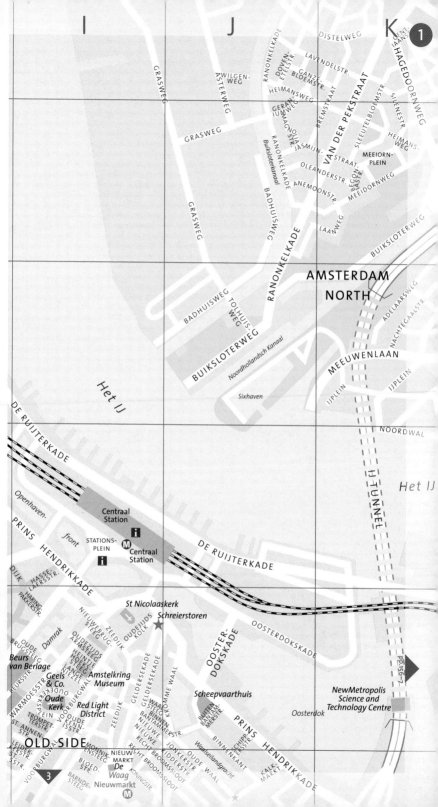

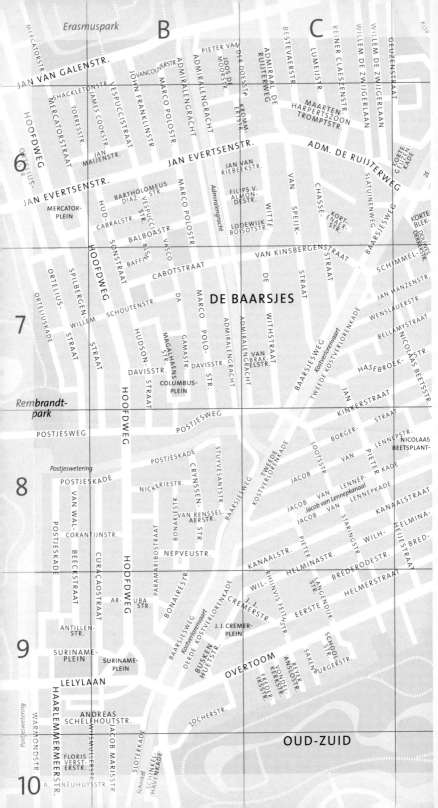

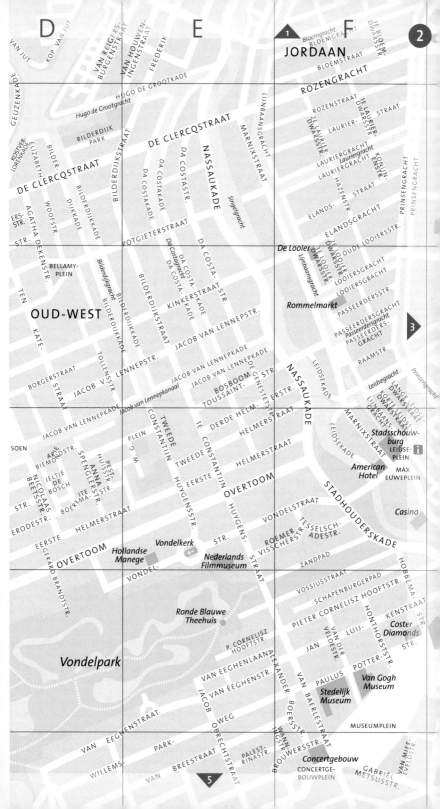

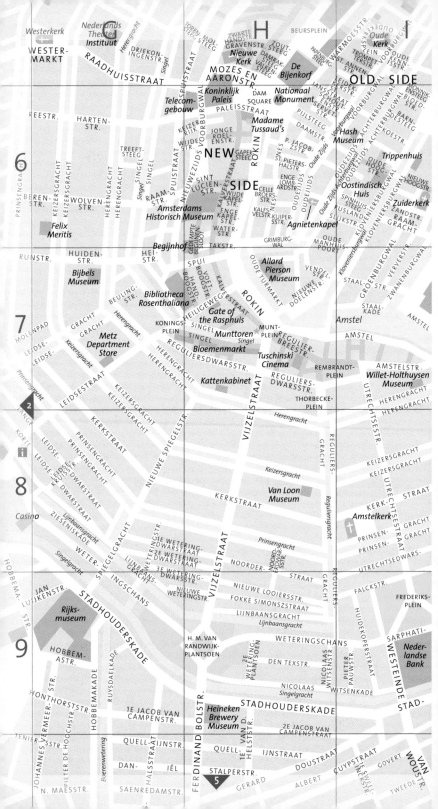

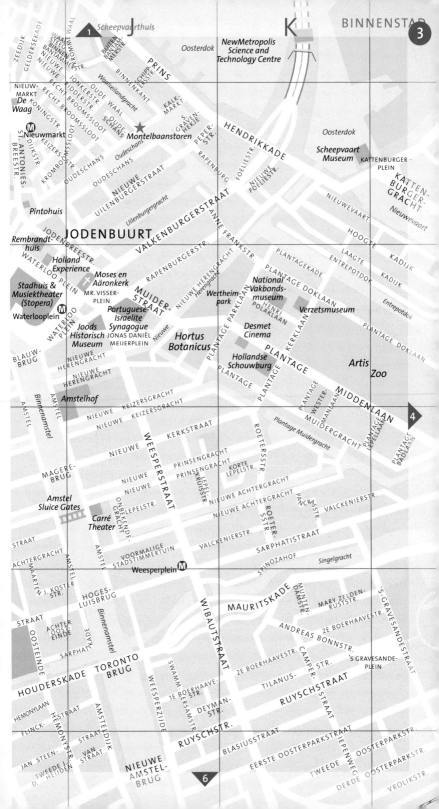

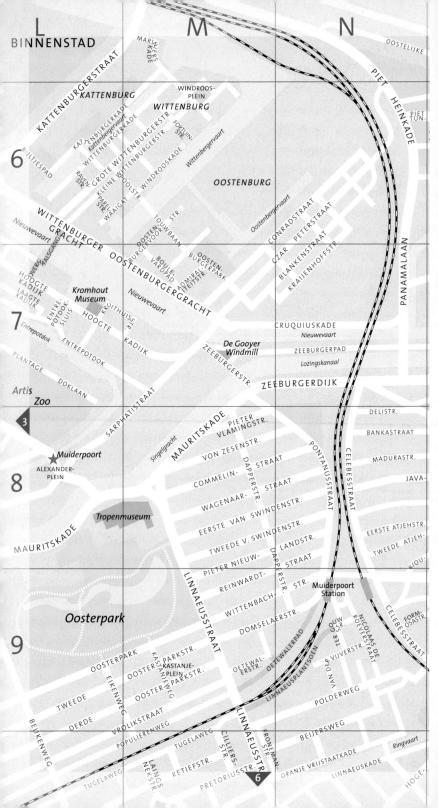

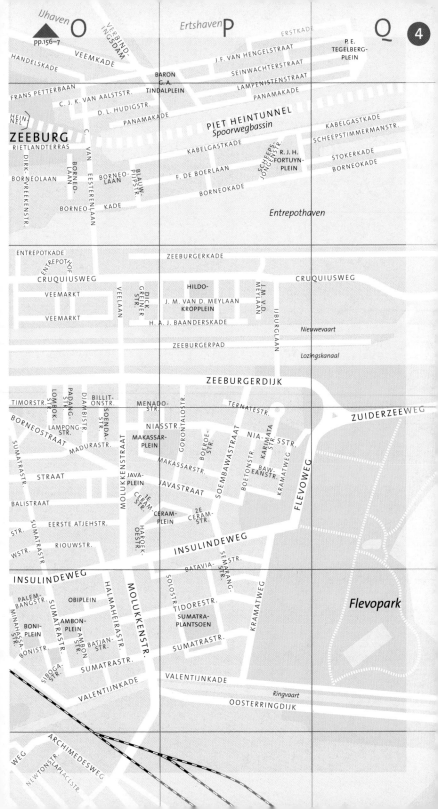

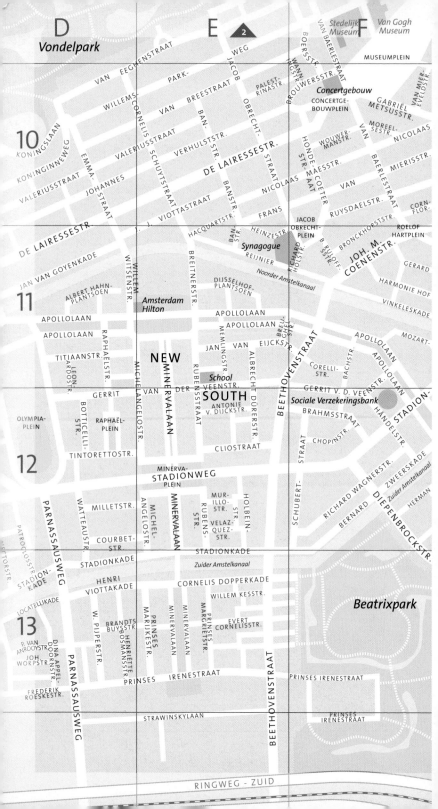

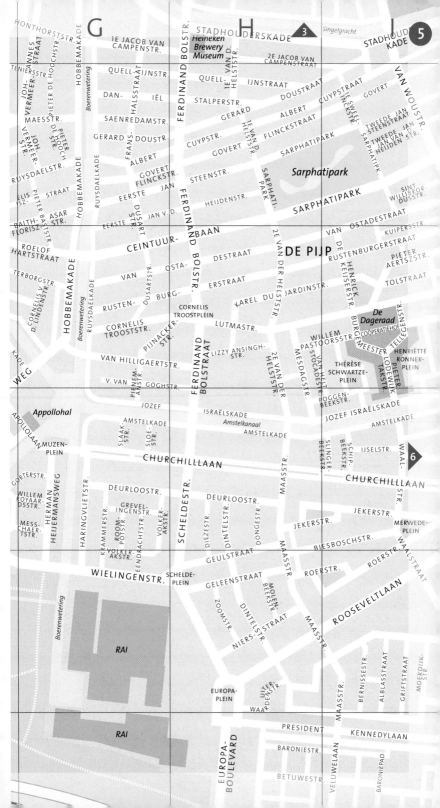

J

K

10

CEINTUURBAAN

HEMONYLAAN

GOVERT FLINCK STRAAT

HEMONY STRAAT

AMSTELDIJK

TWEEDE JAN STEEN STRAAT

TWEEDE VAN D. HEIJDEN STR.

SINT

WILLIBRORDUSSTRAAT

VAN OSTADESTR.

KUIPERSSTR.

RUSTENBURGERSTR.

KUIPERSSTR.

AMSTELDIJK

Binnenamstel

1e BOERHAAVE-STR.

WAMM-STRAAT

JRASAMSTR.

WEESPERZIJDE

3

DEYMAN-STR.

RUYSCHSTR.

RUYSCHSTR.

RUYSCHSTRAAT

CAMPERSTR.

BLASIUSSTRAAT

EERSTE OOSTERPARKSTRAAT

TWEEDE OOSTERPARKSTR.

IEPENWEG

DERDE OOSTERPARKSTR.

OETGENSSTR.

BURMAN-STR.

GRENSSTR.

G. VAN AEMSTELSTR.

WEESPERZIJDE

NIEUWE AMSTEL-BRUG

WIBAUTSTRAAT

Wibautstr.

M

Wibautstr.

VROLIKSTR.

VROLIKSTR.

OLMEN-WEG

POPULIERENWEG

VROLIKSTRAAT

PLATANENWEG

TUGELAWEG

PRESBRAND

REITZ-

JOUBERTSTR.

BEN VILJOEN-STR.

DANIE THERON-

KRUGERSTR.

HOFMEYRSTRAAT

PRES. STEYN

PLANTSOEN

WIBAUTSTRAAT

Ringvaart

11

VAN WOUSTRAAT

PIETER AERTSZSTR.

TOLSTRAAT

TOLSTRAAT

MSTR.

TALMASTR.

HENRIËTTE RONNER-PLEIN

DAVID BLESSTR.

MAUVESTR.

CORNELIS SPRINGERSTR.

JAN LIEVENSSTR.

TOLSTRAAT

DIAMANT-STRAAT

LUTMASTR.

SAFFI- ERSTR.

SMARAGDSTR.

GRANAAT-STR.

SAFFIERSTR.

TOPAASSTR.

JOZEF ISRAËLSKADE

Amstelkanaal

AMSTELKADE

KRAMER-BRUG

GRAAF FLORISSTR.

MARCUS-STR.

OVER-AMSTELSTR.

JAN BERNAR-DUSSTR.

SCHOLLEN-BRUGPAD

SCHOLLEN-BRUGSTR.

12

CHURCHILLLAAN

JOZEF ISRAËLSKADE

AMSTELKADE

5

OUDEIJSELSTR.

SELSTRAAT

REGGESTR.

BERKELSTR.

RIJNSTRAAT

VECHTSTR.

BORSSENBURGSTR.

KORTE MEERHUIZENSTR.

MEERHUIZENSTR.

UITHOORNSTR.

HOLEN-DRECHTSTR.

VRIJHEIDSLAAN

VICTORIE-PLEIN

MERWEDE-PLEIN

WEESPERZIJDE

BERLAGE BRUG

MR. TREUBLAAN

RINGDIJK

ROCKET-STR.

VAN DER KUNST.

GOUDRIAAN-STR.

Amstel

M

Amstel-Station

RIVIERENBUURT

LEKSTR.

VECHTSTR.

WAV- ERSTRAAT

KROMME

LEKSTR.

MIJDRECHTSTR.

GAASP

AMSTELDIJK

WEESPERZIJDE

Weespertrekvaart

13

UITERWAARDENSTR.

WAALSTRAAT

LEKSTR.

KINDERDIJK-STR.

WINTER-DIJKSTR.

LEKSTR.

HUNZESTRAAT

RIJNSTRAAT

TROMPENBURGSTRAAT

STR.

UITERWAARDENSTR.

HOENDIEPSTR.

UITER-WAARDEN-STR.

MOEDIJKSTR.

WAALSTRAAT

KINDERDIJKSTR.

KRIBBESTR.

ZOMER-DIJKSTR.

HUNZESTR.

KUINDERSTR.

VECHTSTR.

EEMSTR.

BOTERDIEPSTR.

PRESIDENT KENNEDYLAAN

AMSTELDIJK

KORTE KERK-

Martin Luther King Prk

Amstel

14

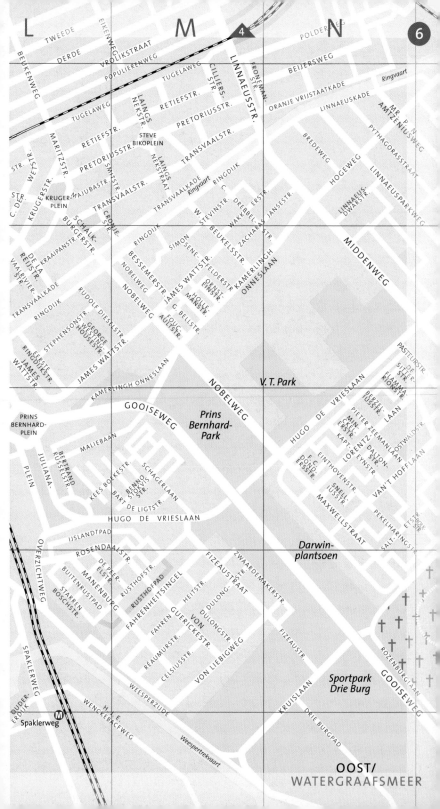

No more
excuses –
just go!

flying visits
ITALY
*great getaways by
budget airline*
CADOGANguide

flying visits
SPAIN
*great getaways
by budget airline & ferry*
CADOGANguides

flying visits
FRANCE
*great getaways by
budget airline, train & ferry*
CADOGANguides

Flying Visits make
travel simple

CADOGANguides
well travelled well read